REVOLUTIONS
A Comparative Study

Edited by

LAWRENCE KAPLAN

With the assistance of

CAROL KAPLAN

Random House · NEW YORK

REVOLUTIONS

A COMPARATIVE STUDY

Library of Congress Cataloging in Publication Data
Kaplan, Lawrence, comp.
Revolutions: a comparative study.
Bibliography: p.
1. Revolution—History. I. Title.
HM283.K3   1972   309.1   72–5335
ISBN 0–394–47371–X

Manufactured in the United States of America by
American Book–Stratford Press, New York, N.Y.
9   8   7   6   5   4   3   2
First Edition

Grateful acknowledgment is made to the following for permission to
reprint material:

Annales E. S. C.: "La place de la Révolution française dans l'histoire du
monde" by Georges Lefebvre, in *Annales—Economics, Sociétés, Civilisations,* No. 3, 1948. (English translation by Peter Amann in *The
Eighteenth Century Revolution,* D. C. Heath.)

Edward Arnold Publishers Ltd: Adapted from Austin Woolrych's "The English Revolution: An Introduction" in E. W. Ives, ed., *The English Revolution 1600–1660*.

The Clarendon Press: "The 'Revolutionary Crowd' in History" from *The Crowd in the French Revolution* by Georges Rudé, 1959.

Doubleday & Co., Inc.: "1848" by Theodore S. Hamerow, from *The Responsibility of Power: Historical Essays in Honor of Hajo Holborn*, edited by Leonard Krieger and Fritz Stern. Copyright © 1967 by Doubleday & Company, Inc.

Europe: "La Commune de Paris" by Jean Gacon, in *Europe*, No. 499–500, November–December 1970. English translation copyright © 1973 by Random House, Inc.

Harcourt Brace Jovanovich, Inc.: "Yenan Communism and the Rise of the Chinese People's Republic" by Maurice Meisner, from *Modern East Asia: Essays in Interpretation*, edited by James B. Crowley. Copyright © 1970 by Harcourt Brace Jovanovich, Inc.

Harvard University Press: "A Historical Turning Point: Marx, Lenin, Stalin" by E. H. Carr, from *Revolutionary Russia*, edited by Richard Pipes. Copyright © 1968 by Richard Pipes.

International Publishers Co., Inc.: From *18th Brumaire of L. Bonaparte* by Karl Marx, 1963. From *The German Ideology* by Karl Marx, 1970. From *State and Revolution* by Lenin, 1932, 1943.

Alfred A. Knopf, Inc.: From *The October Revolution* by E. H. Carr. Copyright © 1969 by E. H. Carr.

McGraw-Hill Book Company: From *Obsolete Communism: The Left-wing Alternative* by Daniel & Gabriel Cohn-Bendit. Copyright © 1968 English translation by André Deutsch Ltd.

Monthly Review Press: "Algeria Unveiled" from *A Dying Colonialism* by Frantz Fanon. English translation copyright © 1965 by Monthly Review Press. First published in France under the title of *L'An Cinq de la Revolution Algérienne*. Copyright © 1959 by François Maspero.

Max Nomad: "Conclusion" from *Rebels and Renegades*. Macmillan, 1932.

Pantheon Books, A Division of Random House, Inc.: From *America's Asia: Dissenting Essays on Asian-American Relations*, edited by Edward Friedman and Mark Selden. Copyright © 1969, 1970, 1971 by Random House, Inc.

The Past and Present Society: "Revolution and Continuity in Early Modern Europe" by J. H. Elliott, in *Past and Present, a journal of historical studies*, no. 42.

Princeton University Press: "Theories of Revolution" by Lawrence Stone, *World Politics*, vol. XVIII, no. 2, Copyright © 1966 by Princeton University Press.

Transaction, Inc.: "Cuba—Revolution Without a Blueprint" by Maurice

Zeitlin in *Transaction,* April 1969. Copyright © 1969 by Transaction, Inc., New Brunswick, New Jersey.

University of Nebraska Press: "The Mexican Revolution, Then and Now" from *Change in Latin America: The Mexican and Cuban Revolutions* by Daniel Cosio Villegas, 1961.

Gordon S. Wood: "Rhetoric and Reality in the American Revolution" by Gordon S. Wood, in *William and Mary Quarterly,* 3rd Ser., XXIII, 1966.

World Publishing Company: From Chapter 3, "The French Revolution," from *The Age of Revolution: Europe 1789–1848* by E. J. Hobsbawm. Copyright © 1962 by E. J. Hobsbawm.

For LAURA and NINA

Preface

The purpose of this book is to encourage the comparative study of revolutions. Its plan is to provide in concise form some of the most perceptive analyses of the major revolutions of modern history. My main criterion in choosing a selection was that it presented the best short account of a particular revolution. I was influenced in my choices by the following considerations: sophistication of analysis, clarity of expression and, wherever possible, the willingness of an author to compare the revolution under discussion with other revolutions. Where special aspects of a revolution require amplification, a second or even a third article has been added. In several instances the writings of revolutionaries themselves have been included to illustrate, among other things, how political activists have drawn "lessons" from the successes and failures of previous revolutions.

An edited work is by definition a cooperative venture, and I would therefore like to acknowledge the help rendered by friends and colleagues. I wish to thank Cyrilly Abels of New York City, Frederick Binder of the City College of New York, Marcia Swislocki of Harvard University, and Hilary Maddux, John J. Simon and Carol Anderson of Random House. Special appreciation is due to Marvin E. Gettleman of the Polytechnic Institute of Brooklyn for his wise counsel, and to Conrad Schirokauer and Martin Waldman, members of the history department of the City College of New York, for help in the selection of certain essays. Carol Kaplan provided the vital assistance that made the preparation of this book possible.

Englewood, New Jersey
October 1971

Contents

Introduction

The subject of revolutions has always attracted great interest. More books are published by historians and biographers on this topic than perhaps any other. Recently, growing numbers of anthropologists, sociologists and political scientists have begun analyzing the nature of revolutions, comparing and defining them from the vantage point of their particular disciplines. The trend toward comparing revolutions has in effect revived an ancient pursuit, for the comparative study of revolutions is a venerable one, going back to the Renaissance and to classical antiquity.

In addition to the timeless curiosity about dramatic episodes of the past, the comparing of revolutions always served a utilitarian purpose. Historians of the ancient world and of the Renaissance were concerned with drawing practical lessons from their investigations. By and large, these writers analyzed previous revolutions in order to gain the requisite knowledge which would help them to avoid revolutions in their own day. Curiously, revolution-prevention has been a major impetus for the contemporary revival of interest in this subject, especially in the United States.[1]

Apart from political considerations, however, the comparative study of revolutions possesses great value as a scholarly discipline, because it helps to weaken the provincialism characteristic of many historians who concentrate on their own countries to the exclusion of all others. For example, students of the

[1] See p. xxii this volume.

American revolution have drawn countless suggestions from R. R. Palmer's *The Age of the Democratic Revolution,* which has placed American events in the pattern of other upheavals occurring throughout the Western world at approximately the same time. Similarly, many French historians who may disagree with Palmer's conclusions regarding the similarity of the democratic revolutions are now forced to refine their conclusions as to the uniqueness of the French revolution.[2] Inevitably the broadening of the historical focus works to the advantage of all scholarly contributions.

Comparative history in general, and the comparative study of revolutions in particular, open up areas of historical research previously ignored. New and different kinds of questions are being asked about specific revolutions, and the answers provide new perspectives on a multitude of historical problems. Lines of approach which have proven fruitful in regard to one revolution are being tried by historians of other such events. Thus, the role of the crowd in the French revolution, which has been so brilliantly treated by Georges Rudé and Albert Soboul,[3] has suggested analyses of the crowd in eighteenth- and nineteenth-century England, in the American revolution and during the revolutions of 1848. Daniel Mornet's able *Les Origines intellectuelles de la Révolution française* has not only stimulated interest in the part played by ideas in causing all revolutions, it has called forth books on the English and American revolutions which have adopted Mornet's format and even his title.[4] The obvious importance of the peasantry during the Chinese revolution has stimulated comparative histories of peasants in revolutions as diverse as the Russian, Mexican, Vietnamese, Cuban and Algerian.[5]

[2] See Selection 7, this volume.

[3] See Selection 9, this volume; and Albert Soboul, *The Parisian Sans-Culottes and the French Revolution,* Oxford, 1964.

[4] Christopher Hill, *Intellectual Origins of the English Revolution,* Oxford, 1965; Bernard Bailyn, *The Ideological Origins of the American Revolution,* Cambridge, Mass., 1967.

[5] See, for example, Eric R. Wolf, *Peasant Wars of the Twentieth Century,* New York, 1969. See also Selection 18, this volume.

The themes which lend themselves to comparison are infinite, yet comparative history does have its pitfalls. Frequently scholars select one revolution as the ideal type and then proceed to analyze others, believing that these will conform to the pattern of the first. This was one of the main defects of Crane Brinton's *Anatomy of Revolution*. The author, originally a historian of the French revolution, took the latter as his model and assumed that the English, American and Russian revolutions passed through similar stages: i.e., moderate, extremist and Thermidorian. He set out to prove his thesis by searching for events that matched his preordained interpretation. This is never a fruitful method of conducting research, and the result of Brinton's efforts was essentially a distortion of historical data. Nevertheless, he provided scholars with a hypothesis that could be tested, modified or more often rejected, but one that forced historians to view their subjects in a new light.[6] This served in many cases to open up uncharted areas of inquiry.

The inclination to view revolutions as similar in all basic respects is a common failing of historians, and it is easy to understand why. Certainly modern revolutions by definition are characterized by rapid, violent and fundamental changes in the political institutions and social structure of the old regime, through rearrangements in class alignments and the participation of masses of people. However, historians who recognize the advantages of making comparisons must also be cognizant of the unique elements present in all revolutions. In many cases it is the original aspects of a particular revolution which determine its success or failure, and these need to be stressed.

Moreover, there exists a changing chronological pattern of revolution: the French revolution of the eighteenth century marks a divide between the modern and early modern periods. Thus, while the English and American revolutions tended to be national in focus and limited to minor social changes, the French carried through their revolution in the name of the rights of man; so that its impact on other countries was greater, while

---

[6] The tendency of historians to regard the final stage of a revolution as Thermidorian can be partially attributed to Brinton's work.

its social transformations were profound and undeniable. Succeeding revolutions, especially the Russian and Chinese, followed the pattern of the French in that they achieved the complete replacement of one class by another. In addition, they widened even further the scope of revolution, placing the masses at the center of revolutionary ideology.

The differences between the earlier and more recent revolutions can also be demonstrated when the role of ideology is studied. In the modern revolutions conflicts of value systems and divergent concepts of legality separate the revolutionary, with his desire for innovation, from the defenders of the status quo. But such conflicts do not characterize the ideological struggles of early modern Europe. The revolutionaries of this epoch did not view themselves as innovators, nor as possessors of a new world view. Rather, their programs called for a restoration of what had been changed by others, usually monarchs who sought greater authority. They expressed a desire to return to old customs and privileges, to the traditional order of society. Thus the Regicides who cut off the head of Charles I maintained that they were restoring ancient liberties.

One finds a similar mental process present at the outset of the eighteenth-century revolutions. In America it was claimed that the English by their treatment of the colonies had violated the spirit of their own institutions. Bernard Bailyn has shown how the colonists regarded the restrictive measures taken by royal officers after 1763 as "evidence of nothing less than a deliberate assault launched surreptitiously by plotters against liberty both in England and in America." Georges Lefebvre and others have observed how the French revolution was precipitated by the aristocracy, who entered the struggle against absolutism as defenders of fundamental laws and as protectors of the French nation. But as Tocqueville realized, "Those traditional institutions with which they [the nobles] opposed the reforms proposed by the royal government were the very institutions which the revolution was to destroy."[7] For when the traditional forms

[7] Bailyn, *op. cit.,* p. 95; Georges Lefebvre, *The Coming of the French Revolution,* Princeton, 1947, p. 36; Alexis de Tocqueville, *The European Revolution and Correspondence with Gobineau,* Garden City, N.Y., 1959, p. 44.

proved incapable of significant flexibility they were discarded, and new institutions and new relationships were then created.

The French revolution of 1789 was to be virtually the last time that revolutionaries would begin a revolution with the program of renovating the ancient constitution.[8] The heirs of Robespierre and Babeuf were to reject the Old Regime totally, making no pretense of restoring what they considered essentially moribund. It is clear, for example, that the Russian and Chinese revolutions both began at a more advanced stage, with revolutionaries intending to build anew.

In modern times the most important contributions to the study of revolutions have been made by Karl Marx. In synthesizing the far-reaching implications of the French and the Industrial revolutions, Marx created a coherent system of thought which still dominates our civilization. As Sartre has astutely observed, almost everything written since Marx has essentially been a commentary on his philosophy.[9] And because Marxism does not merely interpret the world but also seeks to change it, almost every important revolution in the twentieth century has been carried out in his name. To study revolution is therefore largely to deal with Marx and his influence.

In Marx's time the impact of the French revolution was still very real, and he shared with many other writers the belief that it was a world historical event which had changed the course of history by demonstrating that progress would have to come about through violence, i.e., struggles between classes.[10] By progress Marx meant the expansion of the productive capacity of both society and individual human beings, leading ultimately to greater equality and freedom and to the fulfillment of man's potential.

The dramatic conflict of classes so intensified during a time of upheaval became for Marx the prototype of a political

---

[8] In the early days of the Mexican revolution certain moderate revolutionaries (e.g., Francisco Madero) called, among other things, for the restoration of the Mexican Constitution of 1857. But even in this case new demands were made as well.

[9] Jean-Paul Sartre, *Search for a Method*, New York, 1968.

[10] The belief in class struggles in history was shared by such well-known historians as Augustin Thierry and François Guizot.

revolution. According to him, revolution occurs when one class seizes the reins of political power from another by force, and sets up a new state apparatus in accordance with its own needs. The struggle takes place in the political arena, and in that sense all revolutions are political. But the social and economic goals of the different classes are what really matter. A successful revolution will remove those social and political institutions which prevent the development of the class in whose name the revolution is being carried out. Just as France witnessed the sudden replacement of its aristocracy by the bourgeoisie, so too would all countries experience their own bourgeois revolutions. This prognosis of class conflict and the necessity for definite stages in history can be found in Marx's best-known general works.[11]

When Marx came to write about specific revolutions he filled in his general outline with a wealth of detail. In his *Eighteenth Brumaire of Louis Bonaparte,* Marx produced a masterpiece of contemporary history which well illustrates the aphorism that truth lies in the nuances. Account was taken by him of the complexity of the revolutionary situation, wherein a multitude of classes (not just two or three) interacted. Moreover, Marx clearly recognized the crucial role played by individuals within the context of the given circumstances.[12] Again, in his brief treatment of the English Civil War, Marx took note of the uniqueness of the English pattern, which involved a bourgeoisie joining forces with large landowners to form a class alliance. Quite obviously this was a development at variance with the French model.[13]

In another context, Marx demonstrated a flexibility of approach when he lent his support to the Paris Commune of 1871. He did so despite the fact that it occurred in a not yet fully

---

[11] See especially *The Communist Manifesto, A Contribution to the Critique of Political Economy* and *The German Ideology.* See Selection 1, this volume, for excerpts.

[12] See Selection 10, this volume.

[13] Karl Marx, "A Review of Guizot's Book 'Why Has the English Revolution Been Successful?' " in *Marx and Engels on Britain,* Moscow, 1962.

industrialized country, with a poorly organized working class and a leadership composed largely of petit bourgeois elements. What is more, he knew in advance that the Commune could never succeed.[14] Marx called attention to the accidental circumstances which enabled the "working classes" of Paris to liberate themselves from the capitalist government of France in a letter to a friend. He then proceeded to make a general observation regarding chance in history. "World history," Marx wrote,

> would indeed be very easy to make, if the struggle were taken only on condition of infallibly favorable chances. It would, on the other hand, be of a very mystical nature if 'accidents' played no part. These accidents themselves fall naturally into the general course of development and are compensated again by other accidents. But acceleration and delay are very dependent upon such accidents, which include the accident of the character of those who at first stand at the head of the movement.[15]

The outstanding Marxist revolutionaries of the twentieth century have been those who were able to combine a general Marxian analysis of history and society with the creativity which characterizes Marx's approach to specific historical problems. Recognizing the unique aspects of their own situations, both Lenin and Mao Tse-tung successfully adapted Marxism to the particular conditions of their countries. Thus, Lenin in 1917 responded to the disintegration of the February revolution and the obvious weakness of the Russian bourgeoisie by calling for the transfer of power to the representatives of workers and peasants. Making use of the spontaneous creation of Soviets, Lenin and his followers carried out the October revolution in the name of socialism and peace. Mao's great achievement was his early recognition that the Bolsheviks' method of seizing power in the cities could not be repeated in China. As a result, the Chinese Communists under Mao's leadership turned from

[14] Shlomo Avineri, *The Social and Political Thought of Karl Marx,* Cambridge, England, 1970, pp. 239–249.

[15] Karl Marx, *The Civil War in France,* New York, 1940, p. 86.

the urban centers to the countryside, and helped mold peasant discontent into "a force so swift and violent that no power, however great, [was] able to hold it back."[16] It was a combination of his Marxist analysis of the class structure of China, and an intimate knowledge of peasant society, which enabled Mao to formulate a strategy of guerrilla war and revolutionary land reform that proved invincible against the Kuomintang.[17] Similar innovations and achievements on a smaller scale were realized by Ho Chi Minh in Vietnam and by Fidel Castro in Cuba. The revolutionaries who have failed to attain their aims are the ones like the Mensheviks in Russia, whose preconception of historical development conflicted with objective conditions in their country; or those like Li Li-san in China and Che Guevara in Bolivia, both of whom rigidly tried to repeat in a new environment a formula that had worked elsewhere. Apparently each country calls forth its own revolutionary strategy.

Despite the necessity of innovating, revolutionaries always study previous revolutions in different countries in order to learn from the past. Roman history, for example, served as an inspiration and a model for some of the leaders of the French revolution. Bolsheviks in Russia not only knew the course of the French revolution by heart, they also endlessly analyzed the Paris Commune so that they could avoid the pitfalls of the latter. The nationalization of the Russian banks in 1917 had symbolic meaning for all Marxists, since the Communards had failed to take over the Paris Bourse during their brief stay in power. A sizable number of Chinese Communists spent years at Sun Yat-sen University in Moscow, where they became thoroughly versed in Leninist theories of revolution. Castro and his followers gave considerable attention to the reasons why the Arbenz government in Guatemala was so easily overthrown. And young radicals around the world have sought ways to imitate the French student uprising of 1968.

A revolution is a spectacularly dramatic event whose occurrence in one country plays the role of influencing consciousness

[16] Mao Tse-tung, "Report on an Investigation of the Peasant Movement in Hunan," in *Selected Works,* I, Peking, 1954, pp. 23–24.
[17] See Selection 17, this volume.

in other countries. American political ideologies of the prerevolutionary period owed a great deal to the radical political
thought of the English Civil War as it was modified by Com-
monwealthmen in the eighteenth century.[18] In turn, the American revolution, by legitimizing the ideas of the Enlightenment,
contributed to the intellectual origins of the French revolution.
Georges Lefebvre believed that the War of Independence in the
colonies "may in fact be considered the principal direct cause of
the French revolution. . . ."[19] The revolution in France
served as a catalyst for change throughout Europe and the
Americas; indeed, it must be considered as a landmark in the
history of a multitude of nations.[20] The October revolution set
off a whole series of revolutionary waves around the world, and
Ho Chi Minh reminds us of the inspiration it gave to the wars of
national liberation.[21] Its greatest impact, however, was on
China. There Dr. Sun Yat-sen, duly impressed by developments
in Russia, attempted to adopt the Bolshevik method of revolution in his homeland. What is more, Marxism as a political
force began to influence Chinese intellectuals only after the
revolution of 1917.[22]

Unfortunately for revolutionaries their opposite numbers,
those in seats of power, have also been avid students of previous revolutions. At least since the French revolution, these
ruling elites have actively sought to prevent any further revolutionary change. In fact, a good case can be made that for the
last two centuries counterrevolution has been a major theme of
world history. The political ideology of conservatism originated
as a response to the French revolution. The "Metternich system" established after the Napoleonic wars worked to maintain
stability not only in Europe, but elsewhere as well. In the nineteenth century the fear of radical uprisings tempered the de-

[18] Bailyn, *op. cit.*, pp. 34–35.
[19] Lefebvre also shows how French loans to the Americans served to
deplete Louis XVI's finances; *op. cit.*, p. 21.
[20] See Selection 7, this volume.
[21] See Selection 15, this volume.
[22] Jerome Ch'en, *Mao and the Chinese Revolution*, New York, 1967,
p. 76; Stuart Schram, *Mao Tse-tung*, Middlesex, 1967, p. 47.

mands of the European middle classes, and made them wary of precipitating revolutions which might get out of their control. Surely the advent of Louis Bonaparte and Bismarck provides evidence that the bourgeoisie of France and Germany were willing to sacrifice genuine parliamentary government for an authoritarian rule which guaranteed security of property. Involvement in World War I by the great powers must be viewed in part as a means by which they avoided pressing domestic crises that were rapidly becoming insoluble. After the First World War the specter of Bolshevism haunted "the peacemakers" at Versailles, and this is the reason why several recent books on the history of the Cold War begin their narrative with 1917 rather than 1945.[23] Fascism as a phenomenon in Europe can be explained largely as the response of the upper classes to the revolution in Russia, and their dread lest it be repeated in their own country. More recently, American foreign policy following World War II has been designed to prevent the spread of revolution in Europe and in all of the Third World as well.

It is indeed the emergence of the United States as a super power, and the increasingly counterrevolutionary character of American foreign policy, that has given present-day studies of revolutions new relevance. Scholars in various disciplines have devoted their energies to helping our government combat revolutions throughout the world. Many of the works produced in this country during the last few decades have not only been antirevolutionary in tone, some of them actually have purported to give general advice on how revolutions are to be prevented. A most significant book of this genre, Chalmers Johnson's *Revolution and the Social System,* has as its main conclusion the idea that all revolutionary upheavals can be avoided. According to Johnson, revolutions have two general causes: a dysfunctional social system and an inflexible elite. The variable element is always the latter. If the elite, instead of being "intransigent," responds to the crisis by allowing for peaceful changes in the system, i.e., by introducing the requisite reforms,

[23] D. F. Fleming, *The Cold War and Its Origins, 1917–1960,* 2 Vols., Garden City, N.Y., 1961; André Fontaine, *History of the Cold War,* 2 Vols., New York, 1970.

INTRODUCTION xxiii

then the dysfunction will be relieved and "no revolution will take place."[24] Thus armed with the foresight to know when to take the proper corrective action, an elite can perpetuate itself in power.

The major difficulty with testing Johnson's thesis is that historical evidence is unsuitable for such a purpose. Quite obviously, the revolutions available for analysis did in fact take place. Consequently, the only argument that can be made from history is one that stresses "might have beens." Even granting this possibility, and acknowledging that elites which have been replaced during revolutions have not responded imaginatively to a crisis, the fact remains that the type of mistake made by elites tends to be socially conditioned. For Chiang Kai-shek to eliminate corruption and inefficiency in his army and institute land reform (possible corrective steps for his survival) would have meant a transformation completely inconceivable for the Kuomintang, and therefore impossible to contemplate. Similarly, for the Provisional Government in Russia to sue for peace after the February revolution (a step which might have undercut the Bolsheviks' appeal) would have meant breaking with those Western nations whose help was needed to stabilize Russian finances. Furthermore, in cases where elites have recognized the urgency of reform during a critical period, as Charles I did when he summoned the Long Parliament and approved its first measures, or Louis XVI when he accepted the juridical changes of 1789, the revolution took place anyway. Indeed, many observers have pointed out how the granting of reforms by an unpopular government generally encourages new demands which can only be satisfied by a complete transformation of institutions. In the context of a revolutionary situation, reforms frequently lead to revolution.[25]

The idea that revolution can be prevented if elites take the

[24] Chalmers Johnson, *Revolution and the Social System*, Stanford, Calif., 1964, pp. 6–7.

[25] Alexis de Tocqueville, for example, writes: ". . . experience teaches us that, generally speaking, the most perilous moment for a bad government is one when it seeks to mend its ways." The *Old Regime and the French Revolution*, Garden City, N.Y., 1955, pp. 176–177.

proper action proved very attractive to ruling circles in America. Particularly compelling was the thought that Third World countries could be manipulated to the extent that they might become subversion-proof. During the 1960's several university and "think tank" social scientists began devising strategies to combat the form of guerrilla warfare which brought Communist governments into being in China, North Vietnam and Cuba. Based, ironically enough, on the teachings of Mao, General Giap and Che Guevara, counterinsurgency purported to use the fundamentals of guerrilla warfare for the purpose of maintaining pro-Western regimes in power. Established and privileged elites would be encouraged to introduce a modicum of reforms that would gain them local support and also serve to deprive the insurgents of an "issue." At the same time special forces like the "Green Berets" would be trained to live among the peasant ⋅ masses, essentially fighting the enemy guerrillas on their own terms. With superior American know-how and wealth, pro-American governments would soon win the "hearts and minds" of the indigenous peoples, thereby assuring victory against the revolutionary forces.

It is now clear how the belief in the efficacy of counterinsurgency contributed to the Kennedy administration's decision to become further involved in the Vietnam war.[26] In a sense, Vietnam served as the testing ground for this new flexible strategy. Yet the events of the last decade in Indochina have clearly revealed the bankruptcy of counterinsurgency: once again a ruling elite and its army have proven unwilling to carry out reforms. Moreover, American strategists, with their mechanistic and rigid formulations of revolutionary typologies, seriously underestimated the humanism and courage of the Vietnamese people.[27] Recently, however, a new variation of

[26] *The Pentagon Papers,* as published by *The New York Times,* New York, 1971, *passim.*

[27] For an example of American strategy at its most mechanistic, see Walt W. Rostow's "Memorandum on 'Victory and Defeat in Guerrilla Wars' " in *The Pentagon Papers, op. cit.,* pp. 447–448. See also Selection 18, this volume. As a further example of a similar phenomenon in another revolution, Frantz Fanon brilliantly illustrates how the French

the original plan has been conceived. Amelioration of the conditions of the masses is now considered irrelevant. Instead, massive American weaponry and fire power, it is currently held, will deny the Communists the support of the peasants by literally eliminating this segment of the population, either by violent death from the air or by forcible evacuation from the countryside.

In a recent article in *Foreign Affairs,* Samuel P. Huntington, chairman of the government department at Harvard University, applauds America's new answer to wars of national liberation. By driving the rural population into overcrowded cities or into refugee camps, he reasons, "the basic assumptions underlying the Maoist doctrine of revolutionary war no longer operate."[28] Without peasants, quite obviously Third World peasant revolutions are an impossibility. The logic of the argument is irrefutable, but the fact that the United States is now willing to destroy people allegedly in order to save them indicates the level to which counterrevolution has sunk in our century.

Despite the many risks and hardships, revolutionaries remain committed to the struggle for change in the world. When the avenues of peaceful reform are bottled up by the agents of privilege, revolution becomes the only means available to those who wish to improve the condition of the earth's masses and help restore their dignity. As long as deprivation and exploitation exist on as large a scale as they do today, revolutions will continue to be an essential part of our experience.

---

colonialists were incapable of understanding the resourcefulness and potential of the Algerian people, which were only realized in the very act of revolution against their oppressors. See Selection 21, this volume.

[28] Samuel P. Huntington, "The Basis of Accommodation," *Foreign Affairs,* Vol. 46, 1968, p. 652.

I.

DEFINITIONS OF REVOLUTION

1

Marx on Revolution

I.   From the *Critique of Political Economy**

The subject of my professional studies was jurisprudence, which I pursued, however, in connection with and as secondary to the studies of philosophy and history. In 1842–43, as editor of the "Rheinische Zeitung," I found myself embarrassed at first when I had to take part in discussions concerning so-called material interests. The proceedings of the Rhine Diet in connection with forest thefts and the extreme subdivision of landed property; the official controversy about the condition of the Mosel peasants into which Herr von Schaper, at that time president of the Rhine Province, entered with the "Rheinische Zeitung"; finally, the debates on free trade and protection, gave me the first impulse to take up the study of economic questions. At the same time a weak, quasi-philosophic echo of French socialism and communism made itself heard in the "Rheinische Zeitung" in those days when the good intentions "to go ahead" greatly outweighed knowledge of facts. I declared myself against such botching, but had to admit at once in a controversy with the "Allgemeine Augsburger Zeitung" that my previous studies did not allow me to hazard an independent judgment as to the merits of the French schools. When, therefore, the publishers of the "Rheinische Zeitung" conceived the illusion that by a less aggressive policy the paper could be saved from the death

* Karl Marx, Preface to *A Contribution to the Critique of Political Economy* (Chicago: Charles H. Kerr & Co., 1904), pp. 10–13. By permission.

The original German edition was published in 1859.

3

sentence pronounced upon it, I was glad to grasp that opportunity to retire to my study room from public life.

The first work undertaken for the solution of the question that troubled me, was a critical revision of Hegel's "Philosophy of Law"; the introduction to that work appeared in the "Deutsch-Französische Jahrbücher," published in Paris in 1844. I was led by my studies to the conclusion that legal relations as well as forms of state could neither be understood by themselves, nor explained by the so-called general progress of the human mind, but that they are rooted in the material conditions of life, which are summed up by Hegel after the fashion of the English and French of the eighteenth century under the name "civic society"; the anatomy of that civic society is to be sought in political economy. The study of the latter which I had taken up in Paris, I continued at Brussels whither I emigrated on account of an order of expulsion issued by Mr. Guizot. The general conclusion at which I arrived and which, once reached, continued to serve as the leading thread in my studies, may be briefly summed up as follows: In the social production which men carry on they enter into definite relations that are indispensable and independent of their will; these relations of production correspond to a definite stage of development of their material powers of production. The sum total of these relations of production constitutes the economic structure of society—the real foundation, on which rise legal and political superstructures and to which correspond definite forms of social consciousness. The mode of production in material life determines the general character of the social, political and spiritual processes of life. It is not the consciousness of men that determines their existence, but, on the contrary, their social existence determines their consciousness. At a certain stage of their development, the material forces of production in society come in conflict with the existing relations of production, or—what is but a legal expression for the same thing—with the property relations within which they had been at work before. From forms of development of the forces of production these relations turn into their fetters. Then comes the period of social revolution. With the change of the economic foundation the entire immense superstructure is more or less rapidly transformed. In considering such transformations the distinction should always be made between the material transformation of the economic conditions of production which can be determined with the precision of natural science, and the legal, political, religious, aesthetic or philosophic—in short ideological forms in which men become conscious of this conflict and fight it out. Just as our opinion of an individual is not based on what he thinks of himself, so can we not judge of such a period of transformation by its own consciousness; on the contrary, this consciousness must rather be explained from the contradictions of material life, from the existing conflict between the social forces of production and the relations of production. No social order ever disappears before all the productive forces, for which there is room in it, have been developed; and new higher relations of production never appear before the material conditions of their existence have matured in the womb of the old society. Therefore, mankind always takes up only such problems as it can solve; since, looking at the matter more closely, we will always find that the problem itself arises only when the material conditions necessary for its solution already exist or are at least in the process of formation. In broad outlines we can designate the Asiatic, the ancient, the feudal, and the modern bourgeois methods of production as so many epochs in the progress of the economic formation of society. The bourgeois relations of production are the last antagonistic form of the social process of production—antagonistic not in the sense of individual antagonism, but of one arising from conditions surrounding the life of individuals in society; at the same time, the productive forces developing in the womb of bourgeois society create the material conditions for the solution of that antagonism. This social formation constitutes, therefore, the closing chapter of the prehistoric stage of human society.

II. From *The German Ideology* *

The ideas of the ruling class are in every epoch the ruling ideas, i.e., the class which is the ruling *material* force of society, is at

---

* Karl Marx and Frederick Engels, *The German Ideology* (New York: International Publishers, 1970), pp. 64–66, 92–95. By permission. The original German edition was published in 1846.

the same time its ruling *intellectual* force. The class which has the means of material production at its disposal, has control at the same time over the means of mental production, so that thereby, generally speaking, the ideas of those who lack the means of mental production are subject to it. The ruling ideas are nothing more than the ideal expression of the dominant material relationships, the dominant material relationships grasped as ideas; hence of the relationships which make the one class the ruling one, therefore, the ideas of its dominance. The individuals composing the ruling class possess among other things consciousness, and therefore think. Insofar, therefore, as they rule as a class and determine the extent and compass of an epoch, it is self-evident that they do this in its whole range, hence among other things rule also as thinkers, as producers of ideas, and regulate the production and distribution of the ideas of their age: thus their ideas are the ruling ideas of the epoch. For instance, in an age and in a country where royal power, aristocracy, and bourgeoisie are contending for mastery and where, therefore, mastery is shared, the doctrine of the separation of powers proves to be the dominant idea and is expressed as an "eternal law."

The division of labor, which . . . [has been] one of the chief forces of history up till now, manifests itself also in the ruling class as the division of mental and material labor, so that inside this class one part appears as the thinkers of the class (its active, conceptive ideologists, who make the perfecting of the illusion of the class about itself their chief source of livelihood), while the others' attitude to these ideas and illusions is more passive and receptive, because they are in reality the active members of this class and have less time to make up illusions and ideas about themselves. Within this class this cleavage can even develop into a certain opposition and hostility between the two parts, which, however, in the case of a practical collision, in which the class itself is endangered, automatically comes to nothing, in which case there also vanishes the semblance that the ruling ideas were not the ideas of the ruling class and had a power distinct from the power of this class. The existence of revolutionary ideas in a particular period presupposes the existence of a revolutionary class. . . .

If now in considering the course of history we detach the ideas of the ruling class from the ruling class itself and attribute to them an independent existence, if we confine ourselves to saying that these or those ideas were dominant at a given time, without bothering ourselves about the conditions of production and the producers of these ideas, if we thus ignore the individuals and world conditions which are the source of the ideas, we can say, for instance, that during the time that the aristocracy was dominant, the concepts honor, loyalty, etc. were dominant, during the dominance of the bourgeoisie the concepts freedom, equality, etc. The ruling class itself on the whole imagines this to be so. This conception of history, which is common to all historians, particularly since the eighteenth century, will necessarily come up against the phenomenon that increasingly abstract ideas hold sway, i.e., ideas which increasingly take on the form of universality. For each new class which puts itself in the place of one ruling before it, is compelled, merely in order to carry through its aim, to represent its interest as the common interest of all the members of society, that is, expressed in ideal form: it has to give its ideas the form of universality, and represent them as the only rational, universally valid ones. The class making a revolution appears from the very start, if only because it is opposed to a *class,* not as a class but as the representative of the whole of society; it appears as the whole mass of society confronting the one ruling class. It can do this because, to start with, its interest really is more connected with the common interest of all other non-ruling classes, because under the pressure of hitherto existing conditions its interest has not yet been able to develop as the particular interest of a particular class. Its victory, therefore, benefits also many individuals of the other classes which are not winning a dominant position, but only insofar as it now puts these individuals in a position to raise themselves into the ruling class. When the French bourgeoisie overthrew the power of aristocracy, it thereby made it possible for many proletarians to raise themselves above the proletariat, but only insofar as they become bourgeois. Every new class, therefore, achieves its hegemony only on a broader basis than that of the class ruling previously, whereas the opposition of the non-ruling class against the new ruling class later develops all the more sharply and profoundly. Both these things determine the fact that the struggle to be waged against this new ruling class, in its turn, aims at a more decided and radical negation of the previous conditions of society than could all previous classes which sought to rule.

This whole semblance, that the rule of a certain class is only the rule of certain ideas, comes to a natural end, of course, as soon as class rule in general ceases to be the form in which society is organized, that is to say, as soon as it is no longer necessary to represent a particular interest as general or the "general interest" as ruling.

Only the proletarians of the present day, who are completely shut off from all self-activity,[1] are in a position to achieve a complete and no longer restricted self-activity, which consists in the appropriation of a totality of productive forces and in the thus postulated development of a totality of capacities. All earlier revolutionary appropriations were restricted; individuals, whose self-activity was restricted by a crude instrument of production and a limited intercourse, appropriated this crude instrument of production, and hence merely achieved a new state of limitation. Their instrument of production became their property, but they themselves remained subordinate to the division of labor and their own instrument of production. In all expropriations up to now, a mass of individuals remained subservient to a single instrument of production; in the appropriation by the proletarians, a mass of instruments of production must be made subject to each individual, and property to all. Modern universal intercourse can be controlled by individuals, therefore, only when controlled by all.

[1] The absence of "self-activity" refers to Marx's crucial concept of the alienation of labor, which has to do with man's estrangement from himself, from nature and from the rest of mankind under capitalism. There is a large body of literature around this important idea. See, for example, Shlomo Avineri, *The Social and Political Thought of Karl Marx,* Cambridge, England, 1970; Erich Fromm, *Marx's Concept of Man,* New York, 1968.

This appropriation is further determined by the manner in which it must be effected. It can only be effected through a union, which by the character of the proletariat itself can again only be a universal one, and through a revolution, in which, on the one hand, the power of the earlier mode of production and intercourse and social organization is overthrown, and, on the other hand, there develops the universal character and the energy of the proletariat, without which the revolution cannot be accomplished; and in which, further, the proletariat rids itself of everything that still clings to it from its previous position in society.

Only at this stage does self-activity coincide with material life, which corresponds to the development of individuals into complete individuals and the casting-off of all natural limitations. The transformation of labor into self-activity corresponds to the transformation of the earlier limited intercourse into the intercourse of individuals as such. With the appropriation of the total productive forces through united individuals, private property comes to an end. Whilst previously in history a particular condition always appeared as accidental, now the isolation of individuals and the particular private gain of each man have themselves become accidental.

The individuals, who are no longer subject to the division of labor, have been conceived by the philosophers as an ideal, under the name "Man." They have conceived the whole process which we have outlined as the evolutionary process of "Man," so that at every historical stage "Man" was substituted for the individuals and shown as the motive force of history. The whole process was thus conceived as a process of the self-estrangement of "Man," and this was essentially due to the fact that the average individual of the later stage was always foisted on to the earlier stage, and the consciousness of a later age on to the individuals of an earlier. Through this inversion, which from the first is an abstract image of the actual conditions, it was possible to transform the whole of history into an evolutionary process of consciousness.

Finally, from the conception of history we have sketched we obtain these further conclusions: (1) In the development of productive forces there comes a stage when productive forces and means of intercourse are brought into being, which, under the existing relationships, only cause mischief, and are no longer productive but destructive forces (machinery and money); and connected with this a class is called forth, which has to bear all the burdens of society without enjoying its advantages, which, ousted from society, is forced into the most decided antagonism to all other classes; a class which forms the majority of all members of society, and from which emanates the consciousness of the necessity of a fundamental revolution, the communist consciousness, which may, of course, arise among the other classes too through the contemplation of the situation of this class. (2) The conditions under which definite productive forces can be applied are the conditions of the rule of a definite class of society, whose social power, deriving from its property, has its *practical*-idealistic expression in each case in the form of the State; and, therefore, every revolutionary struggle is directed against a class, which till then has been in power. (3) In all revolutions up till now the mode of activity always remained unscathed and it was only a question of a different distribution of this activity, a new distribution of labor to other persons, while the communist revolution is directed against the preceding *mode* of activity, does away with *labor,* and abolishes the rule of all classes with the classes themselves, because it is carried through by the class which no longer counts as a class in society, is not recognized as a class, and is in itself the expression of the dissolution of all classes, nationalities, etc. within present society; and (4) Both for the production on a mass scale of this communist consciousness, and for the success of the cause itself, the alternation of men on a mass scale is necessary, an alteration which can only take place in a practical movement, a *revolution;* this revolution is necessary, therefore, not only because the *ruling* class cannot be overthrown in any other way, but also because the class *overthrowing* it can only in a revolution succeed in ridding itself of all the muck of ages and become fitted to found society anew.

2

Max Nomad: Intellectuals and Revolution*

The deeper aspects of a historical event or process are seldom fully realized by its contemporaries or by its main personages. The actual economic implications behind the religious and idealist verbiage surrounding the Crusades, the Reformation, the French Revolution, though hardly understood by contemporaries and participants, are now self-evident to even the most superficial student of history.

There is no doubt at present that the socialist movement of the nineteenth and twentieth centuries constitutes the beginning of a new historical epoch. Only a few of the momentous events in the evolution of humanity can be compared to it. Its foremost pioneers have not only succeeded in arousing the masses of the dissatisfied; they have also permeated their contemporaries with a more realistic conception and interpretation of historical events. Naturally enough, they have applied that method to their own movement as well and have proudly declared that theirs is the first movement on a world scale to be conscious of its own historical significance. It is a boast which, given the profound scholarship of its authors, sounds almost convincing.

The socialist critics of the existing system pierced through all

* Max Nomad, Conclusion to *Rebels and Renegades* (New York: Macmillan Co., 1932), pp. 392–406. By permission.

Max Nomad is the author of *Apostles of Revolution* and *Aspects of Revolt,* as well as numerous other books and articles.

the shams, and laid bare the real motives of the defenders of capitalist privilege, just as their liberal predecessors saw through those of the feudal apologists. They discerned the general interests which united their privileged enemies, as clearly as the various cross- and under-currents which created internal conflicts within their ranks. These critics likewise penetrated through the unconscious "rationalizing" mental processes which had accompanied both the struggles of the capitalist bourgeoisie for domination and their efforts to maintain it when won: processes which had permitted the capitalists to identify their own specific interests with the interests of all the other dissatisfied classes; to consider the wrongs from which *they* suffered as the wrongs of the "people" at large, and to see in their own access to power the liberation of the country.

According to the socialist scholars, such deception and self-deception as that caused by the predatory character of the ruling class of today is alien to the socialist movement—including in that term all the traditional currents of anticapitalist protest. Aiming, as it does, at the defense not of any privilege, but of the common interests of the majority—the manual and mental workers—it is not predatory in character; it needs no "rationalizing" psychological processes, and it can afford to be fully conscious of its motives and aims.

The theory of the community of interests of all wage- and salary-earning toilers of brawn and brain has long seemed simple and convincing. Yet, just as convincing seemed also that earlier theory of the community of interests of all members of the "third estate"—capitalists and peasants, workers and intellectuals—as opposed to the feudal lords; or Thomas Jefferson's theory of the community of interests of all "producers"—manufacturers, large landowners and the rest—as against the "speculators"; or Henry George's theory of the community of interests of all the people, as against the owners of land.

The theory of the "third estate" rallied the less favored classes of the population around the banner of the capitalist bourgeoisie. The theory of Jefferson could have served a similar purpose, with the money lender substituted as enemy for the non-existent feudal lord; and Henry George's "single tax" was, in the words of Karl Marx, "the last attempt to save the capitalist system." But in the mind of that great scholar—as in that of any other socialist thinker—there was no fallacy in the theory that the hired manager, engineer, professor, all the innumerable more-or-less privileged salaried intellectual workers, were, along with the manual laborers, at bottom, wage-earning, propertyless, proletarians, belonging to the same class as opposed to the property-owning capitalists. Nor did he see, or want to see, that this fallacy was to serve a specific class-purpose: to rally the manual workers around the banner of a new, rising bourgeois class—the intellectual workers.

The development of modern industrialism and of the modern State has made higher education accessible to wider groups of the population than in previous periods. Originally the educated elements belonged chiefly to the priesthood. There was also a restricted group of descendants of the privileged classes who, for one reason or another, were willing to take up politics, the arts and the sciences, usually as the privileged minions of some king or feudal lord. The upper sections of this feudal intelligentsia enjoyed the same privileges and comforts as their property-holding lords. Its lower strata, as represented by the poorer clergy, had often grounds for dissatisfaction. In many cases the more energetic and adventurous elements of this section revolted against their more fortunate superiors. Spiritually, these revolts expressed themselves in heresies drawn from the primitive communism of the Scriptures; materially, in the support of ever-recurring uprisings of the downtrodden urban and rural masses. Whatever the conscious ideal of these heretics, their real subconscious aim is now plainly evident: the theocratic rule of the victorious lesser clergy.

Where the exclusive mental sway of the clergy was either absent, as in classical Greece, or vanishing, as in the Europe of the seventeenth and eighteenth centuries, the dissatisfaction of the intellectuals expressed itself in philosophical or fictional dreams of the perfect State, as a protest of the owners of intellect and culture against the predominance of the owners of land, money, serfs and other material goods. Consciously or unconsciously, these utopian dreams were the compensatory "wish-fulfilments" of a social group which was still too weak to express its ambition for domination in any other way.

The political and industrial revolutions of the declining eighteenth century saw the intellectuals arrayed with the various groups of the rising middle classes in their struggles against the feudal past—and among themselves. With the emerging of capitalist rule, hampered as it still was by many encumbering feudal remainders, the independent strivings of the intellectuals began to come to the fore. A part of the educated scions of the property-holding classes were provided for as members of the State bureaucracy and of the liberal professions, not to speak of the clergy and of the officers' caste. These were entirely satisfied with the status quo and defended it against its critics and opponents. Industries were still largely managed by their owners, but a separate class of managers, engineers and technicians was gradually becoming more and more indispensable for the growing scope of economic development. The rewards of this last group were not very generous as yet, and many of them began to visualize the possibilities of a social order managed by themselves in a more efficient, more scientific, way than by the often ignorant capitalist upstarts, whose blind greed and ruthless exploitation of the workers was pregnant with calamitous possibilities. They remembered the miseries that had followed in the wake of the French revolution, and they wished to avoid their repetition. Their aspirations found expression in the ideas and proposals of various divergent currents, usually referred to as "utopian," "philanthropic," "conservative," or "Christian" socialism.

However widely the advocates of these currents differed in their vocabulary or their point of departure, most of them had actually much in common with the moderate Socialists of the present time. Middle-class or upper-middle-class intellectuals in social status or in sympathies, they feared the impending uprising of the submerged masses. Aside from a few visionary plans for human brotherhood to be realized as a result of the benevolence of the privileged classes, their proposals had in view practical improvements for immediate application, tending in the direction of government ownership. Their hierarchical state was to compensate the capitalists, lavishly to reward the higher abilities of the educated managers and organizers of the nation's economic and cultural life, and to perpetuate the social status of the performers of manual labor. Their postulate for a socialized or regulated form of exploitation—or economic inequality, which amounts to the same thing—can be found in undisguised form in the ideas of the followers of Saint-Simon or in the theories of the "conservative" Socialist, Rodbertus. Anxious to preserve existing privileges, advocates of these ideas were to be found among the staunchest supporters of the Caesarism of Napoleon III and the monarchical principle of Hohenzollern Germany.

But in the first part of the nineteenth century the time had not yet come for the adoption of those proposals. Private capitalism was still at the beginning of its career, and the danger threatening from below could still be coped with by other methods than government ownership or similar schemes.

That danger from below was represented not only by the underpaid manual workers. It threatened likewise from a numerous group of lower-middle-class intellectuals—students without the prospect of comfortable positions after graduation, teachers without appointments, journalists without purchasers for their intellectual wares, and all the other varieties of unemployed or underpaid mental workers with hearty appetites and empty stomachs.

Early in the nineteenth century, Napoleon, with his promise of the "career open to talent," regardless of origin or wealth, had been for a long time the ideal of that educated but almost hopeless younger generation. "Napoleon was indeed the man sent by God to help the youth of France!" was the sigh of Stendhal's hero of that period, Julien Sorel, in *Le Rouge et le Noir*. "Who is to take his place? What will the poor wretches do without him, who have just the few crowns needed to procure them a good education, and then not enough money . . . to launch themselves in a career?"

But Napoleon was not to return, and the young men with an education had to fall back upon another hero of the Great Revolution in decline: Babeuf, the organizer of the "Conspiracy

of the Equals"—the first attempt of a group of communist intellectuals to seize the government with the help of the workers.
Babeuf's gospel was revived a few decades later and was known
first as "Babouvism" and then called after Blanqui, its most
outstanding apostle and martyr. During a whole generation
impecunious intellectuals kept on organizing conspiracies and
coups aiming at the establishment of a revolutionary dictatorship.

That economic depression of the early nineteenth century
which inspired the more desperate section of the French intelligentsia with ideas rather like those of the Russian Communists
of three generations later, had its revolutionary effects in England as well. A powerful radical movement, known as Chartism, was on foot on the other side of the Channel. Headed by
lower-middle-class intellectuals, it enlisted the working masses
in a struggle for more democracy, as expressed by universal
suffrage. It was in many respects the prototype of the continental socialist parties, with their propaganda for universal
franchise of about half a century later.

Greatly differing from each other in their external manifestations and in their vocabulary, the French and the English radicals of nearly a century ago had two important features in
common. Headed by lower-middle-class intellectuals, both
movements aimed at a change in the political form of the existing system—but not at the immediate seizure and nationalization of capital. Socialism, though generally professed by the
French conspirators and partly current among the Chartists,
was reserved for a more-or-less-distant future; but the seizure of
power, or participation in the government with the help of a
democratic suffrage, was put forward as an immediate objective.
Power for the intellectuals and hope for the workers—that division of . . . spoils has remained to the present day.

Both Blanquism and Chartism disappeared under the impact
of new conditions. The economic upswing that took place in
England around the middle of the nineteenth century brought
the trade unions to the fore, as an instrument for immediate
improvement in the situation of labor. For many decades, trade
unionism pure and simple reigned supreme over the minds of

the English workers. An analogous process, though under other forms, took place in France, where a similar revulsion against purely political radicalism led to a development of various coöperative schemes. In both France and England, the parvenu manual worker who had acquired a smattering of education forced out his white-collar competitor for leadership.

A coördination of the political radicalism of the lower-middle-class intelligentsia with the trade-unionist aspirations of the upper stratum of the manual workers was effected by a group, originally German, centered around Karl Marx and Frederick Engels. Their ideas served as inspiration for three generations of socialists of the various schools. "Regular" socialists of the German prototype, Communists of the Russian brand, Syndicalists of the French and American (I.W.W.) varieties, even Anarchists, at least those of the Bakunin tradition—all were under the spell of the Marx-Engels class-struggle theory. That theory proclaimed an irreconcilable antagonism between the proletariat and the capitalist class, the final outcome of which was to be the expropriation of the propertied classes and the establishment of a collectivist form of production.

In the conception, currently accepted by all divisions of modern socialism, the word "proletariat" includes both manual workers and brain workers—all those who have to rely for their livelihood on wages or salaries. In his *Communist Manifesto,* Marx found ardent speech to present the miserable plight of the intellectual workers who had become paid wage slaves of the capitalist class. That plight was very real indeed during the early period of the nineteenth century, and Marx, himself one of them, could not help identifying their fortunes with those of the manual workers. Yet poor as they were, there was a substantial difference between their misery and that of the manual workers. Their middle-class or lower-middle-class families had spent a certain capital "to procure them a good education"—their mental, invisible means of production. That investment was bearing no dividends as yet. But a change in the politico-administrative structure—without essentially altering the status of the manual workers—could remedy their situation. Political democracy with its opportunities for underpaid or unemployed talent, meant not only "dividends" on their investment—it was also the starting point from which the malcontent intelligentsia could eventually obtain a controlling interest in the nation's business: dispossess the capitalists and take charge of the government and of the management of the nationalized industries. In Marxian language this was called "conquest of political power" by the working class.

The second half of the nineteenth century saw the inauguration of political democracy or near-democracy in most western countries. In accomplishing this the radical intelligentsia secured the assistance of the manual workers by helping them, in turn, in their struggles for their bread-and-butter demands.

This was to be succeeded by the second stage: the revolutionary struggle proper, for the removal of capitalism and the establishment of socialism. The establishment of socialism meant, of course, one thing to the intellectuals and self-taught ex-workers, who headed the movement, and another thing to the manual workers, who made up their following. The latter saw in it the fulfillment of their dreams of economic equality; while in the conception of the former, "socialism" was only an euphemistic expression for State Capitalism—that is, government ownership of industries managed by a bureaucracy composed of intellectuals, self-taught ex-workers and former capitalists.

Even so, that second step has never been attempted, in democratic Western Europe, at least. The Paris Commune of 1871, in spite of all the red glamor associated with it, was a venture in radical democracy rather than in socialism. The advent of democracy, coupled with a great upswing in industrial development, had cooled the ardor of the former implacable enemies of the existing system. The starving intellectuals, who in the middle of the nineteenth century had been ready, side by side with the factory workers, to fight on the barricades for democracy or even for a dictatorship as the first step to socialism, were starving no longer. There were plenty of well-paid positions at their disposal, and as a group they had become perfectly respectable bourgeois. A certain section of the intelligentsia continued, however, to dabble in "labor" politics. These were ambitious men who saw in the socialist and labor movement a career that offered unlimited possibilities. There was, of course, a sprinkling of idealists, who joined the movement because the socialist ideal appealed to their outraged sense of justice; and also, to be sure, the common adventurers and "cranks" who infest every heterodox movement.

But these leaders were no revolutionists. That specific capital which they possessed, the privilege of a higher education, placed them above the working masses and enabled them to establish themselves as one of the many privileged groups of the bourgeois world. They were editors, politicians, organizers; preachers of the new gospel of a Proletarian Kingdom, apparently not of this world—or, at least, several generations away. The prospect did not dismay them, for they had time to wait. . . . A peaceful, unprecipitated transition to State Capitalism was the apex of their revolutionary longings. In the interval they were ready to defend the existing system against unwarranted interference with the normal course of affairs. In this they were supported by a section of the working class, the highly skilled workers, who, to a certain extent, were allowed to participate in the benefits of industrial expansion and colonial exploitation.

Nevertheless, theirs was no bed of roses. They were beset by many dangers. There were, first, the too-eager careerists, who were ever ready to jump out of the ranks and to play openly capitalist politics, thus affecting the *morale* of the followers. There were also some younger leaders who were afraid lest the moderation of the official party policy might eventually alienate the more impatient elements of their own party's working-class following; these often indulged in too much loose talk about revolution, with a view to taking over the leadership from the party "fossils." Friction and jealousy were continually occurring between the college-bred "highbrows," in charge of the political end of the movement, and the self-taught ex-workers, controlling the trade unions in coöperation with the party. Finally there were the anarchist and syndicalist heretics who also aspired to leadership of the laboring masses.

In time, however, the inexorable laws of life under democracy took care of the radical competitors, both within and without the party. The oppositionists within became very reasonable as soon as they were themselves admitted to the highest councils of the great organization. The anarchist intellectuals who often succeeded in attracting the most rebellious elements opposed to the existing system could represent no serious menace to the socialist politicians. With their far-away ideal and their rejection of the class struggle (or acceptance of it only for propagandist purposes) they were bound to become an insignificant sect of peaceful preachers, demolishing the existing order in spirit only. The syndicalists, their more realistic counterparts within the trade unions, were likewise bound to lose their revolutionary souls. Wherever they have succeeded in getting control of the trade unions, they have gradually succumbed to the allurements of regular trade-union leadership with its steady rewards. In France, the classical country of its origin, syndicalism has made peace with the existing order, indignant protests of uninfluential groups notwithstanding. Spanish syndicalism, with a long tradition of heroic struggles under the semi-absolutist Bourbon régime, entered shortly after the downfall of the latter upon a similar road of evolution towards respectability. Over and over again the democratic opportunities of the more advanced countries have enabled intellectuals, semi-intellectuals and self-taught ex-workers, as leaders of the various forms of the labor movement, to avail themselves of the revolutionary discontent of the masses in order to divert it into futile political campaigns, into peaceful trade unionism, or into some utopian cult.

But the democratic idyll did not last forever. There came a time when industrial expansion ceased to keep pace with increasing opportunity for higher education. Once more, there were not enough soft jobs to go around. Colonial possessions could provide for a part only of the educated surplus of the population—and not all countries had that outlet. Moreover, there were two great countries of the east which had not yet passed through the democratic stage—Russia and China. Economically and politically undeveloped, they had an enormous army of hungry intellectuals with no share in the national income.

Again, as in the early part of the nineteenth century, the civilized world was confronted by a host of desperate, impecunious, lower-middle-class intellectuals, whose only hope was in a violent overthrow of the existing system. The War and the unrest coming in its wake made an opportunity for this section of the intelligentsia to assert itself. While the official socialist parties, representing the more prosperous and sedate labor politicians and trade-union leaders, rallied to the defense of existing conditions and were accepted as full-fledged members of the various government coalitions—or at best adopted a weak-kneed, temporizing attitude—the more desperate elements openly challenged in one way or another the prevailing status quo. The communist reversion to the Blanquist tradition of revolutionary dictatorship and the Fascist reversion to a sort of military dictatorship in the Napoleonic tradition, represent the final outcome of these revolutionary developments of the War and post-War periods.

In Russia that section of the intelligentsia and semi-intelligentsia (including a large percentage of self-taught ex-workers) which is organized in the Communist Party, has succeeded in eliminating the capitalists and large landowners, and in imposing its rule over the rest of the population, including the other sections of the intelligentsia. It is tirelessly at work establishing a well-knit system of State Capitalism headed by an all-powerful bureaucracy. In the other countries communist leadership represents the younger and more adventurous set of socialist politicians. They are mainly concerned with taking over the inheritance of the decaying and discredited socialist parties. In exceptionally desperate situations, particularly in countries devoid of political liberties like Italy or Poland, some of them may attempt to emulate the Russian example. In the democratic countries, their policy resembles more or less that of the left wing of the socialist parties prior to the War—with more revolutionary talk than action; particularly as the Russian Communists upon whom they depend for inspiration, have shelved the idea of "world revolution"—being now more interested in industrializing their country and in avoiding international complications.

Those of the intellectuals who have joined the Fascist camp in Italy and Poland,[1] are mainly deserters from the radicals—in quest of a short cut to power and influence. In Germany and elsewhere, they are mostly scions of the ruined "newly-poor" middle classes. Their terminology and their "principles" change from country to country, and . . . from one meeting to another; but their purpose is unmistakable: to gain as much power as possible, both by helping the capitalists to cow the workers, and occasionally also by forcing the capitalists to make concessions to other classes of the population. Their chief support is drawn from those sections of the educated middle and lower middle classes whose economic security and prospects have been destroyed by the post-War developments.

Simultaneously with the struggle of the various sections of the educated lower middle classes for power and influence, there seethes, deep below the surface, a potential revolt of those laboring masses, who, subconsciously of course, continue to think in other terms than their leaders. Whatever theories and panaceas they may be offered, they *feel,* so to speak, in terms of wages and employment, and from time to time their violent outbursts give expression to their inarticulate longings for their own emancipation. To be sure, every demand for higher wages implies a step in that direction, a step towards economic equality. Extended to the dimensions of a general strike of all manual workers, skilled and unskilled, the struggle for higher wages and work for the unemployed may culminate in the total absorption of profits and the reduction of the excessive incomes of the higher salaried men. Faced by demands they are unable to meet, the private capitalist corporations may be forced to yield their place to a higher form of industrial management, the system of government ownership, or State Capitalism, which Socialists sometimes call "State Socialism."

This higher form of industrial management has ceased to be the mere theoretical fancy that it was in the early part of the past century, when it was first proposed by various schools of

[1] This article was published in 1932—ed.

socialism. To avoid its violent inauguration as an alternative to gradual economic disintegration otherwise conservative men have ceased to "view with alarm" the idea of state control of the nation's economic life. Remembering the services rendered by socialist parties and cabinet ministers to the cause of social peace during and after World War I, a confused and frightened bourgeois world may entrust these former alleged enemies with the task of reorganization.

Whether the new system is ushered in as a result of sweeping peaceful reforms adopted under the continuous, threatening pressure of the dissatisfied masses, or as a result of a violent cataclysm; whether the new government machine is headed by moderate Socialists and neo-Liberals, or by extreme left radicals, inequality of income, perpetuated in the higher wages assigned for mental work, remains the outstanding characteristic of State Capitalism. On this point, at least, there is no difference of opinion between Communists and Socialists, between the more impecunious and violent enemies, and the more contented and patient critics, of private capitalist privilege. That principle of inequality has been propounded by their common teacher, Karl Marx, in his famous statement on the "first phase of communism"—his euphemistic term for State Capitalism under the management of the socialist intelligentsia. (*On the Gotha Program.*)

Both Socialists and Communists assume that the progress of economic development will automatically result in the later disappearance of these inequalities of the "first phase"; though, like their teacher, they relegate the "higher phase of communism" to a rather distant and nebulous future. Forgetful of their Marxian realism, they candidly attribute to the educated, privileged, beneficiaries of the "first phase" a truly unworldly disinterestedness. Voluntarily they are to level their own incomes with those of the manual workers, thus creating equal educational opportunities for all, and wiping out their own intellectual monopoly and class predominance.

It is not very likely that such promises will keep the workers in their place. The continuous mass struggle for higher and higher wages will remain an accompaniment of State Capitalism (the "first phase of communism") as it is of private capitalism. Discontented groups of intellectuals will continue to embrace the cause of the manual workers and to assist them in their struggle, prompted either by an heroic urge to the good fight, or by their own ambition for leadership.

With the eventual equalization of wages for manual and mental workers, the apparent goal of such struggle, higher education becomes accessible to all alike. The rest is a new page in human history.[2]

[2] I no longer believe that the manual workers' struggle for higher wages will ever result in the equalization of incomes and thus in the establishment of what is called a "classless society." All revolutionary struggles being led by *educated* men, the victorious leaders will, as they did in the Russian, Chinese, and other anticapitalist orbits, establish the rule of a new privileged elite whose higher education (a sort of "invisible capital") enables it to *establish* and to *maintain* its neo-bourgeois or neo-aristocratic ascendancy over the uneducated majority—with the human race remaining, as under all preceding social systems, divided into a privileged ruling minority and an underprivileged, uneducated majority. I also reject the term "state capitalism" for a system which—while sometimes called "socialism" or "communism"—actually deserves the designation of the French term "étatisme," i.e., statism or government monopoly, denoting the class rule of officeholders, managers, and persons of education in general. I also want to point out that I used the term "intellectual" not in its specific American meaning, but in the sense of intellectual workers, whether college-bred or self-educated, including labor-union functionaries.—MAX NOMAD.

3

Lawrence Stone: Recent Academic Views of Revolution*

In attacking the problem of revolution, as most others of major significance in history, we historians should think twice before we spurn the help offered by our colleagues in the social sciences, who have, as it happens, been particularly active in the last few years in theorizing about the typology, causes, and evolutionary patterns of this particular phenomenon. The purpose of this article is not to advance any new hypothesis, but to provide a summary view and critical examination of the work that has been going on.

The first necessity in any inquiry is a careful definition of terms: what is, and what is not, a revolution? According to one view, it is change, effected by the use of violence, in government, and/or regime, and/or society.[1] By *society* is meant the consciousness and the mechanics of communal solidarity, which may be tribal, peasant, kinship, national, and so on; by *regime* is meant the constitutional structure—democracy, oligarchy, monarchy; and by *government* is meant specific political and

---

* Lawrence Stone, "Theories of Revolution," *World Politics* (Princeton: Princeton University Press, 1966), pp. 159–176. By permission.

Lawrence Stone, professor of history at Princeton University, is the author of *The Crisis of the Aristocracy, An Elizabethan: Sir Horatio Palavicino* and numerous articles.

[1] Chalmers Johnson, *Revolution and the Social System,* Hoover Institution Studies 3 (Stanford, 1964).

administrative institutions. Violence, it should be noted, is not the same as force; it is force used with unnecessary intensity, unpredictably, and usually destructively.[2] This definition of revolution is a very broad one, and two historians of the French Revolution, Crane Brinton and Louis Gottschalk, would prefer to restrict the use of the word to the major political and social upheavals with which they are familiar, the "Great Revolutions" as George S. Pettee calls them.[3]

Even the wider definition allows the historian to distinguish between the seizure of power that leads to a major restructuring of government or society and the replacement of the former elite by a new one, and the coup d'état involving no more than a change of ruling personnel by violence or threat of violence. This latter is the norm in Latin America, where it occurred thirty-one times in the ten years 1945–1955. Merle Kling has arrived at a suggestive explanation of this Latin American phenomenon of chronic political instability, limited but frequent use of violence, and almost complete lack of social or institutional change. He argues that ownership of the principal economic resources, both agricultural and mineral, is concentrated in the hands of a tiny, very stable, elite of enormously wealthy monoculture landlords and mining capitalists. This elite is all-powerful and cannot be attacked by opposition groups within the country; externally, however, it is dependent on foreign interests for its markets and its capital. In this colonial situation of a foreign-supported closed plutocracy, the main avenue of rapid upward social mobility for nonmembers of the elite leads, via the army, to the capture of the government machine, which is the only accessible source of wealth and power. This political instability is permitted by the elite on the condition that its own interests are undisturbed. Instability, limited violence, and the absence of social or institutional change are therefore all the

[2] Sheldon S. Wolin, "Violence and the Western Political Tradition," *American Journal of Orthopsychiatry,* xxxiii (January 1963), pp. 15–28.

[3] Crane Brinton, *The Anatomy of Revolution* (New York, 1938); Gottschalk, "Causes of Revolution," *American Journal of Sociology,* i (July 1944), pp. 1–8; Pettee, *The Process of Revolution* (New York, 1938).

product of the contradiction between the realities of a colonial economy run by a plutocracy and the facade of political sovereignty—between the real, stable power of the economic elite and the nominal, unstable control of politicians and generals.[4]

The looser definition of revolution thus suits both historians of major social change and historians of the palace coup. It does, however, raise certain difficulties. Firstly, there is a wide range of changes of government by violence which are neither a mere substitution of personalities in positions of power nor a prelude to the restructuring of society; secondly, conservative counterrevolutions become almost impossible to fit into the model; and lastly, it remains hard to distinguish between colonial wars, civil wars, and social revolution.

To avoid these difficulties, an alternative formulation has recently been put forward by a group of social scientists working mainly at Princeton. They have dropped the word "revolution" altogether and put "internal war" in its place.[5] This is defined as any attempt to alter state policy, rulers, or institutions by the use of violence, in societies where violent competition is not the norm and where well-defined institutional patterns exist.[6] This concept seems to be a logical consequence of the preoccupation of sociologists in recent years with a model of society in a stable, self-regulating state of perpetual equipoise. In this utopian world of universal harmony, all forms of violent conflict are anomalies, to be treated alike as pathological disorders of a similar species. This is a model which, although it has its uses for analytical purposes, bears little relation to the reality familiar to the historian. It looks to a society without change, with universal consensus on values, with complete social harmony, and isolated from external threats; no approxi-

---

[4] "Toward a Theory of Power and Political Instability in Latin America," *Western Political Quarterly,* IX (1956).

[5] Harry Eckstein, ed., *Internal War* (New York 1964), and "On the Etiology of Internal War," *History and Theory,* IV, No. 2 (1965), 133–63. I am grateful to Mr. Eckstein for allowing me to read this article before publication.

[6] The formula has been used by a historian, Peter Paret, in *Internal War and Pacification: The Vendée, 1793–96* (Princeton 1961).

mation to such a society has ever been seen. An alternative model, which postulates that all societies are in a condition of multiple and perpetual tension held in check by social norms, ideological beliefs, and state sanctions, accords better with historical fact, as some sociologists are now beginning to realize.[7]

The first objection to the all-embracing formula of internal war is that, by covering all forms of physical conflict from strikes and terrorism to civil war, it isolates the use of violence from the normal processes of societal adjustment. Though some of the users of the term express their awareness that the use of violence for political ends is a fairly common occurrence, the definition they have established in fact excludes all times and places where it *is* common. It thus cuts out most societies the world has ever known, including Western Europe in the Middle Ages and Latin America today. Secondly, it isolates one particular means, physical violence, from the political ends that it is designed to serve. Clausewitz's famous definition of external war is equally applicable to internal war, civil war, or revolution: "War is not only a political act, but a real political instrument; a continuation of political transactions, an accomplishment of them by different means. That which remains peculiar to war relates only to the peculiar nature of its means."[8]

It is perfectly true that any means by which society exercises pressure or control, whether it is administrative organization, constitutional law, economic interest, or physical force, can be a fruitful field of study in its own right, so long as its students

[7] Barrington Moore, "The Strategy of the Social Sciences," in his *Political Power and Social Theory* (Cambridge, Mass., 1958); Ralph Dahrendorf, "Out of Utopia: Toward a Reorientation of Sociological Analysis," *American Journal of Sociology,* LXIV (September 1958), 115–27; C. Wright Mills, *The Sociological Imagination* (New York 1959); Wilbert E. Moore, *Social Change* (Englewood Cliffs 1963). It should be noted that both the equilibrium and the conflict views of society have very respectable ancestries. The equilibrium model goes back to Rousseau—or perhaps Aquinas; the conflict model to Hobbes, Hegel, and Marx.

[8] Quoted in Edward Mead Earle, ed., *Makers of Modern Strategy* (Princeton 1943), 104–5.

remain aware that they are looking at only one part of a larger whole. It is also true that there is something peculiar about violence, if only because of man's highly ambivalent attitude towards the killing of his own species. Somehow, he regards physical force as different in kind from, say, economic exploitation or psychological manipulation as a means of exercising power over others. But this distinction is not one of much concern to the historian of revolution, in which violence is a normal and natural occurrence. The concept of internal war is too broad in its comprehension of all types of violence from civil wars to strikes, too narrow in its restriction to normally nonviolent societies, too limited in its concern with one of many means, too arbitrary in its separation of this means from the ends in view, and too little concerned with the complex roots of social unrest to be of much practical value to him.

The most fruitful typology of revolution is that of Chalmers Johnson, set out in a pamphlet that deserves to be widely read.[9] He sees six types, identified by the targets selected for attack, whether the government personnel, the political regime, or the community as a social unit; by the nature of the carriers of revolution, whether a mass or an elite; and particularly by the goals and the ideologies, whether reformist, eschatological, nostalgic, nation-forming, elitist, or nationalist. The first type, the *Jacquerie,* is a spontaneous mass peasant rising, usually carried out in the name of the traditional authorities, Church and King, and with the limited aims of purging the local or national elites. Examples are the Peasant Revolt of 1381, Ket's Rebellion of 1549, and the Pugachev rebellion in Russia in 1773–1775. The second type, the *Millenarian Rebellion,* is similar to the first but with the added feature of a utopian dream, inspired by a living messiah. This type can be found at all times, in all parts of the world, from the Florentine revolution led by Savonarola in 1494, to the Anabaptist Rebellion in Münster led by John Mathijs and John Beukels in 1533–1535, to the Sioux Ghost-Dance Rebellion inspired by the Paiute prophet Wovoka in 1890. It has attracted a good deal of atten-

[9] *Revolution and the Social System.*

tion from historians in recent years, partly because the career of Hitler offered overwhelming proof of the enormous historical significance of a charismatic leader, and partly because of a growing interest in the ideas of Max Weber.[10] The third type is the *Anarchistic Rebellion,* the nostalgic reaction to progressive change, involving a romantic idealization of the old order: the Pilgrimage of Grace and the Vendée are examples.

The fourth is that very rare phenomenon, the *Jacobin Communist Revolution.* This has been defined as "a sweeping fundamental change in political organization, social structure, economic property control and the predominant myth of a social order, thus indicating a major break in the continuity of development."[11] This type of revolution can occur only in a highly centralized state with good communications and a large capital city, and its target is government, regime, and society—the lot. The result is likely to be the creation of a new national consciousness under centralized, military authority, and the erection of a more rational, and hence more efficient, social and bureaucratic order on the ruins of the old ramshackle structure of privilege, nepotism, and corruption.

The fifth type is the *Conspiratorial Coup d'État,* the planned work of a tiny elite fired by an oligarchic, sectarian ideology. This qualifies as a revolutionary type only if it in fact anticipates mass movement and inaugurates social change—for example the Nasser revolution in Egypt or the Castro revolution in Cuba; it is thus clearly distinguished from the palace revolt, assassination, dynastic succession-conflict, strike, banditry, and other forms of violence, which are all subsumed under the "internal war" rubric.

Finally, there is the *Militarized Mass Insurrection,* a new phenomenon of the twentieth century in that it is a deliberately

[10] N. R. C. Cohn, *Pursuit of the Millennium* (New York 1961); Eric J. Hobsbawm, *Primitive Rebels* (Manchester 1959); S. L. Thrupp, *Millennial Dreams in Action,* Supplement II, Comparative Studies in Society and History (The Hague 1962); A. J. F. Köbben, "Prophetic Movements as an Expression of Social Protest," *Internationales Archiv für Ethnographie,* XLIX, No. 1 (1960), 117–64.

[11] Sigmund Neumann, quoted in Johnson, p. 2.

planned mass revolutionary war, guided by a dedicated elite. The outcome of guerrilla warfare is determined by political attitudes, not military strategy or matériel, for the rebels are wholly dependent on broad popular support. In all cases on record, the ideology that attracts the mass following has been a combination of xenophobic nationalism and Marxism, with by far the greater stress on the former. This type of struggle has occurred in Yugoslavia, China, Algeria, and Vietnam.

Although, like any schematization of the historical process, this six-fold typology is concerned with ideal types, although in practice individual revolutions may sometimes display characteristics of several different types, the fact remains that this is much the most satisfactory classification we have so far; it is one that working historians can recognize and use with profit. The one obvious criticism is semantic, an objection to the use of the phrase "Jacobin Communist Revolution." Some of Johnson's examples are Communist, such as the Russian or Chinese Revolutions; others are Jacobin but not Communist, such as the French Revolution or the Turkish Revolution of 1908–1922. It would be better to revert to Pettee's category of "Great Revolutions," and treat Communist revolutions as a subcategory, one type, but not the only type, of modernizing revolutionary process.

Given this classification and definition of revolution, what are its root causes? Here everyone is agreed in making a sharp distinction between long-run, underlying causes—the preconditions, which create a potentially explosive situation and can be analyzed on a comparative basis—and immediate, incidental factors—the precipitants, which trigger the outbreak and which may be nonrecurrent, personal, and fortuitous. This effectively disposes of the objections of those historians whose antipathy to conceptual schematization takes the naïve form of asserting the uniqueness of each historical event.

One of the first in the field of model-building was Crane Brinton who, as long ago as 1938, put forward a series of uniformities common to the four great Western revolutions: English, French, American, and Russian. These included an economically advancing society, growing class and status antagonisms, an alienated intelligentsia, a psychologically insecure and politically inept ruling class, and a governmental financial crisis.[12]

The subjectivity, ambiguity, and partial self-contradiction of this and other analyses of the causes of specific revolutions—for example the French Revolution—have been cruelly shown up by Harry Eckstein.[13] He has pointed out that commonly adduced hypotheses run the spectrum of particular conditions, moving from the intellectual (inadequate political socialization, conflicting social myths, a corrosive social philosophy, alienation of the intellectuals) to the economic (increasing poverty, rapid growth, imbalance between production and distribution, long-term growth plus short-term recession) to the social (resentment due to restricted elite circulation, confusion due to excessive elite recruitment, anomie due to excessive social mobility, conflict due to the rise of new social classes) to the political (bad government, divided government, weak government, oppressive government). Finally there are explanations on the level of general process, such as rapid social change, erratic social change, or a lack of harmony between the state structure and society, the rulers and the ruled. None of these explanations are invalid in themselves, but they are often difficult or impossible to reconcile one with the other, and are so diverse in their range and variety as to be virtually impossible to fit into an ordered analytical framework. What, then, is to be done?

Fundamental to all analyses, whether by historians like Brinton and Gottschalk or by political scientists like Johnson and Eckstein, is the recognition of a lack of harmony between the social system on the one hand and the political system on the other. This situation Johnson calls *dysfunction,* a word derived from the structural-functional equilibrium model of the sociologists. This dysfunction may have many causes, some of which are merely cyclical, such as may develop because of personal weaknesses in hereditary kingships or single-party

12 *Anatomy of Revolution.*
13 "On the Etiology of Internal War."

regimes. In these cases, the revolution will not take on serious proportions, and will limit itself to attacks on the governing institutions, leaving regime and society intact. In most cases, however, including all those of real importance, the dysfunction is the result of some new and developing process, as a result of which certain social subsystems find themselves in a condition of relative deprivation. Rapid economic growth, imperial conquest, new metaphysical beliefs, and important technological changes are the four commonest factors involved, in that order. If the process of change is sufficiently slow and sufficiently moderate, the dysfunction may not rise to dangerous levels. Alternatively, the elite may adjust to the new situation with sufficient rapidity and skill to ride out the storm and retain popular confidence. But if the change is both rapid and profound, it may cause the sense of deprivation, alienation, anomie to spread into many sectors of society at once, causing what Johnson calls multiple dysfunction, which may be all but incurable within the existing political system.

In either case the second vital element in creating a revolutionary situation is the condition and attitude of the entrenched elite, a factor on which Eckstein rightly lays great stress. The elite may lose its manipulative skill, or its military superiority, or its self-confidence, or its cohesion; it may become estranged from the nonelite, or overwhelmed by a financial crisis; it may be incompetent, or weak, or brutal. Any combination of two or more of these features will be dangerous. What is ultimately fatal, however, is the compounding of its errors by intransigence. If it fails to anticipate the need for reform, if it blocks all peaceful, constitutional means of social adjustment, then it unites the various deprived elements in single-minded opposition to it, and drives them down the narrow road to violence. It is this process of polarization into two coherent groups or alliances of what are naturally and normally a series of fractional and shifting tensions and conflicts within a society that both Peter Amann and Wilbert Moore see as the essential preliminary to the outbreak of a Jacobin Revolution.[14] To conclude,

[14] Peter Amann, "Revolution: A Redefinition," *Political Science Quarterly*, LXXVII (1962).

therefore, revolution becomes *possible* when a condition of
multiple dysfunction meets an intransigent elite: just such a
conjunction occurred in the decades immediately before the
English, the French, and the Russian Revolutions.

Revolution only becomes *probable* (Johnson might say "certain"), however, if certain special factors intervene: the "precipitants" or "accelerators." Of these, the three most common
are the emergence of an inspired leader or prophet; the formation of a secret, military, revolutionary organization; and the
crushing defeat of the armed forces in foreign war. This last is
of critical importance since it not only shatters the prestige of
the ruling elite, but also undermines the morale and discipline of
the soldiers and thus opens the way to the violent overthrow of
the existing government.

The first defect of Johnson's model is that it concentrates too
much on objective structural conditions, and attempts to relate
conditions directly to action. In fact, however, as Eckstein
points out, there is no such direct relationship; historians can
point to similar activity arising from different conditions, and
different activity arising from similar conditions. Standing between objective reality and action are subjective human attitudes. A behaviorist approach such as Brinton's, which lays
equal stress on such things as anomie, alienation of the intellectuals, frustrated popular aspirations, elite estrangement, and
loss of elite self-confidence, is more likely to produce a satisfactory historical explanation than is one that sticks to the objective social reality. Secondly, Johnson leaves too little play for
the operation of the unique and the personal. He seems to
regard his accelerators as automatic triggers, ignoring the area
of unpredictable personal choice that is always left to the ruling
elite and to the revolutionary leaders, even in a situation of
multiple dysfunction exacerbated by an accelerator. Revolution
is never inevitable—or rather the only evidence of its inevitability is that it actually happens. Consequently the only way to
prove this point is to indulge in just the kind of hypothetical
argument that historians prudently try to avoid. But it is still
just possible that modernization may take place in Morocco
and India without revolution. The modernization and industrial-

ization of Germany and Britain took place without revolution in the nineteenth century (though it can be argued that in the latter case the process was slow by twentieth-century standards, and that, as is now becoming all too apparent, the modernization was far from complete). Some think that a potentially revolutionary situation in the United States in the 1930's was avoided by political action.

Lastly it is difficult to fit into the Johnson model the fact that political actions taken to remedy dysfunction often themselves precipitate change. This produces the paradoxical hypothesis that measures designed to restore equilibrium in fact upset equilibrium. Because he begins with his structural-functional equilibrium model, Johnson is a victim of the fallacy of intended consequences. As often as not in history it is the *unintended* consequences that really matter: to mention but one example, it was Louis XVI's belated and half-hearted attempts at reform that provoked the aristocratic reaction, which in turn opened the way to the bourgeois, the peasant, and the sansculotte revolutions. Finally the dysfunction concept is not altogether easy to handle in a concrete historical case. If societies are regarded as being in a constant state of multiple tension, then some degree of dysfunction is always present. Some group is always in a state of relative deprivation due to the inevitable process of social change.

Recognition of this fact leads Eckstein to point out the importance of forces working *against* revolution. Historians, particularly those formed in the Western liberal tradition, are reluctant to admit that ruthless, efficient repression—as opposed to bumbling, half-hearted repression—involving the physical destruction of leading revolutionaries and effective control of the media of communication, can crush incipient revolutionary movements. Repression is particularly effective when governments know what to look for, when they have before their eyes the unfortunate example of other governments overthrown by revolutionaries elsewhere. Reaction, in fact, is just as infectious as revolution. Moreover diversion of energy and attention to successful—as opposed to unsuccessful—foreign war can ward off serious internal trouble. Quietist—as opposed to activist—religious movements may serve as the opiate of the people, as Halévy suggested about Methodism in England. Bread and circuses may distract popular attention. Timely —as opposed to untimely—political concessions may win over moderate opinion and isolate the extremists.

Basing himself on this suggestive analysis, Eckstein produces a paradigm for universal application. He sees four positive variables—elite inefficiency, disorienting social process, subversion, and available rebel facilities—and four negative variables —diversionary mechanisms, available incumbent facilities, adjustive mechanisms, and effective repression. Each type of internal war, and each step of each type, can, he suggests, be explained in terms of these eight variables. While this may be true, it is fair to point out that some of the variables are themselves the product of more deep-seated factors, others mere questions of executive action that may be determined by the accidents of personality. Disruptive social process is a profound cause; elite inefficiency a behavior pattern; effective repression a function of will; facilities the by-product of geography. One objection to the Eckstein paradigm is therefore that it embraces different levels of explanation and fails to maintain the fundamental distinction between preconditions and precipitants. Secondly, it concentrates on the factors working for or against the successful manipulation of violence rather than on the underlying factors working to produce a revolutionary potential. This is because the paradigm is intended to apply to all forms of internal war rather than to revolution proper, and because all that the various forms of internal war have in common is the use of violence. It is impossible to tell how serious these criticisms are until the paradigm has been applied to a particular historical revolution. Only then will its value become apparent.

If we take the behaviorist approach, then a primary cause of revolutions is the emergence of an obsessive revolutionary mentality. But how closely does this relate to the objective material circumstances themselves? In every revolutionary situation one finds a group of men—fanatics, extremists, zealots —so convinced of their own righteousness and of the urgent need to create a new Jerusalem on earth (whether formally religious or secular in inspiration is irrelevant) that they are prepared to smash through the normal restraints of habit, custom, and convention. Such men were the seventeenth-century English Puritans, the eighteenth-century French Jacobins, the twentieth-century Russian Bolsheviks. But what makes such men is far from certain. What generates such ruthlessness in curbing evil, such passion for discipline and order? Rapid social mobility, both horizontal and vertical, and particularly urbanization, certainly produces a sense of rootlessness and anxiety. In highly stratified societies, even some of the newly-risen elements may find themselves under stress.[15] While some of the *arrivistes* are happily absorbed in their new strata, others remain uneasy and resentful. If they are snubbed and rebuffed by the older members of the status group to which they aspire by reason of their new wealth and position, they are likely to become acutely conscious of their social inferiority, and may be driven either to adopt a pose *plus royaliste que le Roi* or to dream of destroying the whole social order. In the latter case they may try to allay their sense of insecurity by imposing their norms and values by force upon society at large. This is especially the case if there is available a moralistic ideology like Puritanism or Marxism to which they can attach themselves, and which provides them with unshakable confidence in their own rectitude.

But why does the individual react in this particular way rather than another? Some would argue that the character of the revolutionary is formed by sudden ideological conversion in adolescence or early adult life (to Puritanism, Jacobinism, or Bolshevism) as a refuge from this anxiety state.[16] What is not acceptable is the fashionable conservative cliché that the revolutionary and the reformer are merely the chance product of unfortunate psychological difficulties in childhood. It is possible that this is the mechanism by which such feelings are generated,

[15] Émile Durkheim, *Suicide* (Glencoe 1951), 246–54; A. B. Hollingshead, R. Ellis, and E. Kirby, "Social Mobility and Mental Illness," *American Sociological Review*, XIX (1954).

[16] Michael L. Walzer, "Puritanism as a Revolutionary Ideology," *History and Theory*, III, No. 1 (1963), 59–90.

though there is increasing evidence of the continued plasticity of human character until at any rate post-adolescence. The main objection to this theory is that it fails to explain why these particular attitudes become common only in certain classes and age groups at certain times and in certain places. This failure strongly suggests that the cause of this state of mind lies not in the personal maladjustment of the individuals or their parents, but in the social conditions that created that maladjustment. Talcott Parsons treats disaffection or "alienation" as a generalized phenomenon that may manifest itself in crime, alcoholism, drug addiction, daytime fantasies, religious enthusiasm, or serious political agitation. To use Robert Merton's formulation, Ritualism and Retreatism are two possible psychological escape-routes; Innovation and Rebellion two others.[17]

Even if we accept this behaviorist approach (which I do), the fact remains that many of the underlying causes both of the alienation of the revolutionaries and of the weakness of the incumbent elite are economic in origin; and it is in this area that some interesting work has centered. In particular a fresh look has been taken at the contradictory models of Marx and de Tocqueville, the one claiming that popular revolution is a product of increasing misery, the other that it is a product of increasing prosperity.

Two economists, Sir Arthur Lewis and Mancur Olson, have pointed out that because of their basic social stability, both preindustrial and highly industrialized societies are relatively free from revolutionary disturbance.[18] In the former societies, people accept with little question the accepted rights and obligations of family, class, and caste. Misery, oppression, and social injustice are passively endured as inevitable features of life on earth. It is in societies experiencing rapid economic growth that

[17] Parsons, *The Social System* (Glencoe 1951); Merton, *Social Theory and Social Structure* (Glencoe 1957), chap. 4.

[18] W. Arthur Lewis, "Commonwealth Address," in *Conference Across a Continent* (Toronto 1963), 46–60; Olson, "Rapid Growth as a Destabilizing Force," *Journal of Economic History*, XXIII (December 1963), 529–52. I am grateful to Mr. Olson for drawing my attention to Sir Arthur Lewis's article, and for some helpful suggestions.

the trouble usually occurs. Lewis, who is thinking mostly about the newly emerging countries, primarily of Africa, regards the sense of frustration that leads to revolution as a consequence of the dislocation of the old status patterns by the emergence of four new classes—the proletariat, the capitalist employers, the urban commercial and professional middle class, and the professional politicians—and of the disturbance of the old income patterns by the sporadic and patchy impact of economic growth, which creates new wealth and new poverty in close and conspicuous juxtaposition. Both phenomena he regards as merely transitional, since in a country fully developed economically there are strong tendencies toward the elimination of inequalities of opportunity, income, and status.

This model matches fairly well the only detailed analysis of a historical revolution in which a conscious effort has been made to apply modern sociological methods. In his recent study of the Vendée, Charles Tilly argues that a counterrevolutionary situation was the consequence of special tensions created by the immediate juxtaposition of, on one hand, parish clergy closely identified with the local communities, great absentee landlords, and old-fashioned subsistence farming, and, on the other, a large-scale textile industry on the putting-out system and increasing bourgeois competition.[19] Though the book is flawed by a tendency to take a ponderous sociological hammer to crack a simple little historical nut, it is nonetheless a suggestive example of the application of new hypotheses and techniques to historical material.

Olson has independently developed a more elaborate version of the Lewis theory. He argues that revolutionaries are déclassé and freed from the social bonds of family, profession, village or manor; and that these individuals are the product of rapid economic growth, which creates both *nouveaux riches* and *nouveaux pauvres*. The former, usually middle-class and urban artisans, are better off economically, but are disoriented, rootless, and restless; the latter may be workers whose wages have failed to keep pace with inflation, workers in technologically outdated and therefore declining industries, or the unemployed

[19] *The Vendée* (Cambridge, Mass., 1964).

in a society in which the old cushions of the extended family and the village have gone, and in which the new cushion of social security has not yet been created. The initial growth phase may well cause a decline in the standard of living of the majority because of the need for relatively enormous forced savings for reinvestment. The result is a revolution caused by the widening gap between expectations—social and political for the new rich, economic for the new poor—and the realities of everyday life.

A sociologist, James C. Davis, agrees with Olson that the fundamental impetus toward a revolutionary situation is generated by rapid economic growth but he associates such growth with a generally rising rather than a generally falling standard of living, and argues that the moment of potential revolution is reached only when the long-term phase of growth is followed by a short-term phase of economic stagnation or decline.[20] The result of this "J-curve," as he calls it, is that steadily soaring expectations, newly created by the period of growth, shoot further and further ahead of actual satisfaction of needs. Successful revolution is the work neither of the destitute nor of the well-satisfied, but of those whose actual situation is improving less rapidly than they expect.

These economic models have much in common, and their differences can be explained by the fact that Lewis and Olson are primarily concerned with the long-term economic forces creating instability, and Davis with the short-term economic factors that may precipitate a crisis. Moreover their analyses apply to different kinds of economic growth, of which three have recently been identified by W. W. Rostow and Barry Supple: there is the expansion of production in a pre-industrial society, which may not cause any important technological, ideological, social, or political change; there is the phase of rapid growth, involving major changes of every kind; and there is the sustained trend toward technological maturity.[21] His-

[20] "Toward a Theory of Revolution," *American Sociological Review,* XXVII (February 1962), 1–19, esp. the graph on p. 6.
[21] W. W. Rostow, *The Stages of Economic Growth* (Cambridge, Mass., 1960); Supple, *The Experience of Economic Growth* (New York 1963), 11–12.

torians have been quick to see that these models, particularly that of Rostow, can be applied only to a limited number of historical cases. The trouble is not so much that in any specific case the phases—particularly the last two—tend to merge into one another, but that changes in the various sectors occur at irregular and unexpected places on the time-scale in different societies. Insofar as there is any validity in the division of the stages of growth into these three basic types, the revolutionary model of Olson and Lewis is confined to the second; that of Davis is applicable to all three.

The Davis model fits the history of Western Europe quite well, for it looks as if in conditions of extreme institutional and ideological rigidity the first type of economic growth may produce frustrations of a very serious kind. Revolutions broke out all over Europe in the 1640's, twenty years after a secular growth phase had come to an end.[22] C. E. Labrousse has demonstrated the existence of a similar economic recession in France from 1778,[23] and from 1914 the Russian economy was dislocated by the war effort after many years of rapid growth. Whatever its limitations in any particular situation, the J-curve of actual satisfaction of needs is an analytical tool that historians can usefully bear in mind as they probe the violent social upheavals of the past.

As de Tocqueville pointed out, this formula of advance followed by retreat is equally applicable to other sectors. Trouble arises if a phase of liberal governmental concessions is followed by a phase of political repression; a phase of fairly open recruitment channels into the elite followed by a phase of aristocratic reaction and a closing of ranks; a phase of weakening status barriers by a phase of reassertion of privilege. The J-curve is applicable to other than purely economic satisfactions, and the apex of the curve is the point at which underlying causes, the preconditions, merge with immediate factors, the precipitants. The recipe for revolution is thus the creation of new expectations by economic improvement and some social

[22] E. J. Hobsbawm, "The Crisis of the Seventeenth Century," in T. H. Aston, ed., *Crisis in Europe, 1560–1660* (London 1965), 5–58.

[23] *La Crise de l'Économie française à la fin de l'Ancien Régime et au début de la Révolution* (Paris 1944).

and political reforms, followed by economic recession, governmental reaction, and aristocratic resurgence, which widen the gap between expectations and reality.

All these attempts to relate dysfunction to relative changes in economic prosperity and aspirations are hampered by two things, of which the first is the extreme difficulty in ascertaining the facts. It is never easy to discover precisely what is happening to the distribution of wealth in a given society. Even now, even in highly developed Western societies with massive bureaucratic controls and quantities of statistical data, there is no agreement about the facts. Some years ago it was confidently believed that in both Britain and the United States incomes were being leveled, and that extremes of both wealth and poverty were being steadily eliminated. Today, no one quite knows what is happening in either country.[24] And if this is true now, still more is it true of societies in the past about which the information is fragmentary and unreliable.

Secondly, even if they can be clearly demonstrated, economic trends are only one part of the problem. Historians are increasingly realizing that the psychological responses to changes in wealth and power are not only not precisely related to, but are politically more significant than, the material changes themselves. As Marx himself realized at one stage, dissatisfaction with the status quo is not determined by absolute realities but by relative expectations. "Our desires and pleasures spring from society; we measure them, therefore, by society, and not by the objects which serve for their satisfaction. Because they are of a social nature, they are of a relative nature."[25] Frustration may possibly result from a rise and subsequent relapse in real income. But it is perhaps more likely to be caused by a rise in aspirations that outstrips the rise in real income; or by a rise in the *relative* economic position in society of the group in question, followed by a period in which its real income continues to

[24] Gabriel Kolko, *Wealth and Power in America* (New York 1962); Richard M. Titmuss, *Income Distribution and Social Change* (London 1962).

[25] Davis, 5, quoting Marx, *Selected Works in Two Volumes* (Moscow 1955), I, 947.

grow, but less fast than that of other groups around it. Alternatively it may represent a rise and then decline of status, largely unrelated to real income; or if status and real income are related, it may be inversely. For example, social scientists seeking to explain the rise of the radical right in the United States in the early 1950's and again in the early 1960's attribute it to a combination of great economic prosperity and an aggravated sense of insecurity of status.[26] Whether or not this is a general formula for right-wing rather than left-wing revolutionary movements is not yet clear.

Moreover the problem is further complicated by an extension of the reference-group theory.[27] Human satisfaction is related not to existing conditions but to the condition of a social group against which the individual measures his situation. In an age of mass communications and the wide distribution of cheap radio receivers even among the impoverished illiterate of the world, knowledge of high consumption standards elsewhere spreads rapidly, and as a result the reference group may be in another, more highly developed, country or even continent. Under these circumstances, revolutionary conditions may be created before industrialization has got properly under way.

The last area in which some new theoretical work has been done is in the formulation of hypotheses about the social stages of a "Great Revolution." One of the best attacks on this problem was made by Crane Brinton, who was thinking primarily about the French Revolution, but who extended his comparisons to the three other major Western revolutionary movements. He saw the first phase as dominated by moderate bourgeois elements; their supersession by the radicals; a reign of terror; a Thermidorian reaction; and the establishment of strong central authority under military rule to consolidate the limited gains of the revolution. In terms of mass psychology he compared revolution with a fever that rises in intensity, affecting nearly all parts of the body politic, and then dies away.

A much cruder and more elementary model has been ad-

[26] Daniel Bell, ed., *The Radical Right* (Garden City 1963).
[27] Merton, chap. 9.

vanced by an historian of the revolutions of 1848, Peter Amann.[28] He sees the modern state as an institution holding a monopoly of physical force, administration, and justice over a wide area, a monopoly dependent more on habits of obedience than on powers of coercion. Revolution may therefore be defined as a breakdown of the monopoly due to a failure of these habits of obedience. It begins with the emergence of two or more foci of power, and ends with the elimination of all but one. Amann includes the possibility of "suspended revolution," with the existence of two or more foci not yet in violent conflict.

This model admittedly avoids some of the difficulties raised by more elaborate classifications of revolution: how to distinguish a coup d'état from a revolution; how to define the degrees of social change; how to accommodate the conservative counterrevolution, and so on. It certainly offers some explanation of the progress of revolution from stage to stage as the various power blocs that emerge on the overthrow of the incumbent regime are progressively eliminated; and it explains why the greater the public participation in the revolution, the wider the break with the habits of obedience, and therefore the slower the restoration of order and centralized authority. But it throws the baby out with the bathwater. It is impossible to fit any decentralized traditional society, or any modern federal society, into the model. Moreover, even where it might be applicable, it offers no framework for analyzing the roots of revolution, no pointers for identifying the foci of power, no means of distinguishing between the various revolutionary types, and its notion of "suspended revolution" is little more than verbal evasion.

Though it is set out in a somewhat confused, overelaborate, and unnecessarily abstract form, the most convincing description of the social stages of revolution is that outlined by Rex D. Hooper.[29] He sees four stages. The first is characterized by indiscriminate, uncoordinated mass unrest and dissatisfaction, the result of dim recognition that traditional values no longer

28 "Revolution: A Redefinition."
29 "The Revolutionary Process," *Social Forces,* xxviii (March 1950), 270–79.

satisfy current aspirations. The next stage sees this vague unease beginning to coalesce into organized opposition with defined goals, an important characteristic being a shift of allegiance by the intellectuals from the incumbents to the dissidents, the advancement of an "evil men" theory, and its abandonment in favor of an "evil institutions" theory. At this stage there emerge two types of leaders: the prophet, who sketches the shape of the new utopia upon which men's hopes can focus, and the reformer, working methodically toward specific goals. The third, the formal stage, sees the beginning of the revolution proper. Motives and objectives are clarified, organization is built up, a statesman leader emerges. Then conflicts between the left and the right of the revolutionary movement become acute, and the radicals take over from the moderates. The fourth and last stage sees the legalization of the revolution. It is a product of psychological exhaustion as the reforming drive burns itself out, moral enthusiasm wanes, and economic distress increases. The administrators take over, strong central government is established, and society is reconstructed on lines that embody substantial elements of the old system. The result falls far short of the utopian aspirations of the early leaders, but it succeeds in meshing aspirations with values by partly modifying both, and so allows the reconstruction of a firm social order.

Some of the writings of contemporary social scientists are ingenious feats of verbal juggling in an esoteric language, performed around the totem pole of an abstract model, surrounded as far as the eye can see by the arid wastes of terminological definitions and mathematical formulae. Small wonder the historian finds it hard to digest the gritty diet of this neo-scholasticism, as it has been aptly called. The more historically-minded of the social scientists, however, have a great deal to offer. The history of history, as well as of science, shows that advances depend partly on the accumulation of factual information, but rather more on the formulation of hypotheses that reveal the hidden relationships and common properties of apparently distinct phenomena. Social scientists can supply a corrective to the antiquarian fact-grubbing to which historians are so prone; they can direct attention to problems of general relevance, and away from the sterile triviality of so much historical research. They can ask new questions and suggest new ways of looking at old ones. They can supply new categories, and as a result may suggest new ideas.[30]

30 See Werner J. Cahnman and Alvin Boskoff, eds., *Sociology and History: Theory and Research* (New York 1964); H. Stuart Hughes, "The Historian and the Social Scientist," *American Historical Review*, LXVI, No. 1 (1960), 20–46; A. Cobban, "History and Sociology," *Historical Studies*, III (1961), 1–8; M. G. Smith, "History and Social Anthropology," *Journal of the Royal Anthropological Institute*, XCII (1962); K. V. Thomas, "History and Anthropology," *Past and Present*, No. 24 (April 1963), 3–18.

II.

REVOLUTIONS IN EARLY MODERN HISTORY

4

J. H. Elliott: Revolution and Continuity in Early Modern Europe*

Of all the debates which have agitated historians during the past few years, none has been more lively, or less conclusive, than the great debate surrounding what has come to be known as "the general crisis of the seventeenth century." While dissenting voices have been raised here and there,[1] the current fashion is to emphasize the more turbulent characteristics of the age. It was in 1954, which seems in retrospect to have been an unusually crisis-conscious year, that Professor Roland Mousnier

* J. H. Elliott, "Revolution and Continuity in Early Modern Europe," *Past and Present*, 42 (Oxford: The Past and Present Society, 1969), pp. 35–36. By permission.

Professor of History at King's College, London, J. H. Elliott has written *The Revolt of the Catalans, Imperial Spain, Europe Divided* and other works.

[1] Many of the contributions to the debate are to be found reprinted in Trevor Aston (ed.), *Crisis in Europe, 1560–1660* (London, 1965). For expressions of dissent, see E. H. Kossmann, "Trevor-Roper's 'General crisis,'" *Past and Present*, no. 18 (Nov., 1960), pp. 8–11; A. D. Lublinskaya, *French Absolutism: The Crucial Phase, 1620–1629* (Cambridge, 1968); and I. Schöffer, "Did Holland's Golden Age coincide with a period of crisis?," *Acta Historiae Neerlandica*, i (1966), pp. 82–107. Dr. Schöffer's admirable article, of which I was unaware when I originally drafted this essay, makes a number of points which coincide closely with my own.

published a general history of sixteenth- and seventeenth-century Europe, in which the seventeenth century was depicted as a century of crisis, and especially of intellectual crisis.[2] In the same year, Dr. Hobsbawm, in an article which now stands as the classic formulation of the "general crisis" theory, argued that the seventeenth century was characterized by a crisis of the European economy, which marked a decisive shift from feudal towards capitalist organization.[3] Since then, Professor Trevor-Roper, with one eye on the political revolutions of the 1640s, and the other on Dr. Hobsbawm, has produced a uniquely personal interpretation of the seventeenth century as an age of crisis for the "Renaissance State."[4]

It is, I think, striking that three such distinguished historians, of very different views and persuasions, should have united in depicting the seventeenth century in such dramatic terms. They all represent some aspect of the age—whether economic, intellectual or political—in terms of discontinuity, in the sense either of a change of direction or a change of pace. The change, too, is a violent one, as the use of the words "crisis" and "revolution" suggests. But the crisis of one historian is a chimera to another, and the consensus collapses as soon as attempts at definition begin.

It is not my intention now to embark on the daunting task of reconciling the irreconcilable. Nor do I intend to examine the evidence for and against an interpretation of the seventeenth century as an age of economic and intellectual crisis. Instead, I have chosen to concentrate on the narrower, but still, I think, important question of the "political" revolutions of the middle years of the century—those revolutions which (in Professor Trevor-Roper's words) "if we look at them together . . . have so many common features that they appear almost as a general revolution."[5]

The revolts and upheavals which may be held to constitute this "general revolution" have frequently been listed: the Puri-

2 *Les XVIe et XVIIe Siècles* (Paris, 1954).
3 Aston, *Crisis in Europe*, pp. 5–58.
4 *Ibid.*, pp. 59–95.
5 *Ibid.*, p. 59.

tan Revolution in England, flanked by the revolts of Scotland and Ireland; the insurrections in the Spanish Monarchy—Catalonia and Portugal in 1640, Naples and Palermo in 1647; the Fronde in France between 1648 and 1653; the bloodless revolution of 1650 which displaced the *stadtholderate* in the Netherlands; the revolt of the Ukraine from 1648–54; and a string of peasant risings across the continent. Nor should we disregard the plea of Professor Michael Roberts that "if we are really determined to bring the Cossacks and the Ironsides within the scope of a single explanation," we should not "leave Sweden out of the reckoning."[6] For did not the year 1650 see a dangerous social and constitutional crisis in the troubled realm of Queen Christina?

This clustering of revolts was a subject of fascinated concern to contemporaries, who saw them as part of a great cosmic upheaval; and it has frequently been commented upon by historians. It is thirty years now since Professor R. B. Merriman published his *Six Contemporaneous Revolutions*. But for Merriman the six revolutions afforded "an admirable example of the infinite variety of history."[7] Since the 1950s, however, the tendency has been to emphasize their similarities rather than their differences; and the concept of a "general revolution" of the 1640s has effectively come to influence the history of seventeenth-century Europe only in our own generation.

Not the least of the attractions of a "crisis" interpretation of the seventeenth century to our own age, is that it offers the possibility of a unified conceptual approach to a complex period. It has, too, the additional advantage of plausibility, with that dramatic decade of the 1640s to bear witness to the turbulence of the times. Opinions may vary about the long-term consequences of the revolutions. Not everyone, for instance, would agree with Professor Trevor-Roper[8] that the seventeenth century "is broken in the middle, irreparably broken, and at the end of it, after the revolutions, men can hardly recognize the beginning." But there would probably be a fairly general

[6] *Ibid.*, p. 221.
[7] Published Oxford, 1938, p. 89.
[8] Aston, *op. cit.*, pp. 62 and 63.

measure of agreement with his view that "the universality" of revolution in the seventeenth century pointed to "serious structural weaknesses" in the European monarchies—weaknesses which gave rise to revolutionary situations.

Whether these weaknesses were more or less serious at this moment than in preceding generations, need not at present concern us. All I wish to do for the time being is to draw attention to the way in which the argument is couched. It is the "universality" of seventeenth-century revolution which points to structural weakness. This argument from universality underlies most of the theories about the "general crisis" of the seventeenth century. Six contemporaneous revolutions (at a minimum count)—does not the very number and pervasiveness of revolutionary movements suggest a moment of unique gravity, and a crisis of unique proportions, in the history of Early Modern Europe?

But supposing this unprecedented epidemic of revolutions was not, after all, unprecedented. . . . Let us look back for a moment to the sixteenth century, and in particular to the decade of the 1560s: 1559–60, revolt in Scotland, culminating in the abdication of Mary Queen of Scots in 1567; 1560, revolt of the Vaudois against Emmanuel Philibert, duke of Savoy; 1562, outbreak of the French civil wars; 1564, revolt of the Corsicans against Genoa; 1566, the beginning of the revolt of the Netherlands; 1568, revolt of the Moriscos of Granada; 1569, the Northern Rebellion in England. Seven "contemporaneous revolutions"; and perhaps I may be allowed to anticipate Professor Roberts and plead that the rising of the Swedish dukes against Eric XIV in 1568, and his subsequent deposition, should not be overlooked.

This sudden rash of revolts would hardly have come as a surprise to that doughty professional rebel John Knox, who was able to announce reassuringly to Mary Queen of Scots in 1561: "Madam, your realm is in no other case at this day, than all other realms of Christendom are."[9] But while contemporaries seem to have felt that they were witnessing the beginnings of a

[9] *John Knox's History of the Reformation in Scotland*, ed. W. C. Dickinson, vol. I (London, 1949), p. 367.

general conflagration, or what Calvin called "Europae con-
cussio,"[10] I am not aware that any historian has grouped them
together under the title of "the general revolution of the 1560s,"
or has used them as evidence for a "general crisis of the sixteenth century."[11]

Perhaps it is not unreasonable to speculate for a moment on
the possible reasons for this apparent discrimination in the
treatment accorded the seventeenth century. Merriman seems to
have been led to his six contemporaneous revolutions partly by
his study of seventeenth-century political histories, and partly
by the preoccupation of the 1930s with the possibility of a
coming "world revolution." He was also influenced by the
example of 1848, which gave him the opportunity to draw
parallels and comparisons. His principal concern was to consider the relationship of the various revolutions to each other,
and his principal conclusion from a study of the 1640s and the
1840s, was that "national rivalries proved stronger than the
virus of revolution"—an encouraging conclusion, no doubt, in
the circumstances of the 1930s.[12]

Merriman's approach to the seventeenth-century revolutions
by way of diplomatic history was of little interest to historians
of the post-war generation. But he had bequeathed them a
magnificent subject, ready for exploitation. In the context of the
post-war historiography of Early Modern Europe, exploitation
proved easy enough. The French economist Simiand had taught
Early Modern historians to see the sixteenth century as an age
of economic expansion, and the seventeenth as a century in
which expansion was first halted, and then, around 1650,

[10] R. Nürnberger, *Die Politisierung des Französichen Protestantismus*
(Tübingen, 1948), p. 91, n. 57.

[11] The links between the Huguenot and the Dutch revolts have, of
course, received considerable attention, especially from nineteenth-century historians. Cf. in particular Kervyn de Lettenhove, *Les Huguenots
et Les Gueux*, 6 vols. (Bruges, 1883–5). See also H. G. Koenigsberger,
"The Organization of Revolutionary Parties in France and the Netherlands," *Jl. of Modern History*, xxvii (1955), which draws interesting
parallels between the organization of the revolts in France, the Netherlands and Scotland.

[12] Merriman, *op. cit.*, pp. 209 and 213.

succeeded by a slump. Given the existence of a major reversal of economic trends in the middle years of the century, Merriman's contemporaneous revolutions seemed both relevant and suggestive. Here, surely, were the social and political manifestations of a crisis affecting the entire European economy. Had his revolutions been those of the 1560s rather than those of the 1640s—the products of an age of expansion rather than of an age of contraction—they might have attracted less attention. Yet even assuming that we can legitimately speak of a general crisis of the European economy in the mid-seventeenth century—and the evidence, though impressive, is not conclusive—it seems odd that the assumed relationship between economic crisis and political revolution has gone unquestioned. Why should we ignore for the seventeenth century de Tocqueville's perception that revolution tends to come with an improvement rather than with a deterioration of economic conditions?

But the decisive element in the concentration of interest on the revolutions of the 1640s is clearly the supreme importance attributed to the Puritan Revolution in England, as the event which precipitates the collapse of Europe's feudal structure and the emergence of a capitalist society. If the Puritan Revolution is seen as the essential prelude to the Industrial Revolution, it is obvious that a constellation of revolutions benefiting from its reflected glory, is likely to outshine any other in the revolutionary firmament. This, at least, seems to be the attitude of the Soviet historian, Boris Porshnev. His Fronde is a bourgeois revolution *manquée*. "It was," he writes, "a French variant of the English bourgeois revolution which was breaking out on the other side of the Channel, and a distant prologue of the French Revolution of the eighteenth century." He presents the sixteenth-century civil wars, on the other hand, as a combination of feudal quarrels and popular insurrections.[13] Yet, given the upsurge of revolt in the towns of the Ligue in 1588, it is not easy to see any intrinsic reason why the French civil wars should not also be categorized as a bourgeois revolution

[13] Boris Porchnev [Porshnev], *Les Soulèvements Populaires en France de 1623 à 1648* (Paris, 1963), pp. 537, 17, 47.

manquée. But perhaps the Ligueurs lacked a progressive ideology.

A contest in the revolution stakes between the 1560s and the 1640s does not seem in itself a particularly profitable enterprise. But it does give rise to a larger and more important question— the question of our general conception of revolution, and its applicability to the study of Early Modern Europe. Here the distinction between Marxist and non-Marxist historian dwindles in importance. The language of our age is pervasive—so pervasive that Professor Mousnier, after cogently criticizing Professor Porshnev for his interpretation of the Fronde in terms of class conflict, can refer to the English civil war, in his most recent book, as "perhaps the first great bourgeois revolution of modern times."[14]

Coming from the pen of a historian whose approach to the history of his own country is as staunchly anti-Marxist as that of Professor Mousnier, these words hint at the existence of what seems to be a central problem in the history of Early Modern European insurrections. We are all of us the children of our age, but in this particular field of historical writing, the tricks of time have proved to be more than usually deceptive. Between us and Early Modern Europe lies the late eighteenth century, dominated for us by two events which seem to have done more than anything else to shape our own civilization—the French Revolution and the Industrial Revolution in England. During the nineteenth century, each of these became a paradigm—an exemplar, in one instance, for political and social development, and in the other for economic development. The twentieth century has appropriated these paradigms from its predecessor, and continues to make use of them as best it can.

How far the current paradigm of the French Revolution actually corresponds to what occurred in the course of that Revolution has been a matter for fierce debate. But the paradigm has not been confined to the French Revolution and the insurrections that have succeeded it. Consciously or unconsciously, nineteenth- and twentieth-century historians have

[14] *Fureurs Paysannes* (Paris, 1967), p. 7.

looked at revolts in Early Modern Europe in the light of the late eighteenth-century revolutions, and of their assessment of them. This has frequently provided them with valuable insights into the origins of great events; but the very fact that they applied to many of these Early Modern revolts the word "revolution" suggests the possibility of unconscious distortions, which may itself give us some cause for unease.

It is true that "revolution" was by no means an unknown word in sixteenth- and seventeenth-century Europe, as applied to upheavals in states. A Spaniard looking back in 1525 on the revolt of the Comuneros expressed his fear of a "revolution of the people";[15] and in 1647 and 1648 two Italians, Giraffi and Assarino, published accounts of recent insurrections, which they entitled "The Revolutions" of Naples and Catalonia.[16] But a close study of the concept of "revolution" by Professor Karl Griewank has shown how slowly, and with what uncertainty, the idea of revolution was brought down from the heavens of Copernicus and applied with any precision to the mutations of states.[17] Sedition, rebellion, *Aufstand,* mutation, revolt, revoltment (John Knox)[18]—these are the words most commonly employed in sixteenth-century Europe. Gardiner's Puritan Revolution was Clarendon's Great Rebellion. Only towards the end of the eighteenth century, under the impact of events in America and France, did "revolution" effectively establish itself in the European political vocabulary, and acquire those connotations by which we recognize it today.

These include the idea of a violent, irresistible and permanent change of the political and constitutional structure; a powerful social content, through the participation of distinctive social groups and broad masses of the people; and the urge to break sharply with the past and construct a new order in accordance

[15] J. A. Maravall, *Las Comunidades de Castilla* (Madrid, 1963), pp. 243–4.

[16] A. Giraffi, *Le Rivolutioni di Napoli* (Venice, 1647); Luca Assarino, *Le Rivolutioni di Catalogna* (Bologna, 1648). See also Vernon F. Snow, "The concept of revolution in seventeenth-century England," *The Historical Jl.,* v (1962), pp. 167–74.

[17] *Der Neuzeitliche Revolutionsbegriff* (Weimar, 1955).

[18] Knox, *op. cit.,* i, p. 193.

with an ideological program.[19] Modern historians, accustomed to expect these ingredients of a revolution, have instinctively sought to detect them in Early Modern revolts. Presuming the existence of social protest and class conflict, they have duly found them in the uprisings of the populace. Conditioned to look for minority parties scheming to subvert the state by violence, they have anatomized with great skill the techniques of revolutionary organization. Expecting of a revolution that it should have an innovating ideology, they have effectively isolated and explored the aspirations of those who sought to establish a new order on earth. The work which has been done along these lines has proved immensely fruitful. It has made us aware of motives and forces behind the movements of unrest which were largely veiled from the participants. It has told us things which we could never have known, or glimpsed only obscurely, about the patterns of political and social cohesion and the underlying causes of failure or success.

But it would be foolish to ignore the possibility that, in using a concept of revolution which is relatively recent in origin, we may unconsciously be introducing anachronisms, or focusing on certain problems which accord with our own preoccupations, at the expense of others which have been played down or overlooked. Some recognition of this is implied in recent discussions and debates, particularly on the question of the applicability of the idea of class conflict to Early Modern European society.[20] Although Professor Mousnier has insisted against Professor Porshnev that the popular uprisings in Richelieu's France were fomented by the upper classes and testified to the closeness of the relationship between the peasants and their lords, it would be unwise to disregard the evidence for the existence of fierce social antagonisms in Early Modern Europe. These found ex-

[19] Griewank, *op. cit.*, p. 7.

[20] See Mousnier, *Fureurs Paysannes,* p. 29, and also p. 322, n. 1 for reference to his debate with Porshnev. Further discussion of the question of class in Early Modern society may be found in R. Mandrou, *Introduction à la France Moderne* (Paris, 1961), pp. 138–64, and F. Mauro, *Le XVIe Siècle Européen. Aspects Economiques* (Paris, 1966), pp. 337–44.

pression at moments of unbearable tension—whether in the fury of the Neapolitan mobs in 1585,[21] or in the assault of the Catalan peasants and populace on the nobles and the rich in the summer of 1640.[22]

But it is one thing to establish the existence of social antagonisms, and another to assume that they are the principal cause of conflict. The Catalan rebels first attack royal officials and royal troops; and it is only after disposing of them that they turn on their own ruling class. A revolt may frequently have started, as in Catalonia, against the agents of the state, and then been transformed into a war on the rich. But the parallels between this and a modern class conflict cannot be automatically taken for granted, if only because the ordering of society in Early Modern Europe tended to militate against class solidarity. A society grouped into corporations, divided into orders, and linked vertically by powerful ties of kinship and clientage, cannot be expected to behave in the same way as a society divided into classes. Intense rivalries between guildsmen and non-guildsmen, and between the guilds themselves, helped to disrupt community action in urban revolts;[23] and it hardly seems a coincidence that one of the rare examples of a fair degree of urban solidarity is provided by the Comuneros of Castile, where guild organization was weak.

The applicability of the modern notion of ideology to Early Modern revolts seems equally open to question. If by ideology we mean "a specific set of ideas designed to vindicate or disguise class interest,"[24] the uncertainties about "class" in Early Modern Europe must also be extended to "ideology." If we employ it more loosely to mean simply the program of a particular movement (and this is presumably the way in which it is employed by most Western historians), there still remain large

[21] R. Villari, *La Rivolta Antispagnola a Napoli* (Bari, 1967), p. 44.

[22] J. H. Elliott, *The Revolt of the Catalans* (Cambridge, 1963), pp. 462–5.

[23] For a classic example, see Gene A. Brucker, *Florentine Politics and Society, 1347–1378* (Princeton, 1962), p. 55.

[24] A. Gerschenkron, *Community in History and Other Essays* (Cambridge, Mass., 1968), p. 65.

unanswered questions about the extent to which it faithfully represents the character of the movement as a whole. To talk, for instance, of Calvinism as the ideology of the Dutch rebels, is to ascribe to the rebellion as a whole, a series of ideals and aspirations which we know to be those of only a small minority—and a minority whose importance may well have been inflated, simply because they are the group whose ideals correspond most closely to our notions of what an ideology should be.

Perhaps our principal expectation of a revolutionary ideology is that it should break with the past and aspire to establish a new social order. In a society dominated, as Early Modern European society was dominated, by the idea, not of progress, but of a return to a golden age in the past, the best hope of finding an ideology of innovation lies in certain aspects of the Christian tradition. In particular, the chiliastic doctrines of later medieval Europe look foward to the coming of a new age on earth—the age of the Holy Ghost, characterized by a new social and spiritual order. Up to a point, therefore, it is possible to see the Bohemian Taborites of the fifteenth century as belonging to the tradition of revolutionary innovation by means of violent action. It is certainly arguable that the Taborites did in practice establish for themselves a society in which new forms of social and political organization predominated over the old.[25] But, on the other hand, the Taborites did not reject the traditional three-fold ordering of society; and although they were attempting to establish a new spiritual order on earth, the character of this order was determined by reference to the past—in this instance to the primitive church.

The same kind of difficulties are likely to bedevil attempts to bring religiously-inspired movements of the sixteenth century into the category of ideological innovation. The peasant movements in early sixteenth-century Germany, for all their millenarian and egalitarian aspirations, were still dominated by the desire to return to a past order, which was held to be eternally valid.[26] The same would also seem to be true of the Calvinist

[25] H. Kaminsky, *A History of the Hussite Revolution* (Berkeley, 1967), pp. 481 ff.
[26] Griewank, *op. cit.,* p. 102.

ideal of the advancement of the kingdom of God—an advancement which was anyhow to be achieved by the winning of the state authorities to the cause, rather than by the action of the revolutionary masses.[27]

Even if we dignify—or debase—these religious aspirations with the name of "ideology," it would be misleading to see them as providing a program of action appealing to the majority of the participants in Early Modern revolts. The Taborites, the Anabaptists and the Calvinists all singularly failed to win anything like universal acceptance of their ideas; and it is not clear why we should regard them as speaking with the true voice of the movements to which they belong, unless it is because they happen to be the most articulate. With our ears straining to catch one particular theme, there is always a danger that, amidst the general uproar, other notes and other voices will go unheard. This danger is not always recognized with such clarity, or expressed with such candor, as it has been by Mr. Michael Walzer, in his reference to the English sectaries: "However important they are to latter-day genealogists, the sects (even, the Levellers) are of very minor importance in seventeenth-century history."[28]

Doubts of this kind might profitably be extended. A fuller recognition of the degree to which our own thinking about revolutions is affected by preconceptions derived from the nineteenth century, might at least enable us to isolate more effectively those points at which distortions are most liable to occur. If we accept this possibility, a number of uncomfortable questions about our method and our approach may suggest themselves. I have already hinted at one such question: how far can historians accustomed to look for *innovation* among revolutionaries, enter into the minds of men who themselves were obsessed by *renovation*—by the desire to return to old customs and privileges, and to an old order of society? How far, too, has our preoccupation with violence as an essential ingredient of revolution concentrated attention on the agitators and the organizers, at the expense of the more passive and the less com-

[27] Nürnberger, *Die Politisierung,* pp. 19–21.
[28] *The Revolution of the Saints* (London, 1966), p. x.

mitted? For all the brilliance of Calvinist organization in the Netherlands, it is arguable that the fate of the revolt was determined elsewhere—by the great mass of people whose religious affiliation was lukewarm or indeterminate,[29] and by those stolid burghers of Holland and Zealand, who edged their way with such extreme caution along the precipitous path that divided loyalty from rebellion.

Most of all, it is open to question whether our persistent search for "underlying social causes" has not led us down blind alleys, and has concealed from us more profitable ways of approach. I speak here, as in so much else, as one of the errant wanderers. Not that I would claim to have received some sudden illumination on the road to Damascus. It is simply that the constant reading of modern accounts of sixteenth- and seventeenth-century insurrections is likely in due course to induce a weariness of the spirit, and to provoke a certain critical questioning. While it is clear that all the major upheavals in Early Modern Europe represent a combination of different revolts, animated by different ideals and reflecting the aspirations of different groups, it is less clear why "social" revolts should be regarded as in some way more "fundamental." Nor is it clear why we should be expected to assume that the outbreak of revolt in itself postulates structural weaknesses in society. Political disagreement may, after all, be no more and no less than political disagreement—a dispute about the control and the exercise of power.

An age as acutely attuned as ours to the distress signals of the poor and the starving, may be correspondingly less sensitive to the cries of the more fortunate for freedom from arbitrary power. The innumerable peasant revolts—the *soulèvements populaires*—which are now being analyzed in such painstaking detail, provide a terrifying revelation of the misery in which most of Europe's population lived. But we should not, I believe, be afraid to ask the apparently brutal question: did they make any difference? Or, indeed, *could* they make any difference, in a world in which technological backwardness had at least as

[29] See J. W. Smit, "The present position of studies regarding the revolt of the Netherlands," *Britain and the Netherlands,* ed. J. S. Bromley and E. H. Kossmann (London, 1960), pp. 23–5.

much to do with the condition of the populace as exploitation by an oppressive ruling class? And if we conclude that they could and did make a difference, we should then go on to determine the precise areas in which that difference was made.

If we can recognize that contemporary preconceptions about the nature of revolution may have helped to shape our treatment of Early Modern revolts, we are at least in some position to attempt remedial action. Our priorities, for instance, can be set against those of contemporaries, in an attempt to discover which of theirs have receded into the background, or have come to be overlooked. It is a salutary experience to watch the development of the French civil wars through the sharp eyes of Estienne Pasquier, whose evaluation of events is that of an intelligent and well-read sixteenth-century layman. "There are three things," he wrote, "of which one should be infinitely afraid in every principality—huge debts, a royal minority, and a disturbance in religion. For there is not one of these three which is not sufficient of itself to bring mutation to a state."[30]

No doubt Pasquier's analysis is inadequate, even by contemporary standards. His historical analogies were essentially political, and he set the unfolding drama of conflict in France into the context of famous faction feuds. "Two miserable words of faction, Huguenot and Papist, have insinuated themselves among us," he wrote in 1560; "and I fear that in the long run they will lead us to the same calamities and miseries as the Guelfs and Ghibellines in Italy, and the White and the Red Rose in England."[31] But this was not an unreasonable assessment of events from the standpoint of 1560; and if he omitted the social and economic considerations—the discontents of the gentry, the social consequences of rising prices—which loom so large in modern accounts of the French wars, this does not necessarily mean that he was unaware of their influence on events. Pasquier and his contemporaries were capable enough of seeing the existence of a relationship between political and social grievance. It was in the degree of significance to be

[30] *Lettres Historiques* (*1556–1594*), ed. D. Thickett (Geneva, 1966), p. 100.
[31] *Ibid.*, p. 47.

accorded to this relationship that a sixteenth-century approach diverges most sharply from our own. An age which has devoted itself to meticulous research into the fortunes of nobles and gentry is likely to find something almost comically casual about the words which Joachim Hopperus slips into his account of the origins of the Dutch revolt: "Several of the principal leaders were at this time very heavily burdened with debts. This is sometimes considered a source of unrest and attempted innovation, since such people hope to take advantage of disturbances in the state to re-establish their fortunes."[32]

But it may be that we have been equally casual in our approach to what contemporaries themselves regarded as important: Pasquier's "royal minorities," for instance, and indeed the whole question of kingship. It is now almost impossible for us to grasp the degree to which changes in the character of kingship affected the dispositions of power in the state. In societies where all the threads of patronage ultimately come to rest in the hands of the king, any of the accidents and hazards to which hereditary kingship is prone, are likely to have profoundly disturbing consequences. The apparent turbulence of politics in the 1560s may therefore not be entirely unrelated to a remarkably high mortality rate among monarchs in the preceding decade, and the accession of new and inexperienced rulers, some of whom were women or children. Similarly, if a comparison is to be made between the histories of France and Castile, it does not seem entirely irrelevant to consider how far Castile's immunity from rebellion after 1521 is to be ascribed to a high degree of social stability, and how far to the accident that it escaped royal minorities and the baneful presence (except for a short period in the reign of Philip IV) of adult cadet princes.[33]

---

[32] J. Hopperus, "Recueil et Mémorial des Troubles des Pays Bas," *Mémoires de Viglius et d'Hopperus sur le commencement des Troubles des Pays Bas,* ed. A. Wauters (Brussels, 1868), p. 237.

[33] It is significant that Olivares was greatly exercised by the problem of how to educate and employ the Infantes Don Carlos and Don Fernando, and complained of the lack of precedents to guide him: British Museum, Egerton M.S. 2081 f. 268, *Papel del Conde Duque sobre los Infantes.*

There is, however, another area in which most modern historiography seems to have been even less at home, and with far more considerable consequences. The search for the causes of discontent is nowadays more likely to lead to religious or social grievance, than to a sense of national loyalty. Yet the apparent uncertainty of modern historians when faced with the question of nationalism in Early Modern Europe stands in marked contrast to the increasingly confident use in the sixteenth century of the words *patria* and *patrie*. When the Corsican leader, Sampiero Corso, turned to Catherine de Medici for help in the early 1560s to free his native island from Genoese domination, she presented him with a number of banners bearing the heroic inscription: *pugna pro patria*.[34] The rebels of Ghent in 1578 not only spoke of defending their *patrie,* but also referred to themselves as *patriotes*.[35] The lawyers and judges in the reign of Charles I gained a reputation with parliament of being "good patriots";[36] and Masaniello, the hero of the Neapolitan revolt of 1647, was hailed as *liberator patriae*.[37]

It is possible that, in approaching these apparent manifestations of patriotic sentiment, we have again been both influenced and inhibited by our nineteenth-century inheritance. "The Commonwealth," wrote Lord Acton, "is the second stage on the road of revolution, which started from the Netherlands, and went on to America and France. . . ."[38] For all the qualifications introduced by Acton himself, there was a strong temptation to look at Early Modern revolts through the lens of the French Revolution, interpreted this time in accordance with the liberal-national tradition. The modern reaction against the historiographical excesses of this tradition is natural enough. But the manifestations of some kind of community consciousness in Early Modern revolts are too numerous and too forceful to

---

[34] A. De Rublé, *Le Traité de Cateau-Cambrésis* (Paris, 1889), p. 77.

[35] G. Malengreau, *L'Esprit particulariste et la Révolution des Pays-Bas au XVIe Siècle* (Louvain, 1936), p. 82, n. 4.

[36] T. Hobbes, *Behemoth,* ed. F. Tönnies (London, 1889), p. 119.

[37] A. Giraffi, *An Exact Historie of the late Revolutions in Naples* (London, 1650), p. 160.

[38] *Lectures on Modern History* (London, 1907), p. 205.

allow the question of nationalism to be left in a kind of historical limbo.

There are obvious difficulties about attempting to equate these various manifestations with a nationalism of the nineteenth-century variety. All too often a supposed allegiance to a national community turns out, on inspection, to be nothing of the kind. The *patria* itself is at least as likely to be a home town or province as the whole nation,[39] and a revolt, like that of the Dutch, which is represented in nineteenth-century historiography as a nationalist uprising, may just as convincingly be depicted as a manifestation of particularist, rather than nationalist, sentiments.[40]

Yet even though *patria* might apply in the first instance to a native city, it could at times be extended, as in the Castile of the Comuneros,[41] to embrace the entire community of the realm. But whether the community was local or national, expressions of allegiance to it assumed the same form: a deep and instinctive antipathy to outsiders. Throughout the Early Modern period, this antipathy was a powerful driving-force behind popular revolt. It moved the Corsican peasants in the 1560s to take up arms against the Genoese, and the Catalan peasants in 1640 to take up arms against the Castilians. *Visca la terra*— long live the land!—is the perennial cry of the Catalan populace as it turns out, to the summons of the church bells, to attack the bands of Castilian soldiers making their way to their embarkation-point at Barcelona.[42]

This popular nationalism figures prominently in the accounts of revolts written by nineteenth-century historians, who were themselves so often the products of a Romantic culture nurtured on the legends and the songs with which the deeds of the rebels were kept alive in folk memory. But in idealizing it, they

[39] Cf. the description of Barcelona as his *pàtria* by Pujades (Elliott, *Catalans*, p. 42).

[40] As it is by Malengreau, *L'Esprit Particulariste.* . . .

[41] Maravall, *Las Comunidades,* p. 55. See also G. Dupont-Ferrier, "Le sens des mots 'patria' et 'patrie' en France au Moyen Age et jusqu'au début du xviie siècle," *Revue Historique,* clxxxviii (1940), pp. 89–104.

[42] Elliott, *Catalans,* p. 253.

helped to discredit it, and oversimplified a complex phenomenon. What was often, at its least attractive, no more than an instinctive hatred of outsiders, was transmuted into a self-conscious identification with a national community, embodying certain specific ideals. But the Romantic historians were not totally mistaken in assuming the existence in Early Modern Europe of some such sense of identification, although they may have expected too often to find it expressed even at the very lowest social levels. For alongside the more obvious manifestations of popular sentiment, there was also to be found another phenomenon, which has yet to receive the attention and the analysis it deserves. This might perhaps best be described as a corporate or national constitutionalism; and while it may have reached down, in some form, to the lower levels of society, it was essentially the preserve of the dominant social and vocational groups in the state—nobles and gentry, urban patriciates, the lawyers, the clergy, the educated.

Perhaps it may be defined as an idealized conception of the various communities to which allegiance was owed; and it embraced, in ever-widening circles, the family and vocational community to which they belonged, the urban or provincial community in which they lived, and ultimately, and sometimes very hazily, the community of the realm. This idealized conception of the community was compounded of various elements. There was first, and most naturally, the sense of kinship and unity with others sharing the same allegiance. But there was also a sense of the corporation or community as a legal and historical entity, which had acquired certain distinctive characteristics with the passage of time, together with certain specific obligations, rights and privileges.

The community was founded on history, law and achievement, on the sharing of certain common experiences and certain common patterns of life and behavior. As such, it was an ideal—indeed an idealized—entity, already perfect in itself. It was, though, forever subject to attacks from enemies, and to erosion at the hands of time. The highest obligation incumbent upon its members was therefore to ensure that in due course it should be transmitted intact to their successors. The plea for the faithful fulfillment of this obligation echoes right through the history of Early Modern Europe, from the Florentine who urged his fellow-citizens in 1368 to "leave to posterity that which was left to us by our ancestors,"[43] to the Catalan canon who begged his brother canons in 1639 not to "let us lose in our own time what our forbears have so bravely won."[44]

The sixteenth century seems to have contributed a new sophistication and a new awareness to the sacred task of defending a community whose rights and liberties were embodied in written constitutions and charters, and kept alive in the corporate memory. In particular, it engaged with enthusiasm in legal and historical research. The great revival of interest in the customary law—a revival symbolized in France by the names of Bodin and Hotman—[45] not only provided new defenses against arbitrary power decked out with the trappings of Roman Law, but also helped to establish the idea that each nation had a distinct historical and constitutional identity.[46] By endowing the community with a genuine or fictitious constitution, set firmly into a unique historical context, the sixteenth-century antiquarian movement gave new meaning to the struggle for the preservation of liberties. The corporation, the community, the *patria* all acquired a firmer identity as the historical embodiment of distinctive rights.

The idea of the *patria* was also fostered by the new humanist education. A governing class which had imbibed the history of Greece and Rome from an early age would have no great diffi-

---

[43] Brucker, *Florentine Politics*, p. 396.

[44] Elliott, *Catalans*, p. 344.

[45] Julian H. Franklin, *Jean Bodin and the Sixteenth-Century Revolution in the Methodology of Law and History* (New York, 1963), esp. ch. iii.

[46] Ralph E. Giesey, *If Not, Not* (Princeton, 1968), p. 245. On the general question of constitutionalism, see in particular J. G. A. Pocock, *The Ancient Constitution and the Feudal Law* (Cambridge, 1957) and Michael Roberts, "On Aristocratic Constitutionalism in Swedish History," *Essays in Swedish History* (London, 1967). I have also greatly benefited from discussions on this subject with Mr. Quentin Skinner of Christ's College, Cambridge, who kindly read an early draft of this essay and made valuable comments on it.

culty in making an identification between its own idealized community and the polities of classical antiquity.[47]

> There were [says Hobbes in the *Behemoth*] an exceeding great number of men of the better sort, that had been so educated, as that in their youth having read the books written by famous men of the ancient Grecian and Roman commonwealths concerning their polity and great actions; in which books the popular government was extolled by the glorious name of liberty, and monarchy disgraced by the name of tyranny; they became thereby in love with their forms of government. And out of these men were chosen the greatest part of the House of Commons.

> The core of rebellion, as you have seen by this, and read of other rebellions, are the Universities . . .

> The *Universities* have been to this nation, as the wooden horse was to the Trojans.[48]

Until a great deal more research has been done on education in Early Modern Europe, it is impossible to determine what degree of importance should be attached to Hobbes's angry denunciations. But the intellectual influences which went to shape the conception of their own community among the governing classes of Europe, are obviously a matter of the greatest interest, since it was the idealized community or the *patria* which gave them the frame of reference by which they determined their own actions and assessed those of others. In his recent book on *The Community of Kent and the Great Rebellion,* Professor Everitt has shown how the political behavior of the dominant groups in Kentish society between 1640 and 1660 can only be understood in the light of their intense devotion to an idealized local community. While the gentry of Kent included convinced royalists and parliamentarians among their number, the principal aim of the majority was to "stand for the defense of the liberties of their unconquered nation" against assaults from either camp.[49]

---

[47] For the influence of classical polities on seventeenth-century English thought, see Zera S. Fink, *The Classical Republicans* (Evanston, 1945).

[48] *Op. cit.,* pp. 3, 58, 40.

[49] Published Leicester, 1966, p. 269.

This devotion to an idealized community can be paralleled all over Europe, on a local, a regional, and a national scale. Everywhere, the instinct of the ruling classes was to preserve a heritage. While in some instances this heritage might become indissolubly bound up with religious loyalties, the preservation of a heritage seems to have outweighed every other cause, including that of religion, in its appeal to the majority of the ruling nation. "If religion be not persuaded unto you," wrote the Lords of the Congregation to the nobility, burghs and community of Scotland in 1559, "yet cast ye not away the care ye ought to have over your commonwealth, which ye see manifestly and violently ruined before your eyes. If this will not move you, remember your dear wives, children and posterity, your ancient heritages and houses. . . ."[50]

Eloquent appeals for action in defense of laws and liberties were obviously likely to carry additional conviction when the arbitrary power that threatened them was also an alien power. In Scotland, Corsica and the Netherlands in the 1560s, in Catalonia and Portugal in the 1640s, the rebels found it easier to rally support, because the oppression came from foreign rulers, foreign officials and foreign troops on native soil. In these circumstances, a revolt originally sparked by religious protest, or sectional discontents, was capable of gathering support and momentum by combining in a common patriotism the constitutionalism of the privileged classes and the general antipathy to the outsider felt by the population at large.

This combination almost always proved fragile and transitory, because the idea of a national community to which all sections of society owed their prime allegiance, was still so weakly developed. The national community was shot through with rival allegiances, and riven by sectional and social hatreds. Moreover, the constitutionalism of the privileged was all too often no more than a convenient device for defending the interests of an exclusive caste on the basis of bogus history and bogus law. Yet, in recognizing this, one must also recognize that the defense of liberties could, in certain circumstances, broaden into the defense of liberty; and that the pursuit of sectional

[50] Knox, *op. cit.,* i, p. 225.

advantage was not necessarily incompatible with the furtherance of a genuinely constitutional cause. For all its obvious
deficiencies, constitutionalism provided the political nation with
an ideal standard against which to measure current realities.
Once this ideal standard existed, it was always capable of extension by a leader of political genius. The *patrie,* as glimpsed by
William of Orange, was something more than a society in which
the rights and liberties of the privileged were safe from the
exercise of arbitrary power. It was also a society which included
freedom of conscience among its liberties; an essentially open
society, in which men were free to come and go and educate
themselves without restrictions from above.[51]

Given the existence of an idealized vision of the community,
however restricted that vision, movements of protest are likely
to occur within the political nation when the discrepancy between the image and the reality comes to seem intolerably wide.
In Early Modern Europe it is these movements of protest from
above, and not the popular uprisings, which are capable of
leading to a "mutation in the state." The problem, though, is to
relate them to other manifestations of discontent, simultaneous
or complementary, which have their origin in religious, fiscal or
social grievances among the general population. "Then is the
danger," as Bacon appreciated, "when the greater sort do but
wait for the troubling of the waters among the meaner, that then
they may declare themselves."[52] But it is impossible to establish here any common pattern of revolt. In the Netherlands of
the 1560s an aristocratic movement benefited from simultaneous movements of religious and patriotic protest. But the aristocratic movement was halted in its tracks by the popular uprising
—the iconoclastic fury—of August 1566. In Catalonia in 1640
the popular uprising, provoked by the behavior of foreign
troops, encouraged the leaders of the political nation to seize
the initiative, and to transform a long-standing movement of
protest into a decisive break with the crown. In the England of
the 1640s, it was only *after* the political nation had seized the

[51] *Apologie ou defense de . . . Prince Guillaume* (Leyden, 1581),
esp. p. 91.
[52] "Of Seditions and Troubles," *The Works of Francis Bacon,* ed.
J. Spedding, vi (London, 1858), p. 411.

initiative, and then itself split down the middle, that the people began to move. In Naples in 1647 the popular movement failed to evoke an effective response among the dominant social classes, and doomed itself to destruction.

In states displaying such varieties of political and social organization great variations in the pattern of revolt are only to be expected. There will always be men bold enough, angry enough, or frightened enough to seize the opportunity afforded by an upsurge of popular fury or by a sudden weakening of the state. The crucial question then becomes the attitude adopted by the mass of the uncommitted among the ruling class. Will they rally behind the crown and the agents of royal authority in an emergency, or will they allow the leaders of the insurrection to have their way? The answer is likely to depend on a delicate balance between the ruling class's persistent fear of social upheaval, and its feeling of alienation from the crown. In the Netherlands in 1566, for example, the political nation rallied to the government of Margaret of Parma when social upheaval threatened it. But in 1572, after five years of repressive government by the duke of Alba, it had become so alienated from a régime which had launched an assault on its liberties, that it adopted a position of neutrality when the emergency came. The same is true of the Catalan political nation in the summer of 1640: the extent to which it had been alienated from Madrid by the policies of Olivares over the past twenty years was sufficient to prevent it making any serious move to check the course of the revolt. In Naples, on the other hand, the nobles and gentry, for all their discontents, had remained closely associated with the viceregal administration, which had bribed them with favors and privileges because it needed their help in mobilizing the resources of Naples for war. This association made them the immediate objects of popular hatred in 1647; and they had nothing to gain from breaking with a régime which had shown itself more responsive to their interests than any that was likely to replace it.[53]

---

[53] The extent of the crown's concessions to the Neapolitan nobility, and the political consequences of this policy, emerge very clearly from R. Villari, *La Rivolta Antispagnola*. . . .

If the 1560s and the 1640s prove to be decades of more than usual unrest in Europe, it does not seem a coincidence that they were both periods in which the traditional loyalty of ruling classes to their princes had been subjected to very considerable strain. In both decades, several states were still engaged in, or were only just emerging from, a long period of warfare which had imposed heavy demands on national resources. In both decades, too, there was deep discontent among the ruling classes over the prevailing style of government. In the 1560s resentment was focused in particular on the rule of secretaries and professional civil servants: Cecil in England, Persson in Sweden,[54] Granvelle in the Netherlands. In the 1640s, it was focused on the rule of favorites—Strafford, Richelieu, Olivares —all of whom had shown a degree of political ruthlessness which was all the more objectionable because, as nobles, they had been traitors to their kind.

At a time when there was already something of a coolness between the crown and the political nation, the situation was aggravated in both periods by signs of unusually energetic activity on the part of the state. In the late 1550s or early 1560s, the state's preoccupation with religious dissidence as a threat to its own authority had made it exceptionally vigorous in its employment of counter-measures. These brought the central power into conflict with sectional interests and those of local communities, and aroused widespread disquiet about the infringement of rights and liberties. In the 1630s and 1640s the main thrust of state power was fiscal rather than religious, but the consequences were not dissimilar. The financial demands of the state brought it into direct conflict with important sections of the political nation, which expressed its discontent through its representative institutions, where these still existed, and through the tacit withdrawal of allegiance.

In these circumstances, a group of determined rebels is well placed to make the running. The crown, and those sections of the governing class immediately dependent upon it, finds itself temporarily isolated. The privileged and propertied classes hold

54 Michael Roberts, *The Early Vasas* (Cambridge, 1968), p. 224.

aloof, or lend their sympathy and support to the rebels. But in practice the rebels have very little time at their dispoal. Not only do their actions give rise to new feuds and vendettas, but a society which thinks essentially in terms of restoration is likely to balk at measures which smack of innovation. "From the beginning of the rebellion," wrote Hobbes, "the method of ambition was constantly this: first to destroy, and then to consider what they should set up."[55] Rebels who contrived to give this impression were bound to alienate the body of uncommitted but conservative opinion in a political nation which was anyhow terrified that its own internal disputes would place power in the hands of the populace.

Rebels, therefore, could not count on continuing support from within the ruling class. Their movement, too, was likely to have only a narrow social base in a vertically articulated society. In the circumstances, they were bound to be driven back on alternative sources of help—and these could only come from outside. Merriman, with world revolution at the back of his mind, was impressed by the lack of cooperation between rebel régimes in different states. But much more impressive is the extent to which rebels sought, and secured, foreign assistance at vital stages in their revolts. Foreign aid, in fact, seems to have been an indispensable requirement for any revolt, if it were to have a chance of perpetuating itself. It was English military assistance which enabled the Scottish rebels to triumph in 1560. It was the French, the Germans and the English who saved William of Orange and the Dutch. It was the support of foreign Protestant or Roman Catholic powers which gave an additional lease of life to the rebel factions in France. In the 1640s, the story was the same. The Scots came to the help of the English, the French to the help of the Catalans, the French and English to the help of the Portuguese.

The dependence of Early Modern revolts on external assistance suggests something of their character and their limitations. Sometimes they were furthered, sometimes impeded, by popular uprisings; but these were ephemeral movements, which

[55] *Behemoth*, p. 192.

could achieve little or nothing without assistance from groups within the ruling class. The prime aim of this class was to conserve and restore; and this aim at once determined the scope of the rebels' action, and the extent of their support. A ruling class alienated from the crown by encroachment upon its liberties was prepared to let royal authority be challenged, and this allowed the rebels such successes as they in fact achieved. But once the heritage had been saved, the political nation reverted to its traditional allegiance, and those rebels who chose to persist in rebellion were compelled to look abroad for help.

The sixteenth and seventeenth centuries did indeed see significant changes in the texture of European life, but these changes occurred inside the resilient framework of the aristocratic-monarchical state. Violent attempts were made at times to disrupt this framework from below, but without any lasting degree of success. The only effective challenge to state power and to the manner of its exercise, could come from within the political nation—from within a governing class whose vision scarcely reached beyond the idea of a traditional community possessed of traditional liberties. But this proved to be less constricting than it might at first sight appear. Renovation, in theory, does not of itself preclude innovation in practice; and the deliberate attempt to return to old ways may lead men, in spite of themselves, into startlingly new departures. There remained, too, sufficient room for the ruling class to be able to challenge the state at the two points where its activities were most likely to influence the character of national life. By resisting the state in the matter of taxation, it might destroy, or prevent the establishment of, a major obstacle to economic development; and by resisting its claims to enforce religious uniformity, it might remove a major obstacle to intellectual advance. If significant change came to certain European societies in the sixteenth and seventeenth centuries, it came because this challenge was effectively carried through.

By the eighteenth century, the growing awareness of man's capacity to control and improve his environment would make it more fashionable than it had been in the seventeenth century to think in terms of innovation. At this point the character of revolt would also begin to change; and rebellion might come to assume the characteristics of revolution. Until then, revolts continued to be played out within the context of the ambitions of the state on the one hand, and the determination of the dominant social groups to preserve their heritage, on the other. If this determination came to be expressed in an increasingly sophisticated language, this was because the political nation itself was becoming more sophisticated. National constitutionalism learned the language of law, of history and antiquity. Perhaps, then, it is to the rise of a literate and educated lay establishment, not to the rise of new social classes, that we should look if we are to understand the eventually decisive achievement of Early Modern revolts—the transformation of liberties into liberty. That one man, at least, guessed as much, we can see from the dialogue of the *Behemoth:*

> B. For aught I see, all the states of Christendom will be subject to these fits of rebellion, as long as the world lasteth.
> A. Like enough; and yet the fault (as I have said) may be easily mended, by mending the Universities.

5

Austin Woolrych: The English Revolution, 1640–1660*

I

A generation ago it would not have seemed too difficult to write a concise introductory essay on what the English Revolution was about and what happened in it. Samuel Rawson Gardiner's great histories had mapped it out so clearly; Sir Charles Firth had completed the work and presented the authorized version to a wider public in his justly famous biography of Cromwell. Building on their foundations, the young George Macaulay Trevelyan produced, in *England under the Stuarts,* an account brimful of the happy certainties of the Whig tradition. Firth passed the mantle to Godfrey Davies, whose volume in the *Oxford History of England,* published in 1937, was still in most respects an epitome of Gardiner's eighteen volumes.

Today it all looks different, and no major event in our history is more hedged about with question-marks than the Great Rebellion. This is not because the older historians were neces-

* Austin Woolrych, "The English Revolution: An Introduction," in E. W. Ives, ed., *The English Revolution, 1600–1660* (New York: Harper & Row, 1971), pp. 1–33. By permission.

This is the introductory article in a book of essays on the English revolution. Minor deletions have been made for purposes of continuity. Austin Woolrych, professor of history at the University of Lancaster, has written *Battles of the English Civil War, Oliver Cromwell* and many articles.

sarily wrong, in any simple sense. The factual accuracy of Gardiner and Firth is generally as remarkable as the heroic scale of their researches. It is rather that we are no longer fully satisfied with the kind of explanations that they offered, or with the limited area of national politics on which they mainly concentrated. We have learned to ask new questions of the past. . . . A tardy awareness of developments in the social sciences has led us to broaden the scope of historical studies and enlarge our notions of historical causation. Whatever we personally think of the doctrines of Karl Marx and Max Weber, to name only two giants, their shadows and many others fall inevitably across our pages. Even sixth-formers seem to be expected nowadays to have their views, for example, on how to interpret the rise of the gentry and the relationship between Puritanism and capitalism.

As the dust began to settle on those particular battlefields, we were left realizing how little we still knew about the distribution of wealth and power in Stuart England, or about the relations between economic circumstances and political and religious attitudes. We are emerging, a little clearer-eyed, from a period of grand speculation and hypothesis in seventeenth-century studies. The value of the hypotheses—especially those about the rising or declining fortunes of the gentry and their effects on political allegiance—may ultimately be seen to lie less in their intrinsic validity than in the stimulus they have given to a mass of more detailed and more disciplined research. They helped to show that we can best advance knowledge now by close and quantitative investigation of particular counties, particular institutions or particular social groups. Historians have grown wary of generalizing about England as though it were a homogeneous community; they take fuller account now of the fact that when a gentleman three hundred years ago spoke of his "country" he meant his county. They see England more realistically as the sum of her many county communities, each an important unit of government, each an arena in which the gentlefolk lived out their social lives and fought out their social rivalries, each inclined to put local interests before national, and in their sum exhibiting a great variety in social make-up and political attitudes. . . .

If we are to comprehend the kind of society in which the political, social and intellectual conflicts of the English Revolution were generated, we should begin by picturing a population less than a tenth as large as that of today and comprising an overwhelming majority of country-dwellers. Out of perhaps four and a half million people in England and Wales, about a quarter of a million lived in London. But London differed in scale from all other towns far more greatly than now. Only a small handful of provincial towns topped the ten thousand mark, and about six Englishmen out of seven lived in communities of less than a thousand souls. There was no mass-association of people in similar jobs such as modern industry and modern urban society provide, and there was therefore no framework in which class-consciousness as we know it today could form itself. The typical community was the village; the commonest occupation small-scale husbandry; the essential social unit the family. Society was a hierarchy, ranging from great nobles down to cottagers and paupers. Before the revolution brought all in doubt, people accepted the fact of social subordination, of differences of degree, and their preachers constantly told them (as Shakespeare had done) that it was part of the divine order of things. For most men, their relations of dependence upon those just above them in the local community and of influence over those just below them mattered much more than any notion of a common class interest with others of the same kind of occupation and income-level in other communities. This is one reason why interpretations of the English Revolution based on modern concepts of class are apt to look anachronistic.

In a society dominated by status rather than class, the crucial dividing line ran between the small minority who could style themselves gentlemen (or above) and the large majority who could not. Perhaps one in twenty-five of the population belonged to families in the former category. Below that level, men might become constables, parish clerks, churchwardens or possibly overseers of the poor, but their small authority would scarcely stir a ripple beyond the bounds of their village. Those who happened to hold freehold land worth forty shillings a year might cast a vote in a parliamentary election, but these were rare occasions and only quite exceptionally involved any judgment upon national political issues. The great majority of the people lay not only below the level of political participation but below that of political consciousness as well. When the events of the Civil War threatened to change this state of affairs and prompted questions such as the Levellers and Agitators raised at Putney, most members of the ruling class felt that the tide of revolution was carrying them a great deal too far.

Even if we think of this ruling segment as numbering about one twenty-fifth of the whole people we may tend to exaggerate its size. Women were not expected to concern themselves with politics. Moreover it was land more than any other form of wealth that gave a man status and political weight, and the number of landowners substantial enough to affect decision-making at either national or county level was not very large. Professor Aylmer has attempted a rough count based on the year 1633, his figures inevitably becoming less definite as he moves down the scale.[1] There were then 122 English peers, twenty-six bishops, and slightly over 300 in a group just below the peerage which included the eldest sons of peers, Englishmen holding Scottish or Irish titles, and the new order of baronets. Then came between 1,500 and 1,800 knights, 7,000–9,000 esquires and 10,000–14,000 mere "gentlemen." The last category comprised the lesser landed gentry and many whose status derived not primarily from land but from commercial wealth, professional or academic standing, or office under the crown. As a body they were rather on the fringe of the ruling class. It was the ten thousand or so men ranked as esquire or above who really counted politically. It was from their ranks that most of the important county offices were filled—lord lieutenant, deputy lieutenant, sheriff, justice of the peace and so on. They furnished most of the king's servants, the men who mattered in the central administration and the royal household. They took most of the seats in the House of Commons. The higher one goes in the social scale, the larger the proportion of men in each category that one finds actively engaged in national or local politics.

[1] G. E. Aylmer, *The King's Servants: the Civil Service of Charles I* (1961), p. 331.

It was a small enough ruling class to be quite close-knit, especially within each county community. Yet as ruling classes went in the monarchies of that time it was reasonably broad, and compared with its counterparts in (say) France or Spain it was much more politically aware and politically responsible. This was partly because English kings had never been rich enough, even if they had felt the need, to erect a bureaucratic local government of professional, salaried officials. They relied on the unpaid services of the peers and leading gentry in the counties and of the most substantial citizens in the corporate towns. The head of the leading county families executed ordinary justice upon malefactors in their quarter sessions, supervised a wide range of local administration, enforced with varying degrees of zeal a host of statutes, collected the subsidies that parliament voted, mustered the militia—the catalogue could go on a long way. In Stuart England most government was necessarily local government, and the county provided its essential framework. The great problem, as Professors Roots and Everitt have shown,[2] was for central government to secure collaboration from the county communities; the Great Rebellion marked its crucial failure. . . .

The social structure of the English landed classes differed from that of their continental counterparts in one way which had had very important consequences for the development of parliament: only a small élite among them enjoyed the status and privileges of nobility. Elsewhere in Europe, most substantial landowners were noblemen, and newcomers to the land from the ranks of the bourgeoisie sought to acquire noble titles and privileges as soon as possible. The great social divide was between nobleman and commoner, and this was reflected in the composition of national representative assemblies, where they survived. These had most commonly comprised the three separate orders of clergy, nobles and commoners (or third estate),

[2] Ivan Roots, "The Central Government and the Local Community," and Alan Everitt, "The County Community," in Ives, ed., *op. cit.*, pp. 34–47; 48–63. See also Alan Everitt, *The Local Community and the Great Rebellion* (Historical Assoc. Pamphlet, London, 1969)—ed.

and in many lands they had been weakened by the built-in antagonism between noble landlords and bourgeois traders or officials. There had been various outcomes: total atrophy (as in the French Estates-General), the withdrawal of the nobles and clergy, leaving only a few impotent representatives of the towns (as in Castile), the tyranny of the landowners over the bourgeoisie (as in Brandenburg and Prussia), or in the unique case of the Dutch Republic the ascendancy of an urban patriciate. Even where the estates preserved a reasonable balance between aristocratic and bourgeois interests (as in Saxony or Aragon), they hardly shared the vitality of the English parliament.

In England the titled nobility were remarkably few. There were only fifty-five English peers in 1603, and no more than 121 in 1641. Professor Lawrence Stone has recently argued that they suffered a serious though temporary fall in power and prestige under the early Stuarts.[3] Although they largely recovered from the financial crisis that had affected most of them in the later sixteenth century, their military power had largely gone, their holdings of land (and hence their territorial influence) were much depleted, their economic recovery was too often at their tenants' expense, their rank was cheapened because the Stuarts sold noble titles for cash, and many of them became absentee landlords, resident at and dependent on a hated royal court. The great bulk of substantial landowners were not nobles but gentry: baronets, knights, esquires and gentlemen. The relative decline of the titled aristocracy gave this squirearchy a greater political and social influence than ever. But proud as the gentry were of their status, in law they were commoners, and they lacked the essential noble privileges that their French or Spanish equivalents enjoyed. The line that divided gentlemen from the social orders below them was an important one, but it was not so exactly drawn as in the continental monarchies, nor did it mark so deep a fissure. Entry into the ranks of the gentry from below required no royal patent,

[3] Lawrence Stone, *The Crisis of the Aristocracy 1558–1641* (1964).

and a coat of arms could be had for a price. Knights and gentlemen could engage in commercial or industrial enterprises without loss of caste, they intermarried with wealthy burgher families relatively freely, and they often apprenticed their younger sons to the better trades.

Above all, if they wished to serve in parliament they had to seek election to the House of Commons. There was thus no serious clash of social interest between the two Houses, for the richest knights of the shire in the Commons rivalled not a few of the Lords in wealth, and many a peer's son sat in the lower house—forty-eight in the Long Parliament, for example. In the Commons, landed gentlemen and rich citizens sat together, though in very unequal proportions. Legally the Long Parliament should have contained just over four hundred resident burgesses and ninety knights of the shire—more than four townsmen to every one country gentlemen. In fact there were more than four landed gentlemen to every one genuine townsman, for the squires had been taking over the borough seats ever since the fifteenth century. Yet the House of Commons was a strikingly homogeneous body and it showed little tendency to split along class lines. So many great merchants had a foot on the land, so many landowners had a finger in commercial enterprise that no clear line separated them, and there was a further blurring because groups like the lawyers, the courtiers and the royal officials commonly had an interest in both town and country. The fifty or so merchants who sat in an average parliament were a respected body, but commercial wealth carried relatively less political weight than broad acres. If it seems undervalued, however, one should remember how few Englishmen outside London were town-dwellers, and how readily merchants who bought land—as they mostly did—acquired the outlook and values of the landed gentry. The ruling class of Stuart England was in a real sense a single class.

Another factor that strengthened this class in its solidarity against any abuse of government was its veneration for the common law. The Inns of Court were not only training-grounds for professional lawyers but finishing schools for sons of the gentry who wanted no more than a taste of the town and a bit of legal know-how to help them manage their estates and hold up their heads among their fellow justices. But the Inns left their stamp on many a parliament-man—on early two-thirds of those originally elected to the Long Parliament, for example. Dr. Ives describes[4] how prone they were to reduce political or constitutional controversies to legal terms, and how ominous it was when the common law, so lately a buttress of the throne, came to be used to erode its foundations. Among the intellectual forebears of the English Revolution none stands so high as Sir Edward Coke.

II

If we are to sketch the sequence of developments that brought England to the brink of revolution, the first problem is where to begin in time. The conventional starting-point is 1603, the year King James traveled south to take up the Tudor inheritance. In some respects it is too late. The long rise in prices had already taken its toll of the crown's revenue and the lands of the aristocracy; the exceptional mobility of noble and gentry estates was already rising towards the peak it reached in the decade 1610–9. The squirearchy, long indispensable in local government, had already consolidated their hold on the House of Commons and explored there the techniques of opposition. By the fifteen-nineties the great age of Tudor government was clearly passing and the standards of public morality among the queen's servants were already slipping.[5]

Yet in other ways it is misleading to push the genesis of revolution back to 1603. For at least another quarter of a century no one aimed consciously at changing the basic structure of either government or society. King's servants, county magistrates and parliament-men alike sought only to preserve their time-honored inheritance and hold in trim the precious balance between the crown's necessary prerogatives and the subject's lawful rights. Professor Everitt rightly emphasizes the

[4] E. W. Ives, "Social Change and the Law," in Ives, ed., *op. cit.*, pp. 115–130—ed.

[5] See J. E. Neale, "The Elizabethan political scene," in *Essays in Elizabethan History* (1958).

conservatism of the representatives of the local communities, even when they came up all angry to the Long Parliament.[6] Nevertheless the advent of the Stuarts soon led to fresh tensions in the body politic, and is as good a point as any at which to take up the story.

The thirty-seven years that separate the general joy at James's accession from the general indignation of 1640 fall into four stages. The first spans the remaining life-time of the last of Elizabeth's great ministers, Robert Cecil, whom James made Earl of Salisbury. Until he died in 1612, Salisbury maintained something of Tudor competence in the royal administration, but his efforts were constantly undermined by the king. James was indolent and extravagant; worse, he looked upon the many offices in his gift less as places of public trust than as rewards to distribute among his friends. "He did not choose men for his jobs, but bestowed jobs on his men."[7] Thereby he not only accelerated the deterioration in the public service but alienated many of his English subjects, who could not bear to see so many coveted prizes go to Scotsmen and boon companions. The long first parliament of the reign, spanning nearly seven years, probed many issues that would lead to greater conflict later. Finance was prominent among them; resentment was growing against the king's feudal rights of wardship and purveyance, and the controversial impositions—additional import duties imposed by royal prerogative—started the Commons on their mounting opposition to the crown's powers of economic regulation. James by his tactlessness provoked more than one wrangle over the Commons' traditional privileges, he claiming that they depended on the favor of his grant, they retorting that their privileges were theirs by right. There were also disputes over religion. The Commons, balked in their own attempts to initiate further reforms in the church, challenged the canons passed by convocation in 1604 and took up the cause of the Puritan ministers who were deprived of their livings under them. But this

[6] Alan Everitt, "The County Community," in Ives, ed., *op. cit.,* pp. 48–63—ed.

[7] H. R. Trevor-Roper, "King James and his bishops," *History Today,* v (1955), 573.

was border-skirmishing compared with what came later, and the Tudor framework of government still held.

The next stage takes us to 1621 and marks a further sharp decline in the quality of government. It was also a period of non-parliamentary rule, for in ten whole years after the dissolution of January 1611, there was only one brief and sterile parliament in 1614. For six years after Salisbury's death a faction led by the Howard clan dominated the king's counsels, and the royal service was steadily undermined by incompetence, corruption and extravagance. These were the years when James's flashy young favorites made their notorious careers out of his weakness; first Robert Carr, who rose to the earldom of Somerset, and then after Carr's scandalous downfall in 1615, George Villiers, created Earl and finally Duke of Buckingham. These were the years also when offices came to be bought and sold as never before, and by 1618 the whole royal patronage was virtually controlled by Buckingham, to his enormous profit. There was a brisk traffic in titles too. The new rank of baronet was created in 1611 simply to be sold, and the trade in peerages began four years later. When offices of state became the sport of minions and the kingdom's highest honors were put up for cash, a growing proportion of the nobility and gentry began to nurse a sense of outrage.

The conduct of national policy deepened their resentment. The Howards did all they could to align England with Spain, and even after Buckingham supplanted them, the man who most influenced James's foreign policy was Count Gondomar, the Spanish ambassador. When James took up the idea of marrying Prince Charles to a Spanish Infanta and increasingly relaxed the penal laws against the Roman Catholics, most of his subjects felt that the nationalist and protestant ideals of their proud Elizabethan past were being betrayed. This feeling intensified after the Thirty Years' War broke out on the continent, and above all when in 1620 James's daughter Elizabeth and her husband the Elector Palatine became refugees, their principality occupied by Spanish troops.

These humiliations and the growing disreputability of the king's service were driving an ominous new division through

the political nation, a division between Court and Country.[8] The
terms came into contemporary usage in just this period. The
"Court interest" included not only what we should call courtiers
but all who served the king in the central government and
administration, all who wrung sinecures and other lucrative
grants from his bounty, and by extension the many gentry in the
counties who looked to his ministers and favorites as patrons.
The Country by contrast embraced all those gentry who were
free of dependence on the Court and were coming to regard it as
a swollen and vicious parasite. The Court-Country cleavage
showed clearly in the Addled Parliament of 1614, whose stormy
sittings demonstrated on the one hand that James's government
had quite lost the Tudor arts of managing parliament, and on
the other that the Commons had not yet thrown up leaders of
their own who could temper the tactics of opposition with responsible statesmanship.

This was a time too when the claims of the royal prerogative
were increasingly questioned by the common lawyers, Coke
chief among them. James's dismissal of Coke from the Chief
Justiceship of the King's Bench in 1616 was a sad landmark, to
be followed by further threats to the independence of the judi-
ciary. To make matters worse, the prosperity of James's earlier
years had by then collapsed, and the main cause was his own ill-
judged decision to transfer the trading rights of the Merchant
Adventurers, who controlled cloth exports to the Low Countries, to a mushroom syndicate headed by Alderman Cockayne.
The crown's prerogative powers over the affairs of merchants
were brought into still further disrepute by the multiplication of
monopolies, and once again Buckingham and is protégés were
the chief profiteers.

After a long lapse in parliamentary activity, the period from
1621 to 1629—our third stage—was one of frequent parliaments and mounting constitutional conflict. It began against a
background of deepening economic depression. After a brief
recovery from the Cockayne fiasco the cloth trade began to

[8] This essay was written before the publication of Perez Zagorin's
admiral book *The Court and the Country* (1970), which now offers the
best general account of the antecedents of the English Revolution.

slump again even more disastrously, and a series of wretched harvests, coinciding with widespread unemployment, brought hunger and misery to many parts of England. This time the government was not to blame, for the causes lay in England's war-wracked continental markets, but the traditional palliatives that the privy council applied never took the measure of the chronic depression in our one major industry. Recovery set in by 1625, but it was never more than partial and precarious.

The parliament of 1621 however was troubled even more by political than by economic discontents. It revived the process of impeachment, which had lain disused since the Wars of the Roses, and employed it to bring down one of the king's greatest ministers, Francis Bacon, now Viscount St. Albans and Lord Chancellor. The charge was that he took bribes, but his real offenses were his association with Buckingham and his championship of the royal prerogative. More impeachments were to follow, and parliament was launched on its long struggle to render the king's ministers accountable to itself. In the same year the Commons dared to challenge the king on the hitherto sacred ground of foreign policy. Their clamor for war with Spain was foolish, yet three years later Buckingham joined the warmongers, and within two years more he had England at war with France as well as Spain. The results were a scale of expenditure that made the government desperate for supplies, and a series of military and naval disgraces that bred a bitter sense of national humiliation and a crescendo of fury against the favorite.

Charles I's accession in 1625 made little immediate difference, for the old king's grip had been slackening for some time and the new one was even more completely under Buckingham's sway. But in the parliament of that year the Commons abused their power of the purse by seeking to grant the customs duties of tonnage and poundage for one year only, and their successors of 1626 refused supplies for the war altogether until their grievances were redressed. They regarded Buckingham as "the grievance of grievances," and only another dissolution prevented them from impeaching him. Charles then appealed directly to the nation for a free gift, and when that failed in face of the gentry's solid resistance he imposed a huge forced loan. Many gentlemen refused to pay and went to jail, and some of them raised an important test case as to the crown's right to imprison them for reasons of state without trial. The judges found for the king, but the next parliament (1628) took up the cause of the subject's liberty most vigorously. The outcome was the Petition of Right, whereby Charles was forced to acknowledge that he could neither raise taxes, gifts nor loans without parliament's consent, nor imprison his subjects without declaring the cause and entitling them to a trial at law. Soon after this victory, the nation celebrated another deliverance: Buckingham was assassinated.

Yet early in 1629 the Commons threw off the statesmanlike restraint that had secured the Petition of Right and flew at the so-called Arminian divines who enjoyed Charles I's special patronage. These high churchmen, of whom William Laud was emerging as the leader, were obnoxious to ordinary protestant Englishmen, whether Puritans or not, on several grounds: their reintroduction of altars, vestments and liturgical practices that seemed to hark back to popery; their reaction—similarly suspect—against Calvinist theology; their high clerical pretensions, especially their claim that the office and authority of bishop were *jure divino,* ordained by the law of God; their preaching that it was sin to raise the least question of the king's authority; and their efforts to recover for the church some of the wealth of which it had been plundered since the reformation. The last parliamentary session before 1640 ended violently, with the Speaker held down weeping in his chair while the Commons acclaimed wild resolutions that anyone who prompted popery and Arminianism, or advised the levying of tonnage and poundage without parliament's consent, "shall be reputed a capital enemy to this kingdom and commonwealth." This suggestion that there were treasons against the state distinct from treasons against the king momentarily opened a glimpse into a terrifying future in which king, Lords and Commons, the three pillars of England's much-vaunted "mixed monarchy," might fall irreparably apart.

Yet a long calm descended upon the country during the last

phase before the Great Rebellion. These eleven years without a parliament have sometimes been called a tyranny, but they were not that. The crown assumed no new despotic powers; the counties went on as before under the rule of their leading families and the law took its customary course. Nor were they really years of personal rule by Charles I, for he quite lacked the zest and energy for such a role. The true center of national government reverted to the privy council, now no longer eclipsed by one imperious favorite but an arena once more for contending factions. Lord Treasurer Weston achieved a certain ascendancy in the early sixteen-thirties, Archbishop Laud in the later. The man of most formidable stature in the king's service, Thomas, Viscount Wentworth, was kept far from the hub of affairs, first in the Council of the North and then in Ireland, and was not admitted to Charles's full trust until 1639. Charles I's councillors were not an imposing lot, but their government was not notably inefficient or corrupt by the lowish standards of the time, and it did renounce some of the worst abuses of the Buckingham period.

Why then did this government become so hated that the political nation would finally accept its direction no longer? Some textbooks account for it too simply in terms of "illegal" taxation and Puritan opposition to Archbishop Laud. The issues were really wider. Obviously, the financial expedients whereby the crown avoided recourse to parliament were disliked in themselves. Distraint of knighthood, the doubled revenues wrung from wardship, the new monopolies under the guise of corporations, the "compositions" exacted for encroaching on long-forgotten royal forests or contravening obsolescent statutes against depopulation or building in the suburbs of London—all these smelled of legal chicanery and often bore harshly upon individuals. Ship money was hated more because it was a land tax in disguise and because it threatened to obviate the necessity for parliaments indefinitely.

Yet England remained one of the most lightly taxed countries in Europe, and Englishmen cared not only about what they had to pay but what they were paying for. More than half Charles's revenue went to sustain his court and courtiers, and the alienation between Court and Country was growing ever deeper. The court was no longer the splendid show-case through which Elizabeth had wooed her public, no longer the natural focus of the whole world of quality, no longer the proper center to which honorable ambition and talent gravitated in the hope of a career of public service. To most of the gentry it seemed a côterie apart, alien to their aspirations and offensive to their prejudices. There were too many papists in high places, not only in the entourage of Queen Henrietta Maria but even in the privy council itself. Neither Charles nor Laud ever wavered in his Anglican loyalties, but the association between popery and Arminianism came naturally to the average protestant Englishman. Foreign policy seemed to bear it out, for the war with Spain was quickly wound up and through most of the 'thirties Charles reverted to the pro-Spanish alignment of his father's time. It went hard that England should aid the Spaniards in their renewed war against the Dutch Republic, where many an Englishman had shed his blood for the protestant cause.

The religion of Laud and the Arminians displayed itself more and more as a court religion. The king upheld the divine right of bishops; the bishops inflated the hitherto accepted divine right of kings into a doctrine of virtual absolutism. The prominent presence of the three highest prelates—the Archbishops of Canterbury and York and the Bishop of London—in the privy council went against a long tradition, and was much disliked. The courts of Star Chamber and High Commission were used more conspicuously to enforce a censorship and repress critics of the régime in church and state; the savage sentences on Prynne, Bastwick, Burton and Lilburne rebounded eventually upon those who inflicted them.

The most general grievance of all came to be that what contemporaries called the fundamental laws, and we would call the constitution, were being deliberately subverted; that parliament was suppressed so that government could pursue policies in church and state that were abhorrent to most of the nation. Resistance, especially to the payment of ship money, was already beginning when in 1638 rebellion broke out in Scotland against the imposition of a prayer book similar to England's.

The king's government in Scotland rapidly collapsed, and Charles's attempt to restore it by English arms failed ignominiously. Too many of his English subjects had sympathy more with the Scots' cause than with his. After this military fiasco, in 1639 Charles at last called Wentworth home to be his chief minister and made him Earl of Strafford. On Strafford's advice he summoned the first parliament for eleven years, but this Short Parliament would do nothing for him unless he redressed a comprehensive list of grievances, and he dissolved it after only three weeks. Strafford advised him that he was now "loose and absolved from all rules of government," and in the brief interval before the reckoning came England caught a whiff of real tyranny. But in the second "Bishops' War" of 1640 the Scots marched first, drove the English militia back from the river Tyne in disorder, and forced Charles to conclude a humiliating truce. They were to remain in occupation of the northern counties, and England was to pay their keep.

III

Nothing could now save Charles, try as he would, from calling another parliament. The Long Parliament met on 3 November 1640, and within ten months it carried through the decisive victory of the Country over the Court. The Court element in the Commons was the smallest on record, and it was helpless against the serried ranks of opposition that John Pym marshaled so skillfully. Strafford and Laud were promptly impeached, and when Strafford's prosecutors failed to pin charges on him that the Lords would accept as treason, they hustled him to the scaffold with an arbitrary act of attainder. By that time Pym and his supporters were already tackling the abuses of the last decade with a momentous series of constitutional bills, and Charles, with two armies to be paid and no resources, was powerless to refuse them.

Yet these Country politicians were mostly conservative rather than revolutionary in spirit. They wanted to restore the equilibrium of the "balanced polity" which they had inherited from the Tudors, and which Charles I had tilted—though not so far as they made out—in the direction of continental absolutism. All the famous statutes that they passed in 1641 claimed a basis in existing law and precedent, though neither their law nor their history was very sound. Taken together, these acts marked a considerable advance towards constitutional monarchy, yet they left the essential prerogatives of the crown intact, and a wiser king than Charles would have accepted them with a better grace. The Triennial Act provided that henceforth not more than three years should ever elapse without a session of parliament. Another act secured that the present parliament—it applied to no others—should not be dissolved without its own consent. Two more acts abolished the court of Star chamber, together with the prerogative jurisdiction of the Councils in the North and in the Marches, and the High Commission. The Tonnage and Poundage Act made all duties levied at the ports, new impositions as well as old customs, subject to parliamentary consent. Further statutes condemned ship money and the other financial expedients of the 'thirties, and closed the remaining loopholes for non-parliamentary taxation. Parliament thus assured its regular summons in the future, strengthened its power of the purse and established the clear supremacy of the common law, but so far it still left England with a monarch who could rule as well as reign.

There remained the question of religion, and on this the members were less united. It was probably only because the Lords rejected a bill to exclude the bishops from the upper House that the Commons debated a more radical one that would have abolished the whole ecclesiastical hierarchy "root and branch." Yet this Root and Branch Bill was dropped in the end, and the signs were that the moderate majority in both Houses would settle for some modifications of episcopal authority and of the prayer book rather than permit the abolition of either.

By the late summer of 1641, when parliament treated itself to its first recess, the fierce tensions of the past year were relaxing. The Scots had signed a treaty and withdrawn, and the English forces that had faced them were being disbanded. The measures already passed were as much as most moderate men wanted, and the country looked forward to a fresh start on the now tolerably secure basis of constitutional monarchy. Yet within a year England was plunged in civil war. Why?

The event which did most to precipitate the crisis was the appalling rebellion which broke out in Ulster in October and then spread rapidly through most of Ireland. The story of massacre and atrocity was heightened a hundredfold in the telling, and it magnified the bogy of popery into a huge specter, menacing England herself. It sharpened acutely the opposition's distrust of Charles, for the Irish rebels falsely claimed his sanction for their seizure of Protestant property. Charles himself gave too much ground for distrust by his absence in Scotland, whither he had gone in August in the hope of building up a party for himself among the Scottish nobles. The Irish terror necessitated the raising of a new army in England, yet if military power were put into the king's hands—and there was neither law nor precedent for putting it in anyone else's—could he be trusted to use it only against the Irish? This question enabled Pym to press for an answer to another that the parliament had so far left still open: the question of how to ensure that the king governed through ministers who commanded parliament's confidence, without encroaching on his hitherto undoubted right to choose his own servants. Pym now launched a frontal attack on that right. On 8 November he carried the Commons in a demand that the king should "employ only such counsellors and ministers as should be approved by his parliament"—or else parliament would take the suppression of the Irish rebellion into its own hands. A fortnight later the Commons passed the Grand Remonstrance, but by a majority of only eleven. Nominally addressed to the king, it was really a manifesto to the nation of all that evil counsellors had done amiss in the past fifteen years and all that parliament intended by way of redress. In December and January Pym went further and bid for parliamentary control over the militia. It was the gravest encroachment on the royal prerogative that the Commons had yet dared.

Outside the walls of the parliament-house the atmosphere of crisis was growing thicker. The crowds that had clamored for Strafford's head were out again in the London streets, rabbling the bishops on their way to the House of Lords. Twelve of them protested that they dared no longer attend and that parliament's proceedings were void in their absence. Pym promptly impeached them. A few days later the annual elections to the Common Council of London swung decisively his way, and he found means soon after of securing the government of the City in the hands of his allies. Then in the first week of 1642 Charles committed his crowning blunder by going to the House of Commons in person to arrest Pym and four other leaders of the opposition. The City gave them refuge and called out its militia, and for a hectic week London wore the aspect of a great capital on the verge of revolution.

The immediate storm died down, and anxious men on both sides labored to avert the threat of civil war. But the essential issues over which the war would be fought were already defined, and from now on the political nation was steadily driven towards one camp or the other. Should parliament wrest control over the militia from the crown? Should the king's choice of ministers and officers of state be subjected to parliamentary approval? Should parliament initiate a thorough reformation of the national church, and if so were episcopacy and the liturgy to be merely reformed or struck down root and branch? The radicals' demands on these points went far beyond the limited constitutional objectives of the acts that the parliament had passed so far. Unlike those acts they could claim no basis in the ancient fundamental laws; no cloak of antiquarian respectability could be thrown over a program that could now fairly be called revolutionary. As the issues changed, so did the alignment of parties. Between the Grand Remonstrance of November 1641 and the outbreak of war nine months later, the nation divided between Royalists and Parliamentarians, and the line of division was very different from that between Court and Country in 1640. Many of the old Country interest that had supported the legislation of 1641 were dismayed at the demands that Pym was now pressing and at his methods of enlisting support for them. Charles rallied them to his side with a series of skilful and conciliatory declarations which were largely the work of one of their own number, Edward Hyde, the future Earl of Clarendon.

The old Court interest was equally split. Although many fought for the king, many others retreated into neutrality, and a sizable minority went over to the Parliamentarians.

Most Englishmen faced the threat of civil war with extreme reluctance, and the division between the two sides was never clear-cut or complete. Recent research has shown what a considerable proportion of the political nation remained neutral, or at least as neutral as it expediently could. There were of course fully committed men on both sides: "old cavaliers" who regarded the parliament-dogs as mere rebels, and radicals who wanted a decisive transfer of executive as well as legislative power to parliament. Without them there would have been no Civil War. But the majority, even of those who engaged themselves on either side, did not see the issues in such black-and-white terms. Many Parliamentarians had no real wish either for further constitutional changes beyond those of 1641 or for the abolition of episcopacy; they were just uneasily persuaded that Charles could not be trusted to honor what he had been forced to concede unless his hands were further tied. Many Royalists on the other hand approved the recent statutes and disliked popery and Arminianism no less than their more moderate opponents. Between these large moderate groups on either side there was no profound difference of principle; their choice mainly depended on whether they regarded the untrustworthiness of the king or the risks and stigma of rebellion as the greater evil. When allegiance was so often divided by a hair's breadth, and when it so often shifted from one side to the other or hung uneasily poised between the two, we should be very wary of entertaining any simple or single explanation of the alignment of parties on the eve of civil war.

The line of division between Royalists and Parliamentarians, though different from that between Court and Country in the recent past, still ran right through the ruling class of Stuart England. Every order of society, every kind of occupation, was represented in considerable numbers on both sides. The motives that inclined men one way or the other were varied. Loyalty to the king might stem from simple sentiment or from a professional career in the royal service, and either way it was commonly reinforced by affection for the Anglican church order and liturgy, attachment to the old fundamental laws of the land, and a dread lest all this whipping up of popular support and arming of the people against their betters should subvert the whole social order that held the ranks and degrees of men in their due places. There was a note of fear in the social contempt which the cavaliers so often professed towards their adversaries. Motivation on the parliamentary side probably ranged still more widely. Radicals like Henry Parker, the pamphleteer, believed that sovereignty derived from the people and that the people's representatives should be the final arbiters in a national crisis like that of 1642—provided that the nobles and gentry in parliament maintained the exclusive right to speak for the people. There were probably some on the fringes of the political nation who questioned even this proviso, though their voices would not be heard much just yet. More general was a negative determination to put it out of the power of "evil counsellors" at court to do the country further harm. Puritans naturally backed parliament's demand for a thorough reformation of religion, and many (like Richard Baxter) whose religious aims were not very radical were swayed by their moral judgment upon the king's party. Others were moved more by wrongs suffered at the hands of the king's agents during the years of arbitrary rule, and others again by frustration in their business enterprises through the crown's abuse of economic regulation. In some counties, moreover, the split ran much along the lines of purely local feuds and factions.

There was a rough geographical division between the two sides. East Anglia, the south-east and south were predominantly Parliamentarian, while the king's cause was strongest in the south-west, in Wales and the border-counties and in the far north. Not surprisingly, Puritanism was strong in most of the former areas and religious conservatism (whether Anglican or Roman Catholic) in the latter. The Parliamentarian regions were also richer, more populous, generally more advanced both in agriculture and industry, the Royalist ones sparser, poorer and more backward. There are many difficulties however in the way of accepting the Marxist thesis that this line of cleavage implied a kind of class antagonism between a "bourgeois" type of landowner on the one side and a "feudal" type on the other. Yet it does look as though impoverished gentility was temperamentally more inclined to Royalism than to its opposite, and this despite Professor Trevor-Roper's theory that the core of radical opposition lay in the declining gentry of the backwoods. The remoter Royalist regions were thick with small, struggling gentlemen who were mostly as loyal as their greater neighbors, and we know that in some divided counties such as Yorkshire a higher proportion of Royalist than of Parliamentarian gentry were in financial straits. The geographical division however was far from clear-cut, for right down the center of England from Yorkshire and Lancashire to Somerset and Wiltshire ran a chain of divided or disputed counties, and no shire in England was without some supporters of each side.

Turning to the main social groups, many more peers fought for the king than against him, though the Parliamentarian minority was quite formidable. The landed gentry however played much the most important part in both the fighting and the politics of the Civil War years and they were much more evenly divided. It is likely that over England as a whole rather more of the leading county families just below the peerage were for the king, though not by any means in every county. About the lesser gentry historians are still busy finding out, for the regional variation was very great. Professor Supple warns us[9] . . . against generalizing glibly about the merchants, but for all the many important exceptions the majority were for the parliament. Over large areas of England the towns stood out in opposition to a predominantly Royalist countryside, as did the rural clothing areas in the West Riding, in Lancashire and elsewhere. Several contemporaries remarked how much support the parliament got from "the middling sort"—yeomen, substantial tenant farmers, traders and clothiers in a modest way of business, solid independent craftsmen and the like. This is broadly true, though the middling sort then did not mean the same as what we under-

---

[9] Barry Supple, "Class and Social Tension: the Case of the Merchant," in Ives, ed., *op. cit.*, pp. 131–143—ed.

stand by the middle classes. Below this level of society it is not safe to generalize, for the degree of involvement varied so much, and so does the surviving evidence.

Perhaps historians concentrate too much on the line-up of parties at the outbreak of war. It had already changed greatly since Court and Country first faced each other in the Long Parliament, and it would change again as the revolution became more radical in the later 'forties. The ranks would realign and further subdivide, for the Civil War engendered more conflicts than it resolved.

As late as February 1642 there seemed nothing inevitable about the drift into civil war. Pym's hold on the parliament could still be precarious; the king's declarations sounded plausible and his concessions tempting. Charles actually assented to an act excluding bishops from the House of Lords. He offered high office to former opponents, even to Pym himself. He was even prepared to treat, too late, over the militia and the objectionable ceremonies in Anglican worship. The trouble was that his public declarations spoke with one voice and his actions with another. Space forbids a retelling of the intrigues and blunders that undermined confidence in him, but they played into Pym's hands. When parliament passed the Militia Ordinance in March and claimed for it the full force of law despite the refusal of the royal assent, the hopes of a peaceful settlement dwindled fast. Charles withdrew to York, and when he summoned the loyal peers and M.P.'s to his side he left the radical men firmly in command at Westminster. Their demands inevitably grew more uncompromising. Both sides raised forces during the summer, and on 22 August Charles gave the formal signal for war by raising his standard at Nottingham.

We cannot follow the course of the fighting, but the changing fortunes of battle gave rise to two developments which greatly affected the political and religious outcome. The first happened when parliament, brought near to defeat in the summer of 1643, allied with the Scots. The Solemn League and Covenant between the two nations gave Scotland a voice in the eventual settlement and pledged England to establish a Presbyterian national church. But although Scottish arms helped to win the great battle of Marston Moor in July 1644, this was not the decisive victory that it should have been. Parliament's generals, the Earls of Essex and Manchester, did not want to fight the war to a finish. They feared that the consequences would go far beyond their original war aims, vague as those were, and they were anxious for a negotiated peace. Death had removed Pym from his struggle to prevent the parliament from splitting between a war party and a peace party, and the split opened wide when Oliver Cromwell charged Manchester, his own general, before the House of Commons for his "backwardness to all action." It was not a personal vendetta, for as soon as the charge was substantiated Cromwell and his allies dropped it in favor of more positive measures: the resignation of all peers and M.P.'s from their military commands and the forging of an instrument of total victory in the New Model Army.

The New Model, with Sir Thomas Fairfax as Lord General and Cromwell at the head of the cavalry, took the field in 1645. It won the decisive battle of Naseby in June and brought the whole war to an end a year later, but its impact on the course of the revolution had only just begun. Charles surrendered to the Scots, knowing how disquieted they were at the radical Independent temper of the New Model Army. Indeed they were inclined to help him back to his throne if he would only take the Covenant and guarantee a Presbyterian settlement of religion in England as well as Scotland. This he would not do; nor would he accept the severe terms offered to him by the English parliament. The Scots handed him over to the parliament's custody, but he was not too dismayed. He had already begun a long game of temporizing and intrigue, and he reckoned to exploit the divisions among his enemies until either they lowered their conditions or he succeeded in raising military assistance abroad.

The parliament was indeed divided, and the broad cleavage between conservative and radical factions extended . . . to the county committees which had managed the war effort at the local level.[10] One set of issues was political, and arose from the

[10] D. H. Pennington, "The County Community at War," in Ives, ed., *op. cit.,* pp. 64–75—ed.

On the political and religious divisions of these years, both in parlia-

problems of settling the kingdom in face of the king's refusal of parliament's terms. The other great issue was religion: . . . the contest between monolithic Presbyterianism and the Independents' plea for liberty of conscience. Contemporaries labeled the two main parliamentary groupings Presbyterian and "Independent," whether the matter of debate was political or religious, and in spite of the fact that in these two quite different contexts the line of division was by no means the same: political conservatives were not necessarily Presbyterians by religious conviction, nor were all the radical men religious Independents. What broadly characterized the "political" Presbyterians was a desire to restore the king as soon as possible, a profound distrust of the New Model's intentions, acute sensitivity to any threat against the established hierarchy of rank and degree (such as they sensed in the army and in the Puritan sects), and reluctance to consider any political changes beyond what were necessary to secure the interests of their own kind. The Independents covered a wider political spectrum, ranging from moderates, who differed from the Presbyterians more in tactics than in principles, to genuine radicals, the nucleus of a republican party. They opposed any sell-out to the king; they were readier to consider constitutional and legal reforms whose benefits would extend beyond the traditional ruling class; they looked to the army as allies, being generally outvoted in parliament; and if they were not tolerationists by conviction (as many were) they were impelled that way by their dependence on the army.

The Presbyterians wanted to disband the army as soon as possible, and in the war-weary, overtaxed, economically depressed England of 1647 they naturally had much support in this aim. But they pursued it with such a shabby disregard for the soldiers' rights, including their arrears of pay, and put such blatant slights upon the men who had won their battles, that the regiments spontaneously elected "Agitators" from the rank and file to represent their grievances. By one provocation after

---

ment and the provinces, David Underdown's *Pride's Purge* (1971) has thrown a flood of new light since this essay was written.

another the Presbyterians drove the army into open revolt. It broke out in June when the regiments marched in defiance of parliament's orders to a general rendezvous at Newmarket. Cornet Joyce carried the king off to join them there, and thither fled Cromwell, threatened now by the Presbyterians with impeachment. Officers and soldiers covenanted together not to disband until their grievances—and not theirs only but the people's—were redressed. They were talking now of much larger matters than their arrears of pay. They demanded that parliament should expel their detractors, fix a date for its own dissolution, reform its whole constitution by a rational redistribution of seats, and provide for future elections at short and regular intervals. The army, in fact, was claiming to speak for the people of England. In order to give it a single voice and to keep the Agitators within bounds, its commanders established a General Council of the Army on which each regiment was represented by two officers and two soldiers, elected by their fellows.

The Presbyterian politicians at first showed some fight, and then, when they began to yield to the army's intimidation, a mob of Londoners invaded the House of Commons and forced it to call the king back to his capital. Fairfax marched his troops in and cowed both parliament and City. But force would not in itself settle the kingdom's problems, and the generals were already seeking another solution by negotiating with Charles themselves. The pacemaker in this as in most other political moves by the army was Cromwell's very gifted son-in-law, Commissary-General Ireton. His "Heads of the Proposals" for a conditional reinstatement of the king were in most ways more statesmanlike than the parliament's terms—more concerned with positive political reforms, more tolerant in religion, more lenient to the beaten Royalists and less of an affront to traditional regal authority. But there were three obstacles to their acceptance. The first was Charles himself, who temporized over them as he had over parliament's offers, vainly confident that time or force would bring them both lower. Then there was the question of how to make parliament accept them, even if Charles did. Finally, a growing section of the army was rebelling against the whole negotiation. The Leveller movement had been taking shape in London since the previous year, and by the autumn of 1647 it had formulated a program for a popular commonwealth that had no place in it for either king or lords. The Levellers were working on the army through its Agitators, and in September five regiments elected new Agitators of a still more radical color who became the spearhead of an effort to enlist the entire soldiery, if necessary in defiance of their officers, in support of a new political deal based on the suffrages of all the free people of England. Faced with the implacable hostility of the parliament and of the ruling class it represented, the Levellers were bidding for control of the army in order to forge it into an instrument of revolutionary action. The crucial confrontation between the army commanders and the Leveller-indoctrinated Agitators took place in the famous Putney Debates. . . .

The whole situation was more tangled and uncertain than at any time since the first outbreak of war. Charles however choose to cut through it with a sword. In November 1647, a few days after the debates at Putney, he fled from the army's custody to Carisbrooke in the Isle of Wight. There, even if he did not win the Governor to his side as he had hoped, he managed to negotiate with certain commissioners from Scotland without the army chiefs breathing down his neck. A new party had taken over from the strict Covenanters in Scotland, a party which was headed by Charles's old councillor the Duke of Hamilton and was ready to fight for his restoration without forcing him or his subjects to take the Covenant against their wills. On 26 December Charles signed a fatal Engagement with Hamilton's commissioners, they undertaking to send an army to his aid, he to call the cavaliers to arms once more.

The secret could not be kept for long. The army closed its ranks; generals and Agitators joined in vowing to bring "Charles Stuart, that man of blood" to account for his crimes. The parliament was more divided, but in January it voted to treat with him no further. The second Civil War began in the spring of 1648 with a series of Royalist risings, the most formidable being in the originally parliamentarian counties of

Kent and Essex. But these Royalists' gallantry was thrown to waste because the Scots failed to march soon enough to support them. They were all either defeated or contained by the time in August that Cromwell fell upon the Scots at Preston and annihilated them in a three-days' running fight. The war was then virtually over, and Charles was a ruined gambler.

Yet even now it seemed that his ruin might not be total. Moderate men had seen in this last war a choice of evils—a choice between a restoration carried by Scottish arms or the final triumph of the army and its Independent allies. The one would bring an unbridled Royalist reaction; the other starkly threatened monarchy itself. And with monarchy the whole system of gentry power and social subordination stood in danger, for even if the Levellers were checked, the displacement of the ruling county families by lesser men, already widely apparent, would be bound to go further. So the Presbyterian politicians reopened negotiations with Charles and desperately sought agreement with him all through the late autumn. It was more than the army could stand. Ireton really took charge now, for Fairfax was miserably torn and Cromwell took refuge from decision in the siege of Royalist Pontefract. The army secured the king once more, marched into London early in December, and purged the parliament by forcibly excluding the Presbyterian majority. Cromwell arrived on the scene at last; his long spell of perplexed self-communing was in process of giving way to a mood of fierce resolution. The Independent remnant of the House of Commons charged the king with waging war upon the people of England and erected a High Court of Justice consisting of its own more radical members and a large stiffening of army officers. Charles refused to plead before this revolutionary tribunal, but its purpose was inexorable. His head fell on a scaffold before Whitehall Palace on 30 January, 1649.

The Rump of the Long Parliament now became the supreme authority in a commonwealth without either king or House of Lords. Thus the conflict between Presbyterians and Independents was resolved by force, but there still remained the latent conflict between the Levellers and the new wielders of power in the Parliament and army. It did not remain latent for long. The

Levellers had been deluded into hoping that the army grandees would sponsor at least a modified version of their plan for a popular commonwealth based on an Agreement of the People. The Council of Officers debated it, diluted it, presented it to the Rump and allowed it to be quietly shelved. Instead of representative government broad-based on the people's suffrages, the Levellers confronted an oligarchy of calculating politicians, many of them elected more than eight years ago and all sustained by the sharp swords of the grandees. Once more they set in motion their machinery of pamphlets, petitions and mass demonstrations, and this time they raised quite serious mutinies in the army. But their hold on the soldiery could not really challenge that of Fairfax and Cromwell, and after the crushing of the mutinies their movement lost cohesion and declined.

To do the army leaders justice, the Rump was not the kind of government they really wanted, but they knew how precariously the young Commonwealth stood and how fatal a genuine appeal to the people would have been after the fearful shock of the king's execution. They faced an immediate threat from Ireland, where Cromwell conducted a ruthless campaign. Within a year a no less serious danger from Scotland called him home, for the young Charles II swallowed his pride and put himself and his cause into the hands of the Scottish Covenanters. Cromwell now took Fairfax's place as Lord General, for Fairfax had scruples about attacking former allies with whom he had sworn the Solemn League and Covenant, and he resigned. But England had either to invade or be invaded. Cromwell never found a tougher enemy than his old comrade-in-arms David Leslie, or saved himself more spectacularly from defeat than in his superb victory at Dunbar on 3 September, 1650. But the young king still had friends and arms to call upon in Scotland, and next summer he staked them all upon a southward march into England. It ended at Worcester, a year to the day after Dunbar—for Cromwell the "crowning mercy," for the Royalists the last appearance on an English battlefield.

After three hard seasons of campaigning, Cromwell and the army now came back into politics. Their dissatisfaction with their parliamentary masters grew steadily stronger. The Rump would not undertake to dissolve itself before November 1654; it temporized endlessly over the settlement of religion and the reform of the law; it kept old sores open by confiscating hundreds of minor Royalist estates; it offended Cromwell's ideal of a united "protestant interest" by making war on the Dutch. The army's accusations of general corruption were much exaggerated, but its basic grievance was that these worldly-minded politicians had no real care for "the interest of the people of God" and were sticking like leeches to their positions of power and profit. The final crisis came in April 1653 when the Rump tried to rush through a bill for a new representative, whose content remains largely unknown but was profoundly unacceptable to the army.[11] Cromwell's answer was that famous file of musketeers which cleared the chamber and locked its doors.

What happened next can only be understood in the light of the mounting religious enthusiasm in the army. . . . A vociferous minority, headed by Major-General Harrison, were convinced that the millennium was at hand, when Antichrist was to be overthrown and "the saints shall take the kingdom and possess it." Cromwell's vision was less crude than Harrison's, but he too thought he glimpsed "the day of the power of Christ." He could not summon an elected parliament anyway; not only had he no legal right, but having made enemies in turn of the Royalist, the Presbyterian and now most of the Independent politicians, he could expect only hostility and confusion from such a body. So he and the Council of Officers decided on a nominated assembly as the new supreme authority, and they chose and summoned 139 "men fearing God, and of approved integrity" to represent England (by counties), Wales, Scotland and Ireland. Unfortunately the officers were not at one in what they expected of this assembly. Cromwell and his more realistic colleagues envisaged a temporary government which was to educate the nation in the blessings of a commonwealth until it could once more safely choose its own governors, and they nominated mostly men of some substance and experience.

11 Blair Worden, "The Bill for a New Representative," *English Historical Review,* July 1971.

Harrison and the fanatics, by contrast, intended a rule of the saints in preparation for the imminent reign of Christ as king, and they named many obscure sectarian zealots. No wonder Barebone's Parliament, as it came to be called, tended to split between a moderate majority and a firebrand minority. The latter attempted to abrogate the whole common law in favor of a simple written code; they aimed to abolish not only tithes but lay patronage over parish livings and indeed any kind of established ministry in the church. To Cromwell they seemed to be threatening not only religion but property too, and he was thoroughly relieved when in December, after five months' sitting, the moderate majority walked out in disgust and resigned their authority back into his hands.

There was nothing for it now but to take up the burden himself, for as he said "we were running headlong into confusion and disorder." He accepted a written constitution, the Instrument of Government, from the hands of a small group of officers headed by Major-General Lambert, and on 16 December, 1653, he was installed as Lord Protector. Government now returned to a more traditional pattern, for Protector, council of state and parliament as defined by the Instrument, were modified versions of monarch, privy council and parliament as envisaged by the reformers of the 'forties. Executive and legislative powers were to be separated, and the old ideal of a "balanced polity" was reaffirmed. The Protector had to obtain the council's consent in all significant decisions of policy, and his power of veto over bills passed by parliament, provided they did not contravene the Instrument itself, was limited to twenty days. Parliaments were to be elected at least every three years under a moderate property franchise, and their seats were completely reapportioned so that the majority went to the counties and only the larger towns got separate representation.

Cromwell and the council were given emergency powers of legislation until the first new parliament met, and they used it to tackle the thorny problem of religious settlement. They rejected the Leveller and sectarian claim that religion should be wholly removed from the civil magistrate's authority. They provided for a parochial ministry, to be approved by a mixed commission of "Triers" and supported by tithes until a less objectionable form of contribution could be devised. But they imposed no set order of worship, no formal confession of faith and no compulsory ecclesiastical discipline, while the Instrument itself guaranteed the freedom of the peaceable sects to associate and worship in their own way.

The Protectorate was not a dictatorship, either in intent or even for the most part in practice. Yet Cromwell's sincere desire for "a government by consent" was frustrated by two harsh facts. Firstly, the constitution had been framed by a junto of officers and depended on the army to sustain it. Secondly, the parliamentary cause had undergone such fragmentation since 1642 that any basis for unity was desperately hard to find. Faced with Royalists, Presbyterians, Rumpers, Levellers, Commonwealthsmen opposed to the rule of any single person and millenarians dedicated to a dictatorship of the saints, "where," cried Cromwell, "shall we find that consent?" Yet "healing and settling" was the constant theme of his speeches. He strove to reconcile the traditional political nation to a government that would set a bulwark against any further threat of social revolution and preserve "the ranks and orders of men, whereby England hath been known for hundreds of years: a nobleman, a gentleman, a yeoman. That," he said, "is a good interest of the nation, and a great one."[12]

It was uphill work, and like the Stuarts before him he found the limits of his success registered in his relations both with parliament and with the county communities. Two parliaments met under his Protectorate, and in each of them only arbitrary measures prevented the republican politicians who had managed the Rump from leading the majority of moderate, uncommitted members in dangerous attacks upon his personal authority and upon the whole constitution under which he ruled. As for the gentry in the counties, it would be a distortion to picture them seething continuously with discontent, for the signs are that their old ties of neighborhood were being steadily re-knit. Yet

[12] *Writings and Speeches of Oliver Cromwell,* ed. W. C. Abbott (Cambridge, Mass., 1937–47), iii. 435.

they shared a common dislike for a "sword government," and most of the older ruling families remained unreconciled either to their regicide masters or to the newer and lesser men who had in so many cases supplanted them in county office. Cromwell's most drastic measure to compel their co-operation was his division of England into eleven districts, each under a major-general. This followed the abortive Royalist risings of 1655, and its prime object was to provide military security against further conspiracy. But as Professor Roots points out . . .[13] the powers of surveillance over local government which Cromwell gave to the major-generals were a measure of his failure to gain the gentry's collaboration, and nothing did his reputation more harm than his commissioning of upstart soldiers to tell the "natural" rulers of the county communities how to go about their business. Yet it should be remembered that when parliament pronounced against the major-generals' régime, less than eighteen months after its inception, Cromwell acquiesced in its sentence.

Cromwell certainly owed some of his difficulties to his innocence of the arts of parliamentary management and to his riding too roughly over the susceptibilities of local interests. But there was more to it than mere tactics. Certain policies which he thought it his mission to uphold were so contrary to the prejudices of most of the nobility and gentry that no amount of politicking would have won their general acceptance in his time. Not even purged parliaments or well-winnowed benches of justices would go all the way with him on liberty of conscience —still less on his ideal of a "reformation of manners" (and here we may sympathize with them). Nor would most of them support him far in humanizing the criminal law, or promoting measures of social justice, or encouraging schemes for popular education. It is a mistake to regard the Protectorate as simply a phase of conservative reaction.

Moreover Cromwell did not wholly fail in his efforts at reconciliation. Very many of the gentry came to accept his rule as preferable to any likely alternative, so long as the Royalist

[13] Roots, *op. cit.*—ed.

cause lay in ruins. Men of conservative and even Royalist backgrounds like Lord Broghill, Charles Howard, George Monck and Sir Charles Wolseley rose high in his service. The trouble was that, as their influence rose and challenged that of the army officers and Puritan radicals, a new division began to appear. It opened wide during parliament's debates on the major-generals, and again when parliament invited Cromwell to assume the crown—a move inspired by these conservative Cromwellians, and sharply and successfully opposed by the officers. When Cromwell died in September 1658 he left his task of reunifying the nation in a sadly unfinished state. Yet paradoxically the short-lived rule of his son Richard probably enjoyed a broader basis of gentry support than any other government in the last ten years or more.

It was not a Royalist reaction that overthrew Richard's Protectorate and opened the way to the collapse of the revolution but a combination of radical groups who felt that the progressive return to more traditional ways was betraying the "Good Old Cause" for which they had fought. The republican politicians of the Rump directed a skillful propaganda at the Commonwealthsmen in the army and the more fanatical sects. The chief officers lost their nerve and deserted Richard's sinking ship, and when they forced him to dissolve his parliament in April 1659 their unruly subordinates soon compelled them to restore the Rump to the supreme authority it had enjoyed down to 1653. But both Rump and army were politically bankrupt. They quarreled again with each other as they had quarreled before, and from October onwards all was in confusion. Behind the futile posturings of these last legatees of the great parliamentary cause that Pym had led in 1642, England drifted into anarchy and the Great Rebellion collapsed from within. Monarchy returned to fill a vacuum; it had rapidly become the only conceivable basis on which to re-establish the rule of law. The cool midwifery of General Monck assisted its rebirth, and a huge wave of popular acclaim for King Charles II threatened to engulf everything both good and bad that the Good Old Cause had stood for. In their haste to put the clock back, few men probably realized how deeply the experience of the past twenty years would remain etched upon the political, social and intellectual life of the nation. Fewer still would have guessed how soon—a mere twenty-eight years—another revolution would vindicate much of what Pym had striven for; or that more than six times that span would elapse before parliament began seriously to reform its own constitution or enlarge the political nation.

6

Gordon Wood: The American Revolution*

If any catch phrase is to characterize the work being done on the American Revolution by this generation of historians, it will probably be "the American Revolution considered as an intellectual movement."[1] For we now seem to be fully involved in a phase of writing about the Revolution in which the thought of the Revolutionaries, rather than their social and economic interests, has become the major focus of research and analysis. This recent emphasis on ideas is not of course new, and indeed right from the beginning it has characterized almost all our attempts to understand the Revolution. The ideas of a period which Samuel Eliot Morison and Harold Laski once described as, next to the English revolutionary decades of the seventeenth century, the most fruitful era in the history of Western political thought could never be completely ignored in any phase of our history writing.[2]

* Gordon S. Wood, "Rhetoric and Reality in the American Revolution," *William and Mary Quarterly*, 3rd Ser., XXIII (1966), pp. 3–32. By permission.
Gordon S. Wood, associate professor of history at Brown University, is the author of *The Creation of the American Republic*.

[1] This is the title of a recent essay by Edmund S. Morgan in Arthur M. Schlesinger, Jr., and Morton White, eds., *Paths of American Thought* (Boston, 1963), 11–33.

[2] Samuel E. Morison, ed., "William Manning's *The Key of Liberty*," *William and Mary Quarterly*, 3d Ser., XIII (1956), 208.

It has not been simply the inherent importance of the Revolutionary ideas, those "great principles of freedom,"[3] that has continually attracted the attention of historians. It has been rather the unusual nature of the Revolution and the constant need to explain what on the face of it seems inexplicable that has compelled almost all interpreters of the Revolution, including the participants themselves, to stress its predominantly intellectual character and hence its uniqueness among Western revolutions. Within the context of Revolutionary historiography the one great effort to disparage the significance of ideas in the Revolution—an effort which dominated our history writing in the first half of the twentieth century—becomes something of an anomaly, a temporary aberration into a deterministic social and economic explanation from which we have been retreating for the past two decades. Since roughly the end of World War II we have witnessed a resumed and increasingly heightened insistence on the primary significance of conscious beliefs, and particularly of constitutional principles, in explaining what once again has become the unique character of the American Revolution. In the hands of idealist-minded historians the thought and principles of the Americans have consequently come to repossess that explanative force which the previous generation of materialist-minded historians had tried to locate in the social structure.

Indeed, our renewed insistence on the importance of ideas in explaining the Revolution has now attained a level of fullness and sophistication never before achieved, with the consequence that the economic and social approach of the previous generation of behaviorist historians has never seemed more anomalous and irrelevant than it does at present. Yet paradoxically it may be that this preoccupation with the explanatory power of the Revolutionary ideas has become so intensive and so refined, assumed such a character, that the apparently discredited social and economic approach of an earlier generation has at the same time never seemed more attractive and relevant. In other words,

[3] Edmund S. Morgan, "The American Revolution: Revisions in Need of Revising," *Wm. and Mary Qtly.*, 3d Ser., XIV (1957), 14.

we may be approaching a crucial juncture in our writing about the Revolution where idealism and behaviorism meet.

I

It was the Revolutionaries themselves who first described the peculiar character of what they had been involved in. The Revolution, as those who took stock at the end of three decades of revolutionary activity noted, was not "one of those events which strikes the public eye in the subversions of laws which have usually attended the revolutions of governments." Because it did not seem to have been a typical revolution, the sources of its force and its momentum appeared strangely unaccountable. "In other revolutions, the sword has been drawn by the arm of offended freedom, under an oppression that threatened the vital powers of society."[4] But this seemed hardly true of the American Revolution. There was none of the legendary tyranny that had so often driven desperate peoples into revolution. The Americans were not an oppressed people; they had no crushing imperial shackles to throw off. In fact, the Americans knew they were probably freer and less burdened with cumbersome feudal and monarchical restraints than any part of mankind in the eighteenth century. To its victims, the Tories, the Revolution was truly incomprehensible. Never in history, said Daniel Leonard, had there been so much rebellion with so "little real cause." It was, wrote Peter Oliver, "the most wanton and unnatural rebellion that ever existed."[5] The Americans' response was out of all proportion to the stimuli. The objective social reality scarcely seemed capable of explaining a revolution.

Yet no American doubted that there had been a revolution. How then was it to be justified and explained? If the American Revolution, lacking "those mad, tumultuous actions which disgraced many of the great revolutions of antiquity," was not a

[4] [William Vans Murray], *Political Sketches, Inscribed to His Excellency John Adams* (London, 1787), 21, 48.

[5] [Daniel Leonard], *The Origin of the American Contest with Great-Britain . . . [by] Massachusettensis . . .* (New York, 1775), 40; Douglass Adair and John A. Schutz, eds., *Peter Oliver's Origin and Progress of the American Rebellion: A Tory View* (San Marino, 1963), 159.

typical revolution, what kind of revolution was it? If the origin of the American Revolution lay not in the usual passions and interests of men, wherein did it lay? Those Americans who looked back at what they had been through could only marvel at the rationality and moderation, "supported by the energies of well weighed choice," involved in their separation from Britain, a revolution remarkably "without violence or convulsion."[6] It seemed to be peculiarly an affair of the mind. Even two such dissimilar sorts of Whigs as Thomas Paine and John Adams both came to see the Revolution they had done so much to bring about as especially involved with ideas, resulting from "a mental examination," a change in "the minds and hearts of the people."[7] The Americans were fortunate in being born at a time when the principles of government and freedom were better known than at any time in history. The Americans had learned "how to define the rights of nature,—how to search into, to distinguish, and to comprehend, the principles of physical, moral, religious, and civil liberty," how, in short, to discover and resist the forces of tyranny before they could be applied. Never before in history had a people achieved "a revolution by reasoning" alone.[8]

The Americans, "born the heirs of freedom,"[9] revolted not to create but to maintain their freedom. American society had developed differently from that of the Old World. From the time of the first settlements in the seventeenth century, wrote Samuel Williams in 1794, "every thing tended to produce, and to estab-

---

[6] Simeon Baldwin, *An Oration Pronounced Before the Citizens of New-Haven, July 4th, 1788* . . . (New Haven, 1788), 10; [Murray], *Political Sketches*, 48; David Ramsay, *The History of the American Revolution* (Philadelphia, 1789), I, 350.

[7] Thomas Paine, *Letter to the Abbé Raynal* . . . (1782) in Philip S. Foner, ed., *The Complete Writings of Thomas Paine* (New York, 1945), II, 243; John Adams to H. Niles, Feb. 13, 1818, in Charles Francis Adams, ed., *The Works of John Adams* (Boston, 1850–56), X, 282.

[8] William Pierce, *An Oration, Delivered at Christ Church, Savannah, on the 4th of July, 1788* . . . (Providence, [1788]), 6; Enos Hitchcock, *An Oration; Delivered July 4th, 1788* . . . (Providence, [1788]), 11.

[9] Petition to the King, Oct. 1774, in Worthington C. Ford, ed., *Journals of the Continental Congress, 1774–1789* (Washington, 1904–37), I, 118.

lish the spirit of freedom." While the speculative philosophers of Europe were laboriously searching their minds in an effort to decide the first principles of liberty, the Americans had come to experience vividly that liberty in their everyday lives. The American Revolution, said Williams, joined together these enlightened ideas with America's experience. The Revolution was thus essentially intellectual and declaratory: it "explained the business to the world, and served to confirm what nature and society had before produced." "All was the result of reason. . . ."[10] The Revolution had taken place not in a succession of eruptions that had crumbled the existing social structure, but in a succession of new thoughts and new ideas that had vindicated that social structure.

The same logic that drove the participants to view the Revolution as peculiarly intellectual also compelled Moses Coit Tyler, writing at the end of the nineteenth century, to describe the American Revolution as "preeminently a revolution caused by ideas, and pivoted on ideas." That ideas played a part in all revolutions Tyler readily admitted. But in most revolutions, like that of the French, ideas had been perceived and acted upon only when the social reality had caught up with them, only when the ideas had been given meaning and force by long-experienced "real evils." The American Revolution, said Tyler, had been different: it was directed "not against tyranny inflicted, but only against tyranny anticipated." The Americans revolted not out of actual suffering but out of reasoned principle. "Hence, more than with most other epochs of revolutionary strife, our epoch of revolutionary strife was a strife of ideas: a long warfare of political logic; a succession of annual campaigns in which the marshalling of arguments not only preceded the marshalling of armies, but often exceeded them in impression upon the final result."[11]

[10] Samuel Williams, *The Natural and Civil History of Vermont* . . . (Walpole, New Hamp., 1794), vii, 372–373; Pierce, *Oration* . . . *4th July, 1788*, p. 8.

[11] Moses Coit Tyler, *The Literary History of the American Revolution, 1763–1783* (New York, 1897), I, 8–9.

II

It is in this historiographical context developed by the end of the nineteenth century, this constant and at times extravagant emphasis on the idealism of the Revolution, that the true radical quality of the Progressive generation's interpretation of the Revolution becomes so vividly apparent. For the work of these Progressive historians was grounded in a social and economic explanation of the Revolutionary era that explicitly rejected the causal importance of ideas. These historians could scarcely have avoided the general intellectual climate of the first part of the twentieth century which regarded ideas as suspect. By absorbing the diffused thinking of Marx and Freud and the assumptions of behaviorist psychology, men had come to conceive of ideas as ideologies or rationalizations, as masks obscuring the underlying interests and drives that actually determined social behavior. For too long, it seemed, philosophers had reified thought, detaching ideas from the material conditions that produced them and investing them with an independent will that was somehow alone responsible for the determination of events.[12] As Charles Beard pointed out in his introduction to the 1935 edition of *An Economic Interpretation of the Constitution,* previous historians of the Constitution had assumed that ideas were "entities, particularities, or forces, apparently independent of all earthly considerations coming under the head of 'economic.'" It was Beard's aim, as it was the aim of many of his contemporaries, to bring into historical consideration "those realistic features of economic conflict, stress, and strain" which previous interpreters of the Revolution had largely ignored.[13] The product of this aim was a generation or more of historical writing about the Revolutionary period (of which Beard's was but the most famous expression) that sought to explain the Revolution and the formation of the Constitution

[12] For a bald description of the assumptions with which this generation of historians worked see Graham Wallas, *Human Nature in Politics,* 3d ed. (New York, 1921), 5, 45, 48–49, 83, 94, 96, 118, 122, 156.

[13] Charles A. Beard, *An Economic Interpretation of the Constitution* (New York, 1935), x, viii.

in terms of socio-economic relationships and interests rather than in terms of ideas.[14]

Curiously, the consequence of this reversal of historical approaches was not the destruction of the old-fashioned conception of the nature of ideas. As Marx had said, he intended only to put Hegel's head in its rightful place; he had no desire to cut it off. Ideas as rationalization, as ideology, remained—still distinct entities set in opposition to interests, now however lacking any deep causal significance, becoming merely a covering superstructure for the underlying and determinative social reality. Ideas therefore could still be the subject of historical investigation, as long as one kept them in their proper place, interesting no doubt in their own right but not actually counting for much in the movement of events.

Even someone as interested in ideas as Carl Becker never seriously considered them to be in any way determinants of what happened. Ideas fascinated Becker, but it was as superstructure that he enjoyed examining them, their consistency, their logic, their clarity, the way men formed and played with them. In his *Declaration of Independence: A Study in the History of Political Ideas* the political theory of the Americans takes on an unreal and even fatuous quality. It was as if ideas were merely refined tools to be used by the colonists in the most adroit manner possible. The entire Declaration of Independence, said Becker, was calculated for effect, designed primarily "to convince a candid world that the colonies had a moral and legal right to separate from Great Britain." The severe indictment of the King did not spring from unfathomable passions but was contrived, conjured up, to justify a rebellion whose sources

---

[14] While the Progressive historians were attempting to absorb and use the latest scientific techniques of the day nonbehaviorists in government departments and others with a traditional approach to political theory—men like Andrew C. McLaughlin, Edwin S. Corwin, William S. Carpenter, Charles M. McIlwain, and Benjamin F. Wright—were writing during this same period some of the best work that has ever been done on Revolutionary constitutional and political thought. However, because most of them were not, strictly speaking, historians, they never sought to explain the causes of the Revolution in terms of ideas.

lay elsewhere. Men to Becker were never the victims of their thought, always the masters of it. Ideas were a kind of legal brief. "Thus step by step, from 1764 to 1776, the colonists modified their theory to suit their needs."[15] The assumptions behind Becker's 1909 behaviorist work on New York politics in the Revolution and his 1922 study of the political ideas in the Declaration of Independence were more alike than they at first might appear.

Bringing to their studies of the Revolution similar assumptions about the nature of ideas, some of Becker's contemporaries went on to expose starkly the implications of those assumptions. When the entire body of Revolutionary thinking was examined, these historians could not avoid being struck by its generally bombastic and overwrought quality. The ideas expressed seemed so inflated, such obvious exaggerations of reality, that they could scarcely be taken seriously. The Tories were all "wretched hirelings, and execrable parricides"; George III, the "tyrant of the earth," a "monster in human form," the British soldier, "a mercenary, licentious rabble of banditti," intending to "tear the bowels and vitals of their brave but peaceable fellow subjects, and *to wash the ground with a profusion of innocent blood.*"[16] Such extravagant language, it seemed, could be nothing but calculated deception, at best an obvious distortion of fact, designed to incite and mold a revolutionary fervor. "The stigmatizing of British policy as 'tyranny,' 'oppression' and 'slavery,' " wrote Arthur M. Schlesinger, the dean of the Progressive historians, "had little or no objective reality, at least prior to the Intolerable Acts, but ceaseless repetition of the charge kept emotions at fever pitch."[17]

[15] Carl L. Becker, *The Declaration of Independence: A Study in the History of Political Ideas* (New York, 1922), 203, 207, 133.

[16] Quoted in Philip Davidson, *Propaganda and the American Revolution, 1763–1783* (Chapel Hill, 1941), 141, 373, 150.

[17] Arthur M. Schlesinger, *Prelude to Independence: The Newspaper War on Britain, 1764–1776* (New York, 1958), 34. For examples of the scientific work on which the propagandist studies drew, see note one in Sidney I. Pomerantz, "The Patriot Newspaper and the American Revolution," in Richard B. Morris, ed., *The Era of the American Revolution* (New York, 1939), 305.

Indeed, so grandiose, so overdrawn, it seemed, were the ideas that the historians were necessarily led to ask not whether such ideas were valid but why men should have expressed them. It was not the content of such ideas but the function that was really interesting. The Revolutionary rhetoric, the profusion of sermons, pamphlets, and articles in the patriotic cause, could best be examined as propaganda, that is, as a concerted and self-conscious effort by agitators to manipulate and shape public opinion. Because of the Progressive historians' view of the Revolution as the movement of class minorities bent on promoting particular social and economic interests, the conception of propaganda was crucial to their explanation of what seemed to be a revolutionary consensus. Through the use of ideas in provoking hatred and influencing opinion and creating at least "an appearance of unity," the influence of a minority of agitators was out of all proportion to their number. The Revolution thus became a display of extraordinary skillfulness in the manipulation of public opinion. In fact, wrote Schlesinger, "no disaffected element in history has ever risen more splendidly to the occasion."[18]

Ideas thus became, as it were, parcels of thought to be distributed and used where they would do the most good. This propaganda was not of course necessarily false, but it was always capable of manipulation. "Whether the suggestions are to be true or false, whether the activities are to be open or concealed," wrote Philip Davidson, "are matters for the propagandist to decide." Apparently ideas could be turned on or off at will, and men controlled their rhetoric in a way they could not control their interests. Whatever the importance of propaganda, its connection with social reality was tenuous. Since ideas were so self-consciously manageable, the Whigs were not actually expressing anything meaningful about themselves but were rather feigning and exaggerating for effect. What the Americans said could not be taken at face value but must be considered as a rhetorical disguise for some hidden interest. The expression of even the classic and well-defined natural rights

[18] Davidson, *Propaganda,* 59; Schlesinger, *Prelude to Independence,* 20.

philosophy became, in Davidson's view, but "the propagandist's rationalization of his desire to protect his vested interests."[19]

With this conception of ideas as weapons shrewdly used by designing propagandists, it was inevitable that the thought of the Revolutionaries should have been denigrated. The Revolutionaries became by implication hypocritical demagogues, "adroitly tailoring their arguments to changing conditions." Their political thinking appeared to possess neither consistency nor significance. "At best," said Schlesinger in an early summary of his interpretation, "an exposition of the political theories of the anti-parliamentary party is an account of their retreat from one strategic position to another." So the Whigs moved, it was strongly suggested, easily if not frivolously from a defense of charter rights, to the rights of Englishmen, and finally to the rights of man, as each position was exposed and became untenable. In short, concluded Schlesinger, the Revolution could never be understood if it were regarded "as a great forensic controversy over abstract governmental rights."[20]

III

It is essentially on this point of intellectual consistency that Edmund S. Morgan has fastened for the past decade and a half in an attempt to bring down the entire interpretive framework of the socio-economic argument. If it could be shown that the thinking of the Revolutionaries was not inconsistent after all, that the Whigs did not actually skip from one constitutional notion to the next, then the imputation of Whig frivolity and hypocrisy would lose its force. This was a central intention of Morgan's study of the political thought surrounding the Stamp Act. As Morgan himself has noted and others have repeated, "In the last analysis the significance of the Stamp Act crisis lies in the emergence, not of leaders and methods and organizations, but of well-defined constitutional principles." As early as 1765 the Whigs "laid down the line on which Americans stood until they cut their connections with England. Consistently from

[19] Davidson, *Propaganda*, xiv, 46.
[20] Schlesinger, *Prelude to Independence*, 44; Arthur M. Schlesinger, *New Viewpoints in American History* (New York, 1923), 179.

1765 to 1776 they denied the authority of Parliament to tax them externally or internally; consistently they affirmed their willingness to submit to whatever legislation Parliament should enact for the supervision of the empire as a whole."[21] This consistency thus becomes, as one scholar's survey of the current interpretation puts it, "an indication of American devotion to principle."[22]

It seemed clear once again after Morgan's study that the Americans were more sincerely attached to constitutional principles than the behaviorist historians had supposed, and that their ideas could not be viewed as simply manipulated propaganda. Consequently the cogency of the Progressive historians' interpretation was weakened if not unhinged. And as the evidence against viewing the Revolution as rooted in internal class-conflict continued to mount from various directions, it appeared more and more comprehensible to accept the old-fashioned notion that the Revolution was after all the consequence of "a great forensic controversy over abstract governmental rights." There were, it seemed, no deprived and depressed populace yearning for a participation in politics that had long been denied; no coherent merchant class victimizing a mass of insolvent debtors; no seething discontent with the British mercantile system; no privileged aristocracy, protected by law, anxiously and insecurely holding power against a clamoring democracy. There was, in short, no internal class upheaval in the Revolution.[23]

[21] Edmund S. Morgan, "Colonial Ideas of Parliamentary Power, 1764–1766," *Wm. and Mary Qtly.*, 3d Ser., V (1948), 311, 341; Edmund S. and Helen M. Morgan, *The Stamp Act Crisis: Prologue to Revolution,* rev. ed. (New York, 1963), 369–370; Page Smith, "David Ramsay and the Causes of the American Revolution," *Wm. and Mary Qtly.*, 3d Ser., XVII (1960), 70–71.

[22] Jack P. Greene, "The Flight From Determinism: A Review of Recent Literature on the Coming of the American Revolution," *South Atlantic Quarterly,* LXI (1962), 257.

[23] This revisionist literature of the 1950's is well known. See the listings in Bernard Bailyn, "Political Experience and Enlightenment Ideas in Eighteenth-Century America," *American Historical Review,* LXVII (1961–62), 341n; and in Greene, "Flight From Determinism," 235–259.

If the Revolution was not to become virtually incomprehensible, it must have been the result of what the American Whigs always contended it was—a dispute between Mother Country and colonies over constitutional liberties. By concentrating on the immediate events of the decade leading up to independence, the historians of the 1950's have necessarily fled from the economic and social determinism of the Progressive historians. And by emphasizing the consistency and devotion with which Americans held their constitutional beliefs they have once again focused on what seems to be the extraordinary intellectuality of the American Revolution and hence its uniqueness among Western revolutions. This interpretation, which, as Jack P. Greene notes, "may appropriately be styled neo-whig," has turned the Revolution into a rationally conservative movement, involving mainly a constitutional defense of existing political liberties against the abrupt and unexpected provocations of the British government after 1760. "The issue then, according to the neo-whigs, was no more and no less than separation from Britain and the preservation of American liberty." The Revolution has therefore become "more political, legalistic, and constitutional than social or economic." Indeed, some of the neo-Whig historians have implied not just that social and economic conditions were less important in bringing on the Revolution as we once thought, but rather that the social situation in the colonies had little or nothing to do with causing the Revoluton. The Whig statements of principle iterated in numerous declarations appear to be the only causal residue after all the supposedly deeper social and economic causes have been washed away. As one scholar who has recently investigated and carefully dismissed the potential social and economic issues in pre-Revolutionary Virginia has concluded, "What remains as the fundamental issue in the coming of the Revolution, then, is nothing more than the contest over constitutional rights."[24]

[24] Greene, "Flight From Determinism," 237, 257; Thad W. Tate, "The Coming of the Revolution in Virginia: Britain's Challenge to Virginia's Ruling Class, 1763–1776," *Wm. and Mary Qtly.*, 3d Ser., XIX (1962), 323–343, esp. 340.

In a different way Bernard Bailyn in a recent article has clarified and reinforced this revived idealistic interpretation of the Revolution. The accumulative influence of much of the latest historical writing on the character of eighteenth-century American society has led Bailyn to the same insight expressed by Samuel Williams in 1794. What made the Revolution truly revolutionary was not the wholesale disruption of social groups and political institutions, for compared to other revolutions such disruption was slight; rather it was the fundamental alteration in the Americans' structure of values, the way they looked at themselves and their institutions. Bailyn has seized on this basic intellectual shift as a means of explaining the apparent contradiction between the seriousness with which the Americans took their Revolutionary ideas and the absence of radical social and institutional change. The Revolution, argues Bailyn, was not so much the transformation as the realization of American society.

The Americans had been gradually and unwittingly preparing themselves for such a mental revolution since they first came to the New World in the seventeenth century. The substantive changes in American society had taken place in the course of the previous century, slowly, often imperceptibly, as a series of small piecemeal deviations from what was regarded by most Englishmen as the accepted orthodoxy in society, state, and religion. What the Revolution marked, so to speak, was the point when the Americans suddenly blinked and saw their society, its changes, its differences, in a new perspective. Their deviation from European standards, their lack of an established church and a titled aristocracy, their apparent rusticity and general equality, now became desirable, even necessary, elements in the maintenance of their society and politics. The comprehending and justifying, the endowing with high moral purpose, of these confusing and disturbing social and political divergences, Bailyn concludes, was the American Revolution.[25]

Bailyn's more recent investigation of the rich pamphlet literature of the decades before Independence has filled out and refined his idealist interpretation, confirming him in his "rather

[25] Bailyn, "Political Experience and Enlightenment Ideas," 339–351.

old-fashioned view that the American Revolution was above all else an ideological-constitutional struggle and not primarily a controversy between social groups undertaken to force changes in the organization of society." While Bailyn's book-length introduction to the first of a multivolumed edition of Revolutionary pamphlets makes no effort to stress the conservative character of the Revolution and indeed emphasizes (in contrast to the earlier article) its radicalism and the dynamic and transforming rather than the rationalizing and declarative quality of Whig thought, it nevertheless represents the culmination of the idealist approach to the history of the Revolution. For "above all else," argues Bailyn, it was the Americans' world-view, the peculiar bundle of notions and beliefs they put together during the imperial debate, "that in the end propelled them into Revolution." Through his study of the Whig pamphlets Bailyn became convinced "that the fear of a comprehensive conspiracy against liberty throughout the English-speaking world—a conspiracy believed to have been nourished in corruption, and of which, it was felt, oppression in America was only the most immediately visible part—lay at the heart of the Revolutionary movement." No one of the various acts and measures of the British government after 1763 could by itself have provoked the extreme and violent response of the American Whigs. But when linked together they formed in the minds of the Americans, imbued with a particular historical understanding of what constituted tyranny, an extensive and frightening program designed to enslave the New World. The Revolution becomes comprehensible only when the mental framework, the Whig world-view into which the Americans fitted the events of the 1760's and 1770's, is known. "It is the development of this view to the point of overwhelming persuasiveness to the majority of American leaders and the meaning this view gave to the events of the time, and not simply an accumulation of grievances," writes Bailyn, "that explains the origins of the American Revolution."[26]

26 Bernard Bailyn, ed., assisted by Jane N. Garrett, *Pamphlets of the American Revolution, 1750–1776* (Cambridge, Mass., 1965—), I, viii, 60, x, 20. The 200-page general introduction is entitled, "The Transforming Radicalism of the American Revolution."

It now seems evident from Bailyn's analysis that it was the Americans' peculiar conception of reality more than anything else that convinced them that tyranny was afoot and that they must fight if their liberty was to survive. By an empathic understanding of a wide range of American thinking Bailyn has been able to offer us a most persuasive argument for the importance of ideas in bringing on the Revolution. Not since Tyler has the intellectual character of the Revolution received such emphasis and never before has it been set out so cogently and completely. It would seem that the idealist explanation of the Revolution has nowhere else to go.[27]

IV

Labeling the recent historical interpretations of the Revolution as "neo-Whig" is indeed appropriate, for, as Page Smith has pointed out, "After a century and a half of progress in historical scholarship, in research techniques, in tools and methods, we have found our way to the interpretation held, substantially, by those historians who themselves participated in or lived through the era of, the Revolution." By describing the Revolution as a conservative, principled defense of American freedom against the provocations of the English government, the neo-Whig historians have come full circle to the position of the Revolutionaries themselves and to the interpretation of the first generation of historians.[28] Indeed, as a consequence of this historical atavism, praise for the contemporary or early historians has become increasingly common.

But to say "that the Whig interpretation of the American Revolution may not be as dead as some historians would have us believe" is perhaps less to commend the work of David Ramsay and George Bancroft than to indict the approach of

[27] This is not to say, however, that work on the Revolutionary ideas is in any way finished. For examples of the re-examination of traditional problems in Revolutionary political theory see Richard Buel, Jr., "Democracy and the American Revolution: A Frame of Reference," *Wm. and Mary Qtly.*, 3d Ser., XXI (1964), 165–190; and Bailyn's resolution of James Otis's apparent inconsistency in *Revolutionary Pamphlets*, I, 100–103, 106–107, 121–123, 409–417, 546–552.

[28] Smith, "Ramsay and the American Revolution," 72.

recent historians.[29] However necessary and rewarding the neo-Whig histories have been, they present us with only a partial perspective on the Revolution. The neo-Whig interpretation is intrinsically polemical; however subtly presented, it aims to justify the Revolution. It therefore cannot accommodate a totally different, an opposing, perspective, a Tory view of the Revolution. It is for this reason that the recent publication of Peter Oliver's "Origin and Progress of the American Rebellion" is of major significance, for it offers us—"by attacking the hallowed traditions of the revolution, challenging the motives of the founding fathers, and depicting revolution as passion, plotting, and violence"—an explanation of what happened quite different from what we have been recently accustomed to.[30] Oliver's vivid portrait of the Revolutionaries with his accent on their vicious emotions and interests seriously disturbs the present Whiggish interpretation of the Revolution. It is not that Oliver's description of, say, John Adams as madly ambitious and consumingly resentful is any more correct than Adams's own description of himself as a virtuous and patriotic defender of liberty against tyranny. Both interpretations of Adams are in a sense right, but neither can comprehend the other because each is preoccupied with seemingly contradictory sets of motives. Indeed, it is really these two interpretations that have divided historians of the Revolution ever since.

Any intellectually satisfying explanation of the Revolution must encompass the Tory perspective as well as the Whig, for if we are compelled to take sides and choose between opposing motives—unconscious or avowed, passion or principle, greed or liberty—we will be endlessly caught up in the polemics of the participants themselves. We must, in other words, eventually dissolve the distinction between conscious and unconscious motives, between the Revolutionaries' stated intentions and

---

[29] Morgan, "Revisions in Need of Revising," 13.

[30] Adair and Schutz, eds., *Peter Oliver's Origin,* ix. In the present neo-Whig context, Sidney S. Fisher, "The Legendary and Myth-Making Process in Histories of the American Revolution," in American Philosophical Society, *Proceedings* LI (Philadelphia, 1912), 53–75, takes on a renewed relevance.

their supposedly hidden needs and desires, a dissolution that involves somehow relating beliefs and ideas to the social world in which they operate. If we are to understand the causes of the Revolution we must therefore ultimately transcend this problem of motivation. But this we can never do as long as we attempt to explain the Revolution mainly in terms of the intentions of the participants. It is not that men's motives are unimportant; they indeed make events, including revolutions. But the purposes of men, especially in a revolution, are so numerous, so varied, and so contradictory that their complex interaction produces results that no one intended or could even foresee. It is this interaction and these results that recent historians are referring to when they speak so disparagingly of those "underlying determinants" and "impersonal and inexorable forces" bringing on the Revolution. Historical explanation which does not account for these "forces," which, in other words, relies simply on understanding the conscious intentions of the actors, will thus be limited. This preoccupation with men's purposes was what restricted the perspectives of the contemporaneous Whig and Tory interpretations; and it is still the weakness of the neo-Whig histories, and indeed of any interpretation which attempts to explain the events of the Revolution by discovering the calculations from which individuals supposed themselves to have acted.

No explanation of the American Revolution in terms of the intentions and designs of particular individuals could have been more crudely put than that offered by the Revolutionaries themselves. American Whigs, like men of the eighteenth century generally, were fascinated with what seemed to the age to be the newly appreciated problem of human motivation and causation in the affairs of the world. In the decade before independence the Americans sought endlessly to discover the supposed calculations and purposes of individuals or groups that lay behind the otherwise incomprehensible rush of events. More than anything else perhaps, it was this obsession with motives that led to the prevalence in the eighteenth century of beliefs in conspiracies to account for the confusing happenings in which men found themselves caught up. Bailyn has suggested that this common fear of conspiracy was "deeply rooted in the political awareness of eighteenth-century Britons, involved in the very structure of their political life"; it "reflected so clearly the realities of life in an age in which monarchical autocracy flourished, [and] in which the stability and freedom of England's 'mixed' constitution was a recent and remarkable achievement."[31] Yet it might also be argued that the tendency to see conspiracy behind what happened reflected as well the very enlightenment of the age. To attribute events to the designs and purposes of human agents seemed after all to be an enlightened advance over older beliefs in blind chance, providence, or God's interventions. It was rational and scientific, a product of both the popularization of politics and the secularization of knowledge. It was obvious to Americans that the series of events in the years after 1763, those "unheard of intolerable calamities, spring not of the dust, come not causeless." "Ought not the PEOPLE therefore," asked John Dickinson, "to watch? to observe facts? to search into causes? to investigate designs?"[32] And these causes and designs could be traced to individuals in high places, to ministers, to royal governors, and their lackeys. The belief in conspiracy grew naturally out of the enlightened need to find the human purposes behind the multitude of phenomena, to find the causes for what happened in the social world just as the natural scientist was discovering the causes for what happened in the physical world.[33] It was a necessary consequence of the search for

31 Bailyn, *Revolutionary Pamphlets*, I, 87, ix.

32 [Moses Mather], *America's Appeal to the Impartial World . . .* (Hartford, 1775), 59; [John Dickinson], *Letters from a Farmer in Pennsylvania to the Inhabitants of the British Colonies* (1768), in Paul L. Ford, ed., *The Life and Writings of John Dickinson* (Historical Society of Pennsylvania, *Memoirs*, XIV [Philadelphia, 1895]), II, 348. Dickinson hinged his entire argument on the ability of the Americans to decipher the "intention" of parliamentary legislation, whether for revenue or for commercial regulation. *Ibid.*, 348, 364.

33 See Herbert Davis, "The Augustan Conception of History," in J. A. Mazzeo, ed., *Reason and the Imagination: Studies in the History of Ideas, 1600–1800* (New York, 1962), 226–228; W. H. Greenleaf, *Order, Empiricism and Politics: Two Traditions of English Political Thought, 1500–1700* (New York, 1964), 166; R. N. Stromberg, "History in the Eighteenth Century," *Journal of the History of Ideas*, XII (1951), 300. It was against this "dominant characteristic of the historical thought of

connections and patterns in events. The various acts of the British government, the Americans knew, should not be "regarded according to the simple force of each, but as parts of a system of oppression."[34] The Whigs' intense search for the human purposes behind events was in fact an example of the beginnings of modern history.

In attempting to rebut those interpretations disparaging the colonists' cause, the present neo-Whig historians have been drawn into writing as partisans of the Revolutionaries. And they have thus found themselves entangled in the same kind of explanation used by the original antagonists, an explanation, despite obvious refinements, still involved with the discovery of motives and its corollary, the assessing of a personal sort of responsibility for what happened. While most of the neo-Whig historians have not gone so far as to see conspiracy in British actions (although some have come close),[35] they have tended to point up the blundering and stupidity of British officials in contrast to "the breadth of vision" that moved the Americans. If George III was in a position of central responsibility in the British government, as English historians have recently said, then, according to Edmund S. Morgan, "he must bear most of

the age," this "tendency to explain events in terms of conscious action by individuals," that the brilliant group of Scottish social scientists writing at the end of the 18th century directed much of their work. Duncan Forbes, " 'Scientific' Whiggism: Adam Smith and John Millar," *Cambridge Journal,* VII (1954), 651, 653–654. While we have had recently several good studies of historical thinking in 17th-century England, virtually nothing has been done on the 18th century. See, however, J. G. A. Pocock, "Burke and the Ancient Constitution—A Problem in the History of Ideas," *The Historical Journal,* III (1960), 125–143; and Stow Persons, "The Cyclical Theory of History in Eighteenth Century America," *American Quarterly,* VI (1954), 147–163.

[34] [Dickinson], *Letters from a Farmer,* in Ford, ed., *Writings of Dickinson,* 388.

[35] Bailyn has noted that Oliver M. Dickerson, in chap. 7 of his *The Navigation Acts and the American Revolution* (Philadelphia, 1951), "adopts wholesale the contemporary Whig interpretation of the Revolution as the result of a conspiracy of 'King's Friends.' " Bailyn, *Revolutionary Pamphlets,* I, 724.

the praise or blame for the series of measures that alienated and lost the colonies, and it is hard to see how there can be much praise." By seeking "to define issues, fix responsibilities," and thereby to shift the "burden of proof" onto those who say the Americans were narrow and selfish and the empire was basically just and beneficent, the neo-Whigs have attempted to redress what they felt was an unfair neo-Tory bias of previous explanations of the Revolution;[36] they have not, however, challenged the terms of the argument. They are still obsessed with why men said they acted and with who was right and who was wrong. Viewing the history of the Revolution in this judicatory manner has therefore restricted the issues over which historians have disagreed to those of motivation and responsibility, the very issues with which the participants themselves were concerned.

The neo-Whig "conviction that the colonists' attachment to principle was genuine"[37] has undoubtedly been refreshing, and indeed necessary, given the Tory slant of earlier twentieth-century interpretations. It now seems clearer that the Progressive historians, with their naive and crude reflex conception of human behavior, had too long treated the ideas of the Revolution superficially if not superciliously. Psychologists and sociologists are now willing to grant a more determining role to beliefs, particularly in revolutionary situations. It is now accepted that men act not simply in response to some kind of objective reality but to the meaning they give to that reality. Since men's beliefs are as much a part of the given stimuli as the objective environment, the beliefs must be understood and taken seriously if men's behavior is to be fully explained. The American Revolutionary ideas were more than cooked-up pieces of thought served by an aggressive and interested minority to a gullible and unsuspecting populace. The concept of propaganda permitted the Progressive historians to account for the presence of ideas but it prevented them from recognizing ideas as an

36 Morgan, "Revisions in Need of Revising," 7, 13, 8; Greene, "Flight From Determinism," 237.

37 Edmund S. Morgan, *The Birth of the Republic, 1763–89* (Chicago, 1956), 51.

important determinant of the Americans' behavior. The weight attributed to ideas and constitutional principles by the neo-Whig historians was thus an essential corrective to the propagandist studies.

Yet in its laudable effort to resurrect the importance of ideas in historical explanation much of the writing of the neo-Whigs has tended to return to the simple nineteenth-century intellectualist assumption that history is the consequence of a rational calculation of ends and means, that what happened was what was consciously desired and planned. By supposing "that individual actions and immediate issues are more important than underlying determinants in explaining particular events," by emphasizing conscious and articulated motives, the neo-Whig historians have selected and presented that evidence which is most directly and clearly expressive of the intentions of the Whigs, that is, the most well-defined, the most constitutional, the most reasonable of the Whig beliefs, those found in their public documents, their several declarations of grievances and causes. It is not surprising that for the neo-Whigs the history of the American Revolution should be more than anything else "the history of the Americans' search for principles."[38] Not only, then, did nothing in the Americans' economic and social structure really determine their behavior, but the colonists in fact acted from the most rational and calculated of motives: they fought, as they said they would, simply to defend their ancient liberties against British provocation.

By implying that certain declared rational purposes are by themselves an adequate explanation for the Americans' revolt, in other words that the Revolution was really nothing more than a contest over constitutional principles, the neo-Whig historians have not only threatened to deny what we have learned of human psychology in the twentieth century, but they have also in fact failed to exploit fully the terms of their own idealist approach by not taking into account all of what the Americans believed and said. Whatever the deficiencies and misunderstand-

[38] Greene, "Flight From Determinism," 258; Morgan, *Birth of the Republic*, 3.

ings of the role of ideas in human behavior present in the propagandist studies of the 1930's, these studies did for the first time attempt to deal with the entirety and complexity of American Revolutionary thought—to explain not only all the well-reasoned notions of law and liberty that were so familiar but, more important, all the irrational and hysterical beliefs that had been so long neglected. Indeed, it was the patent absurdity and implausibility of much of what the Americans said that lent credence and persuasiveness to their mistrustful approach to the ideas. Once this exaggerated and fanatical rhetoric was uncovered by the Progressive historians, it should not have subsequently been ignored—no matter how much it may have impugned the reasonableness of the American response. No widely expressed ideas can be dismissed out of hand by the historian.

In his recent analysis of Revolutionary thinking Bernard Bailyn has avoided the neo-Whig tendency to distort the historical reconstruction of the American mind. By comprehending "the assumptions, beliefs, and ideas that lay behind the manifest events of the time," Bailyn has attempted to get inside the Whigs' mind, and to experience vicariously all of what they thought and felt, both their rational constitutional beliefs and their hysterical and emotional ideas as well. The inflammatory phrases "slavery," "corruption," "conspiracy," that most historians had either ignored or readily dismissed as propaganda, took on a new significance for Bailyn. He came "to suspect that they meant something very real to both the writers and their readers: that there were real fears, real anxieties, a sense of real danger behind these phrases, and not merely the desire to influence by rhetoric and propaganda the inert minds of an otherwise passive populace."[39] No part of American thinking, Bailyn suggests—not the widespread belief in a ministerial conspiracy, not the hostile and vicious indictments of individuals, not the fear of corruption and the hope for regeneration, not any of the violent seemingly absurd distortions and falsifications of what we now believe to be true, in short, none of the frenzied

[39] Bailyn, *Revolutionary Pamphlets,* I, vii, ix.

rhetoric—can be safely ignored by the historian seeking to understand the causes of the Revolution.

Bailyn's study, however, represents something other than a more complete and uncorrupted version of the common idealist interpretations of the Revolution. By viewing from the "interior" the Revolutionary pamphlets, which were "to an unusual degree, *explanatory*," revealing "not merely positions taken but the reasons why positions were taken," Bailyn like any idealist historian has sought to discover the motives the participants themselves gave for their actions, to re-enact their thinking at crucial moments, and thereby to recapture some of the "unpredictable reality" of the Revolution.[40] But for Bailyn the very unpredictability of the reality he has disclosed has undermined the idealist obsession with explaining why, in the participants' own estimation, they acted as they did. Ideas emerge as more than explanatory devices, as more than indicators of motives. They become as well objects for analysis in and for themselves, historical events in their own right to be treated as other historical events are treated. Although Bailyn has examined the Revolutionary ideas subjectively from the inside, he has also analyzed them objectively from the outside. Thus, in addition to a contemporary Whig perspective, he presents us with a retrospective view of the ideas—their complexity, their development, and their consequences—that the actual participants did not have. In effect his essay represents what has been called "a Namierism of the history of ideas,"[41] a structural analysis of thought that suggests a conclusion about the movement of history not very different from Sir Lewis Namier's, where history becomes something "started in ridiculous beginnings, while small men did things both infinitely smaller and infinitely greater than they knew."[42]

In his *England in the Age of the American Revolution*

[40] *Ibid.*, vii, viii, 17.

[41] J. G. A. Pocock, "Machiavelli, Harrington, and English Political Ideologies in the Eighteenth Century," *Wm. and Mary Qtly.*, 3d Ser., XXII (1965), 550.

[42] Sir Lewis Namier, *England in the Age of the American Revolution*, 2nd ed. (London, 1961), 131.

Namier attacked the Whig tendency to overrate "the importance of the conscious will and purpose in individuals." Above all he urged us "to ascertain and recognize the deeper irrelevancies and incoherence of human actions, which are not so much directed by reason, as invested by it *ex post facto* with the appearances of logic and rationality," to discover the unpredictable reality, where men's motives and intentions were lost in the accumulation and momentum of interacting events. The whole force of Namier's approach tended to squeeze the intellectual content out of what men did. Ideas setting forth principles and purposes for action, said Namier, did not count for much in the movement of history.[43]

In his study of the Revolutionary ideas Bailyn has come to an opposite conclusion: ideas counted for a great deal, not only being responsible for the Revolution but also for transforming the character of American society. Yet in his hands ideas lose that static quality they have commonly had for the Whig historians, the simple statements of intention that so exasperated Namier. For Bailyn the ideas of the Revolutionaries take on an elusive and unmanageable quality, a dynamic self-intensifying character that transcended the intentions and desires of any of the historical participants. By emphasizing how the thought of the colonists was "strangely reshaped, turned in unfamiliar directions," by describing how the Americans "indeliberately, half-knowingly" groped toward "conclusions they could not themselves clearly perceive," by demonstrating how new beliefs and hence new actions were the responses not to desire but to the logic of developing situations, Bailyn has wrested the explanation of the Revolution out of the realm of motivation in which the neo-Whig historians had confined it.

With this kind of approach to ideas, the degree of consistency and devotion to principles become less important, and indeed the major issues of motivation and responsibility over which historians have disagreed become largely irrelevant. Action becomes not the product of rational and conscious calculation but of dimly perceived and rapidly changing thoughts and situa-

[43] *Ibid.*, 129.

tions, "where the familiar meaning of ideas and words faded away into confusion, and leaders felt themselves peering into a haze, seeking to bring shifting conceptions somehow into focus." Men become more the victims than the manipulators of their ideas, as their thought unfolds in ways few anticipated, "rapid, irreversible, and irresistible," creating new problems, new considerations, new ideas, which have their own unforeseen implications. In this kind of atmosphere the Revolution, not at first desired by the Americans, takes on something of an inevitable character, moving through a process of escalation into levels few had intended or perceived. It no longer makes sense to assign motives or responsibility to particular individuals for the totality of what happened. Men were involved in a complicated web of phenomena, ideas, and situations, from which in retrospect escape seems impossible.[44]

By seeking to uncover the motives of the Americans expressed in the Revolutionary pamphlets, Bailyn has ended by demonstrating the autonomy of ideas as phenomena, where the ideas operate, as it were, over the heads of the participants, taking them in directions no one could have foreseen. His discussion of Revolutionary thought thus represents a move back to a deterministic approach to the Revolution, a determinism, however, which is different from that which the neo-Whig historians have so recently and self-consciously abandoned. Yet while the suggested determinism is thoroughly idealist—indeed never before has the force of ideas in bringing on the Revolution been so emphatically put—its implications are not. By helping to purge our writing about the Revolution of its concentration on constitutional principles and its stifling judicial-like preoccupation with motivation and responsibility, the study serves to open the way for new questions and new appraisals. In fact, it is out of the very completeness of his idealist interpre-

[44] Bailyn, *Revolutionary Pamphlets,* I, 90, x, 169, 140. See Hannah Arendt, *On Revolution* (New York, 1963), 173: "American experience had taught the men of the Revolution that action, though it may be started in isolation and decided upon by single individuals for very different motives, can be accomplished only by some joint effort in which the motivation of single individuals . . . no longer counts. . . ."

tation, out of his exposition of the extraordinary nature—the very dynamism and emotionalism—of the Americans' thought that we have the evidence for an entirely different, a behaviorist, perspective on the causes of the American Revolution. Bailyn's book-length introduction to his edition of Revolutionary pamphlets is therefore not only a point of fulfillment for the idealist approach to the Revolution, it is also a point of departure for a new look at the social sources of the Revolution.

V

It seems clear that historians of eighteenth-century America and the Revolution cannot ignore the force of ideas in history to the extent that Namier and his students have done in their investigations of eighteenth-century English politics. This is not to say, however, that the Namier approach to English politics has been crucially limiting and distorting. Rather it may suggest that the Namier denigration of ideas and principles is inapplicable for American politics because the American social situation in which ideas operated was very different from that of eighteenth-century England. It may be that ideas are less meaningful to a people in a socially stable situation. Only when ideas have become stereotyped reflexes do evasion and hypocrisy and the Namier mistrust of what men believe become significant. Only in a relatively settled society does ideology become a kind of habit, a bundle of widely shared and instinctive conventions, offering ready-made explanations for men who are not being compelled to ask any serious questions. Conversely, it is perhaps only in a relatively unsettled, disordered society, where the questions come faster than men's answers, that ideas become truly vital and creative.[45]

Paradoxically it may be the very vitality of the Americans' ideas, then, that suggests the need to examine the circumstances in which they flourished. Since ideas and beliefs are ways of perceiving and explaining the world, the nature of the ideas

[45] See Sir Lewis Namier, *The Structure of Politics at the Accession of George III*, 2d ed. (London, 1961), 16; Sir Lewis Namier, "Human Nature in Politics," in *Personalities and Power: Selected Essays* (New York, 1965), 5–6.

expressed is determined as much by the character of the world being confronted as by the internal development of inherited and borrowed conceptions. Out of the multitude of inherited and transmitted ideas available in the eighteenth century, Americans selected and emphasized those which seemed to make meaningful what was happening to them. In the colonists' use of classical literature, for example, "their detailed knowledge and engaged interest covered only one era and one small group of writers," Plutarch, Livy, Cicero, Sallust, and Tacitus—those who "had hated and feared the trends of their own time, and in their writing had contrasted the present with a better past, which they endowed with qualities absent from their own, corrupt era."[46] There was always, in Max Weber's term, some sort of elective affinity between the Americans' interests and their beliefs, and without that affinity their ideas would not have possessed the peculiar character and persuasiveness they did. Only the most revolutionary social needs and circumstances could have sustained such revolutionary ideas.[47]

When the ideas of the Americans are examined comprehensively, when all of the Whig rhetoric, irrational as well as rational, is taken into account, one cannot but be struck by the predominant characteristics of fear and frenzy, the exaggerations and the enthusiasm, the general sense of social corruption and disorder out of which would be born a new world of benevolence and harmony where Americans would become the "eminent examples of every divine and social virtue."[48] As Bailyn and the propaganda studies have amply shown, there is

[46] Bailyn, *Revolutionary Pamphlets,* I, 22. The French Revolutionaries were using the same group of classical writings to express their estrangement from the *ancien régime* and their hope for the new order. Harold T. Parker, *The Cult of Antiquity and the French Revolutionaries: A Study in the Development of the Revolutionary Spirit* (Chicago, 1937), 22–23.

[47] The relation of ideas to social structure is one of the most perplexing and intriguing in the social sciences. For an extensive bibliography on the subject see Norman Birnbaum, "The Sociological Study of Ideology (1940–60)," *Current Sociology,* IX (1960).

[48] Jacob Duché, *The American Vine, A Sermon, Preached . . . Before the Honourable Continental Congress, July 20th, 1775 . . .* (Philadelphia, 1775), 29.

simply too much fanatical and millennial thinking even by the best minds that must be explained before we can characterize the Americans' ideas as peculiarly rational and legalistic and thus view the Revolution as merely a conservative defense of constitutional liberties. To isolate refined and nicely-reasoned arguments from the writings of John Adams and Jefferson is not only to disregard the more inflamed expressions of the rest of the Whigs but also to overlook the enthusiastic extravagance—the paranoiac obsession with a diabolical Crown conspiracy and the dream of a restored Saxon era—in the thinking of Adams and Jefferson themselves.

The ideas of the Americans seem, in fact, to form what can only be called a revolutionary syndrome. If we were to confine ourselves to examining the Revolutionary rhetoric alone, apart from what happened politically or socially, it would be virtually impossible to distinguish the American Revolution from any other revolution in modern Western history. In the kinds of ideas expressed the American Revolution is remarkably similar to the seventeenth-century Puritan Revolution and to the eighteenth-century French Revolution: the same general disgust with a chaotic and corrupt world, the same anxious and angry bombast, the same excited fears of conspiracies by depraved men, the same utopian hopes for the construction of a new and virtuous order.[49] It was not that this syndrome of ideas was simply transmitted from one generation or from one people to another. It was rather perhaps that similar, though hardly identical, social situations called forth within the limitations of inherited and available conceptions similar modes of expression. Although we need to know much more about the sociology of revolutions and collective movements, it does seem possible

[49] For recent discussions of French and Puritan revolutionary rhetoric see Peter Gay, "Rhetoric and Politics in the French Revolution," *Amer. Hist. Rev.*, LXVI (1960–61), 664–676; Michael Walzer, "Puritanism as a Revolutionary Ideology," *History and Theory*, III (1963), 59–90. This entire issue of *History and Theory* is devoted to a symposium on the uses of theory in the study of history. In addition to the Walzer article, I have found the papers by Samuel H. Beer, "Causal Explanation and Imaginative Re-enactment," and Charles Tilly, "The Analysis of a Counter-Revolution," very stimulating and helpful.

that particular patterns of thought, particular forms of expression, correspond to certain basic social experiences. There may be, in other words, typical modes of expression, typical kinds of beliefs and values, characterizing a revolutionary situation, at least within roughly similar Western societies. Indeed, the types of ideas manifested may be the best way of identifying a collective movement as a revolution. As one student of revolutions writes, "It is on the basis of a knowledge of men's beliefs that we can distinguish their behavior from riot, rebellion or insanity."[50]

It is thus the very nature of the Americans' rhetoric—its obsession with corruption and disorder, its hostile and conspiratorial outlook, and its millennial vision of a regenerated society —that reveals as nothing else apparently can the American Revolution as a true revolution with its sources lying deep in the social structure. For this kind of frenzied rhetoric could spring only from the most severe sorts of social strain. The grandiose and feverish language of the Americans was indeed the natural, even the inevitable, expression of a people caught up in a revolutionary situation, deeply alienated from the existing sources of authority and vehemently involved in a basic reconstruction of their political and social order. The hysteria of the Americans' thinking was but a measure of the intensity of their revolutionary passions. Undoubtedly the growing American alienation from British authority contributed greatly to this revolutionary situation. Yet the very weakness of the British imperial system and the accumulating ferocity of American antagonism to it suggests that other sources of social strain were being fed into the revolutionary movement. It may be that the Progressive historians in their preoccupation with internal social problems were more right than we have recently been willing to grant. It would be repeating their mistake, however, to expect this internal social strain necessarily to take the form of coherent class conflict or overt social disruption. The sources of revolu-

[50] Bryan A. Wilson, "Millennialism in Comparative Perspective," *Comparative Studies in Society and History*, VI (1963–64), 108. See also Neil J. Smelser, *Theory of Collective Behaviour* (London, 1962), 83, 120, 383.

tionary social stress may have been much more subtle but no less severe.

Of all of the colonies in the mid-eighteenth century, Virginia seems the most settled, the most lacking in obvious social tension. Therefore, as it has been recently argued, since conspicuous social issues were nonexistent, the only plausible remaining explanation for the Virginians' energetic and almost unanimous commitment to the Revolution must have been their devotion to constitutional principles.[51] Yet it may be that we have been looking for the wrong kind of social issues, for organized conflicts, for conscious divisions, within the society. It seems clear that Virginia's difficulties were not the consequence of any obvious sectional or class antagonism, Tidewater versus Piedmont, aristocratic planters versus yeomen farmers. There was apparently no discontent with the political system that went deep into the social structure. But there does seem to have been something of a social crisis within the ruling group itself, which intensely aggravated the Virginians' antagonism to the imperial system. Contrary to the impression of confidence and stability that the Virginia planters have historically acquired, they seemed to have been in very uneasy circumstances in the years before the Revolution. The signs of the eventual nineteenth-century decline of the Virginia gentry were, in other words, already felt if not readily apparent.

The planters' ability to command the acquiescence of the people seems extraordinary compared to the unstable politics of the other colonies. But in the years before independence there were signs of increasing anxiety among the gentry over their representative role. The ambiguities in the relationship between the Burgesses and their constituents erupted into open debate in the 1750's. And men began voicing more and more concern over the mounting costs of elections and growing corruption in the soliciting of votes, especially by "those who have neither natural nor acquired parts to recommend them."[52] By the late

---

[51] Tate, "Coming of the Revolution in Virginia," 324–343.

[52] Robert E. and B. Katherine Brown, *Virginia, 1705–1786: Democracy or Aristocracy?* (East Lansing, Mich., 1964), 236; Alexander White to Richard Henry Lee, 1758, quoted in J. R. Pole, "Representation and

sixties and early seventies the newspapers were filled with warnings against electoral influence, bribery, and vote seeking. The freeholders were stridently urged to "strike at the Root of this growing Evil; be influenced by Merit alone," and avoid electing "obscure and inferior persons."[53] It was as if ignoble ambition and demagoguery, one bitter pamphlet remarked, were a "Daemon lately come among us to disturb the peace and harmony, which had so long subsisted in this place."[54] In this context Robert Munford's famous play, *The Candidates,* written in 1770, does not so much confirm the planters' confidence as it betrays their uneasiness with electoral developments in the colony, "when coxcombs and jockies can impose themselves upon it for men of learning." Although disinterested virtue eventually wins out, Munford's satire reveals the kinds of threats the established planters faced from ambitious knaves and blockheads who were turning representatives into slaves of the people.[55]

Authority in Virginia from the Revolution to Reform," *The Journal of Southern History,* XXIV (1958), 23.

[53] Purdie and Dixon's *Virginia Gazette* (Williamsburg), Apr. 11, 1771; Rind's *Virginia Gazette,* Oct. 31, 1771. See Lester J. Cappon and Stella F. Duff, eds., *Virginia Gazette Index, 1736–1780* (Williamsburg, 1950), I, 351, for entries on the astounding increase in essays on corruption and cost of elections in the late 1760's and early 1770's.

[54] *The Defence of Injur'd Merit Unmasked; or, the Scurrilous Piece of Philander Dissected and Exposed to Public View. By a Friend to Merit, wherever found* (n.p., 1771), 10. Robert Carter chose to retire to private life in the early 1770's rather than adjust to the "new system of politicks" that had begun "to prevail generally." Quoted in Louis Morton, *Robert Carter of Nomini Hall: A Virginia Tobacco Planter of the Eighteenth Century* (Williamsburg, 1941), 52.

[55] Jay B. Hubbell and Douglass Adair, "Robert Munford's *The Candidates,*" *Wm. and Mary Qtly.,* 3d Ser., V (1948), 246, 238. The ambivalence in Munford's attitude toward the representative process is reflected in the different way historians have interpreted his play. Cf. *ibid.,* 223–225, with Brown, *Virginia,* 236–237. Munford's fear of "men who aim at power without merit" was more fully expressed in his later play, *The Patriots,* written in 1775 or 1776. Courtlandt Canby, "Robert Munford's *The Patriots,*" *Wm. and Mary Qtly.,* 3d Ser., VI (1949), 437–503, quotation from 450.

By the eve of the Revolution the planters were voicing a growing sense of impending ruin, whose sources seemed in the minds of many to be linked more and more with the corrupting British connection and the Scottish factors, but for others frighteningly rooted in "our Pride, our Luxury, and Idleness."[56] The public and private writings of Virginians became obsessed with "corruption," "virtue," and "luxury." The increasing defections from the Church of England, even among ministers and vestrymen, and the remarkable growth of dissent in the years before the Revolution, "so much complained of in many parts of the colony," further suggests some sort of social stress. The strange religious conversions of Robert Carter may represent only the most dramatic example of what was taking place less frenziedly elsewhere among the gentry.[57] By the middle of the eighteenth century it was evident that many of the planters were living on the edge of bankruptcy, seriously overextended and spending beyond their means in an almost frantic effort to fulfill the aristocratic image they had created of themselves.[58] Perhaps the importance of the Robinson affair in the 1760's lies not in any constitutional changes that resulted but in the shattering effect the disclosures had on that virtuous image.[59] Some of the planters expressed openly their fears for the future, seeing the products of their lives being destroyed in the

[56] [John Randolph], *Considerations on the Present State of Virginia* ([Williamsburg], 1774), in Earl G. Swem, ed., *Virginia and the Revolution: Two Pamphlets, 1774* (New York, 1919), 16; Purdie and Dixon's *Virginia Gazette*, Nov. 25, 1773.

[57] Rind's *Virginia Gazette*, Sept. 8, 1774; Brown, *Virginia*, 252–254; Morton, *Robert Carter*, 231–250.

[58] See George Washington to George Mason, Apr. 5, 1769, in John C. Fitzpatrick, ed., *The Writings of George Washington* (Washington, 1931–44), II, 502; Carl Bridenbaugh, *Myths and Realities: Societies of the Colonial South* (New York, 1963), 5, 10, 14, 16; Emory G. Evans, "Planter Indebtedness and the Coming of the Revolution in Virginia," *Wm. and Mary Qtly.*, 3d Ser., XIX (1962), 518–519.

[59] Rind's *Virginia Gazette*, Aug. 15, 1766. See Carl Bridenbaugh, "Violence and Virtue in Virginia, 1766: or The Importance of the Trivial," Massachusetts Historical Society, *Proceedings*, LXXVI (1964), 3–29.

reckless gambling and drinking of their heirs, who, as Landon
Carter put it, "play away and play it all away."[60]

The Revolution in Virginia, "produced by the wantonness of
the Gentleman," as one planter suggested,[61] undoubtedly
gained much of its force from this social crisis within the gentry.
Certainly more was expected from the Revolution than simply a
break from British imperialism, and it was not any crude avoidance of British debts.[62] The Revolutionary reforms, like the
abolition of entail and primogeniture, may have signified something other than mere symbolic legal adjustments to an existing
reality. In addition to being an attempt to make the older Tidewater plantations more economically competitive with lands
farther west, the reforms may have represented a real effort to
redirect what was believed to be a dangerous tendency in social
and family development within the ruling gentry. The Virginians
were not after all aristocrats who could afford having their entailed families' estates in the hands of weak or ineffectual eldest
sons. Entail, as the preamble to the 1776 act abolishing it
stated, had often done "injury to the morals of youth by render-
ing them independent of, and disobedient to, their parents."[63]
There was too much likelihood, as the Nelson family sadly
demonstrated, that a single wayward generation would virtually
wipe out what had been so painstakingly built.[64] George Mason

[60] Quoted in Bridenbaugh, *Myths and Realities*, 27. See also Morton,
Robert Carter, 223–225.

[61] John A. Washington to R. H. Lee, June 20, 1778, quoted in Pole,
"Representation and Authority in Virginia," 28.

[62] Evans, "Planter Indebtedness," 526–527.

[63] Julian P. Boyd and others, ed., *The Papers of Thomas Jefferson*
(Princeton, 1950—), I, 560. Most of our knowledge of entail and
primogeniture in Virginia stems from an unpublished doctoral dissertation, Clarence R. Keim, "Influence of Primogeniture and Entail in the
Development of Virginia" (University of Chicago, 1926). Keim's is a
very careful and qualified study and conclusions from his evidence—
other than the obvious fact that much land was held in fee simple—are
by no means easy to make. See particularly pp. 56, 60–62, 110–114,
122, 195–196.

[64] Emory S. Evans, "The Rise and Decline of the Virginia Aristocracy
in the Eighteenth Century: The Nelsons," in Darrett B. Rutman, ed.,

bespoke the anxieties of many Virginians when he warned the Philadelphia convention in 1787 that "our own Children will in a short time be among the general mass."[65]

Precisely how the strains within Virginia society contributed to the creation of a revolutionary situation and in what way the planters expected independence and republicanism to alleviate their problems, of course, need to be fully explored. It seems clear, however, from the very nature of the ideas expressed that the sources of the Revolution in Virginia were much more subtle and complicated than a simple antagonism to the British government. Constitutional principles alone do not explain the Virginians' almost unanimous determination to revolt. And if the Revolution in the seemingly stable colony of Virginia possessed internal social roots, it is to be expected that the other colonies were experiencing their own forms of social strain that in a like manner sought mitigation through revolution and republicanism.

It is through the Whigs' ideas, then, that we may be led back to take up where the Progressive historians left off in their investigation of the internal social sources of the Revolution. By working through the ideas—by reading them imaginatively and relating them to the objective social world they both reflected and confronted—we may be able to eliminate the unrewarding distinction between conscious and unconscious motives, and eventually thereby to combine a Whig with a Tory, an idealist with a behaviorist, interpretation. For the ideas, the rhetoric, of the Americans was never obscuring but remarkably revealing of their deepest interests and passions. What they expressed may not have been for the most part factually true, but it was always psychologically true. In this sense their rhetoric was never detached from the social and political reality; and indeed it becomes the best entry into an understanding of that reality. Their repeated overstatements of reality, their incessant talk of

---

The Old Dominion: Essays for Thomas Perkins Abernethy (Charlottesville, 1964), 73–74.

[65] Max Farrand, ed., *The Records of the Federal Convention of 1787* (New Haven, 1911), I, 56; Bridenbaugh, *Myths and Realities*, 14, 16.

"tyranny" when there seems to have been no real oppression, their obsession with "virtue," "luxury," and "corruption," their devotion to "liberty" and "equality"—all these notions were neither manipulated propaganda nor borrowed empty abstractions, but ideas with real personal and social significance for those who used them. Propaganda could never move men to revolution. No popular leader, as John Adams put it, has ever been able "to persuade a large people, for any length of time together, to think themselves wronged, injured, and oppressed, unless they really were, and saw and felt it to be so."[66] The ideas had relevance; the sense of oppression and injury, although often displaced onto the imperial system, was nonetheless real. It was indeed the meaningfulness of the connection between what the Americans said and what they felt that gave the ideas their propulsive force and their overwhelming persuasiveness.

It is precisely the remarkable revolutionary character of the Americans' ideas now being revealed by historians that best indicates that something profoundly unsettling was going on in the society, that raises the question, as it did for the Progressive historians, why the Americans should have expressed such thoughts. With their crude conception of propaganda the Progressive historians at least attempted to grapple with the problem. Since we cannot regard the ideas of the Revolutionaries as simply propaganda, the question still remains to be answered. "When 'ideas' in full cry drive past," wrote Arthur F. Bentley in his classic behavioral study, *The Process of Government,* "the thing to do with them is to accept them as an indication that something is happening; and then search carefully to find out what it really is they stand for, what the factors of the social life are that are expressing themselves through the ideas."[67] Precisely because they sought to understand both the Revolutionary ideas and American society, the behaviorist historians of the

[66] John Adams, "Novanglus," in Charles F. Adams, ed., *The Works of John Adams* (Boston, 1851), IV, 14.

[67] Arthur F. Bentley, *The Process of Government: A Study of Social Pressures* (Chicago, 1908), 152.

Progressive generation, for all of their crude conceptualizations, their obsession with "class" and hidden economic interests, and their treatment of ideas as propaganda, have still offered us an explanation of the Revolutionary era so powerful and so comprehensive that no purely intellectual interpretation will ever replace it.

III.

THE GREAT
FRENCH REVOLUTION

7

E. J. Hobsbawm: The Uniqueness of the French Revolution*

If the economy of the nineteenth-century world was formed mainly under the influence of the British Industrial Revolution, its politics and ideology were formed mainly by the French. Britain provided the model for its railways and factories, the economic explosive which cracked open the traditional economic and social structures of the non-European world; but France made its revolutions and gave them their ideas, to the point where a tricolor of some kind became the emblem of virtually every emerging nation, and European (or indeed world) politics between 1789 and 1917 were largely the struggle for and against the principles of 1789, or the even more incendiary ones of 1793. France provided the vocabulary and the issues of liberal and radical-democratic politics for most of the world. France provided the first great example, the concept and the vocabulary of nationalism. France provided the codes of law, the model of scientific and technical organization, the metric system of measurement, for most countries. The ideology of the modern world first penetrated the ancient civilizations which

* E. J. Hobsbawm, Selection from chapter 3, "The French Revolution," in *The Age of Revolution, 1789–1848* (New York: Mentor Books, 1962), pp. 74–77. By permission.

E. J. Hobsbawm, the author of *Primitive Rebels, Labouring Men* and numerous other works, is a reader in history at Birkbeck College, University of London.

had hitherto resisted European ideas through French influence. This was the work of the French Revolution.[1]

The later eighteenth century, as we have seen, was an age of crisis for the old regimes of Europe and their economic systems, and its last decades were filled with political agitations sometimes reaching the point of revolt, of colonial movements for autonomy sometimes reaching that of secession: not only in the USA (1776–83), but also in Ireland (1782–4), in Belgium and Liège (1787–90), in Holland (1783–7), in Geneva, even—it has been argued—in England (1779). So striking is this clustering of political unrest that some recent historians have spoken of an "age of democratic revolution" of which the French was only one, though the most dramatic and far-reaching.[2]

In so far as the crisis of the old regime was not purely a French phenomenon, there is some weight in such observations. Just so it may be argued that the Russian Revolution of 1917 (which occupies a position of analogous importance in our century) was merely the most dramatic of a whole cluster of similar movements, such as those which—some years before 1917—finally ended the age-old Turkish and Chinese empires. Yet this is to miss the point. The French Revolution may not have been an isolated phenomenon, but it was far more fundamental than any of the other contemporary ones and its consequences were therefore far more profound. In the first place, it occurred in the most powerful and populous state of Europe (leaving Russia apart). In 1789 something like one European out of every five was a Frenchman. In the second place it was, alone of all the revolutions which preceded and followed it, a mass *social* revolution, and immeasurably more radical than any comparable upheaval. It is no accident that the American

[1] This difference between the British and French influences should not be pushed too far. Neither center of the dual revolution confined its influence to any special field of human activity, and the two were complementary rather than competitive. However, even when both converged most clearly—as in *socialism,* which was almost simultaneously invented and named in both countries—they converged from somewhat different directions.

[2] See R. R. Palmer, *The Age of Democratic Revolution* (1959); J. Godechot, *La Grande Nation* (1956), Vol. I, chapter 1.

revolutionaries, and the British "Jacobins" who migrated to France because of their political sympathies, found themselves moderates in France. Tom Paine was an extremist in Britain and America; but in Paris he was among the most moderate of the Girondins. The results of the American revolutions were, broadly speaking, countries carrying on much as before, only minus the political control of the British, Spaniards, and Portuguese. The result of the French Revolution was that the age of Balzac replaced the age of Mme Dubarry.

In the third place, alone of all the contemporary revolutions, the French was ecumenical. Its armies set out to revolutionize the world; its ideas actually did so. The American revolution has remained a crucial event in American history, but (except for the countries directly involved in and by it) it has left few major traces elsewhere. The French Revolution is a landmark in all countries. Its repercussions, rather than those of the American revolution, occasioned the risings which led to the liberation of Latin America after 1808. Its direct influence radiated as far as Bengal, where Ram Mohan Roy was inspired by it to found the first Hindu reform movement and the ancestor of modern Indian nationalism. (When he visited England in 1830, he insisted on traveling in a French ship to demonstrate his enthusiasm for its principles.) It was, as has been well said, "the first great movement of ideas in Western Christendom that had any real effect on the world of Islam,"[3] and that almost immediately. By the middle of the nineteenth century the Turkish word "vatan," hitherto merely describing a man's place of birth or residence, had begun to turn under its influence into something like "patrie"; the term "liberty," before 1800 primarily a legal term denoting the opposite to "slavery," had begun to acquire a new political content. Its indirect influence is universal, for it provided the pattern for all subsequent revolutionary movements, its lessons (interpreted according to taste) being incorporated into modern socialism and communism.[4]

[3] B. Lewis, "The Impact of the French Revolution on Turkey," *Journal of World History,* I (1953–54, p. 105).

[4] This is not to underestimate the influence of the American Revolution. It undoubtedly helped to stimulate the French, and in a narrower

The French Revolution thus remains *the* revolution of its time, and not merely one, though the most prominent, of its kind. And its origins must therefore be sought not merely in the general conditions of Europe, but in the specific situation of France. Its peculiarity is perhaps best illustrated in international terms. Throughout the eighteenth century France was the major international economic rival of Britain. Her foreign trade, which multiplied fourfold between 1720 and 1780, caused anxiety; her colonial system was in certain areas (such as the West Indies) more dynamic than the British. Yet France was not a power like Britain, whose foreign policy was already determined substantially by the interests of capitalist expansion. She was the most powerful and in many ways the most typical of the old aristocratic absolute monarchies of Europe. In other words, the conflict between the official framework and the vested interests of the old regime and the rising new social forces was more acute in France than elsewhere.

The new forces knew fairly precisely what they wanted. Turgot, the physiocrat economist, stood for an efficient exploitation of the land, for free enterprise and trade, for a standardized, efficient administration of a single homogeneous national territory, and the abolition of all restrictions and social inequalities which stood in the way of the development of national resources and rational, equitable administration and taxation. Yet his attempt to apply such a program as the first minister of Louis XVI in 1774–6 failed lamentably, and the failure is characteristic. Reforms of this character, in modest doses, were not incompatible with or unwelcome to absolute monarchies. On the contrary, since they strengthened their hand, they were, as we have seen, widely propagated at this time among the so-called "enlightened despots." But in most of the countries of "enlightened despotism" such reforms were either inapplicable, and therefore mere theoretical flourishes, or unlikely to change the general character of their political and social structure; or

---

sense provided constitutional models—in competition and sometimes alternation with the French—for various Latin American states, and inspiration for democratic-radical movements from time to time.

else they failed in the face of the resistance of the local aristocracies and other vested interests, leaving the country to relapse
into a somewhat tidied-up version of its former state. In France
they failed more rapidly than elsewhere, for the resistance of the
vested interests was more effective. But the results of this failure
were more catastrophic for the monarchy, and the forces of
bourgeois change were far too strong to relapse into inactivity.
They merely transformed their hopes from an enlightened monarchy to the people or "the nation. . . ."

Georges Lefebvre: The French Revolution in the Context of World History*

On the eve of the French Revolution, almost all of Europe was governed by what we now call the *ancien régime*. The prince enjoyed absolute power. The Church looked upon him as God's viceroy and in return he upheld the Church's authority by imposing his religion on his subjects. He had cast aside the concept of natural law, originating with the Stoics and developed during the Middle Ages by theologians like Thomas Aquinas, which assumed a society founded on free contract between governor and governed. Indeed, power had then been conceived only in terms of community welfare and was justified as a guarantee of the inviolable and legitimate rights of the individual.

To achieve absolute power, the prince had undermined seignorial authority and the political authority of the clergy, though allowing them to retain their social preeminence. In becoming subjects, the nobility and the clergy kept their privileges;

* Georges Lefebvre, "The French Revolution in the Context of World History," in Peter Amann, ed., *The Eighteenth Century Revolution* (Boston: D. C. Heath & Co., 1963), pp. 83–91. By permission.

Georges Lefebvre (1874–1959), perhaps the greatest historian of the French revolution in this century, wrote numerous works, among which the following have been translated: *The French Revolution* (2 Vols.), *The Coming of the French Revolution,* and *Napoleon* (2 Vols.).

the king, himself anointed and first gentleman of his realm, did not intend to submerge these orders in the masses. The Old Regime was indeed aristocratic in its structure.

There was a third feature characteristic of France and some other states. In these countries, while the prince had created a territorial and administrative framework, he had not carried this process to its logical conclusion. National unification was therefore incomplete, not only because of the diversity of legal systems, weights and measures, and the customs barriers which impeded the emergence of a national market, but also because the prince had granted or yielded special privileges to provinces and cities. In addition, he granted similar advantages to groupings, usually organized along professional lines, such as the nobility and clergy, so that society was hierarchical and partly "corporative." These estates implied privilege and therefore inequality. Absolutism, relying on "divide and rule," personified inequality . . . and besides, each estate, united by privilege and jealous of its superiority, demanded submission from those lower in the social scale. Nonetheless, the nation, created by submission to a single leader, by ties of material progress, language, and culture, remained divided territorially and socially. Even so, the French were better off than other nations: elsewhere the state, viewed as the personal property of the prince, took no account of national minorities, many of which were scattered among rival or enemy powers.

This regime faced two internal problems that were both political and social. The aristocracy (in other words, the nobility, since the clergy lacked social unity) resented the political impotence to which it had been reduced by the monarch whose power it dreamed of sharing. The nobleman, himself occasionally a victim of despotism, yearned for a freedom consonant with his dignity. This problem was a legacy from the past.

The other problem looked to the future. Ever since the tenth century there had developed a new class based on commerce, industry, finance, on personal rather than on landed property. This new bourgeois class had emerged from the Third Estate in a society in which land, as sole instrument of production, had entitled its owner to seignorial authority over those who farmed for a living. The king had drawn on these bourgeois both for money and officials, and they came to enjoy not only wealth but education and culture as well. Since the Renaissance, moreover, the new rationalism, exemplified by recent empirical science, provided an intellectual orientation consonant with bourgeois interests. Capitalism, which in its beginning phase had enjoyed mercantilistic state patronage, spread beyond the bounds of commerce to industry. The introduction of machinery opened such unlimited horizons for the bourgeoisie that the profits enticed even aristocrats to join in the exploitation of the world.

The bourgeoisie sought to obtain some share of power and therefore was willing to ally itself with the aristocracy against the king, yet bourgeoisie and aristocracy also were in opposition to each other. For centuries the middle class had striven for nobility; though this objective had not been altogether abandoned, the aristocracy was becoming more exclusive at the very time that the middle class, greatly increased in numbers, could no longer hope for mass ennoblement. The bourgeois, therefore, went beyond the nobles' demand for power and freedom to claim the end of all privileges as well as equality before the law.

At the end of the eighteenth century, because of the unequal pace of economic development, these problems appeared in a different guise in the various parts of Europe. Central and eastern Europe, which had long been backward by west European standards, did not partake in the new maritime trade routes and the exploitation of the New World which the great discoveries of the fifteenth and sixteenth centuries had opened up. The gap between East and West thus tended to widen. In this eastern and central European area newly-formed large states had adopted mercantilist policies and relied on the bourgeoisie for economic development and political organization. These states practiced what has been called "enlightened despotism." The mercantile middle class was, however, small in numbers, and the Enlightenment had more substantial influence on government officials, professors, and writers. The prince also confronted a threatening aristocracy. In Poland this nobility had seized power, while in Sweden only the *coup d'état* of Gustavus III had prevented a similar eventuality. In Hungary and Belgium the aristocracy had fought Joseph II to a standstill. In Prussia and Russia the monarchy had compromised, the aristocracy trading obedience and submission to the ruler for a free hand in dealing with their peasants whose serfdom, as one moved east, approached slavery.

In the countries of the south, particularly in the Iberian peninsula, the Counter Reformation had impeded free intellectual development. While Italy had been bypassed by the great overseas discoveries, Spain, in any case poorly endowed by nature, had been ruined by war. The nobility was somnolent, while the bourgeoisie grew only slowly. The peasant, as in France, did enjoy royal protection.

The maritime nations, Holland, England and a newcomer, the United States, offered a striking contrast to these land-based states. All of the former were Protestant. Holland and England had been the greatest beneficiaries of the rise of the European economy since the sixteenth century. In Holland the bourgeoisie was in control of the republic despite the nobility's support of the monarchist ambitions of the House of Orange. Since in this struggle neither constitutionalism nor liberty was at stake, it may be argued that a compromise between these three forces had either been reached already or was at least within sight.

While Holland had long been regarded as enjoying the greatest degree of freedom, the fame of the English and American revolutions, Britain's power and brilliant intellectual contribution made the Anglo-Saxon countries favorite antitheses to the absolutist regimes.

In England an aristocracy that enjoyed few privileges and no exemption from taxes differed markedly from its counterpart on the continent. Above all, only the lords formed a distinct legal estate, yet even their prerogatives were passed on to their eldest sons only. The younger children were commoners on a level with the gentry and squires who were represented in the House of Commons. The lords themselves could scarcely trace their genealogy beyond the Tudor era, since the nobility had been decimated by the massacres of the Wars of the Roses; hence they were not far removed from their middle-class origins. Above all, however, since England was an island, the military character of the nobility had been attenuated or had disappeared altogether, to the point where military service was merely a matter of personal inclination. Consequently nothing stood in the way of the nobleman, even of the peer, going into business, and the distinction between the upper middle class and nobility was only a matter of ancestry and the kind of prestigious distinctions which were even within reach of the bourgeoisie. Nowhere else was there such social mobility: money alone defined class lines. The maritime and colonial expansion had consolidated a community of interest between the aristocracy and the capitalist middle classes. The Reformation, by sanctifying the struggle for naval and world supremacy waged against Spain and France, had heightened this solidarity. After the Catholic and Francophile Stuarts had, in the course of the seventeenth century, succeeded in rousing the whole nation against themselves, two revolutions had insured the final defeat of royal despotism. Yet neither the aristocracy nor the upper middle classes had directed their alliance against the monarchy as such. The Revolution of 1688 was a compromise establishing constitutional government which balanced king, lords, and a combination of gentry and middle class in the House of Commons. The latter was elected by a limited franchise which by its very lack of system insured the absolute control of the wealthy.

History was a source of precedents to be used against royal despotism. More than once the aristocracy had succeeded in extracting concessions from a monarchy that had appeared all-powerful since the Norman conquest, the most famous of these concessions being Magna Carta. English liberties were founded on such precedents and customs, in short, on tradition rather than on philosophical speculation. Even so, natural law had not been forgotten. It inspired Locke's justification of the Revolution of 1688. The importance of his works, which served as bible of all the continental *philosophes* of the eighteenth century, can hardly be exaggerated. However, once the Whig oligarchy had gained power, it gradually abandoned Locke as its intellectual mentor, since the contract theory, the recourse to natural right, could also justify democratic movements which loomed on the horizon threatening its power. On the eve of the French Revolution, Burke agreed with George III in considering the British constitution to be the most perfect imaginable. For Burke the constitution recognized not the rights of man but the rights of Englishmen: only the English had been able to conquer these liberties and they alone had clear title to them.

Not only did English liberty make no claim to universality, but the English state itself did not grant complete freedom of thought. Even though, like Holland, England enjoyed broader toleration than Catholic countries, the state religion was maintained. More important, equality before the law had never become a fighting issue. Because the aristocracy was allied with wealth, the upper middle class had never had to appeal to this equality. Political freedom had never undermined a determination to maintain the existing social hierarchy.

Anglo-Saxon America did not have to become quite so empirically minded. Natural right remained a vital force in these Puritan communities that had left Europe to escape, not only religious intolerance, but the weight of despotism and of aristocratic society. In breaking with the home country, the colonists appealed to natural right to justify their secession, while their declarations proclaimed the rights of man, not merely the rights of Americans. Their public law reflected this universality of natural law. At the same time the Protestant sects sought to safeguard their independence by insisting on religious liberty. There were, however, notable limitations: no one claimed any rights for black men, and slaves remained slaves. Freedom of thought was not the rule and even though state and church were separated, it was taken for granted that religious liberty was confined to Christians. As in England, there was no insistence on equality. As the United States had never had peers or privileged persons the issue of privilege had never divided gentlemen and rich bourgeoisie. There were gentlemen descended from the British gentry who, living as noblemen on their plantations in Virginia and other Southern colonies, ruled over their enslaved blacks. Among these were the men who, like Washington, led the War of Independence and governed the republic during the first decades of its existence. However, men of a very different social background, such as Jefferson, had also become planters. Nothing prevented a Benjamin Franklin, printer turned merchant and journalist, from taking his place on the outer fringe of the ruling elite. Equality before the law for all whites, irrelevant as an issue in the struggle against Great Britain, had thus never been raised, nor was it ever considered a challenge to a social hierarchy based on wealth. Actually this equality before the law did not extend to politics, since the state constitutions restricted the franchise. What was called "democracy" in France during the first months of the Revolution was a government belonging not to the ruler or the aristocracy but to the nation. The actual procedures allowed, however, for the dominance of the moneyed class.

The English and American examples exercised a profound influence as the birthplaces of freedom. America, moreover, had stressed the universal validity of natural right. In practice this equality of rights, however admitted in principle, was not wholly applied, and in any case was not the basis for these revolutions. It is understandable that the example of these countries should have swayed not only the middle classes but also the continental aristocracy opposing royal power. For both, liberty seemed the pertinent catchword. Since equality had not been one of the consequences of these revolutions, it did not occur to the continental aristocracy, that liberty might endanger its social predominance.

The Anglo-Saxon revolutions had been directed against absolutism in behalf of a bourgeois-aristocratic alliance. The French Revolution was to be a very different affair.

From the socioeconomic as well as the geographical point of view our country occupied an intermediate position in Europe. Just as in other continental states, intermittent warfare had helped the nobility to preserve its military character. The very fact that this nobility faced impoverishment only increased its exclusiveness and its tendency to become a closed caste. Yet as a maritime nation France had also participated in European colonial expansion: its commerce was second only to that of

Great Britain, while its industrial capitalism, though backward in comparison to the latter, nonetheless enjoyed the most advanced development on the continent. The French bourgeoisie, though closer to the land than the English middle class, was infinitely larger and more influential than that of any other continental monarchy. Perhaps most peculiar to French society was the important role played by saleable offices. The king had tapped middle-class wealth by putting many official positions on the auction block. In order to increase their saleability or to gain the support of the officeholders, the king had endowed some of these positions not only with corporate privileges but even with personal or hereditary nobility. Just as in England, the infiltration of bourgeois families meant a renewal of the aristocracy. By the eighteenth century few nobles could produce a genealogy going back to the Crusades. This new nobility of the robe was establishing an increasingly intimate relationship to the military nobility. Nonetheless the nobility of the robe was not only businesslike in the management of its own affairs, but also kept up contact with other officeholders who had not graduated to the nobility. It also maintained ties with a socially less prestigious group, namely the lawyers. An intermediate class had thus developed which included these nobles at the top with officeholders in the middle, and commoners at the bottom. As a result of common professional outlook it shared the concept of law, of a legal order, of a monarchy whose prerogatives were limited by the sovereign courts' privilege of registration and remonstrance. Within this class a quite Cartesian rationalism and a tradition of the monarchy governing in cooperation with the wellborn and the well-to-do found special favor. Locke's ideas of natural right had fallen on fertile ground. In this respect, too, France occupied an intermediate position. While the absolute monarchy did cooperate with the Church in thought control, in contrast to Spain, Italy and Belgium, the Counter Reformation had not succeeded in stifling the development of philosophy and scientific inquiry. Finally, the French king had not had to yield power to the nobles; unlike England where a dominant aristocracy had uprooted the peasantry by enforcing enclosure, the majority of France's peasants were for all practical purposes free landowners.

Down to the time of the Fronde, the French nobility had often countered royal power with armed resistance. Even at that time the judicial officeholders had shown that they too could resist the monarch's authority. This reappeared once the hiatus imposed by Louis XIV was over, although its nature had altered as society had evolved. By the eighteenth century, armed outbreaks had become obsolete: the sovereign courts relied instead on a bourgeois appeal to public opinion, to constitutional tradition, to natural right. At the same time the aristocratically-dominated provincial estates played an increasingly important administrative role, particularly in Languedoc and Brittany. The office of *intendant* was preempted by nobles, as were the bishoprics. Commoners, already excluded from the sovereign courts in 1781 were barred from becoming professional officers, though they could still be promoted from the ranks. Aristocratic theorists, among whom Boulainvilliers and Montesquieu stood out, justified seignorial power by claiming that the aristocracy was descended from the Germanic conquerors of Gaul. Peasants complained over what historians have called the "feudal reaction," namely the increasingly exacting collection of manorial dues. It is clear, in any case, that some great landed proprietors benefited from royal ordinances permitting them to enclose land and to divide the commons. It is customary to concentrate on the eighteenth-century growth of the bourgeoisie and the rise of the Enlightenment which reflected its aspirations. This period, however, was equally notable for the growing influence of the aristocracy, who attacked royal authority and successfully resisted all reform attempts that would have undermined their privileges, particularly exemption from taxation.

The French Revolution, in its first phase a revolution of the nobles, represented the climax of this rebirth of aristocratic opposition. By September 1788 when Louis XVI had been forced to call the Estates General, an aristocratic triumph seemed in sight. If, as anticipated, the Estates were to meet in three separate orders with the clergy dominated by the aristocratic episcopate, the nobility would be in control. This nobility was willing to help the king bring order out of financial chaos, but only at the price of certain concessions.

What were these concessions? The aristocrats demanded what they called liberty, that is, a constitutional government relying on regular meetings of an Estates General dominated by the nobility. In the provinces they would displace the *intendant*.

The nobility had no inkling that it was undermining the bulwark of its own privileges by weakening royal power. The nobility did not foresee that once the Estates had been called, the bourgeoisie would find its voice. Much as in England, the price of their cooperation was likely to be equality of rights. When this price was demanded the French nobility refused to make this concession. As a result the Estates General, intended as a battering ram against royal authority, saw the nobility thrown back on the defensive. A second phase of the Revolution had begun—the bourgeois revolution.

When Louis XVI accepted both freedom and constitutional government on June 23, 1789, some of the national objectives seemed to have been met. When, however, he threw his support to the nobility and clergy, this was tantamount to rejecting equality which henceforth became the crux of the struggle.

Actually the king, by means of his army, seemed capable of ending the conflict on his own terms. The artisans and peasants, however, whose own interest was unmistakable, supported the bourgeoisie. The popular and peasant revolutions, culminating in the night of August 4, broke the power both of the monarchy and the nobility. Unlike the bourgeoisie which had not aimed for the ruin of the aristocracy, the popular revolution wiped the slate clean and soon completed the social revolution by nationalizing church property.

In practice the consequences of this social revolution were not carried to their logical conclusion in 1789. A part of the manorial dues had to be redeemed; the Catholic clergy retained its monopoly of public religious services, its state financial support, its control of marriage, education, and welfare work. When the aristocracy and the monarchy looked abroad for support, civil war broke out. This civil war persuaded some of the middle classes to throw in their lot with the lower classes to complete the destruction of the aristocracy by confiscating the *émigrés'* property and by seeking to crush the clergy's influence. In these circumstances the revolution turned democratic: it adopted manhood suffrage, proclaimed a republic, freed the slaves, separated State from Church, and secularized education, welfare, and personal status.

This is the way in which the French Revolution gained its distinctive place in the history of the world. Although the revolution appealed to natural law (as the American Revolution had also done), its achievements left a universal imprint quite alien to British liberty. Its sheer momentum, moreover, was much greater. Not only did the revolution establish a republic but it insisted on manhood suffrage. Freedom for whites was not enough: the slaves were freed. Not content with toleration, the revolution admitted Protestants and Jews to full citizenship and, by secularizing personal status, recognized the individual's right not to belong to any religion.

All this, however, was secondary to the real mission of the revolution which was to be the revolution of equality. While in England and America the alliance of aristocracy and upper middle class had precluded a stress on civil equality, in France the bourgeoisie had been forced to emphasize it by the unbending attitude of the nobility. Indeed, by abolishing manorial rights, the peasants initiated equality with a vengeance. Since by revolutionary definition liberty was tantamount to obedience to lawful authority alone, liberty and equality were complementary in that liberty by itself would lead to privilege for the few.

In gaining freedom and equality, the French had become the Nation One and Indivisible. This new interpretation of national sovereignty is a third outstanding characteristic of the revolution from which grew France's claim that nations, like individuals, should be liberated. Thus France claimed Alsace, Avignon, and Corsica by appealing to free consent rather than to conventional treaties between rulers. International law was being revolutionized just as internal civil law had been. In this early phase the revolution looked forward to peace and cooperation among free nations united by the ideal of a society of nations, even of a universal Republic.

These characteristics explain the French Revolution's impact on the world and its long-range significance. At the same time, although these principles have since registered gains, it would be a mistake to attribute their dissemination solely to the revolution. The example of England and the United States had certainly not been forgotten. It would be equally false—and this is a widespread idea—to credit this ideological expansion solely to the magnetism of ideas: in areas adjoining France, the *ancien régime* fell victim mainly to the revolutionary armies led by Napoleon. Since that time capitalism has become the chief vehicle by which these new principles have conquered the world. These principles, as historians have sought to show during the last several decades, reflected the interest of the middle class who championed them. In granting economic freedom, abolishing serfdom, freeing the land from the burden of tithe and manorial dues, bringing church property back into the dynamic channels of the economy, the bourgeoisie was paving the way for capitalism. Wherever capitalism has penetrated—and thanks to its inner dynamic it has become ubiquitous—the same kinds of transformations have occurred. By strengthening or creating a middle class, capitalism has helped the triumph of liberty and civil equality as well as the development of nationalism, in our own day even among colonial peoples once dominated by the white man.

Nonetheless the French Revolution has retained an emotional drawing power unrelated to any selfish interest. It is associated with popular insurrection symbolized by the storming of the Bastille and the wars of liberation which the *Marseillaise* commemorates. This is the work of those who died for the revolution. To ignore the influence of class interests and economics on a movement of ideas would be a mutilated history. To forget that the bourgeoisie was convinced that its rise was identified with justice and the welfare of all mankind would be no less of a distortion. The fighters of July 14 and August 10, the soldiers of Valmy, Jemmapes and Fleurus risked their lives not from self-interest but because they enthusiastically embraced a universal cause.

Nonetheless this equality of rights, this essential principle of the French Revolution by which the bourgeoisie of 1789 rationalized the abolition of aristocratic privilege based on birth, had some unexpected consequences. The middle class, confident in its ability, power and prospect, had ignored the ill-tempered warnings of its opponents in this respect.

For this middle class, as for the Anglo-Saxons, equality meant equality of opportunity. Although everyone was free to take advantage of these opportunities, obviously not everyone had the requisite ability. What significance could freedom of the press or free access to public office have for someone who was illiterate? Yet public instruction was contingent upon being well-off if not actually wealthy. The bourgeoisie of 1789 interpreted the right to vote and to be elected in a similar spirit. This right, like others, required certain prerequisites, in this case the payment of a given amount of taxes as evidence of a certain standard of economic independence. Thus the rights of man and of the citizen, formulated by the bourgeoisie, were to remain largely academic and theoretical. There was little doubt, and none after Thermidor, that in the eyes of the middle class only property owners were entitled to actual, as against theoretical, power. Property being hereditary meant that privilege due to birth had not, as counterrevolutionaries observed, been eliminated after all. Democrats were soon to point out that private ownership of the means of production led to the subjection of the wage earners. Private property in workshops, the sole source of employment, made illusory the rights of the propertyless.

The lower classes, aware of these implications, had always opposed economic freedom which led to capitalism and the triumph of big business. Their ideal was a nation of peasant proprietors and independent artisans. In any case they sought state protection for the wage earner from the omnipotence of the rich. In order to gain power and organize the defense of the revolution after August 10, 1792, the republican bourgeoisie had accepted universal suffrage and continued its alliance with the so-called "sans-culottes." This alliance resulted in a compromise between the middle-class aspirations of 1789 and the masses who called for government intervention to secure a more widespread distribution of property, public education for all, economic controls to keep prices and wages in balance, and a minimum social security system. This policy of "social democracy," initiated by the Mountain during the Year II, horrified and frightened the bourgeoisie and seemed to be banished forever after 9 Thermidor. When, however, republicanism reappeared after 1830, some of its followers took up Montagnard principles. With the re-establishment of universal suffrage in 1848, the application of these principles became one of the facts of political life.

Even during the revolutionary period, however, some groups had gone even farther by calling for the abolition of the private ownership of the means of production and the creation of a communist democracy intended to fulfill the promise of equality. This same intention has, in the final analysis, also made socialist theoreticians, particularly in France, present their systems as the completion of the French revolutionary achievements left unfinished by the middle classes. This is not to claim that the tradition of the French Revolution is the sole element in this development. Religious and humanitarian feelings have also been instrumental in aiding social progress. Above all, the transformation of the economy has had a powerful influence on the broad extension of equality of rights. The victories of capitalism led to trade union and political organization of the proletariat made possible by the concentration of business and labor, which defined and accelerated the class struggle. These organized elements could not be ignored. At the same time, the phenomenal productive growth engendered by capitalism, by increasing the resources available to human society, has brought a variety of welfare services, such as education and social security, within the realm of feasibility, whereas during and long after the revolution the cost of such services relegated them to Utopia.

Leaving aside differing approaches to history, the fundamental problem of our contemporary world appears to be the problem of equality within each nation and equality among nations. It is not the historian's job to prophesy how mankind will resolve such a problem; yet the historian can attest that the French Revolution not only raised this issue but also indicated various directions in which a solution might be sought. One may conclude, therefore, that, admired or loathed, the name of the French Revolution will long remain on men's lips.

9

Georges Rudé: The Revolutionary Crowd in History*

We return to our central question—the nature of the crowds that took part in the great events of the Revolution in Paris. From our analysis these crowds have emerged as active agents in the revolutionary process, composed of social elements with their own distinctive identities, interests, and aspirations. Yet these were not at variance with, or isolated from, those of other social groups. In fact we have seen that the Revolution was only able to advance—and, indeed, to break out—because the *sans-culottes,* from whom these elements were largely drawn, were able to assimilate and to identify themselves with the new political ideas promoted by the liberal aristocracy and *bourgeoisie.* But, even when revolutionary crowds were impregnated with and stimulated by such ideas, they cannot for that reason be dismissed as mere passive instruments of middle-class leaders and interests; still less can they be presented as inchoate "mobs" without any social identity or, at best, as drawn from criminal elements or the dregs of the city population. While these played a part, it was an altogether minor one and on no occasion corresponded to the unsympathetic picture of the all-prevailing *canaille* painted by Taine and other writers.

* Georges Rudé, "The 'Revolutionary Crowd' in History," in *The Crowd in the French Revolution* (New York: Oxford University Press, 1959), pp. 232–239. By permission.

Georges Rudé has also authored *The Crowd in History* and *Wilkes and Liberty.*

Michelet's use of *le peuple* corresponds, of course, far more closely to the facts: we have seen Barnave, for one, applying the term to those participants in revolutionary events who were neither of the aristocracy nor of the *bourgeoisie*. Yet it is too indefinite; for while the *menu peuple,* or *sans-culottes,* taken collectively, formed the main body of rioters and insurgents, the part played by their constituent elements—women, wage-earners, craftsmen, journeymen, petty traders, or workshop masters—varied widely from one occasion to another. This, of course, merely emphasizes the point that revolutionary crowds, far from being social abstractions, were composed of ordinary men and women with varying social needs, who responded to a variety of impulses, in which economic crisis, political upheaval, and the urge to satisfy immediate and particular grievances all played their part.

Are such conclusions only valid within the comparatively restricted context of the French Revolution, or have they a certain validity, as well, in the case of other "revolutionary crowds," whom historians have been inclined, either for convenience or from lack of sympathy, to depict as "mobs" or as social riff-raff?[1] It would, of course, be both presumptuous and misleading to generalize too freely and too confidently from the cases examined in the course of the present study; yet, even if we admit that there are no exact historical parallels, there are certain features that are common both to these and to other popular movements arising in Britain and France during the

[1] Sometimes, of course, crowds are given Michelet's more sympathetic, if not more discriminating, label of "the people" or "the patriots." This has generally been the case in British historians' descriptions of the European and South American national movements of the nineteenth century in which crowds were promoting causes with which the writers were manifestly in sympathy. Even, on occasion, from a change of fashion or of official policy, a "switch" is made, in estimating a given movement, from one attitude to the other. Thus the "bandits" of yesterday become the "patriots" or "freedom fighters" of today. (For an amusing illustration, see Mr. R. H. S. Crossman's account of the "switch" from Mihailovitch to Tito in the Second World War in the *New Statesman and Nation* of 15 December 1956.)

eighteenth and early nineteenth centuries. To that extent, at least, we may perhaps apply our conclusions to a wider field.

We have already noted the similarities between certain "economic" movements of the Revolution and those of the latter years of the old régime in France—particularly that of 1775. Here we have the same spontaneous reaction to the rising cost of flour and bread; rioting in markets and bakers' shops; the imposition of popular price-control, the terms of which were carried by word of mouth from market to market; the same almost unquestioning faith in the efficacy and benevolence of the royal authority; the role of rumor in stimulating activity; the active participation of different groups of the *menu peuple* of towns and villages, among whom criminal elements and down-and-outs played an altogether insignificant part.[2] Several of these features, though by no means all, reappear in French rural riots as late as 1848.[3] In the urban revolutions of the early nineteenth century, too, a large measure of continuity with that of 1789 still persists, though new features emerge with industrial advance and gradual social change. The external appearance of Paris and the geographical distribution of its population remained much the same in 1848 as sixty years before;[4] the small workship still predominated and, far from disappearing, was increasing its hold;[5] while the main centers of the *menu peuple* were still the Faubourgs Saint-Antoine and Saint-Marcel and the districts north of the markets.[6] As far as can be told from limited records, the composition of the participants in the "trois glorieuses" of July 1830 was not very different from that

[2] See the conclusions to my article on the grain riots of 1775, G. Rudé, "La Taxation populaire de Mai 1775 à Paris et dans la région parisienne," *Ann. hist. Rév. franç.*, no. 143, 1956, p. 148.

[3] See R. Gossez's "carte des troubles" in E. Labrousse (ed.), *Aspects de la crise et de la dépression de l'économie française au milieu du xix siècle (1846–1851)* (Paris, 1956); G. Lefebvre, *La Grande Peur de 1789*, pp. 61–65.

[4] See C. Seignobos, *La Révolution de 1848* (Paris, 1921), pp. 344–5.

[5] L. Chevalier, *La Formation de la population parisienne au XIXe siècle* (Paris, 1950), p. 77.

[6] G. Vauthier, "La Misère des ouvriers en 1831," *La Révolution de 1848*, xxii (1925), 607–17.

of the captors of the Bastille.[7] Like their forbears of 10 August 1792 the *ouvriers* of 1830 left their workshops to take up arms and, far from encouraging looting, shot those who engaged in it out of hand.[8] In 1848, again, masters and journeymen marched together, and jointly manned the barricades and occupied the Chamber of Deputies in the February days.[9] De Tocqueville's descriptions of the popular invasion of the parliamentary sessions of 24 February and 15 May of that year read like accounts of the great demonstrations in the National Convention in Germinal and Prairial of the Year III,[10] and even in the June revolution that followed, when *bourgeois* and *ouvriers* found themselves ranged in armed conflict on opposing sides, we find the insurgents largely belonging to the familiar trades of those who stormed the Bastille and reduced the Tuileries: of 11,693 persons arrested and charged in this affair, there were 554 stonemasons, 510 joiners, 416 shoemakers, 321 cabinet-makers, 285 locksmiths, 286 tailors, 283 painters, and 191 wine-merchants.[11] But the differences are equally, if not more, striking. Even in February the proportion of wage-earners among the insurgents was far greater than it was in 1789: de Tocqueville actually believed that the victors of the Revolution—up to May, at least—were the working classes and that its sole victims were the *bourgeoisie*.[12] This is an exaggeration; yet the fact remains that the wage-earners and independent craftsmen, who played the principal part in the insurrections and

[7] See the very incomplete lists of those killed and decorated as a result of their participation in the events of 27–29 July 1830 in Paris (Arch. Préf. Pol., Aa 369–70, 420).

[8] "Une Lettre inédite sur les journées de juillet 1830," *La Révolution de 1848*, vii (1910), 272–5. In 1848, too, de Tocqueville noted (without surprise, he added) the absence of looting (*The Recollections of Alexis de Tocqueville*, ed. J. P. Mayer (London, 1948), p. 80).

[9] A. Crémieux, "La Fusillade du boulevard des Capucines du 23 février 1848," *La Révolution de 1848*, viii (1911), 99–124; F. Dutacq, "Un Récit des journées de février 1848," *ibid.* (1912), 266–70.

[10] *Recollections*, pp. 51–59, 135–45.

[11] *Liste générale en ordre alphabétique des inculpés de juin 1848.* Arch. Nat., F7* 2585–6.

[12] *Recollections*, pp. 78 ff.

journées of the period, were now organized in their own political clubs, marched under their own banners and leaders, and, far from responding to the ideas and slogans of the *bourgeoisie,* were deeply imbued with the new ideas of Socialism.[13] The Industrial Revolution of Louis-Philippe's reign had brought in railways and the beginnings of mechanized industry: among the arrested insurgents of June, we note, alongside the joiners, cabinet-makers, and locksmiths of the traditional crafts and small workshops, the names of some eighty railwaymen and 257 *mécaniciens.*[14] As June 1848 marks the first great armed collision between *ouvriers* and *bourgeoisie,* so it marks the final eclipse of the *sans-culottes* and the emergence of the wage-earners as the new shock-troops of insurrection and the predominant element in revolutionary crowds.

We find a similar process taking place in Britain, though it begins at an earlier date. Even more than in France the typical rural riot of the eighteenth century had its origins in the high price of corn, flour, or bread and expressed itself in various forms of direct action, ranging from personal assaults on mill-owners, farmers, or magistrates, the destruction of fences, turnpikes, houses, or mills, the seizure of stocks of grain and stoppage of food convoys, to great demonstrations of farm-workers, miners, and rural craftsmen in the local market towns. Such activities are, of course, reminiscent of those engaged in by French peasants and village tradesmen during the same period; but none is more strikingly similar than the widespread resort to the *taxation populaire,* or popular price-control, examples of which seem to have been even more abundant in the English countryside than in the French: for the year 1766 alone Dr. Wearmouth has recorded no less than twenty-two such instances from market towns and villages all over the coun-

[13] Seignobos, *op. cit.,* pp. 24–25, 57–58, 67–70, 89–106, 138–9; Suzanne Wasserman, "Le Club de Raspail en 1848," La Révolution de *1848,* v (1908–9), 589–605, 655–74, 748–62; R. Gossez, "L'organisation ouvrière à Paris sous la Seconde République," *1848. Revue des révolutions contemporaines,* xli (1949), 31–45.

[14] Archives Nationales (Registres), 2585–6. See also G. Duveau, *La Vie ouvrière en France sous le Second Empire* (Paris, 1946), pp. 42–43.

try;[15] and local records would no doubt reveal many more. It was only in the rural districts of England and Wales that this type of riot—with its emphasis on popular, or "natural," justice—persisted well into the nineteenth century, at a time when such manifestations had long been superseded in urban communities. Perhaps the latest, and certainly the most spectacular, example of it was seen in the Rebecca Riots which broke out in West Wales in 1839 and again in 1842—ostensibly directed against toll-gates, but actually expressing the accumulated grievances of the Welsh peasantry over tithe, "alien" landowners, tyrannical magistrates, church rates, high rents, and the New Poor Law, besides.[16] Here again, even at this late date, there are striking resemblances with certain of the French riots and insurrections, both urban and rural, of the late eighteenth century—the appeal to tradition in both the propaganda and the costume of the rioters,[17] the sporadic emergence of local leaders or "Rebeccas";[18] the visible expression of "natural justice" in the destruction of toll-gates and workhouses; the joint action of farmers and farm-laborers; and the spontaneous spreading of rioting, as though by contagion, from one area to another.[19] But new social forces were at work; and it is certainly significant that "Rebecca's" nocturnal antics were called off and gave way to mass meetings and petitions to Parliament—not so much owing to successful government repres-

[15] R. W. Wearmouth, *Methodism and the Common People of the Eighteenth Century* (London, 1945), pp. 19–50, 51–76, 77–91.

[16] David Williams, *The Rebecca Riots* (Univ. of Wales Press, 1955).

[17] "Rebecca's" letters reminded the Welsh of their enslavement by the English "sons of Hengist" (*ibid.*, p. 192) [cf. the English radical tradition that Englishmen had been enslaved by the "Norman yoke"]; and rioters commonly disguised themselves by blackening their faces or by dressing up as women (the last was a charge insistently made against the Parisians who marched to Versailles on 5 October 1789).

[18] These were most often tenant farmers, though occasional reports speak of "gentlemen," publicans, and even laborers (*ibid.*, pp. 190, 195, 198, 221, 250).

[19] *Ibid.*, p. 212. Some of these features appear in the English agricultural laborers' revolt of 1830–1, the last movement of its kind in rural England.

sion as to the farmers' change of heart when faced with their laborers' insistence on pressing their own particular claims.[20]

It was similar changes in the relations of social classes that transformed the nature of English urban riots. During the eighteenth century, despite the wide variety of issues involved, there is a certain continuity of pattern which, again, is reminiscent of the French. In market towns and all but the largest cities the prevailing form continued to be the food riot. In London it rarely took this form, though the high price of food might be a contributory cause of disturbance.[21] The constant repetition by historians of such catch-phrases as Tory or Wilkite "mobs" has of course tended to obscure the true nature of such disturbances and the fact that crowds taking part in them were both socially identifiable and were impelled by specific grievances and by motives other than those of loot or monetary gain. The East London riots of July 1736 were largely the work of journeymen and laborers, who had been roused to violence against the local Irish by the employment of Irish workers at lower rates of wages;[22] yet other factors, such as the Gin Act of that year and memories of Walpole's threatened Excise, entered into the picture. In the "Wilkes and Liberty" riots of 1768–9 and the Gordon Riots of a dozen years later, those taking part were mainly journeymen, apprentices, servants, laborers, small craftsmen, and petty traders. Though the immediate causes of disturbance were very different in the two cases, both movements were movements of social protest, in which the underly-

[20] *Ibid.,* pp. 243, 262.

[21] This was probably so in the anti-Irish and Gin Riots of 1736 and in the "Wilkes and Liberty" riots of March–May 1768, though probably not so in the Wilkes movements of 1763 or 1769, or in the Gordon Riots of 1780. (For these and other points relating to these movements see G. Rudé, " 'Mother Gin' and the London Riots of 1736," *The Guildhall Miscellany,* no. 10, 1959; "Wilkes and Liberty, 1768–69," *ibid.,* no. 8, 1957, pp. 3–24; "The Gordon Riots: a Study of the Rioters and their Victims," *Transactions of the Royal Historical Society,* 5th series, vol. vi, 1956, pp. 93–114.)

[22] Despite their origins, these riots, like the Paris Réveillon riots of fifty years later, had little in common with the nineteenth-century type of wages movement.

ing conflict of poor against rich (though not yet of labor against capital) is clearly visible beneath the surface. All these movements are typical of French and English urban popular movements of the period, in which the *menu peuple* of wage-earners, craftsmen, and small tradesmen, led by local captains, dispense a rough and ready kind of natural justice by breaking windows, burning their enemies of the moment in effigy, or "pulling down" their dwelling-houses, pubs, or mills.[23] In the Gordon Riots this activity reached alarming proportions, settled claims for damage to private buildings and personal property alone amounting to over £70,000. This particular feature was due not so much to the deeper social antagonisms as to the immediate panic-fear of the consequences of the believed increase in the numbers and influence of the Roman Catholics: it was even rumored that Lord Mansfield, the Lord Chief Justice, "had made the king one" overnight! An interesting by-product of all this was that the merchants and householders of the City of London, facing a double threat—to their liberties from the Government's military measures and to their properties from the destructive zeal of "the inferior set of people"—anticipated the request made nine years later by their counterparts in Paris for the institution of a *milice bourgeoise* to defend their interests.[24]

Such forms of popular demonstration did not long survive the arrival of the new industrial age. With the growth of urban population and the dawn of the factory system at the end of the century, trade unions became more frequent and more stable, and direct conflicts between wage-earners and employers a more common feature of industrial and urban communities. From the 1780's onwards strikes were beginning to eclipse food riots and other movements of natural justice as the typical form of social protest. At the same time, as we have seen, the wage-earners

[23] These features also appear in the "Church and King" riots of 1790–2 in Birmingham and Manchester; but in these cases other elements enter which require to be separately studied.

[24] G. Rudé, "I 'tumulti di Gordon' (1780)," *Movimento Operaio* (Milan), 1955, p. 852. Not surprisingly the request was coldly received and had to be dropped.

were beginning to replace such social groupings as "the urban poor," "the inferior set of people," or the *menu peuple*—terms appropriate to an earlier age—as the main participants in urban social movements. In Britain this process was not attended by as much violence or as rapid a maturing of political ideas as was witnessed in France in 1848; but the general process started sooner and, by the advent of Chartism in the 1830's, it was already completed.

From these few examples it would appear, then, that a new type of "revolutionary crowd"—to use the term in its broadest possible sense—with new social objectives and new modes of expression was evolving in western Europe in the first part of the nineteenth century; with the advance of capitalist industry it was to spread rapidly elsewhere. This newer type of crowd is probably easier to identify than the older type that prevailed at the time of the French Revolution, and historians of the Trade Union and Labour movement, in particular, have not been backward in using available sources of inquiry to bring it to light. But bad old habits die hard, and the general historian is inclined in such matters to cover up his tracks by resorting to a convenient and ready-to-hand vocabulary which, though hallowed by time, is none the less misleading and inadequate. The term "mobs," in the sense of hired bands operating on behalf of external interests, doubtless has its place in the writing of social history; but it should be invoked with discretion and only when justified by the particular occasion. In so far as any conclusion of general validity emerges from the present study it is, perhaps, that such occasions are rare and that Taine's "mob" should be seen as a term of convenience, or as a frank symbol of prejudice, rather than as a verifiable historical phenomenon.

IV. NINETEENTH-CENTURY REVOLUTIONS

10

Karl Marx: The French Revolution of 1848*

I

Hegel remarks somewhere that all facts and personages of great importance in world history occur, as it were, twice. He forgot to add: the first time as tragedy, the second as farce. Caussidière for Danton, Louis Blanc for Robespierre, the *Montagne* of 1848 to 1851 for the *Montagne* of 1793 to 1795, the Nephew for the Uncle. And the same caricature occurs in the circumstances attending the second edition of the eighteenth Brumaire![1]

Men make their own history, but they do not make it just as they please; they do not make it under circumstances chosen by themselves, but under circumstances directly encountered, given and transmitted from the past. The tradition of all the dead generations weighs like a nightmare on the brain of the living. And just when they seem engaged in revolutionizing themselves and things, in creating something that has never yet existed, precisely in such periods of revolutionary crisis they anxiously conjure up the spirits of the past to their service and borrow from them names, battle cries and costumes in order to present

---

* Karl Marx, *The Eighteenth Brumaire of Louis Bonaparte* (New York: International Publishers, 1963), pp. 15–41. By permission.

[1] On the eighteenth of Brumaire (November 9, 1799), Napoleon I seized power in France. On December 2, 1851 his nephew, Louis Bonaparte, carried out a successful *coup d'état*—ed.

the new scene of world history in this time-honored disguise and this borrowed language. Thus Luther donned the mask of the Apostle Paul, the Revolution of 1789 to 1814 draped itself alternately as the Roman republic and the Roman empire, and the Revolution of 1848 knew nothing better to do than to parody, now 1789, now the revolutionary tradition of 1793 to 1795. In like manner a beginner who has learnt a new language always translates it back into his mother tongue, but he has assimilated the spirit of the new language and can freely express himself in it only when he finds his way in it without recalling the old and forgets his native tongue in the use of the new.

Consideration of this conjuring up of the dead of world history reveals at once a salient difference. Camille Desmoulins, Danton, Robespierre, Saint-Just, Napoleon, the heroes as well as the parties and the masses of the old French Revolution, performed the task of their time in Roman costume and with Roman phrases, the task of unchaining and setting up modern bourgeois society. The first ones knocked the feudal basis to pieces and mowed off the feudal heads which had grown on it. The other created inside France the conditions under which alone free competition could be developed, parceled landed property exploited and the unchained industrial productive power of the nation employed; and beyond the French borders he everywhere swept the feudal institutions away, so far as was necessary to furnish bourgeois society in France with a suitable up-to-date environment on the European Continent. The new social formation once established, the antediluvian Colossi disappeared and with them resurrected Romanity—the Brutuses, Gracchi, Publicolas, the tribunes, the senators, and Caesar himself. Bourgeois society in its sober reality had begotten its true interpreters and mouthpieces in the Says, Cousins, Royer-Collards, Benjamin Constants and Guizots; its real military leaders sat behind the office desks, and the hog-headed Louis XVIII was its political chief. Wholly absorbed in the production of wealth and in peaceful competitive struggle, it no longer comprehended that ghosts from the days of Rome had watched over its cradle. But unheroic as bourgeois society is, it neverthe-less took heroism, sacrifice, terror, civil war and battles of peoples to bring it into being. And in the classically austere traditions of the Roman republic its gladiators found the ideals and the art forms, the self-deceptions that they needed in order to conceal from themselves the bourgeois limitations of the content of their struggles and to keep their enthusiasm on the high plane of the great historical tragedy. Similarly, at another stage of development, a century earlier, Cromwell and the English people had borrowed speech, passions and illusions from the Old Testament for their bourgeois revolution. When the real aim had been achieved, when the bourgeois transformation of English society had been accomplished, Locke supplanted Habakkuk.

Thus the awakening of the dead in those revolutions served the purpose of glorifying the new struggles, not of parodying the old; of magnifying the given task in imagination, not of fleeing from its solution in reality; of finding once more the spirit of revolution, not of making its ghost walk about again.

From 1848 to 1851 only the ghost of the old revolution walked about, from Marrast, the Republican in kid gloves who disguised himself as the old Bailly, down to the adventurer, who hides his commonplace repulsive features under the iron death mask of Napoleon. An entire people, which had imagined that by means of a revolution it had imparted to itself an accelerated power of motion, suddenly finds itself set back into a defunct epoch and, in order that no doubt as to the relapse may be possible, the old dates arise again, the old chronology, the old names, the old edicts, which had long become a subject of antiquarian erudition, and the old minions of the law, who had seemed long decayed. The nation feels like that mad Englishmen in Bedlam who fancies that he lives in the times of the ancient Pharaohs and daily bemoans the hard labor that he must perform in the Ethiopian mines as a gold digger, immured in this subterranean prison, a dimly burning lamp fastened to his head, the overseer of the slaves behind him with a long whip, and at the exits a confused welter of barbarian mercenaries, who understand neither the forced laborers in the mines nor one another, since they speak no common language. "And all this is expected of me," sighs the mad Englishman, "of me, a free-born Briton, in order to make gold for the old Pharaohs." "In order to pay the debts of the Bonaparte family," sighs the French nation. The Englishman, so long as he was in his right mind, could not get rid of the fixed idea of making gold. The French, so long as they were engaged in revolution, could not get rid of the memory of Napoleon, as the election of December 10[2] proved. They hankered to return from the perils of revolution to the fleshpots of Egypt, and December 2, 1851 was the answer. They have not only a caricature of the old Napoleon, they have the old Napoleon himself, caricatured as he must appear in the middle of the nineteenth century.

The social revolution of the nineteenth century cannot draw its poetry from the past, but only from the future. It cannot begin with itself before it has stripped off all superstition in regard to the past. Earlier revolutions required recollections of past world history in order to drug themselves concerning their own content. In order to arrive at its own content, the revolution of the nineteenth century must let the dead bury their dead. There the phrase went beyond the content; here the content goes beyond the phrase.

The February Revolution was a surprise attack, a taking of the old society unawares, and the people proclaimed this unexpected stroke as a deed of world importance, ushering in a new epoch. On December 2 the February Revolution is conjured away by a cardsharper's trick, and what seems overthrown is no longer the monarchy but the liberal concessions that were wrung from it by centuries of struggle. Instead of society having conquered a new content for itself, it seems that the state only returned to its oldest form, to the shamelessly simple domination of the saber and the cowl. This is the answer to the unexpected stroke of February 1848, given by the rash act of December 1851. Easy come, easy go. Meanwhile the interval of time has not passed by unused. During the years 1848 to 1851 French society has made up, and that by an abbreviated, because revolutionary, method, for the studies and experiences which, in a regular, so to speak, textbook course of develop-

---

[2] The day Louis Bonaparte was elected President of the Republic—ed.

ment would have had to precede the February Revolution, if it was to be more than a ruffling of the surface. Society now seems to have fallen back behind its point of departure; it has in truth first to create for itself the revolutionary point of departure, the situation, the relations, the conditions under which alone modern revolution becomes serious.

Bourgeois revolutions, like those of the eighteenth century, storm swiftly from success to success; their dramatic effects outdo each other; men and things seem set in sparkling brilliants; ecstasy is the everyday spirit; but they are short-lived; soon they have attained their zenith, and a long crapulent depression lays hold of society before it learns soberly to assimilate the results of its storm-and-stress period. On the other hand, proletarian revolutions, like those of the nineteenth century, criticize themselves constantly, interrupt themselves continually in their own course, come back to the apparently accomplished in order to begin it afresh, deride with unmerciful thoroughness the inadequacies, weaknesses and paltrinesses of their first attempts, seem to throw down their adversary only in order that he may draw new strength from the earth and rise again, more gigantic, before them, recoil ever and anon from the indefinite prodigiousness of their own aims, until a situation has been created which makes all turning back impossible, and the conditions themselves cry out:

> Here is Rhodes, leap here!
> Here is the rose, here dance!

For the rest, every fairly competent observer, even if he had not followed the course of French developments step by step, must have had a presentiment that an unheard-of fiasco was in store for the revolution. It was enough to hear the self-complacent howl of victory with which Messieurs the Democrats congratulated each other on the expected gracious consequences of the second Sunday in May 1852.[3] In their minds the second Sunday in May 1852 had become a fixed idea, a dogma, like the day on which Christ should reappear and the millennium begin,

[3] This was the day on which, according to the Constitution, Bonaparte was to have retired as president—ed.

in the minds of the Chiliasts. As ever, weakness had taken
refuge in a belief in miracles, fancied the enemy overcome when
he was only conjured away in imagination, and it lost all understanding of the present in a passive glorification of the future
that was in store for it and of the deeds it had in reserve but
which it merely did not want to carry out as yet. Those heroes
who seek to disprove their demonstrated incapacity by mutually
offering each other their sympathy and getting together in a
crowd had tied up their bundles, collected their laurel wreaths
in advance and were just then engaged in discounting on the
exchange market the republics *in partibus*[4] for which they had
already providently organized the government personnel with all
the calm of their unassuming disposition. December 2 struck
them like a thunderbolt from a clear sky, and the peoples that in
periods of pusillanimous depression gladly let their inward
apprehension be drowned by the loudest bawlers will perchance
have convinced themselves that the times are past when the
cackle of geese could save the Capitol.

The Constitution, the National Assembly, the dynastic
parties, the blue and the red republicans, the heroes of Africa,
the thunder from the platform, the sheet lightning of the daily
press, the entire literature, the political names and the intellectual reputations, the civil law and the penal code, the *liberté,
égalité, fraternité* and the second Sunday in May 1852—all has
vanished like a phantasmagoria before the spell of a man whom
even his enemies do not make out to be a sorcerer. Universal
suffrage seems to have survived only for a moment, in order
that with its own hand it may make its last will and testament
before the eyes of all the world and declare in the name of the
people itself: All that exists deserves to perish.

It is not enough to say, as the French do, that their nation
was taken unawares. A nation and a woman are not forgiven
the unguarded hour in which the first adventurer that came
along could violate them. The riddle is not solved by such turns
of speech, but merely formulated differently. It remains to be
explained how a nation of thirty-six millions can be surprised

[4] In foreign parts, i.e., existing only on paper—trans.

and delivered unresisting into captivity by three *chevaliers d'industrie.*

Let us recapitulate in general outline the phases that the French Revolution went through from February 24, 1848, to December 1851.

Three main periods are unmistakable: the February period; May 4, 1848, to May 28, 1849: the period of the constitution of the republic, or of the Constituent National Assembly; May 28, 1849, to December 2, 1851: the period of the constitutional republic or of the Legislative National Assembly.

The first period, from February 24, or the overthrow of Louis Philippe, to May 4, 1848, the meeting of the Constituent Assembly, the February period proper, may be described as the prologue to the revolution. Its character was officially expressed in the fact that the government improvised by it itself declared that it was provisional and, like the government, everything that was mooted, attempted or enunciated during this period proclaimed itself to be only provisional. Nothing and nobody ventured to lay claim to the right of existence and of real action. All the elements that had prepared or determined the revolution, the dynastic opposition, the republican bourgeoisie, the democratic-republican petty bourgeoisie and the social-democratic workers, provisionally found their place in the February government.

It could not be otherwise. The February days originally intended an electoral reform, by which the circle of the politically privileged among the possessing class itself was to be widened and the exclusive domination of the aristocracy of finance overthrown. When it came to the actual conflict, however, when the people mounted the barricades, the National Guard maintained a passive attitude, the army offered no serious resistance and the monarchy ran away, the republic appeared to be a matter of course. Every party construed it in its own way. Having secured it arms in hand, the proletariat impressed its stamp upon it and proclaimed it to be a social republic. There was thus indicated the general content of the modern revolution, a content which was in most singular contradiction to everything that, with the material available, with the degree of education attained by the masses, under the given circumstances and relations, could be immediately realized in practice. On the other hand, the claims of all the remaining elements that had collaborated in the February Revolution were recognized by the lion's share that they obtained in the government. In no period do we, therefore, find a more confused mixture of high-flown phrases and actual uncertainty and clumsiness, of more enthusiastic striving for innovation and more deeply-rooted domination of the old routine, of more apparent harmony of the whole of society and more profound estrangement of its elements. While the Paris proletariat still reveled in the vision of the wide prospects that had opened before it and indulged in seriously meant discussions on social problems, the old powers of society had grouped themselves, assembled, reflected and found unexpected support in the mass of the nation, the peasants and petty bourgeois, who all at once stormed on to the political stage, after the barriers of the July Monarchy had fallen.

The second period, from May 4, 1848, to the end of May 1849, is the period of the constitution, the foundation, of the bourgeois republic. Directly after the February days not only had the dynastic opposition been surprised by the republicans and the republicans by the Socialists, but all France by Paris. The National Assembly, which met on May 4, 1848, had emerged from the national elections and represented the nation. It was a living protest against the pretensions of the February days and was to reduce the results of the revolution to the bourgeois scale. In vain the Paris proletariat, which immediately grasped the character of this National Assembly, attempted on May 15, a few days after it met, forcibly to negate its existence, to dissolve it, to disintegrate again into its constituent parts the organic form in which the proletariat was threatened by the reacting spirit of the nation. As is known, May 15 had no other result save that of removing Blanqui and his comrades, that is, the real leaders of the proletarian party, from the public stage for the entire duration of the cycle we are considering.

The bourgeois monarchy of Louis Philippe can be followed

only by a bourgeois republic, that is to say, whereas a limited section of the bourgeoisie ruled in the name of the king, the whole of the bourgeoisie will now rule in the name of the people. The demands of the Paris proletariat are utopian nonsense, to which an end must be put. To this declaration of the Constituent National Assembly the Paris proletariat replied with the June Insurrection, the most colossal event in the history of European civil wars. The bourgeois republic triumphed. On its side stood the aristocracy of finance, the industrial bourgeoisie, the middle class, the petty bourgeois, the army, the *lumpenproletariat* organized as the Mobile Guard, the intellectual lights, the clergy and the rural population. On the side of the Paris proletariat stood none but itself. More than three thousand insurgents were butchered after the victory, and fifteen thousand were transported without trial. With this defeat the proletariat passes into the background of the revolutionary stage. It attempts to press forward again on every occasion, as soon as the movement appears to make a fresh start, but with ever decreased expenditure of strength and always slighter results. As soon as one of the social strata situated above it gets into revolutionary ferment, the proletariat enters into an alliance with it and so shares all the defeats that the different parties suffer, one after another. But these subsequent blows become the weaker, the greater the surface of society over which they are distributed. The more important leaders of the proletariat in the Assembly and in the press successively fall victims to the courts, and ever more equivocal figures come to head it. In part it throws itself into doctrinaire experiments, exchange banks and workers' associations, hence into a movement in which it renounces the revolutionizing of the old world by means of the latter's own great, combined resources, and seeks, rather, to achieve its salvation behind society's back, in private fashion, within its limited conditions of existence, and hence necessarily suffers shipwreck. It seems to be unable either to rediscover revolutionary greatness in itself or to win new energy from the connections newly entered into, until all classes with which it contended in June themselves lie prostrate beside it. But at least it succumbs with the honors of the great, world-historic struggle; not only France, but all Europe trembles at the June earthquake, while the ensuing defeats of the upper classes are so cheaply bought that they require bare-faced exaggeration by the victorious party to be able to pass for events at all, and become the more ignominious the further the defeated party is removed from the proletarian party.

The defeat of the June insurgents, to be sure, had now prepared, had leveled the ground on which the bourgeois republic could be founded and built up, but it had shown at the same time that in Europe the questions at issue are other than that of "republic or monarchy." It had revealed that here bourgeois republic signifies the unlimited despotism of one class over other classes. It had proved that in countries with an old civilization, with a developed formation of classes, with modern conditions of production and with an intellectual consciousness in which all traditional ideas have been dissolved by the work of centuries, the republic signifies in general only the political form of revolution of bourgeois society and not its conservative form of life, as, for example, in the United States of North America, where, though classes already exist, they have not yet become fixed, but continually change and interchange their elements in constant flux, where the modern means of production, instead of coinciding with a stagnant surplus population, rather compensate for the relative deficiency of heads and hands, and where, finally, the feverish, youthful movement of material production, which has to make a new world its own, has left neither time nor opportunity for abolishing the old spirit world.

During the June days all classes and parties had united in the party of Order against the proletarian class as the party of Anarchy, of Socialism, of Communism. They had "saved" society from "the enemies of society." They had given out the watchwords of the old society, "property, family, religion, order," to their army as passwords and had proclaimed to the counterrevolutionary crusaders: "In this sign thou shalt conquer!" From that moment, as soon as one of the numerous parties which had gathered under this sign against the June insurgents seeks to hold the revolutionary battlefield in its own class interest, it goes down before the cry: "Property, family, religion, order." Society is saved just as often as the circle of its rulers contracts, as a more exclusive interest is maintained against a wider one. Every demand of the simplest bourgeois financial reform, of the most ordinary liberalism, of the most formal republicanism, of the most shallow democracy, is simultaneously castigated as an "attempt on society" and stigmatized as "Socialism." And, finally, the high priests of "the religion and order" themselves are driven with kicks from their Pythian tripods, hauled out of their beds in the darkness of night, put in prison-vans, thrown into dungeons or sent into exile; their temple is razed to the ground, their mouths are sealed, their pens broken, their law torn to pieces in the name of religion, of property, of the family, of order. Bourgeois fanatics for order are shot down on their balconies by mobs of drunken soldiers, their domestic sanctuaries profaned, their houses bombarded for amusement—in the name of property, of the family, of religion and of order. Finally, the scum of bourgeois society forms the holy phalanx of order and the hero Crapulinski[5] installs himself in the Tuileries as the "savior of society."

II

Let us pick up the threads of the development once more.

The history of the Constituent National Assembly since the June days is the history of the domination and the disintegration of the republican faction of the bourgeoisie, of that faction which is known by the names of tricolor republicans, pure republicans, political republicans, formalist republicans, etc.

Under the bourgeois monarchy of Louis Philippe it had formed the official republican opposition and consequently a recognized component part of the political world of the day. It had its representatives in the Chambers and a considerable sphere of influence in the press. Its Paris organ, the *National,* was considered just as respectable in its way as the *Journal des Débats.* Its character corresponded to this position under the constitutional monarchy. It was not a faction of the bourgeoisie

---

[5] An allusion to the hero of Heine's poem "Two Nights." Here Marx is identifying Bonaparte with this spendthrift Polish nobleman—ed.

held together by great common interests and marked off by specific conditions of production. It was a clique of republican-minded bourgeois, writers, lawyers, officers and officials that owed its influence to the personal antipathies of the country against Louis Philippe, to memories of the old republic, to the republican faith of a number of enthusiasts, above all, however, to French nationalism, whose hatred of the Vienna treaties and of the alliance with England it stirred up perpetually. A large part of the following that the *National* had under Louis Philippe was due to this concealed imperialism, which could conse-quently confront it later, under the republic, as a deadly rival in the person of Louis Bonaparte. It fought the aristocracy of finance, as did all the rest of the bourgeois opposition. Polemics against the budget, which were closely connected in France with fighting the aristocracy of finance, procured popularity too cheaply and material for puritanical leading articles too plenti-fully, not to be exploited. The industrial bourgeoisie was grate-ful to it for its slavish defense of the French protectionist system, which it accepted, however, more on national grounds than on grounds of national economy; the bourgeoisie as a whole, for its vicious denunciation of Communism and Social-ism. For the rest, the party of the *National* was purely republi-can, that is, it demanded a republican instead of a monarchist form of bourgeois rule and, above all, the lion's share of this rule. Concerning the conditions of this transformation it was by no means clear in its own mind. On the other hand, what was clear as daylight to it and was publicly acknowledged at the reform banquets in the last days of Louis Philippe, was its unpopularity with the democratic petty bourgeois and, in par-ticular, with the revolutionary proletariat. These pure republi-cans, as is, indeed, the way with pure republicans, were already on the point of contenting themselves in the first instance with a regency of the Duchess of Orleans, when the February Revolu-tion broke out and assigned their best-known representatives a place in the Provisional Government. From the start, they naturally had the confidence of the bourgeoisie and a majority in the Constituent National Assembly. The socialist elements of the Provisional Government were excluded forthwith from the

Executive Commission which the National Assembly formed when it met, and the party of the *National* took advantage of the outbreak of the June insurrection to discharge the Executive Commission also, and therewith to get rid of its closest rivals, the petit-bourgeois, or democratic, republicans (Ledru-Rollin, etc.). Cavaignac, the general of the bourgeois-republican party who commanded the June massacre, took the place of the Executive Commission with a sort of dictatorial power. Marrast, former editor-in-chief of the *National,* became the perpetual president of the Constituent National Assembly, and the ministries, as well as all other important posts, fell to the portion of the pure republicans.

The republican bourgeois faction, which had long regarded itself as the legitimate heir of the July Monarchy, thus found its fondest hopes exceeded; it attained power, however, not as it had dreamed under Louis Philippe, through a liberal revolt of the bourgeoisie against the throne, but through a rising of the proletariat against capital, a rising laid low with grape-shot. What it had conceived as the most revolutionary event turned out in reality to be the most counterrevolutionary. The fruit fell into its lap, but it fell from the tree of knowledge, not from the tree of life.

The exclusive rule of the bourgeois republicans lasted only from June 24 to December 10, 1848. It is summed up in the drafting of a republican constitution and in the state of siege of Paris.

The new Constitution was at bottom only the republicanized edition of the constitutional Charter of 1830. The narrow electoral qualification of the July Monarchy, which excluded even a large part of the bourgeoisie from political rule, was incompatible with the existence of the bourgeois republic. In lieu of this qualification, the February Revolution had at once proclaimed direct universal suffrage. The bourgeois republicans could not undo this event. They had to content themselves with adding the limiting proviso of a six months' residence in the constituency. The old organization of the administration, of the municipal system, of the judicial system, of the army, etc., continued to exist inviolate, or, where the Constitution changed them, the change concerned the table of contents, not the contents; the name, not the subject matter.

The inevitable general staff of the liberties of 1848, personal liberty, liberty of the press, of speech, of association, of assembly, of education and religion, etc., received a constitutional uniform, which made then invulnerable. For each of these liberties is proclaimed as the absolute right of the French *citoyen,* but always with the marginal note that it is unlimited so far as it is not limited by the "equal rights of others and the public safety" or by "laws" which are intended to mediate just this harmony of the individual liberties with one another and with the public safety. For example: "The citizens have the right of association, of peaceful and unarmed assembly, of petition and of expressing their opinions, whether in the press or in any other way. The enjoyment of these rights has no limit save the equal rights of others and the public safety." (Chapter II of the French Constitution, § 8.)—"Education is free. Freedom of education shall be enjoyed under the conditions fixed by law and under the supreme control of the state." (*Ibidem,* § 9).— "The home of every citizen is inviolable except in the forms prescribed by law." (Chapter II, § 3.) Etc., etc.—The Constitution, therefore, constantly refers to future organic laws which are to put into effect those marginal notes and regulate the enjoyment of these unrestricted liberties in such manner that they will collide neither with one another nor with the public safety. And later, these organic laws were brought into being by the friends of order and all those liberties regulated in such manner that the bourgeoisie in its enjoyment of them finds itself unhindered by the equal rights of the other classes. Where it forbids these liberties entirely to "the others" or permits enjoyment of them under conditions that are just so many police traps, this always happens solely in the interest of "public safety," that is, the safety of the bourgeoisie, as the Constitution prescribes. In the sequel, both sides accordingly appeal with complete justice to the Constitution: the friends of order, who abrogated all these liberties, as well as the democrats, who demanded all of them. For each paragraph of the Constitution contains its own antithesis, its own Upper and Lower House, namely, liberty in the general phrase, abrogation of liberty in the marginal note. Thus, so long as the name of freedom was respected and only its actual realization prevented, of course in a legal way, the constitutional existence of liberty remained intact, inviolate, however mortal the blows dealt to its existence in actual life.

This Constitution, made inviolable in so ingenious a manner, was nevertheless, like Achilles, vulnerable in one point, not in the heel, but in the head, or rather in the two heads in which it wound up—the Legislative Assembly, on the one hand, the President, on the other. Glance through the Constitution and you will find that only the paragraphs in which the relationship of the President to the Legislative Assembly is defined are absolute, positive, noncontradictory, and cannot be distorted. For here it was a question of the bourgeois republicans safeguarding themselves. §§ 45–70 of the Constitution are so worded that the National Assembly can remove the President constitutionally, whereas the President can remove the National Assembly only unconstitutionally, only by setting aside the Constitution itself. Here, therefore, it challenges its forcible destruction. It not only sanctifies the division of powers, like the Charter of 1830, it widens it into an intolerable contradiction. The play of the constitutional powers, as Guizot termed the parliamentary squabble between the legislative and executive power, is in the Constitution of 1848 continually played *va-banque*.[6] On one side are seven hundred and fifty representatives of the people, elected by universal suffrage and eligible for re-election; they form an uncontrollable, indissoluble, indivisible National Assembly, a National Assembly that enjoys legislative omnipotence, decides in the last instance on war, peace and commercial treaties, alone possesses the right of amnesty and, by its permanence, perpetually holds the front of the stage. On the other side is the President, with all the attributes of royal power, with authority to appoint and dismiss his ministers independently of the National Assembly, with all the resources of the executive power in his hands, bestowing all posts and disposing thereby in

[6] Staking everything on one roll of the dice—trans.

France of the livelihoods of at least a million and a half people, for so many depend on the five hundred thousand officials and officers of every rank. He has the whole of the armed forces behind him. He enjoys the privilege of pardoning individual criminals, of suspending National Guards, of discharging, with the concurrence of the Council of State, general, cantonal and municipal councils elected by the citizens themselves. Initiative and direction are reserved to him in all treaties with foreign countries. While the Assembly constantly performs on the boards and is exposed to daily public criticism, he leads a secluded life in the Elysian Fields, and that with Article 45 of the Constitution before his eyes and in his heart, crying to him daily: "Brother, you must die." Your power ceases on the second Sunday of the lovely month of May in the fourth year after your election! Then your glory is at an end, the piece is not played twice and if you have debts, look to it betimes that you pay them off with the six hundred thousand francs granted you by the Constitution, unless, perchance, you should prefer to go to Clichy[7] on the second Monday of the lovely month of May!—Thus, whereas the Constitution assigns actual power to the President, it seeks to secure moral power for the National Assembly. Apart from the fact that it is impossible to create a moral power by paragraphs of law, the Constitution here abrogates itself once more by having the President elected by all Frenchmen through direct suffrage. While the votes of France are split up among the seven hundred and fifty members of the National Assembly, they are here, on the contrary, concentrated on a single individual. While each separate representative of the people represents only this or that party, this or that town, this or that bridgehead, or even only the mere necessity of electing some one as the seven hundred and fiftieth, without examining too closely either the cause or the man, *he* is the elect of the nation and the act of his election is the trump that the sovereign people plays once every four years. The elected National Assembly stands in a metaphysical relation, but the elected President in a personal relation, to the nation. The National

[7] The debtors' prison in Paris—ed.

Assembly, indeed, exhibits in its individual representatives the manifold aspects of the national spirit, but in the President this national spirit finds its incarnation. As against the Assembly, he possesses a sort of divine right; he is President by the grace of the people.

Thetis, the sea goddess, had prophesied to Achilles that he would die in the bloom of youth. The Constitution, which, like Achilles, had its weak spot, had also, like Achilles, its presentiment that it must go to an early death. It was sufficient for the constitution-making pure republicans to cast a glance from the lofty heaven of their ideal republic at the profane world to perceive how the arrogance of the royalists, the Bonapartists, the Democrats, the Communists as well as their own discredit grew daily in the same measure as they approached the completion of their great legislative work of art, without Thetis on this account having to leave the sea and communicate the secret to them. They sought to cheat destiny by a catch in the Constitution, through § 111 of it, according to which every motion for a revision of the Constitution must be supported by at least three-quarters of the votes, cast in three successive debates between which an entire month must always lie, with the added proviso that not less than five hundred members of the National Assembly must vote. Thereby they merely made the impotent attempt still to exercise a power—when only a parliamentary minority, as which they already saw themselves prophetically in their mind's eye—a power which at the present time, when they commanded a parliamentary majority and all the resources of governmental authority, was slipping daily more and more from their feeble hands.

Finally the Constitution, in a melodramatic paragraph, entrusts itself "to the vigilance and the patriotism of the whole French people and every single Frenchman," after it had previously entrusted in another paragraph the "vigilant" and "patriotic" to the tender, most painstaking care of the High Court of Justice, the *"haute cour,"* invented by it for the purpose.

Such was the Constitution of 1848, which on December 2, 1851, was not overthrown by a head, but fell down at the touch of a mere hat; this hat, to be sure, was a three-cornered Napoleonic hat.

While the bourgeois republicans in the Assembly were busy devising, discussing and voting this Constitution, Cavaignac outside the Assembly maintained the state of siege of Paris. The state of siege of Paris was the midwife of the Constituent Assembly in its travail of republican creation. If the Constitution is subsequently put out of existence by bayonets, it must not be forgotten that it was likewise by bayonets, and these turned against the people, that it had to be protected in its mother's womb and by bayonets that it had to be brought into existence. The forefathers of the "respectable republicans" had sent their symbol, the tricolor, on a tour round Europe. They themselves in turn produced an invention that of itself made its way over the whole Continent, but returned to France with ever renewed love until it has now become naturalized in half her Departments—the state of siege. A splendid invention, periodically employed in every ensuing crisis in the course of the French Revolution. But barrack and bivouac, which were thus periodically laid on French society's head to compress its brain and render it quiet; saber and musket, which were periodically allowed to act as judges and administrators, as guardians and censors, to play policeman and do night watchman's duty; moustache and uniform, which were periodically trumpeted forth as the highest wisdom of society and as its rector—were not barrack and bivouac, saber and musket, moustache and uniform finally bound to hit upon the idea of rather saving society once and for all by proclaiming their own regime as the highest and freeing civil society completely from the trouble of governing itself? Barrack and bivouac, saber and musket, moustache and uniform were bound to hit upon this idea all the more as they might then also expect better cash payment for their higher services, whereas from the merely periodical state of siege and the transient rescues of society at the bidding of this or that bourgeois faction little of substance was gleaned save some killed and wounded and some friendly bourgeois grimaces. Should not the military at last one day play state of siege in their own interest and for their own benefit, and at the same time besiege the citizens' purses? Moreover, be it noted in passing, one must not forget that Colonel Bernard, the same military commission president who under Cavaignac had 15,000 insurgents deported without trial, is at this moment again at the head of the military commissions active in Paris.

Whereas, with the state of siege in Paris, the respectable, the pure republicans planted the nursery in which the praetorians[8] of December 2, 1851 were to grow up, they on the other hand deserve praise for the reason that, instead of exaggerating the national sentiment as under Louis Philippe, they now, when they had command of the national power, crawled before foreign countries, and, instead of setting Italy free, let her be reconquered by Austrians and Neapolitans. Louis Bonaparte's election as President on December 10, 1848, put an end to the dictatorship of Cavaignac and to the Constituent Assembly.

In § 44 of the Constitution it is stated: "The President of the French Republic must never have lost his status of a French citizen." The first President of the French republic, L. N. Bonaparte, had not merely lost his status of a French citizen, had not only been an English special constable, he was even a naturalized Swiss.

I have worked out elsewhere the significance of the election of December 10. I will not revert to it here. It is sufficient to remark here that it was a reaction of the peasants, who had had to pay the costs of the February Revolution, against the remaining classes of the nation, a reaction of the country against the town. It met with great approval in the army, for which the republicans of the *National* had provided neither glory nor additional pay, among the big bourgeoisie, which hailed Bonaparte as a bridge to monarchy, among the proletarians and petit-bourgeois, who hailed him as a scourge for Cavaignac. I shall have an opportunity later of going more closely into the relationship of the peasants to the French Revolution.

The period from December 20, 1848, until the dissolution of the Constituent Assembly, in May 1849, comprises the history

[8] Marx here refers to Bonaparte's bodyguards, using the word for bodyguards in ancient Rome—ed.

of the downfall of the bourgeois republicans. After having founded a republic for the bourgeoisie, driven the revolutionary proletariat out of the field and reduced the democratic petit-bourgeoisie to silence for the time being, they are themselves thrust aside by the mass of the bourgeoisie, which justly impounds this republic as its property. This bourgeois mass was, however, royalist. One section of it, the large landowners, had ruled during the Restoration and was accordingly Legitimist. The other, the aristocrats of finance and big industrialists, had ruled during the July Monarchy and was consequently Orleanist. The high dignitaries of the army, the university, the church, the bar, the academy and of the press were to be found on either side, though in various proportions. Here, in the bourgeois republic, which bore neither the name Bourbon nor the name Orleans, but the name Capital, they had found the form of state in which they could rule conjointly. The June Insurrection had already united them in the "party of Order." Now it was necessary, in the first place, to remove the coterie of bourgeois republicans who still occupied the seats of the National Assembly. Just as brutal as these pure republicans had been in their misuse of physical force against the people, just as cowardly, mealy-mouthed, broken-spirited and incapable of fighting were they now in their retreat, when it was a question of maintaining their republicanism and their legislative rights against the executive power and the royalists. I need not relate here the ignominious history of their dissolution. They did not succumb; they passed out of existence. Their history has come to an end forever, and, both inside and outside the Assembly, they figure in the following period only as memories, memories that seem to regain life whenever the mere name of Republic is once more the issue and as often as the revolutionary conflict threatens to sink down to the lowest level. I may remark in passing that the journal which gave its name to this party, the *National,* was converted to Socialism in the following period.

Before we finish with this period we must still cast a retrospective glance at the two powers, one of which annihilated the other on December 2, 1851, whereas from December 20, 1848, until the exit of the Constituent Assembly, they had lived in conjugal relations. We mean Louis Bonaparte, on the one hand, and the party of the coalesced royalists, the party of Order, of the big bourgeoisie, on the other. On acceding to the presidency, Bonaparte at once formed a ministry of the party of Order, at the head of which he placed Odilon Barrot, the old leader, *nota bene,* of the most liberal faction of the parliamentary bourgeoisie. M. Barrot had at last secured the ministerial portfolio, the specter of which had haunted him since 1830, and what is more, the premiership in the ministry; but not, as he had imagined under Louis Philippe, as the most advanced leader of the parliamentary opposition, but with the task of putting a parliament to death, and as the confederate of all his archenemies, Jesuits and Legitimists. He brought the bride home at last, but only after she had been prostituted. Bonaparte seemed to efface himself completely. This party acted for him.

The very first meeting of the council of ministers resolved on the expedition to Rome, which, it was agreed, should be undertaken behind the back of the National Assembly and the means for which were to be wrested from it by false pretenses. Thus they began by swindling the National Assembly and secretly conspiring with the absolutist powers abroad against the revolutionary Roman republic. In the same manner and with the same maneuvers Bonaparte prepared his *coup* of December 2 against the royalist Legislative Assembly and its constitutional republic. Let us not forget that the same party which formed Bonaparte's ministry on December 20, 1848, formed the majority of the Legislative National Assembly on December 2, 1851.

In August the Constituent Assembly had decided to dissolve only after it had worked out and promulgated a whole series of organic laws that were to supplement the Constitution. On January 6, 1849, the party of Order had a deputy named Rateau move that the Assembly should let the organic laws go and rather decide on its own dissolution. Not only the ministry, with Odilon Barrot at its head, but all the royalist members of the National Assembly told it in bullying accents then that its dissolution was necessary for the restoration of credit, for the consolidation of order, for putting an end to the indefinite provisional arrangements and for establishing a definitive state of affairs; that it hampered the productivity of the new government and sought to prolong its existence merely out of malice; that the country was tired of it. Bonaparte took note of all this invective against the legislative power, learnt it by heart and proved to the parliamentary royalists, on December 2, 1851, that he had learnt from them. He reiterated their own catchwords against them.

The Barrot ministry and the party of Order went further. They caused petitions to the National Assembly to be made throughout France, in which this body was politely requested to decamp. They thus led the unorganized popular masses into the fire of battle against the National Assembly, the constitutionally organized expression of the people. They taught Bonaparte to appeal against the parliamentary assemblies to the people. At length, on January 29, 1849, the day had come on which the Constituent Assembly was to decide concerning its own dissolution. The National Assembly found the building where its sessions were held occupied by the military; Changarnier, the general of the party of Order, in whose hands the supreme command of the National Guard and troops of the line had been united, held a great military review in Paris, as if a battle were impending, and the royalists in coalition threateningly declared to the Constituent Assembly that force would be employed if it should prove unwilling. It was willing, and only bargained for a very short extra term of life. What was January 29 but the *coup d'état* of December 2, 1851, only carried out by the royalists with Bonaparte against the republican National Assembly? The gentlemen did not observe, or did not wish to observe, that Bonaparte availed himself of January 29, 1849, to have a portion of the troops march past him in front of the Tuileries, and seized with avidity on just this first public summoning of the military power against the parliamentary power to foreshadow Caligula.[9] They, to be sure, saw only their Changarnier.

A motive that particularly actuated the party of Order in forcibly cutting short the duration of the Constituent Assem-

[9] A despotic Roman emperor, A.D. 37–41—ed.

bly's life was the organic laws supplementing the Constitution, such as the education law, the law on religious worship, etc. To the royalists in coalition it was most important that they themselves should make these laws and not let them be made by the republicans, who had grown mistrustful. Among these organic laws, however, was also a law on the responsibility of the President of the republic. In 1851 the Legislative Assembly was occupied with the drafting of just such a law, when Bonaparte anticipated this *coup* with the *coup* of December 2. What would the royalists in coalition not have given in their parliamentary winter campaign of 1851 to have found the Responsibility Law ready to hand, and drawn up, at that, by a mistrustful, hostile, republican Assembly!

After the Constituent Assembly had itself shattered its last weapon on January 29, 1849, the Barrot ministry and the friends of order hounded it to death, left nothing undone that could humiliate it and wrested from the impotent, self-despairing Assembly laws that cost it the last remnant of respect in the eyes of the public. Bonaparte, occupied with his fixed Napoleonic idea, was brazen enough to exploit publicly this degradation of the parliamentary power. For when on May 8, 1849, the National Assembly passed a vote of censure of the ministry because of the occupation of Civitavecchia by Oudinot, and ordered it to bring back the Roman expedition to its alleged purpose, Bonaparte published the same evening in the *Moniteur* a letter to Oudinot, in which he congratulated him on his heroic exploits and, in contrast to the ink-slinging parliamentarians, already posed as the generous protector of the army. The royalists smiled at this. They regarded him simply as their dupe. Finally, when Marrast, the President of the Constituent Assembly, believed for a moment that the safety of the National Assembly was endangered and, relying on the Constitution, requisitioned a colonel and his regiment, the colonel declined, cited discipline in his support and referred Marrast to Changarnier, who scornfully refused him with the remark that he did not like intellectual bayonets. In November 1851, when the royalists in coalition wanted to begin the decisive struggle with Bonaparte, they sought to put through in their notorious

Quaestors' Bill, the principle of the direct requisition of troops by the President of the National Assembly. One of their generals, Le Flô, had signed the bill. In vain did Changarnier vote for it and Thiers pay homage to the far-sighted wisdom of the former Constituent Assembly. The War Minister, Saint-Arnaud, answered him as Changarnier had answered Marrast—and to the acclamation of the *Montagne!*

Thus the party of Order, when it was not yet the National Assembly, when it was still only the ministry, had itself stigmatized the parliamentary regime. And it makes an outcry when December 2, 1851, banished this regime from France!

We wish it a happy journey.

11

Theodore S. Hamerow: The German Revolution of 1848*

The Revolution of 1848 remains one of the enigmas of German history. What other uprising succeeded at first so swiftly and bloodlessly? What other uprising failed in the end so dismally and utterly? In the exultation of the "springtime of peoples" the Baden liberal Karl Mathy wrote to his wife from Frankfurt am Main: "I live here not among men but among angels, and I sleep in a fairy temple." A year later he stood amid the ruins of that temple, contemplating the disintegration of the revolutionary movement. The gulf between the promise and the accomplishment seemed so vast that only some fundamental flaw, some congenital and irremediable weakness could account for it. The usual categories of historical explanation appeared too ordinary to make intelligible the enormity of the disaster. There had to be a unique and compelling reason for a defeat of such magnitude. For more than a hundred years scholars have been looking for that fatal defect which doomed the liberal uprising in Central Europe. And while unanimity regarding its nature is no closer today than it was a century ago, there is at least

* Theodore S. Hamerow, "1848," in Leonard Krieger and Fritz Stern, eds., *The Responsibility of Power: Historical Essays in Honor of Hajo Holborn* (New York: Doubleday & Co., Inc., 1967), pp. 145–161. By permission.

Theodore S. Hamerow is the author of *Restoration, Revolution, Reaction: Economics and Politics in Germany, 1815–1871*.

widespread agreement that the answer lies in a basic deficiency of either the political leadership or the social class or the entire nation involved in the revolution.

The most popular explanation of the failure of 1848 has been that the men who directed the revolutionary movement lacked the practicality to transform theory into reality. Toward the end of his life Carl Schurz, looking back at the insurrection he had defended in his youth, concluded that the Frankfurt Parliament "suffered from an excess of intellect, erudition, and virtue, and from a lack of that political experience and insight which recognize that the better is often the enemy of the good, and that the true statesman will beware of forfeiting the favorable moment by endangering the achievement of the essential through an obstinate insistence on the less essential." This is the familiar thesis of the visionariness of German parliamentarians immortalized in a thousand textbooks.

A more subtle interpretation of 1848, favored by historians on the left, maintains that the middle class, after gaining control of the revolution, betrayed it to the reaction rather than accept the emancipation of the proletariat. Jürgen Kuczynski restated this classic Marxian position on the occasion of the centenary of the March days:

> We know that the bourgeoisie failed in its struggle to win political power. It failed because it fought on two fronts, against the feudal nobility and against the working class. It fought against the working class, because it was afraid that it would have to share with it a part of the political power to be won. And it fought against the nobility in order to win in the first place the power which it did not want to share with the working class. But because in the past it had been accustomed to becoming a millionaire without political self-determination, its leadership in the course of the revolution inclined more and more toward a war on one front against the working class and in alliance with the feudal nobility.

Finally, in the years since 1933 the horrors of National Socialism encouraged the view that the failure of the revolution was the result of an innate deficiency of the German national character. Especially in countries that had fought against the Third Reich there was a feeling that Auschwitz and Buchenwald betokened a depravity whose roots extended deep into the history of Central Europe. Thus Edmond Vermeil wrote that "if one investigates the reason for the dramatic and disastrous climax to the events of 1848 and 1849 within the German Confederation, one discovers that they lie not so much in external causes as in the mentality of the German people." There were even some Germans who reached a similar conclusion regarding the civic incapacity of their nation. For example, Theodor Heuss, soon to become the first president of the German Federal Republic, conceded that the revolution revealed "the narrowness of the German character, which we may praise or revile, but which we must accept as something given." In this thesis the specific weaknesses of liberal leaders and bourgeois Phillistines are subsumed under the generic weaknesses of a people's mentality.[1]

Yet the attempt to explain 1848 through ideas and policies pursued in Germany ignores the fact that the revolutionary movement was not confined to Germany. It was a European phenomenon affecting the entire Continent from the English Channel to the Black Sea. Its course, moreover, proved everywhere the same. First there was a popular uprising which forced the old order to capitulate almost without a struggle. Then came a period of jubilation at the triumph of liberty, jubilation tempered by the awareness that the victors were divided over the use to be made of their victory. As these divisions became more pronounced, the defeated conservatives, recovering from their confusion, began to take the offensive. The last stage was the successful assault of the counterrevolution and the re-estab-

[1] Gustav Freytag, *Karl Mathy: Geschichte seines Lebens,* 2nd ed. (Leipzig, 1872), p. 263; Carl Schurz, *Lebenserinnerungen* (3 vols., Berlin, 1906–12), I, 168; Jürgen Kuczynski, *Die wirtschaftlichen und sozialen Voraussetzungen der Revolution von 1848–1849* (Berlin, 1948), p. 20; Edmond Vermeil, "An Historical Paradox: The Revolution of 1848 in Germany," in *The Opening of an Era: 1848,* François Fejto, ed. (London, 1948), p. 223; Theodor Heuss, *1848: Werk und Erbe* (Stuttgart, 1948), p. 166.

lishment of the political and social status quo. This was the basic pattern of development not only in Germany, but in France, Italy, Austria, and Hungary as well. It implies that everywhere in Europe the same cause produced the same effect, in other words, that the factors leading to the uprising transcended state boundaries.

Almost half a century after the outbreak of the revolution Friedrich Engels in his introduction to Marx's *The Class Struggles in France* explained that "what [Marx] had earlier deduced, half *a priori,* from defective material, was made absolutely clear to him by the facts themselves, namely, that the world trade crisis of 1847 had been the true mother of the February and March Revolutions and that the industrial prosperity which had been returning gradually since the middle of 1848, and which attained full bloom in 1849 and 1850, was the revivifying force of the newly strengthened European reaction." To be sure, there is little in Marx's writing or activities in 1848 to suggest that he realized the effect economic recovery was bound to have on the course of the uprising. Even two years later, when he wrote the articles comprising *The Class Struggles in France,* he was more interested in proving the inevitability of a new insurrection than in analyzing the failure of the old. "A new revolution is only possible in consequence of a new crisis," he expounded. "It is, however, also just as certain as this." He even predicted the time of the next depression: "If the new cycle of industrial development which began in 1848 follows the same course as that of 1843-47, the crisis will break out in the year 1852." But to Engels in 1895 the perspective of almost fifty years clearly revealed what he and Marx had only vaguely surmised in the heat of battle, namely, that the revival of the European economy had deprived the revolution of the urgency and militancy essential for its success.[2]

There is ample statistical evidence that the food shortage which helped produce the international wave of insurrection had already passed its crisis when the victorious revolutionaries prepared to consolidate their initial successes. In Germany the

[2] Karl Marx, *The Class Struggles in France (1848–1850)* (New York, 1964), pp. 10–11, 135; *Neue Rheinische Zeitung: Politische-ökonomische Revue* (Berlin, 1955), p. 312.

index of wholesale prices for agricultural products (1913 = 100) fell from 88 in 1847 to 58 in 1848 and 48 in 1849, while for cereal foodstuffs alone the figures were 122, 68, and 54. In Prussia the cost of a scheffel of wheat, 50 liters, declined during those 3 years from 11.03 marks to 6.30 and 6.17. Rye went from 8.62 to 3.82 and 3.18, and potatoes from 3.00 to 1.72 and 1.37. A pound of butter for which the consumer paid 68 pfennigs in 1847 could be bought for 62 in 1848 and 55 in 1849. The price of a pound of beef fell from 32 pfennigs to 31 and 21, and of a pound of pork from 44 to 43 and 36. In other words, the cost of living which had risen rapidly in the middle years of the decade, reaching its apex in 1847, began to drop with equal rapidity just as the revolution broke out.[3]

The business depression ended later than the famine, but it was never as intense. The per capita value of foreign trade in the Zollverein declined from 39.40 marks in 1847 to 36.60 in 1848 and 35.60 in 1849. The output of the anthracite mines of Prussia diminished from 19,145,000 tons in 1847 to 17,572,-000 in 1848, but then increased again to 18,197,000 in 1849. The Zollverein index of production for iron manufacture (1860 = 100) fell rapidly from 50 in 1847 to 40 in 1848 and then to 37 in 1849. The average for the entire decade, however, was only 36. The volume of capital investment in the Prussian railroads dropped from 109,989,000 marks in 1847 to 42,938,000 in 1848 and 52,111,000 in 1849. Yet revenues continued to climb from 22,500,000 marks in 1847, to 26,665,000 in 1848, and 32,349,000 in 1849. The nominal earnings of industrial labor, moreover, were generally unaffected by the hard times. Indeed, the index of average gross real wages in Germany (1900 = 100) rose from 57 in 1847 to 79 in 1848 and 86 in 1849, a reflection of the decline in the price of food.[4]

[3] Alfred Jacobs and Hans Richter, *Die Grosshandelspreise in Deutschland von 1792 bis 1934* (Hamburg, 1934), p. 82; "*Durchschnittspreise der wichtigsten Lebensmittel für Menschen und Thiere in den bedeutensten Marktorten der preussischen Monarchie*," *Zeitschrift des königlich preussischen Statistischen Bureaus*, XI (1871), 243.

[4] Gerhard Bondi, *Deutschlands Aussenhandel, 1815–1870* (Berlin, 1958), p. 145; Jürgen Kuczynski, *A Short History of Labour Conditions under Industrial Capitalism: Germany, 1800 to the Present Day* (London, 1945), pp. 29, 32, 58, 84; *Jahrbuch für die amtliche Statistik des*

In any case, for a country that was still largely agricultural the increase in farm output proved more important than the stagnation of business. The pattern of demographic change reflected the ups and downs of the cost of living with remarkable fidelity. For Germany as a whole the number of marriages per 1000 inhabitants was 7.2 in 1847, 7.7 in 1848, and 8.2 in 1849. The figures varied from state to state, but they were almost without exception on the rise: 7.8, 8.3, and 9.2 in Prussia; 6.3, 6.6, and 6.7 in Bavaria; 7.7, 8.0, and 8.5 in Saxony; and 6.5, 6.6, and 6.8 in Württemberg. Only in Baden was there a slight decline from 6.7 to 6.6 and 6.5. The over-all birth rate increased from 34.6 in 1847 to 34.7 in 1848 and 39.7 in 1849, while the death rate first rose from 29.7 to 30.5, and then dropped sharply to 28.6. Emigration statistics, however, are the most sensitive measure of the economic recovery which coincided with the coming of the revolution. The outflow of population has been estimated at 78,800 in 1847, 59,000 in 1848, and 61,700 in 1849. The destination of the vast majority of the emigrants was the New World, for the number of Germans entering the United States during these years was reported at 74,300, 58,500, and 60,200 respectively. In Prussia there were 14,900 authorized departures between October 1, 1846, and September 30, 1847; during the next twelve months the figure was 8300; and during the succeeding twelve it was 8800. The net increase in the population of the kingdom, representing the cumulative effect of changes in the birth, death, and emigration rates, was 44,200 in 1847, 8300 in 1848, and 165,800 in 1849.[5]

---

preussischen Staats, I (1863), 513; *Statistisches Handbuch für den preussischen Staat*, II (1893), 304.

[5] Paul Mombert, *Studien zur Bevölkerungsbewegung in Deutschland in den letzten Jahrzehnten mit besonderer Berücksichtigung der ehelichen Fruchtbarkeit* (Karlsruhe, 1907), pp. 48, 105; Marcus L. Hansen, "The Revolutions of 1848 and German Emigration," *Journal of Economic and Business History*, II (1930), 635, n. 8; *Statistisches Jahrbuch für das Deutsche Reich*, I (1880), 19; T. Bödiker, "Die Auswanderung und die Einwanderung des preussischen Staates," *Zeitschrift des königlich preussischen Statistischen Bureaus*, XIII (1873), 2–3; *Statistisches Handbuch für den preussischen Staat*, II (1893), 96.

The Revolution of 1848 thus differs from the two classic revolutions of the modern period, the French and the Russian, in that it did not originate in a financial or military crisis that the old order could not resolve. It was rather a belated reaction against hard times, a protest against material privations that were already diminishing as a result of economic recovery. Nor was the ruling caste, which it temporarily displaced, a decorative court aristocracy enjoying exalted status without a corresponding civic function. The nobility of Central Europe, particularly in Prussia, was still a robust social class occupying a strategic position in the army, the bureaucracy, and agriculture. Its defeat during the March days had been the result of a failure of nerve, not the penalty for ineptitude. The sudden collapse of established authority on the Continent had surprised and demoralized the Junker landowners of the east. In Frederick William IV, moreover, they had a ruler incapable of withstanding misfortune. Alarmed by peasant unrest and discouraged by the pusillanimity of their King, they reluctantly acquiesced in the establishment of a new order that promised to save them from anarchy through constitutionalism. Even an uncompromising conservative like Bismarck admitted: "The estate owners, like all other reasonable men, tell themselves that it would be senseless and impossible to want to arrest or dam up the current of the time."

But the recovery of the economy during the spring months revived the courage of the landed aristocrats. It created the opportunity for restoring royal authority and noble prerogative through an alliance of the upper with the lower classes. An intensification of the famine and depression would have forced the revolution farther to the left. It would have produced an irreparable breach between the old order and the new by encouraging both to adopt desperate expedients. The liberals would have become more radical, the conservatives more reactionary. A compromise would have proved impossible. The alleviation of hard times, on the other hand, had the effect of moderating political passion. It suggested to the court the strategy of appeasing the bourgeoisie with political reform, while conciliating the proletariat with economic reform. The idea of rallying the masses to the support of the crown appealed especially to the opponents of the revolution. As early as the March days Joseph von Radowitz was assuring Frederick William IV that "the proletariat as such is by no means republican. This is a common error. Any form of government that would boldly and wisely take its interests in hand, that would devote itself to the system of progressive taxation, the entire problem of poor relief, and the regulation of the inequality between capital and labor, would have the 'common man' on its side and thereby an enormous force. To be sure, this is a dangerous course, but what is not dangerous now?"

The conservative policy of moderation gained support as the return of economic stability vitiated the justification for political radicalism. The program the rightist members of the Prussian national assembly published in June was reasonableness itself. "We want to develop political and religious freedom in keeping with the promises made to the people," it proclaimed. "We assert that in accordance with the concept of a constitutional form of government the rights of sovereignty are exercised jointly by the King and the people." Most important, "we seek in the realm of material interests the welfare of the people and especially of the working class, a fair criterion of the obligation to pay taxes based on the ability to pay taxes, the abolition of the feudal system with all its consequences, the elimination of manorial and domanial authority. Liberation of landed property from all servile obligations to which it is subject, the right of the proprietor to dispose of his land with complete freedom, and the limitation of the regalia." Who could take exception to such conciliatory proposals? A month later a correspondent for Marx's *Neue Rheinische Zeitung* reported from Stettin that a "part of our landowners is intelligent enough to consider the elimination of the privileges they have had until now a necessary condition for the acquisition by large landed property of the political influence that they need for the advancement of their interests." And in August, at the "General Assembly for the Protection of the Interests of Landowners and for the Advancement of the Welfare of All Classes of the Population," which the Junkers convoked in Berlin, Ernst von Bülow-Cummerow advocated a conservatism based on economic interest rather than ideological orthodoxy: "If this honorable assembly shares my views, we will refrain from all political debates. We will thereby avoid conflicts leading to disunion. Material interests have a significance outweighing all others. By pursuing them we will always be on firm ground. Let us exert all our energies to advance them, and if we are successful, we can count on the approval of the great mass of the people and of all propertied groups." This became the strategy of the successful counter-offensive the old order launched in the fall of 1848.[6]

The economic recovery that made the conservatives less conservative made the revolutionaries less revolutionary. It strengthened the hand of the middle-of-the-roaders to whom liberalism meant essentially the establishment of a social system dominated by individual talent rather than hereditary privilege. To them, free private property was the basis of civic progress, and any attempt to regulate its ownership would conflict with the underlying laws of economics. A government that tried to tamper with the natural interplay of material interests invited disaster. "The unequal distribution of goods is not artificial," expounded Konrad von Rappard before the Frankfurt Parliament. "It is established deep in the cumulative nature of landed property and capital that in a populous state they will always remain in the hands of only a small part of the nation. Legislation can change nothing in this regard. It should only remove the barriers that exclude individuals or entire classes from property." According to the moderates the social purpose of the revolution was to win freedom of opportunity for the gifted and the energetic, to create a new aristocracy of ability in place of the old aristocracy of birth. That is what Joseph Schneider meant when he argued in the national assembly for the abolition of titles of nobility: "I am certainly well aware that we will have an aristocracy of wealth and we will have an aristocracy of

[6] Otto von Bismarck, *Die gesammelten Werke* (15 vols., Berlin, 1924–35), XV, 28; Paul Hassel, *Joseph Maria v. Radowitz* (Berlin, 1905), pp. 577–78; *Die deutschen Parteiprogramme,* Felix Salomon, ed. (2 vols., Leipzig and Berlin, 1907), I, 23–24; *Neue Rheinische Zeitung,* July 25, 1848; *Neue Preussische Zeitung,* August 22, 1848.

intellect, human nature unfortunately being what it is. But those, gentlemen, are natural aristocracies for which everyone is qualified and to which everyone can ascend. But an aristocracy of birth is never natural nor is it necessary."

Belief in a basic inequality in society led logically to belief in a basic inequality in politics. The liberal bourgeoisie that came to power during the spring uprising opposed the egalitarian demands of the proletariat as resolutely as the hierarchical prejudices of the aristocracy. For how could the ignorant and the propertyless be expected to resist the blandishments of rabble-rousers? "No civic order," maintained the constitutional committee of the Frankfurt Parliament, "of whatever sort it may be, monarchical or republican, will endure or achieve any kind of stability, if the right of decision in all political questions is placed in the hands of the great mass, which only too often lets itself be led without a will of its own, and which capriciously follows one leader today and another one tomorrow." Participation in public affairs had to be restricted to those who could demonstrate their intelligence and ability through the accumulation of property. Heinrich von Gagern, prime minister in the national government, was convinced that "the tendency of our time is to secure for the middle classes the preponderant influence in the state. While we have granted the individual all personal freedoms, the right of association, freedom of the press, fullest freedom of conscience, and whatever the individual might require to assert himself and establish the conditions for the exercise of political rights, we must provide for a wise exercise of political rights through such authoritative measures that the property owner is secure in his property, and . . . the state is not threatened by a mass influence which is not suited to our conditions."[7]

The end of the depression intensified the reluctance of the bourgeoisie to abandon its cozy theories of timocratic politics and laissez-faire economics. A firm alliance between the middle

[7] *Stenographischer Bericht über die Verhandlungen der deutschen constituirenden Nationalversammlung zu Frankfurt am Main*, Franz Wigard, ed. (9 vols., Frankfurt am Main, 1848–49), VII, 5303. Cf. *ibid.*, II, 1313, VII, 2222, 5296.

and lower classes might have saved the revolution despite the return of prosperity. Such an alliance, however, would have required a fundamental change in the economic relationships and institutions of Central Europe. A vigorous program of agrarian reform, for example, could have won for liberalism the support of the peasantry, the most numerous class of the population, but only at the expense of established property rights. And that was a price bourgeois parliamentarians, heartened by the upturn of business conditions, refused to pay. Marx, on the other hand, advocated the total destruction of the system of manorial obligations precisely because he recognized that it would create an irreparable breach with the past and make impossible any compromise between the new order and the old:

[Consider] the most striking evidence that the German Revolution of 1848 is only the parody of the French Revolution of 1789. On August 4, 1789, three weeks after the attack on the Bastille, the French people in one day disposed of the feudal burdens. On July 11, 1848, four months after March barricades, the feudal burdens are disposing of the German people. . . . The French bourgeoisie of 1789 did not for one moment desert its allies, the peasants. It knew that the basis of its power was the destruction of feudalism in the countryside, the creation of a free, landowning peasant class. The German bourgeoisie of 1848 betrays without any scruple these peasants who are its most natural allies, flesh of its flesh, and without whom it is powerless against the nobility.

Yet the comparison was not altogether valid. The French people did not dispose of the feudal burdens in one day, and the creation of a free, landowning peasant class was a gradual process which became possible only as the revolution moved farther to the left under the pressure of financial and military exigency. It was the National Convention that liquidated the last remnants of feudalism in France. The men who guided the revolution in Germany, however, were no Jacobins. They were cautious middle-class liberals who refused to adopt desperate expedients in the absence of desperate needs. Their purpose was not to save freedom from reaction, but to defend it against attacks from the left as well as the right. And that meant defending the principle of private ownership, the basis of freedom. The economic committee of the national assembly maintained that "every private property, whether it consists of land or dues, is equally sacred and inviolable, and must be safeguarded by civil society, whatever political form of state the latter may assume. By destroying the protection of right and property it would destroy its foundations and vital elements, and so destroy itself." To acquiesce in the expropriation of the nobility might ultimately lead to the expropriation of the bourgeoisie. For was there any logical distinction between estates and factories, between rural and urban wealth? That was the danger against which Paul Pfizer warned the Württemberg legislature:

> Every demand to abolish the still existing feudal dues and to destroy completely rights which have until now been recognized by the state and protected by the courts because of the injustice, the severity, and oppressiveness which may partly be connected with them, every such demand . . . to end right and wrong by a stroke of the pen had to be rejected, for we know that from the destruction of land registers and stock ledgers it is only a step to the destruction of mortgage records and promissory notes, and from the destruction of promissory notes it is again only a step to the division of property or a general community of goods.

Most of the liberals of 1848 wanted to maintain the existing structure of society in Central Europe. They believed that the object of the revolution was not to abolish established rights of ownership, but to adapt them to the demands of a free capitalistic economy. This required first of all the transformation of manorial dues into money rents extinguishable by lump payment, and secondly, the removal of class restrictions on the acquisition of land. In other words, the same underlying principles that governed property relationships in industry would now be applied to agriculture. Economic obligations were to be based on written contact rather than common custom, while the prohibition of entailment was to make ability the only condition of rural proprietorship. The distinction in the forms of possession between manufacture and farming would disappear to make way for the untrammeled rule of laissez faire. The free interaction of private interests in pursuit of material gain was to solve the agrarian problem by ensuring the survival of the fittest. Wilhelm Löwe of Kalbe attacked entailed estates in language that anticipated Herbert Spencer: "I personally do not in the least wish that this property should always remain immovably in one hand, and when I consider the development of the people and the development of humanity, I want no one to have any longer this security which is born on the bed of ease. . . . Everyone should strive and toil; this struggle should not cease; everyone should also wage this struggle every moment in his small circle. In this way character will be steeled, self-confidence will be strengthened, in a word, the moral personality will be raised to a higher level." To such men rugged individualism was the best cure for the ills of the peasantry.[8]

The leaders of the revolution applied the same austere dogmas of laissez-faire liberalism to problems facing the urban working class. The latter consisted largely of skilled artisans whose livelihood was being threatened by the advance of industrialization. The economist Bruno Hildebrand pointed out to the members of the Frankfurt Parliament that "the German proletariat is not a factory but a handicraft proletariat. In the middle-sized and smaller towns there are the many small master tradesmen who have sunk, who are starving, and who must at present be considered proletarians. There are especially the numerous unfortunate master tradesmen who are engaged in homecrafts and compete with the machines. . . . The greater part of the master tradesmen is unfortunately made up of nothing more than proletarians who live from hand to mouth just like the day laborers." The artisan masses which had marched in demonstrations and fought on the barricades during the March days might have become the *sans-culottes* of the revolu-

[8] *Neue Rheinische Zeitung,* July 30, 1848; *Verhandlungen der Nationalversammlung,* F. Wigard, ed., IV, 2403, 2549; *Verhandlungen der württembergischen Kammer der Abgeordneten auf dem Landtage von 1848* (Stuttgart, 1848), pp. 229–30.

tion in Central Europe. Hungry and embittered, they were the victims of the mechanization of production which had been growing steadily since the end of the Napoleonic wars. What they wanted above all was a corporative regulation of manufacture, which would enable them to withstand the competition of the factory system. "It was found," proclaimed an assembly of journeymen, "that through the introduction of [industrial freedom] the rich became richer and richer, the poor poorer and poorer; that the middle class was ruined and the working class reduced to begging; [and] that the freedom which had been sought was no true freedom but only a caricature." Any political movement that undertook to protect the independent handicraftsman against industrialism could have won his backing.

This was a bargain, however, that the middle-of-the-road liberals were unwilling to make. It would have meant imposing new burdens on the business community, which was just beginning to recover from a serious depression. It would have meant tampering with the eternal laws of economics. They were determined to avoid experiments in mass welfare like those that had led to civil war in France during the June Days. Their credo could be found in the reports the economic committee submitted to the national assembly: "It is a demand of natural law that everyone be allowed to employ his individual skill profitably for his own advantage as much as he can, and to choose his occupation in accordance with his own inclination. If conditions make the choice of another form of employment necessary or desirable, the change to another form of livelihood should not be rendered difficult. . . . In competition lies an irresistible force of progress. Whoever does not accept it will be left behind." Not even the realization that the revolution was losing support could shake their rigid adherence to principle. It was better to risk a restoration of the old order than to shackle the economic energies of the nation. For what was the good of political liberty won by the sacrifice of economic freedom?[9]

9 *Verhandlungen der Nationalversammlung*, F. Wigard, ed., VII, 5285; W. Ed. Biermann, *Karl Georg Winkelblech (Karl Marlo): Sein Leben und sein Wirken* (2 vols., Leipzig, 1909), II, 451–52; *Verhandlungen der deutschen verfassunggebenden Reichs-Versammlung zu Frankfurt am*

The same logic made it impossible for the leaders of the revolution to establish an effective alliance with the industrial working class. Whether such an alliance could in any case have saved the new order is an open question. The factory proletariat was numerically weak and politically indifferent. Made up in large part of uprooted peasants driven from their villages by overpopulation, it lacked a sense of community and purpose. Nor had it yet developed an effective form of organization such as the guild system had once provided for the artisan masses. Most important of all, the factory proletariat was still without a collective feeling of social grievance. Employed in an expanding sector of the economy, it had not suffered the material and psychological hardships to which the independent skilled handicraftsman was exposed. Its earnings had generally remained stable during the years of the depression, and with the return of good times its economic position was improving. That is what Hermann Kriege, a former disciple of Marx, meant when he reported that "we cannot rely on the proletariat; the ideal proletariat does not exist." Even under the most favorable circumstances the liberal statesmen of 1848 may not have succeeded in transforming the labor force of the factories into an instrument of their policy. And such an attempt was certainly bound to fail without an extensive program of social reform, which they were unwilling to contemplate.

The Frankfurt Parliament rejected out of hand proposals for the establishment of minimum wage rates: "Aside from the fact that legal determination of the proceeds of labor presupposes a police state such as has not yet existed anywhere, a minimum wage would necessary pull with it all prices of goods and even extend to the produce of the soil. . . . A fixed wage rate would furthermore deprive of their bread the workers who are less energetic, less able, who are weak from old age, but who now find work because a lower wage makes up for their inferior ability." A state guarantee of work for all citizens was worse still: "Such a guarantee would be the paralysis of diligence, a

---

Main, K. D. Hassler, ed. (6 vols., Frankfurt am Main, 1848–49), II, 899, IV, 146.

sanction of laziness, a paralysis of the energy which above all should animate and elevate this populace, if it is to overcome the harshness of its lot. . . . It is our duty to steel the trust in their strength of these classes on which the Providence of God has imposed labor as a necessity of life, . . . and to steel their moral courage by directing their trust to Providence." The only way to enable the worker to get ahead in economics as in politics was by establishing freedom of opportunity, the open-sesame of laissez-faire liberalism: "Germany should also consider labor sacred, but she should honor it by opening for the industrious worker the avenue to every position, even the highest in the fatherland. He must never be excluded, but he must also never be enfranchised if he has not demonstrated by what he accomplishes that he meets the criterion of capacity for a wise exercise of the political vocation." The rigorous ethic of the *juste-milieu* had only one answer for all problems of state and society.[10]

The revolution, to be sure, also had its democratic adherents. Some of them sat in the legislative assemblies of 1848, waiting patiently for an unexpected turn of events to thrust power into their hands. Others, afraid that legalistic scruples would only strengthen the predominance of the moderates, preached sedition and organized hopeless putsches. All of them, however, believed in popular sovereignty and manhood suffrage. Their ideal was not a constitutional monarchy of property and education, but the Jacobin republic of virtue. The faction of the *Donnersberg* in the Frankfurt Parliament proclaimed "liberty, equality, and fraternity as the principles whose realization is its task," while the militants congregating in the *Deutscher Hof* dreamed of a radical democracy in Central Europe:

> The party of the left . . . wants a popular representation arising out of the free choice of all Germans who are of age. . . . It wants the right of the individual German states to determine their constitutions, whether in the form of the

[10] Veit Valentin, *Geschichte der deutschen Revolution von 1848–49* (2 vols., Berlin, 1930–31), II, 256; *Verhandlungen der Nationalversammlung,* F. Wigard, ed., VII, 5102, 5114, 5246.

democratic monarchy or in the form of the democratic free state. . . . It wants humanity. It accordingly wants in particular a system of education which has been completely altered, penal legislation based on humanity, and a military system built on a popular militia. It wants the elimination of all immoral state revenues, and a method of taxation in keeping with the ability to pay. It wants in general a thoroughgoing improvement in the social conditions of the people.

Nor did these radicals hesitate to subordinate the abstractions of classical economics to the vital needs of the community. Bernhard Eisenstuck, for example, advocated a system of social insurance: "You must create institutions that will impose on every employer, in proportion to the labor force that he uses, the obligation of paying during the use of the labor force, that is, during the actual continuance of the contract, a tax solely for the benefit of the workers. This tax must flow into the state treasury and be publicly administered. And the use of this tax should be nothing other than the compensation of the labor force after it has been expended, that is, for the material support of invalid workers, the establishment of retirement homes, etc." Ludwig Simon on the far left was even ready to defend the appropriation of public funds for the relief of unemployment and want: "I for my part at least deplore far less the money that was spent in France for the 200,000 workers in the national workshops, or that was spent in Berlin by the state and municipal treasury for some 6000 workers in the time of anarchy, than the Silesians and Irishmen who died of hunger in a condition of law and order." Here was an incipient awareness of the social problems engendered in industrialization, an awareness that, if translated into government policy, might have won for the new order the lower-class support essential for its survival.[11]

Yet the radicals never came to power, because the times were not propitious for political or economic experiment. What the revolution needed was a great galvanizing crisis capable of evoking the hidden energies and resources of society. Under the

[11] *Parteiprogramme*, F. Salomon, ed., pp. 29–31; *Verhandlungen der Nationalversammlung*, F. Wigard, ed., VII, 5119, 5135.

pressure of national disaster a small faction of dogmatists and visionaries created the Jacobin republic and the Bolshevik dictatorship, successfully defying the world. The men of 1848, on the other hand, never matched these achievements, because they never grappled with the same elemental urgencies. How could they effect the transition from Mirabeau to Robespierre, from Kerensky to Lenin? Among them might have been found "some Cromwell guiltless of his country's blood," guiltless for lack of opportunity. Yet only the desperation born of military defeat or economic collapse could have produced a widespread resolve to break once and for all with the beliefs and loyalties of the past. The nineteenth century, the golden age of the European bourgeoisie, was too prosperous, too optimistic for great uprisings. It could produce theories, ideals, enthusiasms, and slogans, but it lacked that mass despair that is indispensable for a violent, fundamental alteration in the structure of society. The revolution failed not because of the weakness of the national character, not because of the treason of the middle class, not even because of the timidity of the leaders, but because of an unshaken faith that the basic civic and material needs of Germany could be met within the framework of established ideas and institutions.

12

Jean Gacon: The Paris Commune of 1871*

The Paris Commune of 1871, which governed Paris for seventy-two days, for years was virtually ignored in the basic history textbooks assigned to all French students. Thus, the huge slanders heaped on the heads of the Communards in the years immediately after the event were succeeded by a faithfully observed unofficial conspiracy of silence. The Commune was excluded from French tradition, a tradition which easily reconciles Henry IV and Danton and puffs up Napoleon, but which still has difficulty integrating Robespierre and Jaurès. It received brief mention as a shameful episode between the Second Empire, with its industrial and commercial growth, and a Third Republic that has been idealized in all respects. The Communards were presented as more or less crazy revolutionaries or Prussian henchmen, brutes without any great ideal and given the benefit of only one excuse: that of having known beforehand the miseries of the siege, the "volcanic fever" that infected besieged Paris. As for the barbaric repression of the Versailles Government, it was for all intents and purposes minimized, and completely and quickly eclipsed by the radiant dawn of a Third Republic capable of bringing happiness to everyone. Such was for many years the "shared knowledge" of the average Frenchman on the subject of the Commune.

* Jean Gacon, "La Commune de Paris," *Europe, revue mensuelle,* no. 499–500 (November-December 1970), pp. 6–17. By permission.

227

Confronted with this official ideology, the working class of France and of the world in their own organizations whole-heartedly celebrated the Commune as the first workers' government, the first earthly incarnation of socialist dreams or theories; in a word, as the dawn of a new day. Marx, Engels and Lenin drew lessons from this attempt at popular power, a daring and premature one, broken quickly a century ago by the bourgeoisie and other property-owning classes using military power. To the admiration of the workers these three added critical lucidity for the advancement of socialist theory. Almost immediately Marxists and Anarchists began to fight over the heritage of the Commune, in a debate which is only one theme in a necessary ideological clarification leading to a true science of socialism.

Historians have until now wished to pass over these significant reflections of class struggles in their presentations of the Commune. The "royalist" school has seen in the Commune the eternal turbulence of Paris, as in the time of Etienne Marcel or the *Fronde,* which Authority—thank God!—suppressed. These simplifications take no account of the differences between eras and of the social make-up of the contesting forces. University historians, in the name of objectivity and research, have concluded that the Commune deserved neither so much opprobrium nor so much honor. The last revolution of the past, it would not be the harbinger of times to come. For the scholar studying the event in the archives, the working class and socialists had forged a kind of "myth of the Commune" which in its turn played an historic role, but which did not stand up to an examination of the facts.

Finally, for the latest chapter to date, on the eve of the Centenary of the Commune it is naturally good taste to rehabilitate the Communards. A vast operation of annexation and recovery seems to be only in its beginnings. Building on certain real as well as instructive similarities, a certain type of Leftist supposes a parallel extremism between 1871 and May–June 1968 in the Latin Quarter. But above all, from the Right apology for the Versailles Government is no longer offered, and camouflage is no longer possible. For more than one Gaullist it has become obvious that the Communards are in some way ancestors to glorify. Meanwhile, the rebel General André Zeller uses his time in prison to study a rebellion totally different from his own, as one way of calling for total amnesty for the O.A.S. He concludes that civil wars lead to injustice.

All those who honestly ask: "What is this Paris Commune that we know so little about and about which we speak so much?" must be answered just as honestly. All the while one must be careful to avoid falling into the traps of a partially changing ruling-class ideology, as well as the more subtle ones of a false objectivity. In truth, if knowledge of the Commune has been increased, it does not deny what Marx, by insight, and the working class, by instinct, had previously felt and revealed. The Paris Commune, although in step with the great movements of the nineteenth century, is really, and above all, the glorious herald of a new era.

In the quasi-majestic history of bourgeois France, revolutions, even if they are made by the common people with their own hands, always end by putting in office a new form of bourgeois state power more fitted to the needs of the moment. How then was it possible that from March 18 to May 28, 1871, the capital of this country could be governed by a Commune, a new form of democracy molded at least in part by workers aspiring toward socialism?

It is seemingly paradoxical that one prime reason for this is patriotism. While Marx wrote, "the working class has no country," Péguy holds that "countries are always defended by beggars and surrendered by the rich."[1] The true meaning of Marx's phrase goes further than this simple statement. One can neither give nor take from a rising but oppressed class what it does not have—a country. But this class ends by taking upon itself responsibility for the national interest. In 1793 the rising bourgeoisie represented the nation, in comparison to a declining aristocracy which betrayed it and emigrated.

In 1871 the bourgeoisie in power believed that the war, desired by the Imperial court in order to consolidate the throne,

[1] Charles Péguy, *Cahiers*, Vol. 7, January 5, 1904.

would be useful to themselves. But after the first defeats and the disaster at Sedan, even though the Republic was proclaimed, the new government of the Jules (Favre, Simon, Ferry) and of Louis-Jules Trochu (despite the fact that it called itself "the Government of National Defense") only wanted to deal with Bismarck so as to preserve the essence of society: the privileges and peace of mind of the possessors of wealth. In opposition, the working class, which had nothing to do with the declaration of war, wanted to break the siege of Paris and chase the invaders from France. The war changed its meaning. It became for the people a just war of liberation, and it was the rising working class which picked up the banner of national independence dropped by the bourgeoisie.

After the humiliation of the armistice, the loss of Alsace-Lorraine and the parade of the Prussians into Paris, working-class bitterness overflowed. The Commune had been demanded from the beginning of the siege by the most politically conscious workers in order to fight to the end against the Prussians; it was the exasperated uprising of a people which refused to accept defeat. But to reduce it to that, as did Georges Bernanos,[2] is to have a narrow view of things, because the armistice also provided for elections. Those of February 1871 resulted in a revealing separation. The Right won in the provinces, above all the countryside; it played on the legitimate wish of simple men for peace. In many regions where landowners and big businessmen wanted to forget the national interest in favor of their own immediate personal interests, people did not understand that to vote for peace was to vote for social stability and political reaction. As a result the normal electoral map of France was bizarrely deformed. For example, the Ariège voted for the Right, which it was never known to do. Later, during the by-elections, the true face of Leftist departments reappeared. But for the moment the damage was done. Only the city of Paris and the areas which suffered voted for the Left republicans and for revolutionary socialists.

Thus was created a chasm not merely patriotic in character.

---

2 Georges Bernanos, *La grande peur des bien-pensants,* p. 64.

At Bordeaux, then at Versailles, sat an assembly of notables (noble landowners and bourgeois creditors) in no way representative of the actual forces in the country, ready to restore the monarchy and defend the established social order. On the other side the popular classes of Paris had other political objectives: a real republic and social change.

These elements in Paris were organized by the pressure of recent events. Even if their organizations did not function smoothly, they had the virtue of existence. During the entire siege, the Central Republican Committee for the Twenty Arrondissements had asked for mobilization of the whole population and denounced those wishing to surrender. The finest of the militants were found in its ranks. Their names were unknown or disdained by the men in power, but they were well regarded and influential in their neighborhoods, where they had in past years led the struggle against the Second Empire. Now they called for a "Commune." For some it was the memory of 1793, for others the clear idea of the structure of a working-class state.

Moreover, after the armistice the National Guard remained the pivot of the political life of Paris. All eligible men were organized into battalions and sections. The officers were elected; only the general was named by the government. The National Guard had its own family welfare associations and mutual aid societies, which had gained importance during the siege by occupying themselves with rations and softening misery as much as possible. These units took the initiative in creating a Republican Federation of the National Guard (from which comes the name of *"fédérés"* that the Communards bear). On February 24, 1871, a Central Committee was elected. The most politically aware of the organizers of the Committee of the Twenty Arrondissements henceforth preferred this larger organization, which had better contacts with the people despite its fluid structure and ideological divisions.

The duel between Paris and the Assembly at Versailles commenced. Thiers, elected February 12 as chief of the executive power, was pushed by financial circles to whom he was submissive to tame Paris, the red city. Vinoy, a detested Bonapartist, was placed at the head of the Army of Paris, and

Aurelle de Paladines at the head of the National Guard. Pay for the National Guard was halted except for indigents. Freedom of the press in Paris was suspended. Thus emerged a political situation more complex than one of mere disagreement over the problem of peace with Prussia.

But one does not really understand this political climate if one does not take account, in depth, of its economic and social causes. The France of 1871 was definitely no longer that of 1793, and therein lay the mistake of those who only spoke of the "Commune" in order to recreate the past: romantics, like Félix Pyat, who called themselves "Jacobins," and whom the young nicknamed with impertinence "the graybeards of 1848."

In reality the Commune occurred in the midst of a period of transition. Journeymen still existed in workshops where they "broke bread" with the master, but workers in the modern sense of the word were growing in number in real factories. The working class was developing in numbers, solidarity and consciousness. It won the right to organize, increased strikes, began trade union committees.

For a long time Parisian workers had been the supporting cast, the sacrificed troops of revolutionary events which ended by the retreat of the old nobility or the advance of a new layer of the bourgeoisie. In June 1848, when they wished to fight for themselves, that pretension was mercilessly drowned in their blood. For a long time also the workers had voted simply for the opposition, the educated and fine-sounding "radical." According to the saying of one of them, "Whether a potato peel or a cabbage skin, what does it matter what I put in the voting urn, so long as it offends!"

But in 1864 the *Manifesto of the Sixty,* although very moderate, proclaimed that the workers wanted "to be represented," i.e., to have their own deputies. To the principle of equality mandated by universal suffrage was to be added the reality of social equality. And above all the working class saw themselves exercising power so as to build socialism.

Of course, on the way to achieving it they divided. Blanqui and his friends thought of armed action by a small number of determined men. Proudhon's disciples had faith in the virtue of example: cooperativism would win step by step. Marxism was still little known in France. However, since 1864 there existed the First International, whose inaugural address was drawn up by Marx. Soon driven to secrecy by Imperial repression, its French section was animated by the bookbinder Varlin. He was Proudhonian at the start, but came to believe more and more, like the jewelry worker Frankel, in mass political struggle.

The International became a bogeyman for the bourgeoisie and the rulers of the country, while purblind historians have spoken of the Commune as a "plot" by the International. In fact, Marx warned the Parisian members that "a premature action would be folly," and advised French workers "to use calmly and firmly the advantages of republican freedom to strengthen their organizations."

There was no plot: the conditions of the time led the "Commune" to power. Marx followed its unfolding with a troubled passion, magnifying its martyrs and drawing theoretical profit from their glorious experience. Because the Commune, which was not a conspiracy, was also not an accident; with its dross and its beauties it was a logical step in working-class struggles.

The conditions of the moment were also the socio-economic realities. The lot of the Parisian people was tragic after the siege. The rich left for the provinces or received packages of food; they could again eat their fill and even find delicacies. The Goncourts' *Journal* remarks their astonishment that the population did not break windows in the well-off neighborhoods, because among the poor frightful shortages continued. The stopping of pay for the National Guards, often their only means of income since unemployment reigned, aggravated the situation still more.

And then the Assembly attacked the shopkeepers and artisans. No bank yet having reopened to offer loans, the law on debts still made commercial debts immediately payable. Thus the shopkeepers, who since the beginning of the war had made hardly any money, were driven to bankruptcy. Napoleon III himself had put a moratorium on rents during the war. This was annulled and thousands of tenants, above all artisans, were at the mercy of the "vultures," as they called the landlords. Thereby uncomprehending deputies sealed the alliance between the working class and a *petite bourgeoisie* which in June 1848 had been hostile to it. "The Commune of 1871" would not be solely working class, but founded upon the alliance of the working class with a part of the middle class.

Thiers wanted to sign a peace treaty with Bismarck, make the Republic a conservative force, assure social order and the profits of businessmen. To do that it would be necessary "to get rid of" the National Guard. On March 18, 1871, he made the move that was to unleash everything! He decided to take away the cannons which belonged to the National Guard and which they had placed for safety in the artillery parks on the hills in the northeast of the city. In the early morning the troops sent to accomplish this mission were drowned in a wave of fraternization, above all at Montmartre. The National Guard mobilized, but against the threat from Versailles.

During the evening of March 18, while the Central Committee moved into the Hôtel de Ville, Thiers gave the order to all his officials to fall back on Versailles. Certainly he was afraid, but perhaps also he wanted to allow the situation in Paris to develop, so that he could accuse the workers of rebellion and more effectively smash their movement. He set off the sparks of civil war, but he wanted the working class to appear responsible for the conflagration.

At the Hôtel de Ville the most ardent spoke of marching on Versailles, the most cautious of negotiating a compromise. (All during the Commune there would be "conciliators," such as Georges Clemenceau, some well meaning, but most rather cunning opponents.) Finally, defensive barricades were raised at the western gates because they were afraid of an immediate counterattack. Nothing happened, and the Central Committee was almost embarrassed by this windfall. The political vacuum suddenly created possibilities for the fervently desired "Commune," but by what means was it to be established? These revolutionaries were so sensitive to the possibility of being accused of usurping power, so attached to democratic formalities, that they did not dream of proclaiming the "Commune" on their own initiative.

They organized elections. These took place on March 26, with scrupulous honesty. The Central Committee slate won by a strong majority and became a municipal council. It extended an offer to the rest of France to create a federation of communes, without considering itself a nationwide source of authority. The blockade and attack by Versailles would change this initial position.

Forced to fight, the Paris Commune would soon call itself the Municipal Council of Paris and a government of the working class. This ambiguity in function was due to the exceptional circumstances which created the Commune. It remains true that the Communards were initially pacific and that the initiation of violence came from Thiers and Versailles.

Within the Communal Council itself could be found tendencies reflecting the diversity of origins and ideological positions of the working class and its *petit bourgeois* allies. Out of sixty-five members there were twenty-five real workers and seventeen members of the International. Doctors like Edouard Vaillant sat next to writers like Jules Vallès and the painter Courbet.[3] The Jacobins kept close to the Blanquists (but Blanqui was in prison first at Cahors then at Fort Taureau, in the Bay of Morlaix) while the "Internationalists," even if they were Proudhonists, were bothered by the defection of the latter's most faithful disciples, like Tolain, who went back to Versailles, or Chaudey, who would be shot as a traitor. That is why they became more and more susceptible to the influence of Marx, which was brought to bear on Bénoît Malon by Frankel, and also by the shoemaker Serailler, who had made the journey from London.

At the beginning the Jacobin majority wanted above all to emphasize political activities; and the socialist minority, socialist measures. Curiously they agreed on this distinction, which seems to us arbitrary, for each group sought to choose between the priorities of political organization or the satisfaction of the

[3] On the social and ideological composition of the Communal Council, see chapter IV of the remarkable work of Bruhat-Dautry-Tersen, *La Commune de 1871* (Paris: Editions Sociales, 1961), a new edition of which is soon to be reissued.

imperative material needs of the masses. However, events would soon settle the matter, since it would be necessary at the same time to govern in favor of the oppressed and to fight against the enemy in Versailles. This is what the Committee of Public Safety would try to do.

On May 10 the newspaper *le Prolétaire* wrote: "The Commune is the people themselves." The most far-seeing of its leaders, despite their quarrels, never thought otherwise. Frankel said: "If we do nothing for the working class I see no reason for the Commune to exist." And the leaders never imagined a government without direct contact with the masses. They consulted the people in its organizations with a watchful concern for direct democracy. Aside from the unions or sections of the National Guard, the clubs were essential. They increased their meetings in theaters and churches. It was not unusual in certain churches for the priest to offer Mass on Sunday while in the evening the pulpit was open to popular speakers, the organs accompanying revolutionary songs.

The masses supported the government and controlled it, often submitting to it their views and suggestions, inviting members of the Commune to come and brief them. This recalls both the *sans-culottes* of 1793 and the Soviets of revolutionary Russia. History should not be disguised: certain Communard leaders balked at coming, certain clubs wanted everything changed— immediately! The machinery sometimes accomplished nothing; control sometimes led to suspiciousness and excess verbiage. This proves only that real democracy demands an *avant garde* better organized and more theoretically sophisticated than the sects of that time.

Nevertheless, the balance sheet remains positive. "The originality of the Commune was precisely its role as a crucible, which in less than eight weeks produced the most daring set of principles and revolutionary laws that any legislative assembly in the nineteenth century could ever have adopted."[4] Despite its

---

[4] George Soria, *Grande histoire de la Commune,* 2 Vols. (Paris: Robert Laffont, 1970–71), II, 190. No one will henceforth be able to study the Commune without referring to this monumental work.

weaknesses, the Commune proved its own superiority over the formal representative system of the bourgeoisie.

It is true that, on the whole, the Commune at first adopted the radical Belleville program drawn up by Gambetta in 1869, in accordance with the wishes of his supporters. It is true that the Commune—that bogeyman—only inscribed on its lawbooks legislation that the bourgeois Republic would take more than a half-century to pass in its own right, bit by bit. It is, however, absurd to deny the fact that the Commune inevitably wedded a specifically socialist character to the hopes of *petit bourgeois* democracy, while the latter was pushed to its furthest limits.

When forced to choose between capital and labor, the Commune always intervened in favor of the working class. It suppressed fines for employees, private employment agencies and nightwork in the bakeries; and it recognized the principle that a guaranteed wage must be registered on the books of every business. If it did not nationalize industries, nor institute the financial reforms recommended by the Paris Section of the International in April 1870, it decided to make cooperatives out of the enterprises abandoned by owners favoring Versailles. It proclaimed the abolition of permanent, professional armies and recognized the National Guard, linked to the people, as the only military force. It emphasized the development of technical education as much as the separation of Church and State. Above all, it established a connection between the simple aspirations of the advanced republicans and the abolition of man's exploitation by man.

Doubtless there was among the Communards an element of utopianism, and sometimes naïveté. Typically utopian was the "practical socialism" of Jourde, who wanted to organize competition between workers' cooperatives and capitalist enterprises. The fact that Beslay, the Commune's delegate at the Bank of France, while maintaining cordial relations with the Bank's Assistant Governor, the Marquis de Ploëuc, failed to confiscate the gold in the Bank borders on complicity with Versailles. But one cannot deny the name of "socialists" to those whose message to the countryside said that "the land must belong to those who work it." Alas, few peasants would hear these words because Thiers had already flooded them with lies about the "Communists." Yet on May 2, 1871, at Coulommiers, a liberty tree was planted to the cries of "long live the Commune."

More to the point, the Parisian working class was isolated from the provinces. The provincial "Communes," which sometimes even preceded that of Paris, were no more than footnotes to the more decisive event. That of Lyon was of anarchist tendencies, inspired by the "secret leaders," so dear to Bakunin, who lived in nearby Switzerland. That of Marseilles, led by Gaston Crémieux, was at most merely radical. The most interesting was probably the Commune at Creusot, led by the worker Dumay, who danced to the tune of the boss, Schneider. Solidarity was evident: at Grenoble on April 16, workers prevented the departure of soldiers and munitions intended for Versailles. But, for the most part, Thiers succeeded in maintaining his *cordon sanitaire.* Paris alone would have to meet and resist the attack of MacMahon's army.

On April 2, the troops of Versailles attacked Courbevoie. The National Guard counterattacked the next day, took Bougival, but fell back because of the artillery fire from the Fort of Mont-Valérien. Thiers had abandoned the Fort on March 19, but in an unfortunate oversight Lullier had not occupied it in time in the name of the Commune. Troops on which the Parisians had mistakenly counted to be neutral opted for Versailles. In the course of the retreat the son of a famous scientist, Gustave Flourens, who went from scholarship to revolution, was captured and murdered by a policeman. At the same time, at Chatou, Galliffet began to have prisoners shot out of hand.[5] The drama had begun.

The final act was "bloody week." At the end of the nineteenth century Camille Pelletan, a radical republican, published under the title *La Semaine de Mai,* a poignant, well documented, and calmly written book, today unfortunately forgotten. In it he shows that in all French history there was no scene of comparable horror. Saint Bartholomew's Day was nothing in

[5] In *A l'assaut du ciel* (Paris: Editions Sociales, 1961), Jacques Duclos admirably recounts the day-to-day happenings of these tragic times.

comparison to the massacres of 1871, above all at Belleville. On May 21, when the army of Versailles entered Paris the Parisians vainly battled them in traditional street fighting. Each neighborhood had its own desperate struggle. Unfortunately, the military leadership of the Commune was inadequate. The first leader of the Army was the mediocre Cluseret, who was replaced by Rossel, a career officer nauseated by Bazaine's treason. A renegade member of the bourgeoisie, he was—wrongly or rightly—suspected of Caesarian ambitions and had to leave his post. The best strategist of the Commune, Dombrowski, fell on the barricade in rue Myrrha on May 23.

Dombrowski and Wroblewski were admirable Polish revolutionaries and patriots who came to serve the Commune. Working-class internationalism was not an empty word, and it would be possible to demonstrate this by citing many other names besides those of the Hungarian Frankel, or the Russian, Elizabeth Dmitrieff. All this served as a pretext for the most hideous xenophobia among bourgeois racists and nationalists after they recovered from their fright. The *Figaro,* which wrote, with attention to nuances, "March against the Prussians, but run after the Communards," trumpeted, "Shady Poles and fantastic Valaques are going to stop running the finest city in the world." And the son of the poet Mickiewicz, who was not involved in anything, was able to note, "After the defeat of the Communards the fact of being Polish was alone enough to get one shot."

At the time, the class struggle was taking place on an international scale. Bismarck was not, as is too often maintained, content to see Frenchmen fighting each other. He feared that the contagion would spread to his own countrymen, including the Prussian soldiers occupying France. That is why, as he admits in a note written on July 15, 1871, he did everything to help Thiers destroy the Commune, offering to him the soldiers and officers held prisoner. That is why the Prince of Saxony cheerfully moved his troops so as to surround Paris completely. Those Communards fleeing the city were stopped by German troops and given over to Versailles policemen who shot them on the spot. However, there were cases, related by survivors, when

Prussian soldiers refused to be party to this filthy job and preferred to let their captives escape. Thus, juxtaposed to the solidarity of the possessors of wealth we see another type of solidarity: that of the people.

This feeling was distributed unevenly: English trade unionists and Americans hardly seem to have understood the Commune, but deep feelings of sympathy were expressed in Germany and Italy. Garibaldi wrote, in disagreement with Mazzini, "The International is the hope of the future," and he magnified the achievements of the Commune.

From its first moment of existence all sorts of slanders about the Commune were broadcast; these have been continually resurrected since then and they must be refuted.[6] Courbet, the soul of the Commune's Fine Arts Committee, was sentenced to six months in prison in June 1871 on the pretext that he had wanted to destroy the Vendôme Column. He was also condemned to pay for the costs of its reconstruction. In fact he did not want to destroy it, but to unfasten this "mass of melted cannons" and transfer it to the Invalides.

More serious is the myth of the "women incendiaries." Among the Communards there are such shining figures as Anna Jaclard and Louise Michel, or the nurse to whom Jean-Baptiste Clément dedicates a posteriori *Le Temps des Cérises,* written in 1867. Women like these infuriated Thiers and his henchmen. The expression "women incendiaries" itself is a symbol. Lacking anything else, they used kerosene during the Commune to heat their food and warm themselves. The term was spread by Thiers across France before any fire had been set in Paris. And these fires that are so often held against the Communards were the reply to the terrible war of extermination conducted by Versailles; they served to slow down the advance of the murderers.

Galliffet shot Communard prisoners. The Commune answered by taking about fifty hostages, suspected of dealing with Versailles. It must be made clear that despite the continuation of the deliberate, cold-blooded execution of prisoners at Ver-

6 Excellent on this matter, as on everything else concerning the Commune, is the work of the late and dearly missed Maurice Choury, *La Commune au Coeur de Paris* (Paris: Editions Sociales, 1970).

sailles, proven by a note in the *Journal Officiel,* these prisoners were spared and were only killed on May 26, in the rue Haxo, despite the opposition of Varlin, Serailler and Jules Vallès, by a crowd which truly had cause to do so! The "massacre on rue Haxo" photograph which gave so much pleasure to the reactionary press, is a forgery concocted on the request of General Appert, an officer charged later by Versailles to examine the Commune and its so-called "crimes."

This same General Appert was nonetheless forced to admit that there were 17,000 dead on the side of the Communards and the Parisian population at large (there were doubtless more than 30,000) and 873 dead in the Versailles army. The latter killed more Parisians in eight days than did the Prussians during the entire war of 1870–71. The Terror of 1793, minutely examined by royalist historians, found at the most 2,600 victims in fifteen months.

The legal repression was as implacable. There were 50,000 arrests. The prisoners, penned at Satory, continued to die there of illness or from the abuse of their jailers. The courts-martial sat up to 1873, and as late as 1874 there was one execution. Out of 270 sentenced to death there were twenty-six executions, because fortunately there were many escapes. But, conversely, how many *déportés* perished in their floating hulk prisons on the Atlantic or before arriving in New Caledonia! Sick prisoners were thrown overboard; "the sharks must eat," said their cruel guards. Many Communards found refuge in Switzerland, Belgium and England, and an amnesty, called for by progressive republicans, only became really effective in 1880.

The blood of the martyrs had not flowed in vain. Those who believed they had destroyed the French working-class movement had given it more reason to fight, and more experience. In 1879 the French Workers' Party was founded. And as for the international movement, Lenin was able to say that the Commune had done more to advance it than a hundred theoretical programs or party manifestos. But this does not mean that we should hide its weaknesses or mistakes. The major reasons for these inadequacies have their roots in the period during which the Commune took place. If the historian has the duty to uncover them, he also must explain them. And above all he must restore to the Commune its essence, which has been so greatly distorted by the ideologues of the privileged classes.

Finally, one must conclude with the words of one of the most courageous Communards, Léon Frankel, who wrote in 1887:

> The great ideal which inspired the warriors of the Commune will continue to be spread until the day when it will lead the oppressed to final victory. For us, March 18 heralds a new world.

13

V. I. Lenin: The Historical Significance of the Paris Commune*

1. What Made the Communards' Attempt Heroic?

It is well known that in the autumn of 1870, a few months before the Commune, Marx warned the Paris workers that any attempt to overthrow the government would be the folly of despair. But when, in March 1871, a decisive battle was *forced* upon the workers and they accepted it, when the uprising had become a fact, Marx greeted the proletarian revolution with the greatest enthusiasm, in spite of unfavorable auguries. Marx did not persist in the pedantic attitude of condemning an "untimely" movement as did the ill-famed Russian renegade from Marxism, Plekhanov, who in November 1905 wrote encouragingly about the workers' and peasants' struggle, but after December 1905 cried, liberal fashion: "They should not have taken up arms."

Marx, however, was not only enthusiastic about the heroism of the Communards, who, as he expressed it, "stormed heaven." Although the mass revolutionary movement did not achieve its aim, he regarded it as a historic experience of enormous importance, as a certain advance of the world proletarian

* V. I. Lenin, "The State and Revolution: Experiences of the Paris Commune of 1871, Marx's Analysis," in *Collected Works*, Vol. 25 (London: Lawrence & Wishart, 1964), pp. 413–432. By permission.

revolution, as a practical step that was more important than hundreds of programs and arguments. Marx endeavored to analyze this experiment, to draw tactical lessons from it and re-examine his theory in the light of it.

The only "correction" Marx thought it necessary to make to the *Communist Manifesto* he made on the basis of the revolutionary experience of the Paris Communards.

The last preface to the new German edition of the *Communist Manifesto,* signed by both its authors, is dated June 24, 1872. In this preface the authors, Karl Marx and Frederick Engels, say that the program of the *Communist Manifesto* "has in some details become out-of-date," and they go on to say:

> ". . . One thing especially was proved by the Commune, viz., that 'the working class cannot simply lay hold of the ready-made state machinery and wield it for its own purposes.' . . ."

The authors took the words that are in single quotation marks in this passage from Marx's book, *The Civil War in France.*

Thus, Marx and Engels regarded one principal and fundamental lesson of the Paris Commune as being of such enormous importance that they introduced it as an important correction into the *Communist Manifesto.*

Most characteristically, it is this important correction that has been distorted by the opportunists, and its meaning probably is not known to nine-tenths, if not ninety-nine-hundredths, of the readers of the *Communist Manifesto.* We shall deal with this distortion more fully farther on, in a chapter devoted specially to distortions. Here it will be sufficient to note that the current, vulgar "interpretation" of Marx's famous statement just quoted is that Marx here allegedly emphasizes the idea of slow development in contradistinction to the seizure of power, and so on.

As a matter of fact, *the exact opposite is the case.* Marx's idea is that the working class must *break up, smash* the "ready-made state machinery," and not confine itself merely to laying hold of it.

On April 12, 1871, i.e., just at the time of the Commune, Marx wrote to Kugelmann:

"If you look up the last chapter of my *Eighteenth Brumaire,* you will find that I declare that the next attempt of the French Revolution will be no longer, as before, to transfer the bureaucratic-military machine from one hand to another, but to *smash* it [Marx's italics—the original is *zerbrechen*], and this is the precondition for every real people's revolution on the Continent. And this is what our heroic Party comrades in Paris are attempting." (*Neue Zeit,* Vol. XX, 1, 1901–02, p. 709. . . .)

The words, "to smash the bureaucratic-military machine," briefly express the principal lesson of Marxism regarding the tasks of the proletariat during a revolution in relation to the state. And it is this lesson that has been not only completely ignored, but positively distorted by the prevailing, Kautskyite, "interpretation" of Marxism!

As for Marx's reference to *The Eighteenth Brumaire,* we have quoted the relevant passage in full above.

It is interesting to note, in particular, two points in the above-quoted argument of Marx. First, he restricts his conclusion to the Continent. This was understandable in 1871, when Britain was still the model of a purely capitalist country, but without a militarist clique and, to a considerable degree, without a bureaucracy. Marx therefore excluded Britain, where a revolution, even a people's revolution, then seemed possible, and indeed was possible, *without* the precondition of destroying the "ready-made state machinery."

Today, in 1917, at the time of the first great imperialist war, this restriction made by Marx is no longer valid. Both Britain and America, the biggest and the last representatives—in the whole world—of Anglo-Saxon "liberty," in the sense that they had no militarist cliques and bureaucracy, have completely sunk into the all-European filthy, bloody morass of bureaucratic-military institutions which subordinate everything to themselves, and suppress everything. Today, in Britain and America, too, "the precondition for every real people's revolution" is the *smashing,* the *destruction* of the "ready-made state machinery" (made and brought up to "European," general imperialist, perfection in those countries in the years 1914–17).

Secondly, particular attention should be paid to Marx's extremely profound remark that the destruction of the bureaucratic-military state machine is "the precondition for every real *people's* revolution." This idea of a "people's" revolution seems strange coming from Marx, so that the Russian Plekhanovites and Mensheviks, those followers of Struve who wish to be regarded as Marxists, might possibly declare such an expression to be a "slip of the pen" on Marx's part. They have reduced Marxism to such a state of wretchedly liberal distortion that nothing exists for them beyond the antithesis between bourgeois revolution and proletarian revolution, and even this antithesis they interpret in an utterly lifeless way.

If we take the revolutions of the twentieth century as examples we shall, of course, have to admit that the Portuguese and the Turkish revolutions are both bourgeois revolutions. Neither of them, however, is a "people's" revolution, since in neither does the mass of the people, their vast majority, come out actively, independently, with their own economic and political demands to any noticeable degree. By contrast, although the Russian bourgeois revolution of 1905–07 displayed no such "brilliant" successes as at times fell to the Portuguese and Turkish revolutions, it was undoubtedly a "real people's" revolution, since the mass of the people, their majority, the very lowest social groups, crushed by oppression and exploitation, rose independently and stamped on the entire course of the revolution the imprint of *their* own demands, *their* attempts to build in their own way a new society in place of the old society that was being destroyed.

In Europe, in 1871, the proletariat did not constitute the majority of the people in any country on the Continent. A "people's" revolution, one actually sweeping the majority into its stream, could be such only if it embraced both the proletariat and the peasants. These two classes then constituted the "people." These two classes are united by the fact that the "bureaucratic-military state machine" oppresses, crushes, exploits them. To *smash* this machine, *to break it up,* is truly in the interest of the "people," of their majority, of the workers and most of the peasants, is "the precondition" for a free alliance of the poor peasants and the proletarians, whereas without such an alliance democracy is unstable and socialist transformation is impossible.

As is well known, the Paris Commune was actually working its way toward such an alliance, although it did not reach its goal owing to a number of circumstances, internal and external.

Consequently, in speaking of a "real people's revolution," Marx, without in the least discounting the special features of the petty bourgeoisie (he spoke a great deal about them and often), took strict account of the actual balance of class forces in most of the continental countries of Europe in 1871. On the other hand, he stated that the "smashing" of the state machine was required by the interests of both the workers and the peasants, that it united them, that it placed before them the common task of removing the "parasite" and of replacing it by something new.

By what exactly?

2. What Is to Replace the Smashed State Machine?

In 1847, in the *Communist Manifesto,* Marx's answer to this question was as yet a purely abstract one; to be exact, it was an answer that indicated the tasks, but not the ways of accomplishing them. The answer given in the *Communist Manifesto* was that this machine was to be replaced by "the proletariat organized as the ruling class," by the "winning of the battle of democracy."

Marx did not indulge in utopias; he expected the *experience* of the mass movement to provide the reply to the question as to the specific forms this organization of the proletariat as the ruling class would assume and as to the exact manner in which this organization would be combined with the most complete, most consistent "winning of the battle of democracy."

Marx subjected the experience of the Commune, meager as it was, to the most careful analysis in *The Civil War in France.* Let us quote the most important passages of this work.

Originating from the Middle Ages, there developed in the nineteenth century "the centralized state power, with its ubiquitous organs of standing army, police, bureaucracy, clergy, and judicature." With the development of class antagonisms between capital and labor, "state power assumed more and more the character of a public force for the suppression of the working class, of a machine of class rule. After every revolution, which marks an advance in the class struggle, the purely coercive character of the state power stands out in bolder and bolder relief." After the revolution of 1848–49, state power became "the national war instrument of capital against labor." The Second Empire consolidated this.

"The direct antithesis to the empire was the Commune." It was the "specific form" of "a republic that was not only to remove the monarchical form of class rule, but class rule itself. . . ."

What was this "specific" form of the proletarian, socialist republic? What was the state it began to create?

". . . The first decree of the Commune . . . was the suppression of the standing army, and its replacement by the armed people. . . ."

This demand now figures in the program of every party calling itself socialist. The real worth of their programs, however, is best shown by the behavior of our Socialist-Revolutionaries and Mensheviks, who, right after the revolution of February 27, actually refused to carry out this demand!

"The Commune was formed of the municipal councilors, chosen by universal suffrage in the various wards of Paris, responsible and revocable at any time. The majority of its members were naturally working men, or acknowledged representatives of the working class. . . . The police, which until then had been the instrument of the Government, was at once stripped of its political attributes, and turned into the responsible and at all times revocable instrument of the Commune. So were the officials of all other branches of the administration. From the members of the Commune downwards, public service had to be done at *workmen's wages*. The privileges and the representation allowances of the high dignitaries of state disappeared along with the dignitaries themselves. . . . Having once got rid of the standing army and the police, the instruments of the physical force of the old Government, the Commune proceeded at once to break the instrument of spiritual suppression, the power of the priests. . . . The judicial functionaries lost that sham independence . . . they were thenceforward to be elective, responsible, and revocable. . . ."

The Commune, therefore, appears to have replaced the smashed state machine "only" by fuller democracy: abolition of the standing army; all officials to be elected and subject to recall. But as a matter of fact this "only" signifies a gigantic replacement of certain institutions by other institutions of a fundamentally different type. This is exactly a case of "quantity being transformed into quality": democracy, introduced as fully and consistently as is at all conceivable, is transformed from bourgeois into proletarian democracy; from the state (= a special force for the suppression of a particular class) into something which is no longer the state proper.

It is still necessary to suppress the bourgeoisie and crush their resistance. This was particularly necessary for the Commune; and one of the reasons for its defeat was that it did not do this with sufficient determination. The organ of suppression, however, is here the majority of the population, and not a minority, as was always the case under slavery, serfdom and wage slavery. And since the majority of the people *itself* suppresses its oppressors, a "special force" for suppression *is no longer necessary!* In this sense, the state *begins to wither away*. Instead of the special institutions of a privileged minority (privileged officialdom, the chiefs of the standing army), the majority itself can directly fulfill all these functions, and the more the functions of state power are performed by the people as a whole, the less need there is for the existence of this power.

In this connection, the following measures of the Commune,

emphasized by Marx, are particularly noteworthy: the abolition of all representation allowances, and of all monetary privileges to officials, the reduction of the remuneration of *all* servants of the state to the level of *"workmen's wages."* This shows more clearly than anything else the *turn* from bourgeois to proletarian democracy, from the democracy of the oppressors to that of the oppressed classes, from the state as a *"special force"* for the suppression of a particular class to the suppression of the oppressors by the *general force* of the majority of the people— the workers and the peasants. And it is on this particularly striking point, perhaps the most important as far as the problem of the state is concerned, that the ideas of Marx have been most completely ignored! In popular commentaries, the number of which is legion, this is not mentioned. The thing done is to keep silent about it as if it were a piece of old-fashioned "naïveté," just as Christians, after their religion had been given the status of a state religion, "forgot" the "naïveté" of primitive Christianity with its democratic revolutionary spirit.

The reduction of the remuneration of high state officials seems to be "simply" a demand of naïve, primitive democracy. One of the "founders" of modern opportunism, the ex-Social-Democrat Eduard Bernstein, has more than once repeated the vulgar bourgeois jeers at "primitive" democracy. Like all opportunists, and like the present Kautskyites, he did not understand at all that, first of all, the transition from capitalism to socialism is *impossible* without a certain "reversion" to "primitive" democracy (for how else can the majority, and then the whole population without exception, proceed to discharge state functions?); and that, secondly, "primitive democracy" based on capitalism and capitalist culture is not the same as primitive democracy in prehistoric or pre-capitalist times. Capitalist culture has *created* large-scale production, factories, railways, the postal service, telephones, etc., and *on this basis* the great majority of the functions of the old "state power" have become so simplified and can be reduced to such exceedingly simple operations of registration, filing and checking that they can be easily performed by every literate person, can quite easily be performed for ordinary "workmen's wages," and that these functions can (and must) be stripped of every shadow of privilege, of every semblance of "official grandeur."

All officials, without exception, elected and subject to recall *at any time,* their salaries reduced to the level of ordinary "workmen's wages"—these simple and "self-evident" democratic measures, while completely uniting the interests of the workers and the majority of the peasants, at the same time serve as a bridge leading from capitalism to socialism. These measures concern the reorganization of the state, the purely political reorganization of society; but, of course, they acquire their full meaning and significance only in connection with the "expropriation of the expropriators" either being accomplished or in preparation, i.e., with the transformation of capitalist private ownership of the means of production into social ownership.

> "The Commune," Marx wrote, "made that catchword of all bourgeois revolutions, cheap government, a reality, by abolishing the two greatest sources of expenditure—the army and the officialdom."

From the peasants, as from other sections of the petty bourgeoisie, only an insignificant few "rise to the top," "get on in the world" in the bourgeois sense, i.e., become either well-to-do, bourgeois, or officials in secure and privileged positions. In every capitalist country where there are peasants (as there are in most capitalist countries), the vast majority of them are oppressed by the government and long for its overthrow, long for "cheap" government. This can be achieved *only* by the proletariat; and by achieving it, the proletariat at the same time takes a step towards the socialist reorganization of the state.

3. Abolition of Parliamentarism

> "The Commune," Marx wrote, "was to be a working, not a parliamentary, body, executive and legislative at the same time . . . .

> "Instead of deciding once in three or six years which member of the ruling class was to represent and repress [ver- und zertreten] the people in parliament, universal suffrage was to serve the people constituted in communes, as individual suf-

frage serves every other employer in the search for workers,
foremen and accountants for his business."

Owing to the prevalence of social-chauvinism and opportunism, this remarkable criticism of parliamentarism, made in
1871, also belongs now to the "forgotten words" of Marxism.
The professional Cabinet Ministers and parliamentarians, the
traitors to the proletariat and the "practical" socialists of our
day, have left all criticism of parliamentarism to the anarchists,
and, on this wonderfully reasonable ground, they denounce *all*
criticism of parliamentarism as "anarchism"!! It is not surprising that the proletariat of the "advanced" parliamentary countries, disgusted with such "socialists" as the Scheidemanns,
Davids, Legiens, Sembats, Renaudels, Hendersons, Vanderveldes, Staunings, Brantings, Bissolatis and Co., has been with
increasing frequency giving its sympathies to anarcho-syndical-
ism, in spite of the fact that the latter is merely the twin brother
of opportunism.

For Marx, however, revolutionary dialectics was never the
empty fashionable phrase, the toy rattle, which Plekhanov,
Kautsky and others have made of it. Marx knew how to break
with anarchism ruthlessly for its inability to make use even of the
"pigsty" of bourgeois parliamentarism, especially when the
situation was obviously not revolutionary; but at the same time
he knew how to subject parliamentarism to genuinely revolutionary proletarian criticism.

To decide once every few years which member of the ruling
class is to repress and crush the people through parliament—
this is the real essence of bourgeois parliamentarism, not only in
parliamentary-constitutional monarchies, but also in the most
democratic republics.

But if we deal with the question of the state, and if we
consider parliamentarism as one of the institutions of the state,
from the point of view of the tasks of the proletariat in *this*
field, what is the way out of parliamentarism? How can it be
dispensed with?

Once again we must say: the lessons of Marx, based on the
study of the Commune, have been so completely forgotten that

the present-day "Social-Democrat" (i.e., present-day traitor to socialism) really cannot understand any criticism of parliamentarism other than anarchist or reactionary criticism.

The way out of parliamentarism is not, of course, the abolition of representative institutions and the elective principle, but the conversion of the representative institutions from talking shops into "working" bodies. "The Commune was to be a working, not a parliamentary, body, executive and legislative at the same time."

"A working, not a parliamentary, body"—this is a blow straight from the shoulder at the present-day parliamentarians and parliamentary "lap dogs" of Social-Democracy! Take any parliamentary country, from America to Switzerland, from France to Britain, Norway and so forth—in these countries the real business of "state" is performed behind the scenes and is carried on by the departments, chancelleries and General Staffs. Parliament is given up to talk for the special purpose of fooling the "common people." This is so true that even in the Russian republic, a bourgeois-democratic republic, all these sins of parliamentarism came out at once, even before it managed to set up a real parliament. The heroes of rotten philistinism, such as the Skobelevs and Tseretelis, the Chernovs and Avksentyevs, have even succeeded in polluting the Soviets after the fashion of the most disgusting bourgeois parliamentarism, in converting them into mere talking shops. In the Soviets, the "socialist" Ministers are fooling the credulous rustics with phrase-mongering and resolutions. In the government itself a sort of permanent shuffle is going on in order that, on the one hand, as many Socialist-Revolutionaries and Mensheviks as possible may in turn get near the "pie," the lucrative and honorable posts, and that, on the other hand, the "attention" of the people may be "engaged." Meanwhile the chancelleries and army staffs "do" the business of "state."

Dyelo Naroda, the organ of the ruling Socialist-Revolutionary Party, recently admitted in a leading article—with the matchless frankness of people of "good society," in which "all" are engaged in political prostitution—that even in the ministries headed by the "socialists" (save the mark!), the whole bureaucratic apparatus is in fact unchanged, is working in the old way and quite "freely" sabotaging revolutionary measures! Even without this admission, does not the actual history of the participation of the Socialist-Revolutionaries and Mensheviks in the government prove this? It is noteworthy, however, that in the ministerial company of the Cadets, the Chernovs, Rusanovs, Zenzinovs and the other editors of *Dyelo Naroda* have so completely lost all sense of shame as to brazenly assert, as if it were a mere bagatelle, that in "their" ministries everything is unchanged!! Revolutionary-democratic phrases to gull the rural Simple Simons, and bureaucracy and red tape to "gladden the hearts" of the capitalists—that is the *essence* of the "honest" coalition.

The Commune substitutes for the venal and rotten parliamentarism of bourgeois society institutions in which freedom of opinion and discussion does not degenerate into deception, for the parliamentarians themselves have to work, have to execute their own laws, have themselves to test the results achieved in reality, and to account directly to their constituents. Representative institutions remain, but there is *no* parliamentarism here as a special system, as the division of labor between the legislative and the executive, as a privileged position for the deputies. We cannot imagine democracy, even proletarian democracy, without representative institutions, but we can and *must* imagine democracy without parliamentarism, if criticism of bourgeois society is not mere words for us, if the desire to overthrow the rule of the bourgeoisie is our earnest and sincere desire, and not a mere "election" cry for catching workers' votes, as it is with the Mensheviks and Socialist-Revolutionaries, and also the Scheidemanns and Legiens, the Sembats and Vanderveldes.

It is extremely instructive to note that, in speaking of the functions of *those* officials who are necessary for the Commune and for proletarian democracy, Marx compares them to the workers of "every other employer," that is, of the ordinary capitalist enterprise, with its "workers, foremen and accountants."

There is no trace of utopianism in Marx, in the sense that he made up or invented a "new" society. No, he studied the *birth* of the new society *out of* the old, and the forms of transition from the latter to the former, as a natural-historical process. He examined the actual experience of a mass proletarian movement and tried to draw practical lessons from it. He "learned" from the Commune, just as all the great revolutionary thinkers learned unhesitatingly from the experience of great movements of the oppressed classes, and never addressed them with pedantic "homilies" (such as Plekhanov's: "They should not have taken up arms" or Tsereteli's: "A class must limit itself").

Abolishing the bureaucracy at once, everywhere and completely, is out of the question. It is a utopia. But to *smash* the old bureaucratic machine at once and to begin immediately to construct a new one that will make possible the gradual abolition of all bureaucracy—this is *not* a utopia, it is the experience of the Commune, the direct and immediate task of the revolutionary proletariat.

Capitalism simplifies the functions of "state" administration; it makes it possible to cast "bossing" aside and to confine the whole matter to the organization of the proletarians (as the ruling class), which will hire "workers, foremen and accountants" in the name of the whole of society.

We are not utopians, we do not "dream" of dispensing *at once* with all administration, with all subordination. These anarchist dreams, based upon incomprehension of the tasks of the proletarian dictatorship, are totally alien to Marxism, and, as a matter of fact, serve only to postpone the socialist revolution until people are different. No, we want the socialist revolution with people as they are now, with people who cannot dispense with subordination, control and "foremen and accountants."

The subordination, however, must be to the armed vanguard of all the exploited and working people, i.e., to the proletariat. A beginning can and must be made at once, overnight, to replace the specific "bossing" of state officials by the simple functions of "foremen and accountants," functions which are already fully within the ability of the average town dweller and can well be performed for "workmen's wages."

We, the workers, shall organize large-scale production on the basis of what capitalism has already created, relying on our own experience as workers, establishing strict, iron discipline backed up by the state power of the armed workers. We shall reduce the role of state officials to that of simply carrying out our instructions as responsible, revocable, modestly paid "foremen and accountants" (of course, with the aid of technicians of all sorts, types and degrees). This is *our* proletarian task, this is what we can and must *start* with in accomplishing the proletarian revolution. Such a beginning, on the basis of large-scale production, will of itself lead to the gradual "withering away" of all bureaucracy, to the gradual creation of an order—an order without inverted commas, an order bearing no similarity to wage slavery—an order under which the functions of control and accounting, becoming more and more simple, will be performed by each in turn, will then become a habit and will finally die out as the *special* functions of a special section of the population.

A witty German Social-Democrat of the seventies of the last century called the *postal service* an example of the socialist economic system. This is very true. At present the postal service is a business organized on the lines of a state-*capitalist* monopoly. Imperialism is gradually transforming all trusts into organizations of a similar type, in which, standing over the "common" people, who are overworked and starved, one has the same bourgeois bureaucracy. But the mechanism of social management is here already to hand. Once we have overthrown the capitalists, crushed the resistance of these exploiters with the iron hand of the armed workers, and smashed the bureaucratic machine of the modern state, we shall have a splendidly-equipped mechanism, freed from the "parasite," a mechanism which can very well be set going by the united workers themselves, who will hire technicians, foremen and accountants, and pay them *all,* as indeed *all* "state" officials in general, workmen's wages. Here is a concrete, practical task which can immediately be fulfilled in relation to all trusts, a task whose fulfillment will rid the working people of exploitation, a task which takes account of what the Commune had already begun to practice (particularly in building up the state).

To organize the *whole* economy on the lines of the postal service so that the technicians, foremen and accountants, as well as *all* officials, shall receive salaries no higher than "a workman's wage," all under the control and leadership of the armed proletariat—this is our immediate aim. This is the state and this is the economic foundation we need. This is what will bring about the abolition of parliamentarism and the preservation of representative institutions. This is what will rid the laboring classes of the bourgeoisie's prostitution of these institutions.

4. Organization of National Unity

"In a brief sketch of national organization which the Commune had no time to develop, it states explicitly that the Commune was to be the political form of even the smallest village. . . ." The communes were to elect the "National Delegation" in Paris.

". . . The few but important functions which would still remain for a central government were not to be suppressed, as has been deliberately mis-stated, but were to be transferred to communal, i.e., strictly responsible, officials.

". . . National unity was not to be broken, but, on the contrary, organized by the communal constitution; it was to become a reality by the destruction of state power which posed as the embodiment of that unity yet wanted to be independent of, and superior to, the nation, on whose body it was but a parasitic excrescence. While the merely repressive organs of the old governmental power were to be amputated, its legitimate functions were to be wrested from an authority claiming the right to stand above society, and restored to the responsible servants of society."

The extent to which the opportunists of present-day Social-Democracy have failed—perhaps it would be more true to say, have refused—to understand these observations of Marx is best shown by that book of Herostratean fame of the renegade Bernstein, *The Premises of Socialism and the Tasks of the Social-Democrats*. It is in connection with the above passage from Marx that Bernstein wrote that "as far as its political content is concerned," this program "displays, in all its essential features, the greatest similarity to the federalism of Proudhon. . . . In spite of all the other points of difference between Marx and the 'petty-bourgeois' Proudhon [Bernstein places the word "petty-bourgeois" in inverted commas to make it sound ironical] on these points, their lines of reasoning run as close as could be." Of course, Bernstein continues, the importance of the municipalities is growing, but "it seems doubtful to me whether the first job of democracy would be such a dissolution [Auflösung] of the modern states and such a complete transformation [Umwandlung] of their organization as is visualized by Marx and Proudhon (the formation of a National Assembly from delegates of the provincial or district assemblies, which, in their turn, would consist of delegates from the communes), so that consequently the previous mode of national representation would disappear." (Bernstein, *Premises,* German edition, 1899, pp. 134 and 136.)

To confuse Marx's views on the "destruction of state power, a parasitic excrescence," with Proudhon's federalism is positively monstrous! But it is no accident, for it never occurs to the opportunist that Marx does not speak here at all about federalism as opposed to centralism, but about smashing the old, bourgeois state machine which exists in all bourgeois countries.

The only thing that does occur to the opportunist is what he sees around him, in an environment of petty-bourgeois philistinism and "reformist'" stagnation, namely, only "municipalities"! The opportunist has even grown out of the habit of thinking about proletarian revolution.

It is ridiculous. But the remarkable thing is that nobody argued with Bernstein on this point. Bernstein has been refuted by many, especially by Plekhanov in Russian literature and by Kautsky in European literature, but neither of them has said *anything* about *this* distortion of Marx by Bernstein.

The opportunist has so much forgotten how to think in a revolutionary way and to dwell on revolution that he attributes "federalism" to Marx, whom he confuses with the founder of anarchism, Proudhon. As for Kautsky and Plekhanov, who claim to be orthodox Marxists and defenders of the theory of revolutionary Marxism, they are silent on this point! Here is one of the roots of the extreme vulgarization of the views on the difference between Marxism and anarchism, which is characteristic of both the Kautskyites and the opportunists, and which we shall discuss again later.

There is not a trace of federalism in Marx's above-quoted observations on the experience of the Commune. Marx agreed with Proudhon on the very point that the opportunist Bernstein did not see. Marx disagreed with Proudhon on the very point on which Bernstein found a similarity between them.

Marx agreed with Proudhon in that they both stood for the "smashing" of the modern state machine. Neither the opportunists nor the Kautskyites wish to see the similarity of views on this point between Marxism and anarchism (both Proudhon and Bakunin) because this is where they have departed from Marxism.

Marx disagreed both with Proudhon and Bakunin precisely on the question of federalism (not to mention the dictatorship of the proletariat). Federalism as a principle follows logically from the petty-bourgeois views of anarchism. Marx was a centralist. There is no departure whatever from centralism in his observations just quoted. Only those who are imbued with the philistine "superstitious belief" in the state can mistake the destruction of the bourgeois state machine for the destruction of centralism!

Now if the proletariat and the poor peasants take state power into their own hands, organize themselves quite freely in communes, and *unite* the action of all the communes in striking at capital, in crushing the resistance of the capitalists, and in transferring the privately-owned railways, factories, land and so on to the *entire* nation, to the whole of society, won't that be centralism? Won't that be the most consistent democratic centralism and, moreover, proletarian centralism?

Bernstein simply cannot conceive of the possibility of voluntary centralism, of the voluntary amalgamation of the communes into a nation, of the voluntary fusion of the proletarian communes, for the purpose of destroying bourgeois rule and the bourgeois state machine. Like all philistines, Bernstein pictures centralism as something which can be imposed and maintained solely from above, and solely by the bureaucracy and the military clique.

As though foreseeing that his views might be distorted, Marx expressly emphasized that the charge that the Commune had wanted to destroy national unity, to abolish the central authority, was a deliberate fraud. Marx purposely used the words: "National unity was . . . to be organized," so as to oppose conscious, democratic, proletarian centralism to bourgeois, military, bureaucratic centralism.

But there are none so deaf as those who will not hear. And the very thing the opportunists of present-day Social-Democracy do not want to hear about is the destruction of state power, the amputation of the parasitic excrescence.

5. Abolition of the Parasite State

We have already quoted Marx's words on this subject, and we must now supplement them.

". . . It is generally the fate of new historical creations," he wrote, "to be mistaken for the counterpart of older and even defunct forms of social life, to which they may bear a certain likeness. Thus, this new Commune, which breaks [*bricht*, smashes] the modern state power, has been regarded as a revival of the medieval communes . . . as a federation of small states (as Montesquieu and the Girondins visualized it) . . . as an exaggerated form of the old struggle against over-centralization. . . .

". . . The Communal Constitution would have restored to the social body all the forces hitherto absorbed by that parasitic excrescence, the 'state,' feeding upon and hampering the free movement of society. By this one act it would have initiated the regeneration of France. . . .

". . . The Communal Constitution would have brought rural producers under the intellectual lead of the central towns of their districts, and there secured to them, in the town working men, the natural trustees of their interests. The very existence of the Commune involved, as a matter of course, local self-government, but no longer as a counterpoise to state power, now become superfluous."

"Breaking state power," which was a "parasitic excrescence"; its "amputation," its "smashing"; "state power, now become superfluous"—these are the expressions Marx used in regard to the state when appraising and analyzing the experience of the Commune.

All this was written a little less than half a century ago; and now one has to engage in excavations, as it were, in order to bring undistorted Marxism to the knowledge of the mass of the people. The conclusions drawn from the observation of the last great revolution which Marx lived through were forgotten just when the time for the next great proletarian revolutions had arrived.

". . . The multiplicity of interpretations to which the Commune has been subjected, and the multiplicity of interests which expressed themselves in it show that it was a thoroughly flexible political form, while all previous forms of government had been essentially repressive. Its true secret was this: it was essentially *a working-class government,* the result of the struggle of the producing against the appropriating class, the political form at last discovered under which the economic emancipation of labor could be accomplished. . . .

"Except on this last condition, the Communal Constitution would have been an impossibility and a delusion. . . ."

The utopians busied themselves with "discovering" political forms under which the socialist transformation of society was to take place. The anarchists dismissed the question of political forms altogether. The opportunists of present-day Social-Democracy accepted the bourgeois political forms of the parliamentary democratic state as the limit which should not be overstepped; they battered their foreheads praying before this "model," and denounced as anarchism every desire to *break* these forms.

Marx deduced from the whole history of socialism and the political struggle that the state was bound to disappear, and that the transitional form of its disappearance (the transition from the transitional form of its disappearance (the transition from state to non-state) would be the "proletariat organized as the ruling class." Marx, however, did not set out to *discover* the political *forms* of this future stage. He limited himself to carefully observing French history, to analyzing it, and to drawing the conclusion to which the year 1851 had led, namely, that matters were moving towards the *destruction* of the bourgeois state machine.

And when the mass revolutionary movement of the proletariat burst forth, Marx, in spite of its failure, in spite of its short life and patent weakness, began to study the forms it had *discovered*.

The Commune is the form "at last discovered" by the proletarian revolution, under which the economic emancipation of labor can take place.

The Commune is the first attempt by a proletarian revolution to *smash* the bourgeois state machine; and it is the political form "at last discovered," by which the smashed state machine can and must be *replaced*.

We shall see further on that the Russian revolutions of 1905 and 1917, in different circumstances and under different conditions, continue the work of the Commune and confirm Marx's brilliant historical analysis.

V.

TWENTIETH-CENTURY REVOLUTIONS: RUSSIAN, CHINESE AND VIETNAMESE

14

E. H. Carr: The Russian Revolution of 1917*

I shall interpret the term "the Russian revolution" broadly. My concern is not so much with the ten days that shook the world in 1917 as with the world-shaking process of which they were the expression and sometimes the starting-point. Revolution automatically raises the familiar issue of continuity and change in history. It is a commonplace that no continuous situation, however static, is exempt from change, and that no change, however revolutionary, wholly breaks the continuity. But two observations are in point here. The first is that conservatives tend to dwell on the element of continuity—Tocqueville or Albert Sorel and the French revolution; in its extreme form, this attitude issues in the belief that revolutions have no fundamental significance, and represent merely the substitution of one ruling group or elite for another. Radicals, on the other hand, insist on the element of sudden and fundamental change— Engels and the leap from the kingdom of necessity into that of freedom, or Mao and the great leap forward. The second observation is that the elements of continuity in any revolution are in the nature of things those pertaining to a particular

* E. H. Carr, "The Russian Revolution: Its Place in History," in *The October Revolution: Before and After* (New York: Alfred A. Knopf, 1969), pp. 1–33. By permission.

E. H. Carr is the author of *The Bolshevik Revolution, The New Society, What Is History?* and many other important works.

country, and the elements of wider or universal application are those of change. Since my interest on the present occasion is in the universal aspects of the Russian revolution, I shall emphasize the elements of change inherent in it, and not the elements of continuity which, in the context of Russian history, it undoubtedly displays. I shall not attempt to suggest that all the major changes which I wish to discuss were directly produced by the Russian revolution. Of these changes the revolution was in part cause, in part result, and in part symptom or symbol. All three intertwined relations constitute the "significance" of the revolution of 1917, and help to explain its place in history.

The concept of revolution comes into modern history with the English revolution of the seventeenth century. For a thousand years, dissent, unrest, political and social change, had expressed themselves in religious terms. The English seventeenth-century revolution had marked religious overtones; the French revolution was the first purely secular revolution. But, when English writers called the events of 1688 "the glorious revolution," and then extended the term backwards to the still more dramatic events of forty years earlier, they were thinking primarily of the achievement of civil liberty, by which they meant a society based on the legally secured rights of individual citizens and not on monarchical authority, divinely or humanly ordained. In the turbulent middle years of the seventeenth century another idea had made a tentative appearance—the principle, broadly speaking, that one man is as good as another, and has the same rights as another—what we should now call the principle of "social justice." This idea seems to have flourished only in a few obscure and fanatical sects, and was safely smuggled out of sight in the glorious revolution. But it never entirely disappeared from the underworld of English history, and survived to become a dominant idea in all modern revolutions.

The French revolution, which stood before 1917 as the great prototype of revolution, was the first total and violent overthrow in modern times of a social and political order: this explains the immense impact it has made on modern history. It made this impact in three principal ways.

In the first place, the French revolution made liberty and equality essential rights of man and accepted goals of political action. The conception of the rights of the individual citizen was borrowed from the English revolution of 1688. English political theory and practice enjoyed an immense prestige among the intellectuals of eighteenth-century France. But the French revolution went beyond the rather simple ideas of political and civil liberty propounded in 1688. The idea of social justice, dimly adumbrated in seventeenth-century England, found more specific expression in the egalitarian ideology of the revolutionaries and, in particular, in the "conspiracy" of Babeuf; and, though these demands were once more crushed when they took concrete form, the idea of equality could no longer be expunged from the revolutionary trinity. The French revolution had deeper social and economic roots than the English revolution, and more far-reaching economic and social consequences. In a phrase said to have been coined by Mirabeau and quoted by Napoleon: "Ce n'est pas la liberté qui fait la révolution, c'est l'égalité."[1]

Secondly, the French revolution—though this was no part of its original design—set its ideals in the future rather than in the past, and thus paved the way for a doctrine of progress. Theorists of the English revolution, true to the age-long habit of looking for authority in the past, had taken the view that what occurred in seventeenth-century England was not a process of innovation, but a reassertion of ancient liberties unjustifiably abrogated by the Stuart kings. The same argument was used a century later by the makers of what used to be called the American revolution; and no less a person than Tom Paine paradoxically attempted to defend the French revolution on precisely the same grounds: "What we now behold may not improperly be called a 'counter-revolution.' Conquest and tyranny, at some earlier period, dispossessed man of his rights, and he is now recovering them."[2] The myth of classical antiquity created by the Renaissance, and still immensely powerful in European eighteenth-century society, formed an anomalous

---

[1] *Annales: Économies, Sociétés, Civilisations*, xiv (1959), 556.
[2] T. Paine, *Rights of Man*, Introduction to Part II.

strand in Jacobin thought and Jacobin oratory. The hopes and the enthusiasms kindled by the revolution superseded and replaced it.[3] Condorcet, more than any other single individual, marked the shift in the golden age of mankind from the past to the future.

Thirdly, the French revolution—here again through its consequences rather than by conscious intention—elevated the concept of productivity to a new and central place in human affairs. In the hierarchical society of the *ancien régime,* the interest of the rulers in economic affairs had been limited to the raising of revenues from their subjects to meet military and administrative needs. From the sixteenth to the eighteenth century, from Machiavelli through Colbert and his successors at the court of Louis XIV to the Prussian cameralists, we can trace the line of slow development from the concept of the administration of the prince's patrimony to that of the administration of the state; and this development was marked by an increasing preoccupation with efficiency in administration. But the ultimate end in view was to meet the financial necessities of the government. It was left for the Physiocrats and Adam Smith to insist that the wealth of nations came not (as the mercantilists had taught) from trade, but from production, to distinguish between outlay of wealth on consumption and outlay on investment to promote further production, and to make the productivity of the whole society the preoccupation of political economy. As Marc Bloch put it: "Toute la doctrine économique du XVIIIe siècle—qui a légué ce tour d'esprit à l'économie 'classique' de l'âge suivant—a été dominée par le souci de la production; et pour la plupart des économistes français du XVIIIe siècle production voulait dire avant tout culture."[4] The influx of wealth into new hands which preceded the French revolution had its original source in trade. But, at the moment when the French revolution was setting the scene for the birth of bourgeois society, the industrial revolution in England was rapidly expanding the sphere of economic activity and altering its

[3] This did not prevent it from retaining its hold on English and German education down to 1914.

[4] *Annales d'Histoire Économique et Sociale* (1930) ii 333–4.

character; in Marxist terms commercial capital was being transformed into industrial capital. Here too, however, the revolutionary cult of liberty had its part to play. The sequel of the French revolution and the industrial revolution was the rise to positions of power and influence of a group of men whose earnings from their individual economic activities provided the foundation of the wealth and power of the state; and the main function of the state was to create and maintain the appropriate conditions of liberty for the untrammeled furtherance of these activities.

When Marx began to elaborate his system in the 1840s, he was the heir to all these revolutionary traditions. Liberty, expressed in Hegelian terms, meant the subordination of necessity to freedom, of blind economic forces to the conscious exercise of human reason; man was to be rescued from the self-alienation to which the existing social order subjected him, and reinstated as a "social being."[5] Equality found its embodiment in his idealization of a proletariat—the class which "has a universal character because its sufferings are universal."[6] Marx fortified the revolutionary faith in progress with faith in history as a meaningful process, and, by combining with it a belief in revolution as "the locomotive of history," created the first theory of revolution. Finally, Marx stood on the shoulders of the Enlightenment thinkers and of the classical economists in treating production as the essential economic activity, to which all other categories were subsidiary:[7] and he was in essence right when he saw the key to the future in the hands of the industrial worker, and treated the individual peasant cultivator of the soil as an obsolescent unit of production. Marx regarded the mode of production as the constitutive element of society; the aim and essence of revolution was to change the mode of production. The *Communist Manifesto* proclaimed it as the aim of the vic-

---

[5] K. Marx, *Economic and Philosophical Manuscripts of 1844*, tr. Milligan (1959) 105.

[6] K. Marx, *Early Writings*, ed. Bottomore (1963) 58.

[7] Marx went further by treating production as *the* specifically human activity [K. Marx and F. Engels, *The Germany Ideology*, Engl. transl. (1965) 164].

torious proletariat "to increase the total of productive forces as rapidly as possible"; and one of the few glimpses afforded by Marx in his later writings of the communist Utopia was that here "the springs of co-operative wealth flow more abundantly."[8] Marx proved the most devastating of all the critics of western bourgeois society, precisely because he was a western thinker rooted in the presuppositions of bourgeois society, which he proceeded to carry to their logical conclusion. Marx's vast synthesis of the French revolution and the industrial revolution embraced the future as well as the past. It was an unfinished revolution, both in the sense that its purposes had been fulfilled only in part, and required to be completed by further revolutionary action, and in the sense that their fulfillment would merely pave the way for further revolutionary aims to be achieved through another revolution. It was in both these senses that Marx once coined, or borrowed, the slogan "permanent revolution." It was appropriate that his name and doctrine should serve as the beacon for the next great revolution.

In the interval between the final elaboration of Marx's system and the next outbreak of revolution much had changed, but much also survived, so that, when we consider the historical significance of the Russian revolution, we see the interaction of a Marxist or pre-Marxist revolutionary tradition and a neo-Marxist or post-Marxist revolutionary environment. One thing which had not changed—or rather had been greatly intensified—was the emphasis on productivity. In the half-century before 1917 applied science was in process of creating a new technology of industrial production; mass production methods revolutionized the economics of industry; the production line and the conveyor belt created new problems of labor organization and discipline. The year 1870 demonstrated that the industrially advanced nation was also the militarily powerful nation; military power, as well as material prosperity, was a function of productivity. The Russian revolution for the first time explicitly proclaimed the goal of increased production, and identified it with socialism: Lenin's remark that socialism meant electrification plus the Soviets was a primitive formulation of this idea. It

8 K. Marx, *Critique of the Gotha Programme* (Engl. transl., n.d.) 14.

was repeated over and over again by Lenin and other Bolsheviks that the test of socialism was that it could organize production more efficiently than capitalism.[9] Modern Marxists have remained faithful to this doctrine, in theory as well as in practice. Among economists, as a distinguished American economist has remarked, "the Marxists . . . have come closest to developing a substantial theory of economic growth."[10]

The Russian revolution looked both backward and forward. It was the peculiarity of Russia's historical condition that she had both the need to catch up with western nineteenth-century achievements and the capacity to pass beyond them. Russia never really belonged to the nineteenth century; the great Russian nineteenth-century literature was a literature of protest not only against Tsarism, but against western bourgeois democracy and bourgeois capitalism. But at the same time the Russian revolution had to incorporate the achievements of the French revolution and of the industrial revolution and to recapitulate the material advances made in the nineteenth century by the west. This was expressed in Marxist terms by saying that the revolution of 1917 was the completion of Russia's bourgeois revolution as well as the inauguration of the socialist revolution. The campaign for industrialization started in the later 1920s aimed at the rapid transformation of the USSR into a modern industrial country—with military power and material prosperity as the twin objectives—through the application of the most advanced industrial technology; American aid and advice were

[9] This did not prevent Lenin from recognizing that "the victory of the workers is impossible without sacrifices, without a temporary worsening of their situation" (*Polnoe Sobranie Sochinenii,* 5th ed. xxxi 233). Bukharin provided a lengthy theoretical justification for the argument: "In revolution the 'husk' of productive relations, i.e. of the organization of human labor is 'exploded' which means, and must mean, a breakdown of the process of production and, consequently, a distinction of productive forces. If this is true—and it is unconditionally true—then it is clear *a priori* that the *proletarian* revolution is accompanied by an extremely steep decline in productive forces, since no revolution has experienced so far-reaching and so profound a break-up of old relations and their re-shaping on new lines." [N. Bukharin, *Ekonomika Perokhodnogo Perioda* (1920) i 95–6.]

[10] E. Domar, *Essays in the Theory of Economic Growth* (1957) 17.

freely sought and obtained in this process, since the United States was technologically the most advanced industrial nation, and hence the most deserving of imitation.

The success of this campaign, which in thirty years, starting from a semi-literate population of primitive peasants, raised the USSR to the position of the second industrial country in the world and the leader in some of the most advanced technological developments, is perhaps the most significant of all the achievements of the Russian revolution. Nor can the achievement be measured purely in material terms. In the time span of half a century, a population almost 60 per cent urban has replaced a population more than 80 per cent peasant; a high standard of general education has replaced near illiteracy; social services have been built up; even in agriculture, which remains the stepchild—or the problem child—of the economy, the tractor has replaced the wooden plough as the characteristic instrument of cultivation. It would be wrong to minimize or condone the sufferings and the horrors inflicted on large sections of the Russian people in the process of transformation. This was a historical tragedy, which has not yet been outlived, or lived down. But it would be idle to deny that the sum of human well-being and human opportunity in Russia today is immeasurably greater than it was fifty years ago. It is this achievement which has most impressed the rest of the world, and has inspired in industrially undeveloped countries the ambition to imitate it. This was the process foreshadowed by Marx in the preface to *Capital:* "The industrially more developed country presents to the industrially less developed country a picture of the latter's future."

The world in which the USSR embarked on industrialization was, however, a very different world from that of Marx. It was not only technology that had advanced. Man's attitude to nature, and his conception of his place in the economic process, had also radically changed. The neo-Marxist world was a world of self-consciousness.[11] The Russian revolution was the first

[11] The terms "self-consciousness" and "consciousness," which are differentiated in Hegel's *Phenomenology*, are used interchangeably by Marx and Engels. Marx appears to prefer "self-consciousness" in his

great revolution in history to be deliberately planned and made. The English revolution received its name *ex post facto* not from the politicians who made it, but from the intellectuals who theorized about it. The men who brought about the French revolution did not seek to make a revolution; the Enlightenment was not in intention a revolutionary movement. The self-declared revolutionaries appeared only after the revolution had begun. The revolution of 1848 was a conscious imitation of the French revolution: this is presumably why Namier called it a "revolution of the intellectuals." But its one positive achievement was to extend to some parts of central Europe (where the peasantry was still a revolutionary force—which it had ceased to be in France, and had not yet become in Russia)[12] some of the results of the French revolution. The Russian revolution was also a revolution of intellectuals, but of intellectuals who not only repeated the past but planned the future, who sought not only to make a revolution, but to analyze and prepare the conditions in which it could be made. It is this element of self-consciousness which gives the Russian revolution its unique place in modern history.

The nature of the change is sometimes explained in terms of the differences between Marx and Lenin, of the transition from Marxism to Leninism. The problem is complicated by the evolution through which Marx himself passed. Marx down to and including the period of the *Communist Manifesto,* when revolution still seemed a live issue in France and Germany, was primarily concerned to propound a program of action: the function of philosophers was not merely to interpret the world, but to change it. Marx, after he settled in London, was primarily concerned to analyze the objective laws of motion of capitalist society and to reveal the causes of its impending overthrow; political activities were the superstructure resting on the economic realities beneath. It was this mature Marxism—the

---

earlier, more Hegelian, writings, and "consciousness" in his later writings, where he was concerned to stress the subordination of "consciousness" to "being"; but the distinction is not rigid.

[12] On this point see G. Lichtheim, *Marxism* (1961) 363.

Marxism of the *Critique of Political Economy* and of *Capital*—
which, with its scientific and determinist emphasis, left its imprint on the rising European workers' movement in the latter
part of the nineteenth century; and Leninism can be depicted as
a return to the earlier Marx.[13] Nevertheless, though nearly
everything that Lenin wrote can be supported by quotations
from Marx, the differences between them were profound and
significant. The differences are sometimes explained as due to
the transplantation of Marxism to Russian soil: Leninism is
Marxism adapted to Russian needs and conditions. There is a
grain of truth in this view. But it is more fruitful to think of the
differences as the product of a difference in time: Leninism is
Marxism of the epoch no longer of objective and inexorable
economic laws, but of the conscious ordering of economic and
social processes for desired ends.

The growth of consciousness begins in the economic sphere.
So long as the individual producer and the small entrepreneur
predominated, nobody seemed to control the economy as a
whole, and the illusion of impersonal laws and processes was
preserved. Marx's world-picture was firmly grounded in the
past. He learned from Adam Smith that individual entrepreneurs
and owners of capital were the essential agents of production in
bourgeois society; and he followed Adam Smith and Hegel in
believing that the activity of individuals, acting in their own
interests, led in virtue of objective laws—the counterpart of the
"hidden hand" or the "cunning of reason"—to results independent of their own will and purpose. Thus nobody consciously
controlled the economic policies; and the product was master of
the men who produced it. This was the realm not of freedom,
but of necessity. The Marxist ideal, as Plekhanov put it, was

[13] Many of Marx's earlier writings which have received much attention in recent Marxist literature were first published in the 1920s and
1930s, and were unknown to Lenin as well as to earlier Marxists. Lenin's
reputation as a philosopher has suffered the opposite mishap; it has
been based mainly on the early and unsatisfactory *Materialism and
Empirio-Criticism,* and not on his much subtler, though of course in-
formal, *Philosophical Notebooks,* first published in 1929–30, and scarcely
known in the west till a decade later.

"the subordination of *necessity to freedom,* of blind *economic forces* to the power of human reason."[14] Though Marx rejected the providential harmony of interests, he did, however, believe that ultimate harmony would result from the economically motivated action of individuals: this absolved him from any deliberate planning for the future. All economic thinkers from Adam Smith to Karl Marx believed in objective economic laws and in the validity of predictions derived from them. This was the essence of "classical economics." The change came when technological advance gave birth to large-scale capitalism. With the arrival of the mammoth manufacturing corporation and trading cartel, the economic scene was dominated by what, in a masterly understatement, was described by economists as "imperfect competition." The notion of a self-regulating economy in which decisions resulted from the uncontrolled interplay of divergent interests was replaced by the notion of identifiable people manipulating social forces to bring about a predetermined objective. Economics had become instrumental—a matter not so much of scientific prediction as of conscious regulation. Spontaneous price adjustment through the law of supply and demand was replaced by price regulation for specific economic ends. It was no longer possible to believe in a world governed by objective economic laws. The hidden hand that pulled the strings was barely concealed by the velvet glove of the great corporations.

These developments made quite unrealistic the old conception of the "night-watchman" state, mounting guard to ensure fair play between a host of small, independent, competitive producers. Friedrich List, about the time when Marx began to think and write, demonstrated the need for state intervention on grounds of national efficiency in the organization of industry. Half a century later in Russia, the first steps in large-scale industrialization undertaken by Witte owed nothing to individual initiative and were an integral part of state policy. The socialists, though they appear to have invented the term "planning," were far behind German industrialists, bankers and academic

---

[14] G. Plekhanov, *In Defence of Materialism,* tr. Rothstein (1947) 292.

economists in their recognition of the direction and the inevitability of the processes at work. The first more or less fully planned national economy in modern times was the German economy at the height of the First World War, with the British and French economies lagging not far behind. When the revolution proved victorious in Russia, the case for planning rested both on socialist precept and on the example of the German war economy. The first long-term plan to be formally adopted in the USSR was the plan of electrification in 1920. In the following years several industries, not excluding agriculture, prepared five-year plans, which were, however, at first regarded as rough estimates and not as mandatory prescriptions. The first "five-year plan of the national economy" was adopted for the period 1928–29 to 1932–33. Since then the USSR, except in the war period, has never been without its long-term plan; and five-year plans (or sometimes six- or seven-year plans) have proliferated round the world. If you wish to assess the historical significance of the Russian revolution in terms of the influence exercised by it, productivity, industrialization and planning are key-words.

The transition from economic *laissez-faire* to economic management by the state, from spontaneity to planning, from the unconscious to the conscious, had corresponding repercussions on social policy. The *Communist Manifesto* had accused the bourgeoisie of "naked, shameless, direct, brutal exploitation" of the worker. Yet, so long as poverty or bad housing or unemployment could be attributed to the operation of objective economic laws, consciences were appeased by the argument that anything done to remedy these misfortunes would be done in defiance of economic laws, and would therefore in the long run only make things worse.[15] Once, however, everything that happened in the economy was seen as the result of a deliberate human decision, and therefore avoidable, the argument for positive action became irrefutable. Compassion for unavoidable suffering was replaced by indignation at unnecessary suffering. The concept of exploitation acquired a new dimension. For

[15] In Great Britain this doctrine, as applied to the evil of unemployment, was preached by leading economists, financiers and politicians of all parties as recently as 1931.

Marx exploitation was not an incidental abuse of which individuals were guilty, but an essential characteristic of the capitalist system, ineradicable so long as that system lasted. Exploitation now became a misdemeanor which could be prevented or mitigated by remedial action. A perceptive English writer in the first decade of the twentieth century diagnosed the change of climate, and defined by implication the character of the next revolution: "The belief in the possibility of social reform by conscious effort is the dominant current of the European mind; it has superseded the belief in liberty as the one panacea. . . . Its currency in the present is as significant and as pregnant as the belief in the rights of man about the time of the French revolution."[16] The revolution of 1917 was the first revolution in history committed to establish social justice through economic controls organized by political action.[17]

The reassertion, due to the advance of technology and economic organization, of the need for political action to direct and control the economy, was reflected in a change of emphasis in Marxist doctrine. Marx's nineteenth-century belief in the primacy of economics over politics had been cautiously qualified, after his death, by Engels's famous remarks about the mutual interaction of structure and superstructure. The change fitted readily into Russian conditions. At the turn of the century, the controversy between the orthodox Russian Social-Democrats and the Economists, who wanted to give priority to the economic demands of the workers, helped to shape and influence early Bolshevik thinking, and encouraged Lenin, in *What Is to Be Done?* and elsewhere, to stress the primary need for political action. The Russian trade unions were too feeble and too

[16] Leathes in *Cambridge Modern History* (1910) xii 15.

[17] Hannah Arendt stresses this aspect of the revolution from the standpoint of a hostile critic: "The whole record of past revolutions demonstrates beyond doubt that every attempt to solve the social question with political means leads into terror. . . . Nothing . . . could be more obsolete than to attempt to liberate mankind from poverty by political means; nothing could be more futile and more dangerous." [*On Revolution* (1964) 108.] But does this say more than that revolution, like war, which also leads to terror, is a bad thing, and that it is better to solve social problems by peaceful means? The argument remains inconclusive—except to total pacifists.

unreliable to play any role in Bolshevik schemes of revolution. The Russian revolution was a political revolution in an economically unripe country. Lenin, in a remarkable *obiter dictum* of May 1918, observed that one half of socialism—the political half—had been realized in Russia, the other half—a planned economy—in Germany. Political action, the dictatorship of the proletariat, was needed to promote an economic result, the building of a socialist economy. The assumption that, once the revolution had triumphed, the economic consequences would look after themselves was, however, falsified. After the political episode of war communism, the introduction of the New Economic Policy (NEP) in 1921 meant a partial reinstatement of economic forces; and throughout the 1920s the battle went on between the market principle as the guiding force of the economy and the principle of planning. In theory everyone accepted the assumption that it was preferable to achieve the socialist goal through economic rather than through administrative action. In practice market forces proved unable to carry the strain of intensive industrialization, and by 1929 had completely broken down. The use of direct and conscious political means to bring about economic ends has been since 1929 a persistent *leitmotiv* of Soviet history, scarcely modified by the play-acting of so-called "market socialism." Stalin in later years, in the short history of the party published in 1938, and in his pronouncement on linguistics in 1950, increasingly emphasized Engels's recognition of the role of the superstructure.

The dichotomy between economics and politics characteristic of western nineteenth-century thought was reflected in the familiar issue of society versus the state. When the Physiocrats in France sought to free trade from the frustrating restrictions of state power, when Adam Smith had his vision of a vast economic process working independently of the state for the greatest benefit of all, when Hegel set "civil society"[18] over

---

[18] "Bürgerliche Gesellschaft" should be translated "civil society," not "bourgeois society"; the term had not yet acquired its distinctive color. Marx defined it as "the form of intercourse determined by the existing productive forces . . . and in its turn determining these" (Marx and Engels, *The German Ideology,* 47–8).

against the state and made this dichotomy the foundation of his political theory, the distinction between economics, which meant civil society, and politics, which meant the state, was clearly established. Civil society was the realm of economic man. Throughout the nineteenth century the argument proceeded about the desirable and practicable relation between society and the state, but not about the reality of the distinction. In the English-speaking world, in particular, the opposition between society and the state, and the natural priority of society, became a fundamental category of political thinking. But Marx fully shared the same view: "Only *political superstition* [he wrote in *The Holy Family*] today supposes that social life must be held together by the state, whereas in reality the state is held together by civil life."[19]

In nineteenth-century Russia an embryonic bourgeois society was too weak to withstand the hypertrophy of state power; and after the revolution of 1917 a paradoxical situation developed. In western countries the persistence of the nineteenth-century liberal-democratic tradition continued to encourage a negative attitude towards the state, and an eagerness to denounce "bureaucratic" abuses of its power, even while the constant encroachments of that power were recognized and accepted. In fascist countries the supremacy of the state over society was openly preached and practiced. In the USSR the Marxist tradition also embodied a deep-seated hostility to the state, enshrined in Lenin's *State and Revolution* and in widespread denunciations of "bureaucratism." But this clashed with the Russian tradition of an absolute state power, and, in a period where the state was everywhere extending its functions and its authority, fought a losing battle. What is happening everywhere today is not so much the assertion of the primacy of the state, by way of reaction against the nineteenth-century assertion of the primacy of society, as a gradual obliteration of the distinction between them. The state becomes predominantly social and economic in character. Society identifies itself with the power of the state. The dividing line between economics and politics

[19] K. Marx and F. Engels, *The Holy Family* (Engl. transl. 1957) 163; both "social" and "civil" in this passage represent "bürgerlich."

which was the essential feature of bourgeois society ceases to exist. These changes are strikingly illustrated by the way in which Soviet thought and practice has turned away from the Marxist attitude to the state.

Here we come to Lenin's most distinctive innovation in revolutionary theory and practice—the substitution of party for class as the motive force of revolution. Lenin once again found himself in verbal agreement, at any rate with the earlier Marx. The *Communist Manifesto* foresaw "the organization of the proletarians into a class, and consequently into a political party"; and Lenin, of course, constantly spoke of the class of which the party was the spearhead or vanguard. But the change of emphasis was marked, and corresponded to the shift from the world of objective economic laws to the world of political action designed to mold and modify the economy. A class was a loose economic group without clear definition or organization or program. A party was a closely knit political organization defined by a common conscious purpose.

Both for Marx and for modern sociologists class remains an elusive concept. A class, for Marx, was an economic and social group bound together by a common relation to the means of production. It had no legal existence and no institutions. Its common action was the unconscious product of innumerable spontaneous actions of individuals pursuing their particular interests. This view of class fitted into *laissez-faire* conceptions of economic action and thought, and of the sharp dichotomy between society and state, which were dominant in the advanced countries throughout the nineteenth century, and was scarcely comprehensible in any other context. The embarrassments of attempting to apply the concept of class to earlier historical periods or to other continents are notorious. All authorities agree that the French revolution was a bourgeois revolution. This is not to say that it was started or led by an identifiable group or class answering to the name of bourgeoisie; the class structure in France on the eve of the revolution was too complicated and mixed up for any such simplification. It is just as difficult to identify the bourgeoisie in pre-revolutionary French history as it is to attach any precise meaning to the term "feudal," used by Marx as its class antithesis.[20] If, however, social revolution is defined as "a social transformation in which the power of the obsolescent class is overthrown, and that of the progressive, revolutionary class is established in its place,"[21] the credentials of the French revolution as a bourgeois revolution are fully vindicated. It was a bourgeois revolution not in the sense that it was made by the bourgeoisie, but in the sense that it substituted for the hierarchical society of the *ancien régime* a new type of society dominated by the bourgeoisie. To speak of a class struggle in France in the context of the French revolution is to anticipate the consequences of the revolution, not to describe its antecedents. "Pre-industrial society," it has been well remarked, ". . . did not invest the concept of class with an operational meaning."[22] It was only after the revolution that class became a useful cutting-tool of analysis, and was wielded as such by Marx with incomparable power.

The only class which really comes to life in Marx's writings is the bourgeoisie; nearly everything written by him about class in general relates, consciously or unconsciously, to the bourgeoisie in particular.[23] The unplanned and unconscious common action of innumerable individuals determined the policies of bourgeois governments, and constituted "the dictatorship of the bourgeoisie." The proletariat as a class was envisaged by Marx on the same model. Increasingly intolerable economic conditions would drive the workers to take action in defense of their interests. The workers of the world would spontaneously unite; and this common action would bring about the overthrow of the

[20] The term "feudal" masks the fact that the nobility and the other "orders" or "estates" of pre-industrial society were legal categories and plainly not classes in the Marxist sense; but a feudal class is still more puzzling.

[21] *Grundlagen der Marxistischen Philosophie,* German transl. (Berlin 1953) 551; this is the current official textbook.

[22] Lichtheim, *Marxism,* 381.

[23] As Wetter says [*Soviet Ideology Today* (1966) 203], Marx's well-known aphorism, "The hand-mill gives you society with the feudal lord; the steam-mill society with the industrial capitalist," has meaning only as a statement about industrial society, not as a statement about feudal society. The hand-mill was not peculiar to feudal society, and is introduced here merely to point a contrast with capitalism.

bourgeoisie and the dictatorship of the proletariat. Marx made it clear that this did not imply consciously planned action: "The question is not what this or that proletarian, or even the whole proletariat at the moment, *considers* as its aim. The question is, *what the proletariat is,* and what, consequent on that *being,* it will be compelled to do."[24]

Marx knew well that only a small proportion of the proletariat was as yet class-conscious (though, living in England, he may have tended to exaggerate this proportion); and he recognized the existence of a *Lumpenproletariat,* an unorganized and unreliable mass of low-grade workers. At the other end of the scale, Engels noted the birth in England of what he called "a bourgeois working class," of a stratum of workers who showed signs of making common cause with the capitalists. But Marxists as a whole were not troubled by these threats to the international solidarity of the proletariat. It was assumed that time would correct these anomalies, and that at the right moment the workers would play their historical role, like the bourgeoisie before them, as a unified class. The contractions of the capitalist system, and the pressures engendered by it, would sap its progressive and expansive capacities, and provoke a revolt by an increasingly numerous and increasingly impoverished proletariat. This would be the last revolution, which would overthrow the last ruling class, the bourgeoisie, and usher in the classless society.

When Lenin surveyed the scene—and the Russian scene in particular—at the turn of the century, the prospect was obscure. In the countries of the Second International, while few signs had appeared of an imminent proletarian revolution, the organization of the workers had made giant strides; and everyone appeared to agree that this was an encouraging token of their growing solidarity and revolutionary potential. In Russia workers' organization was primitive, and revolutionary hopes seemed infinitely remote. In *What Is to Be Done?* Lenin wrote: "The spontaneous struggle of the proletariat will not become a genuine 'class struggle' until it is led by a strong organization of

[24] Marx and Engels, *The Holy Family,* 53.

revolutionaries."[25] Logically Lenin set to work to create a party to galvanize the Russian workers into action; and in Russian conditions the work of a party on Russian soil was necessarily secret and conspiratorial. These preparations seemed in no sense a departure from the Marxist tradition or from the models created by the great Social-Democratic parties of the west; they were merely another desperate Russian attempt to "catch up" with the west. What was bewildering and decisive was what happened in 1914 and 1917—the negative and positive sides of the same medal. The outbreak of war in 1914 struck a crucial and long-awaited blow at the nineteenth-century capitalist system, and found the workers of the advanced countries rallying to its defense in their respective national uniforms; the traumatic effect on Lenin of this incredible experience is well known. The revolution of 1917 put in power the first government professing allegiance to Marxism and dedicated to the overthrow of capitalism; and this occurred in an economically backward country with a small, undeveloped and relatively unorganized proletariat. This reversal of the expected order of events confronted the Bolsheviks with the task of maintaining and defending the victorious Russian revolution in a hostile environment with woefully inadequate resources, human and material, at their disposal.

This crisis evoked a response already familiar in Russian revolutionary history. For the best part of a century, the Russian intelligentsia—a group without precise counterpart elsewhere—had provided the leadership and the inspiration for a series of revolutionary movements. When Lenin, in *What Is to Be Done?*, published in 1902, pleaded for a party of professional revolutionaries under intellectual leadership to spearhead the proletarian revolution, Trotsky contemptuously observed that the Marxist beliefs of intellectuals were "no substitute for a politically developed proletariat," and accused the Bolshevik Party of attempting "to *substitute* itself for the working class."[26]

[25] Lenin, *Polnoe Sobranie Sochinenii*, 5th ed. vi 135.
[26] N. Trotsky, *Nashi Politicheskie Zadachi* (Geneva, 1904) 23, 50 and *passim*. Later Trotsky evidently became more reconciled to the idea; in an article of 1908 (*Sochineniya,* xx 327–42), he described the De-

When, however, the survival of the revolutionary regime was placed in jeopardy by the inadequacy, quantitative and qualitative, of the proletariat, the party, led and organized mainly by intellectuals, stepped into the gap. The Russian revolution was made and saved not by a class, but by a party proclaiming itself to be the representative and vanguard of a class. It was a solution consonant with the Russian revolutionary tradition. But, more important, it was a solution which marked the distance traveled since the days of Marx. That Leninism was not exclusively or primarily a product of Russian conditions is suggested by the fact that the two major Marxist theorists after Lenin, who further elaborated the Leninist notion of creative vanguards, were both non-Russians: Lukacs and Gramsci. The Leninist gloss on Marxism belonged to an age which thought of effective force as the product, no longer of the spontaneous action of a mass of individuals, but of conscious political planning.

The *Communist Manifesto* recognized the role of leadership exercised by communists as the only fully class-conscious members of the proletariat and of proletarian parties. But it was a condition of the proletarian revolution that communist consciousness should spread to a majority of the workers. Marx attributed to Blanqui, and rejected as heretical, a belief in the revolutionary seizure of power by a disciplined minority. But for Marx consciousness was still primarily consciousness of a process which remained outside conscious control. Lenin's conception of the party as the vanguard of the class contained elitist elements absent from Marx's writings, and was the product of a period when political writers were turning their attention more and more to the problem of elites. The party was to lead and inspire the mass of workers; its own membership was to remain small and select. In the months between February and October 1917, it was a favorite Menshevik taunt that Lenin was a disciple of Blanqui or Bakunin, not of Marx. On the eve of

cembrists of 1825 as substituting themselves for a not yet existing bourgeoisie. He did not cite the intellectual leaders of the narodnik movement, whose "going to the people" campaign in the 1870s enjoyed little success.

the February revolution of 1917 the Bolsheviks appear to have numbered no more than 23,000; and, though members flowed in between February and October, the party in whose name the revolution was made and governmental power assumed probably did not much exceed 100,000.[27] But it would be an error to suppose that Lenin regarded the revolution as the work of a minority. His fullest account of what created a revolutionary situation was given in the pamphlet *The Infantile Disease of "Leftism"* which he prepared for the Second Congress of the Communist International in 1920. "Only when '*the lower layers* (nizy)' *are not willing* to put up with the old, and '*the top layers* (verkhi)' *are not able to go on in the old way,* only then can the revolution triumph. In other words, this truth can be expressed as follows: revolution is impossible without a general national crisis affecting both exploited and exploiters."[28] The task of leading the masses was not, properly understood, a task of indoctrination, of creating a consciousness that was not there, but of evoking a latent consciousness; and this latent consciousness of the masses was an essential condition of revolution. Lenin, within the circle of party leaders, was capable of taking up the position of a dictator. But he never did so in relation to the masses of the workers; and to this he owed much of his immense hold over them. His profession of willingness to learn from the masses was never an empty pretense. Lenin emphatically did not believe in revolution from above. Already in April 1917 he had written: "The commune, i.e. the Soviets, does not 'introduce,' does not propose to 'introduce,' and must not 'introduce,' any transformations which have not matured both absolutely and in economic reality, and in the consciousness of the overwhelming majority of the people."[29] And a year later,

[27] Official party statistics put the membership at 23,000 in January 1917 and 115,000 in January 1918 (*Bol'shaya Sovetskaya Entsiklopediya,* 1st ed. (1930) xi 531); much larger estimates quoted elsewhere look like exaggerations made either at the time to encourage optimism, or *ex post facto* to refute the impression that the revolution was the work of an insignificant minority.

[28] Lenin, *Polnoe Sobranie Sochinenii,* 5th ed. xli 69–70.

[29] *Ibid.* xxxi 163–4.

at the party congress which approved the ratification of the Brest-Litovsk treaty, he repeated still more emphatically: "Socialism cannot be introduced by a minority—the party. It can be introduced only by tens of millions when they learn to do it themselves."[30]

Some critics have found an element of political casuistry in this attempt to combine an elite leadership with mass consciousness. The embarrassed and sometimes contradictory utterances of the Bolshevik leaders about class contrast with their precise and rigid conceptions of party. After Lenin's death, sinister developments occurred, the seeds of which had undoubtedly been sown in Lenin's lifetime. Before the revolution some attention had been paid to the growth, in western political parties, of central party organizations and party bureaucracies which effectively determined party policy, and controlled the rank and file of party members.[31] In the Russian Social-Democratic Party tension had existed from the first between divergent conceptions of the party as a mass organization and as a vanguard leading and instructing the masses. After the revolution, the problems of survival and material progress confronting a revolutionary regime isolated in a hostile world were so vast and so pressing that Lenin's successors lacked the capacity or the patience to evoke that measure of mass consciousness and mass support which Lenin had had behind him in the period of the revolution and the civil war, and took the short cut—always the temptation that lies in wait for an elite—of imposing their will, by measures of increasingly naked force, on the mass of the population and on the mass of the party. Stalin's once famous short history of the Communist Party called the collectivization of agriculture "a revolution from above, on the initiative of state power, with direct support from below"; and, though the phrase "revolution from above" has since been condemned as heretical, it was symptomatic of the Stalinist epoch.

These developments were due in part to the peculiarly exacting nature of the problems which the revolutionary regime in Russia had to face, and in part to the peculiar conditions of a

30 *Ibid.* xxxvi 53.
31 The classical works of Ostrogorski and R. Michels are frequently quoted in this context.

country where primitive peasants formed more than 80 per cent of the population, and the number of trained and politically conscious workers, comparable to the organized workers of the west, was infinitesimally small. But they were also, and more significantly, a product of the period. The French revolutionary slogan of equality was a necessary and effective protest against privilege in a highly stratified society. For Marx this problem, like every social problem, was a problem of the relations of production. Capitalist society was based on the exploitation of man by man; the principle of inequality was built into the capitalist division of labor. In a famous passage of *Capital,* Marx reiterated the belief, common to many nineteenth-century writers, that large-scale industry would "make an end of the manufacturing division of labor in which each man is tied for life to a single detail operation."[32] The Marxist Utopia contemplated the breaking down of the differentiation between different forms of labor—notably between manual and intellectual work. Lenin's *State and Revolution,* with its vision of the work of administration performed by ordinary workers in rotation, and the initial experiments of the Bolshevik revolution in workers' control in the factories, were the last belated tributes to this conception.

The vision quickly faded, and the experiments ended in failure. Marx himself, in a later chapter of *Capital* which appeared posthumously in the third volume, took a more realistic view of the future of labor:

> Freedom in this field can only consist in socialized man, the associated producers, rationally regulating their interchange with nature, bringing it under their common control, instead of being ruled by it as the blind forces of nature. . . . But it nonetheless still remains a realm of necessity. Beyond it begins that development of human energy which is an end in itself, the true realm of freedom, which can, however, only blossom forth with this realm of necessity as its basis.[33]

[32] K. Marx, *Capital,* I (transl. Moore and Aveling 1954) 522.
[33] Marx, *Capital,* 3 (Engl. transl. 1960) 800. In his note-books Marx remarked that "labor cannot become play, as Fourier wants to make it" [*Grundrisse der Kritik der Politischen Ökonomie* (1953) 599]; con-

Lenin, as early as March 1918, came out in support of what was later called "one-man management" (edinonachalie) in factories in terms so emphatic that the passage has sometimes been unfairly quoted out of context as a defense of political dictatorship.[34] The problem is not confined to the degree of discipline required to enforce performance of a necessary minimum of arduous and repellent physical labor. It is correct that both the scope and the harsh character of such labor have diminished over the past century, though its total elimination still seems a utopian dream. But the bold nineteenth-century assumption that technological progress would reduce the need of specialization and thus obliterate distinctions between different forms of labor, and especially between intellectual and manual labor, has been signally falsified. A new kind of stratification has entered into every branch of administration and production. The need for technological and administrative elites declares itself at every level—in government, in industrial organization, on the factory floor and on the farm—and is likely to increase with the increasing complexity of administrative and productive processes.

When, therefore, Stalin shocked the world in June 1931 by denouncing egalitarianism or "leveling" (uravnilovka), and remarked that "every industry, every enterprise, every workshop" had its "leading groups," and later accused supporters of egalitarianism of "petty-bourgeois views,"[35] he struck a shrewder blow than was realized by his critics at the time. The ideal of equality launched by the French revolution found increasingly widespread acceptance and application in the western world of the nineteenth century; before the end of the century, the need to extend it from the political to the economic sphere had begun to be recognized. Since 1917 dramatic strides have been made, in the Soviet Union and in other countries, towards improving the standards of living of the industrial worker. But

---

trast this with Engels's naïve optimism: "Productive labor will become a pleasure instead of a burden." [*Anti-Dühring* (Engl. transl. 1954) 408].

[34] Lenin, *Polnoe Sobranie Sochinenii*, 5th ed. xxxvi 200.

[35] J. Stalin, *Sochineniya*, xiii 58–60, 357.

this process has been accompanied by an insidious spread of elitist doctrines, avowed or disguised, and by a growing recognition of the difficulty of reconciling the need for administrative and technological elites with the egalitarian aspirations which mass democracy inherited from the French revolution. The fact that many of these elites would call themselves nonpolitical does not mean that they do not wield decisive political influence. "Bureaucracy" and "technocracy" are not empty words. The autocrats of the past have been replaced by anonymous Kafka-like figures, whom we cannot control and often cannot identify. The need, with which Lenin wrestled and which Stalin contemptuously dismissed, of reconciling elite leadership with mass democracy has emerged as a key problem in the Soviet Union today. Nor is the problem, though spotlighted by the sequel of the Bolshevik revolution, of exclusive significance to a single country. It would be rash to dismiss the Russian experience as irrelevant to our own, or to be unduly complacent about our own solutions. It would be rasher still to think of it as irrelevant to the problems of countries all over the world which have no experience of an established democracy in the past.

The educational function of the elite was strongly emphasized by Lenin in *What Is to Be Done?* Marx, like Adam Smith and Hegel, believed that individuals conformed to, and were the agents or victims of, objective social and economic laws of which they were, nevertheless, unconscious. "Conceptions which arise about the laws of production in the heads of the agents of capitalist production and circulation diverge drastically from these real laws"; and "individuals have become enslaved under a power alien to them."[36] These conceptions, which did not correspond with reality, were what Marx called "ideology." Ideology for Marx was necessarily false consciousness—the false idea of their motives formed by men who were unconscious of the real laws governing their actions. As Engels put it: "That the material life-conditions of persons inside whose heads the thought process goes on determine in the last resort the course of this process, remains of necessity unknown

[36] Marx, *Capital*, 3, 307; Marx and Engels, *The German Ideology*, 48.

to these persons, for otherwise there would be an end of all ideology."[37] What were decisive were the unconscious, not the conscious, motives and actions of those engaged in production. It was only the communists who, in the words of the *Communist Manifesto,* "have, over the mass of the proletariat, the advantage of clearly understanding the line of march." Marx did not consider it his function to issue positive injunctions—much less to propound a new ideology. His aim was to unmask error and illusion. Marx, following Hegel, identified the historical process with the growth of consciousness, and the growth of consciousness with the growth of freedom. Thus the final revolution leading to the Marxist Utopia of the classless society would also mean the ending of the rift between reality and ideology, and the realization of true freedom and true consciousness.

This belief in the liberating character of the understanding, traduced and caricatured in the aphorism that "freedom is the recognition of necessity," gave Marx a place in two worlds. He was primarily concerned with analysis. But analysis was a condition of therapy. Marx was the real founder of the social sciences, in which man is both the object of investigation and the investigator; and man cannot investigate himself without changing himself. Marx looked forward to "the full development of man's control over the forces of nature—including his own nature."[38] Marx, however, who lived in a world where the supremacy of the individual entrepreneur and the climate of *laissez-faire* had not yet been seriously disturbed, could not fully emancipate himself from the iron laws of classical economics: these continued to dominate his thinking. The period between the death of Marx and the Russian revolution witnessed a rapid transition. Freud, like Marx, uncovered the reality that lay behind unconscious behavior. Freud, like Marx, rejected the assumption of an unchanging human nature. But analysis was subordinated to therapy. Science became more specifically instrumental. The aim was no longer to ascertain objective facts,

[37] F. Engels, *Ludwig Feuerbach* (Engl. transl. 1934) 65–6.
[38] K. Marx, *Pre-Capitalist Economic Formations,* ed. E. Hobsbawm (1964) 84.

but to establish working hypotheses which led to positive results; human behavior and human impulses are molded by means which can be studied and applied by psychiatrists. What Freud did was to add a new dimension to reason. Reason can investigate, understand and utilize the irrational.

The Russian revolution stands on the highroad of this transition. Lenin remained formally within the Marxist framework. But, while the *Communist Manifesto* had counted on "the gradual, spontaneous class organization of the proletariat," Lenin treated "spontaneity" as the bane of the Russian workers' movement and as the converse of "consciousness." Socialism was a more rational method of organizing the productive process than capitalism precisely because it was "conscious." For Marx, communist consciousness arises only when "an alteration of men on a mass scale" takes place, i.e., by a revolution.[39] In Lenin's scheme a highly conscious elite party was needed to bring revolutionary consciousness to the mass of workers. Marx believed that the new man would arise "spontaneously" out of the new society; Lenin realized that it was necessary to create the new man in order to create the new society. With the recognition of this need, the word "ideology" changed its meaning. Ideology for Lenin was no longer necessarily false consciousness. Its character was dependent on its content. Revolutionary or socialist ideology was what the party and its leaders strove to inculcate in the workers. "Ideology," declares the current Soviet *Philosophical Dictionary,* "may be a true or a false, a scientific or an unscientific, reflection of reality."

Lenin remained in one respect rooted in the nineteenth century. While he proclaimed the need to instruct and influence the masses, he continued to believe in instruction by rational persuasion or by force of experience. By the middle of the twentieth century this belief had lost much of its validity both in the Soviet Union and elsewhere. This was perhaps the fundamental difference which marked the transition from Lenin to Stalin. Lenin regarded persuasion or indoctrination as a rational process in the sense that it sought to implant a rational conviction in

[39] Marx and Engels, *The German Ideology,* 86.

the minds of those to whom it was directed. Stalin regarded it as
a rational process only in the sense that it was planned and
conducted by a rational elite. Its aim was to induce large
numbers of people to behave in a desired way. How to achieve
this aim was a technical problem which was the object of
rational study. But the most effective means to employ in
achieving this aim did not always, or not often, appeal to the
reason. It would be erroneous to suppose that this transition
was peculiar to the USSR, or to any particular form of government. A similar development in western democratic countries
has often been attributed to the influence of commercial adver-
tising, the techniques of which, and sometimes the practitioners
who applied them, were transferred from the commercial world
to that of politics. The candidate is sold to the voter by the same
means used to sell patent medicines or refrigerators. The enormous expansion of media of mass communication has clearly
also been a factor. But deeper underlying causes have been at
work. The professional, politically neutral, public relations con-
sultant, setting out to create a favorable image for his clients
and to mold opinion, by every known technical and psychological device, in the sense desired by them, is a now familiar
phenomenon, difficult to reconcile with the principles of Lincoln
or Gladstone, but apparently inseparable from contemporary
mass democracy. The future of democracy, in any part of the
world, is today a disturbing problem. Here, as in other respects,
the transition from liberal democracy to mass democracy in the
western world has reflected the experience of the Russian revolution.

The other phenomenon of the modern world in which the
Russian revolution has played a significant part has been the
movement for the liberation of the so-called backward peoples.
In the aftermath of the French revolution, the proposition that
one man is as good as another was extended to the proposition
that one nation is as good as another. Equality of rights for
individuals was held to include equality of rights for nations,
and the liberation of nations became a purpose as vital, and as
intoxicating, as the liberation of man. This conception remained

as one of the most durable legacies of the French revolution to the nineteenth and twentieth centuries. Marx, though he postulated the ultimate goal of a world without nations as well as without classes, regarded the liberation of subject nations as a milestone on the road to revolution, and as a cause worthy of the support of radicals and revolutionaries; he was himself concerned in particular with the wrongs of the Irish and the Poles. While, however, some attention was given, by Marx and by others, to the problems of India and China, the nineteenth century scarcely thought of the undeveloped peoples of Asia and Africa as candidates for nationhood and liberation. Nationalism remained primarily a European phenomenon, and could be fitted by Marxist thinkers into the scheme of successive bourgeois and proletarian revolutions. As Lenin put it, the proletariat, as the oppressed class which possessed no rights, was the natural "standard-bearer of all peoples in the struggle for liberty."[40]

These attitudes were profoundly affected by the intensive commercial and political penetration of other continents by the European Powers which occupied the last quarter of the nineteenth century, and came to be known by the generic term "imperialism." It is difficult to dissociate this process from the broad wave of prosperity enjoyed by the capitalist economies of western Europe at the turn of the century. But, though imperialism seemed in the short run to have brought a powerful reinforcement to capitalism, it could also be seen from another angle as the Achilles' heel of the capitalist Powers. In the decade before 1917, both Rosa Luxemburg and Lenin were heavily preoccupied with the question of imperialism. Differences between them existed, and were magnified in later polemics. But both agreed in regarding imperialism as the last fling of capitalism in decline; and anything that served to sap and destroy imperialism would therefore hasten the downfall of capitalism. All socialists feared and expected that imperialist policies would lead sooner or later to war between the Great Powers, and believed in theory that war would spell the down-

[40] Lenin, *Polnoe Sobranie Sochinenii,* 5th ed. v 334.

fall of capitalism; Rosa Luxemburg, Lenin and every Bolshevik looked forward to the war as providing a heaven-sent opportunity to work actively for this result.

This picture had, however, its reverse side. The prosperity of capitalism in its imperialist phase had an important, though at first unnoticed, by-product: the growth of "revisionism" in the German Social-Democratic Party and of similar tendencies in other socialist and labor parties of western Europe. The grievances of the workers had become less acute. The prospect loomed large of mitigating them further by peaceful pressure on governments, or by bargains and compromises with them. To use democratic procedures in order to influence, to control, and perhaps eventually to take over, governments began to make sense. The entry of an isolated socialist into a French bourgeois government in 1900 created a scandal in the French socialist movement. But this act evidently paved the way for socialist-controlled French governments in the future. The first successes of British labor on the parliamentary scene belonged to the same period. The view that all reforms under a capitalist regime were illusory was sharply challenged by the view that a peaceful revolution was possible. In western countries, the Marxist program of the overthrow of capitalist governments was relegated to a distant future, and had no apparent relevance to the present.

These developments had no counterpart in eastern Europe, and Lenin continued to bask in the illusion that revisionism had been soundly defeated in the west. His discovery in August 1914 of the extent to which the workers' parties of western Europe had identified themselves with their national governments convinced him of the need to build a new international movement from the foundations. This was attempted at Zimmerwald in 1915. The unexpected victory of the Russian revolution provided a solid national base for the attempt. The sectarian Zimmerwald movement was replaced by a world-wide organization for the overthrow of capitalism: the Third or Communist International. Had the Russian revolution been quickly followed—as the Bolsheviks at first expected—by revolutions in western Europe, its priority would have been no more than a chronological anomaly in the total scheme. But when the cause of revolution, having proved barren in the west, flourished in the fertile soil of Asia, the shape of things to come radically changed. The abortive Russian revolution of 1905 had appeared to provide an impulse, in the ensuing years, for revolutions in Turkey, Persia and China. The extension to other continents of a movement for national liberation hitherto confined mainly to Europe was the most conspicuous international achievement of the revolution of 1917. In Central Asia, in Persia, Turkey and Egypt and throughout the Middle East, Soviet Russia seemed the natural ally of the underdog against the arch-imperialist Power, Great Britain. In India and Afghanistan the nationalist movement looked naturally to Moscow; in China Soviet Russia won prestige and sympathy as the first Power which voluntarily abandoned extra-territorial rights. As the revolutions of 1789 and 1848 spread from France, not to England, but eastward to less advanced countries of central Europe, so the Russian revolution spread, not westward into Europe, but eastward into the less advanced Asian continent. The revolution could now be seen not only as a revolt against bourgeois capitalism in the most backward western country, but as a revolt against western imperialism in the most advanced eastern country. Lenin, in the last article he ever wrote, consoled himself for the failure of the revolution in Europe with the reflection that "the east has already entered the revolutionary movement" and that "Russia, India, China etc. contribute a huge majority of the population of the world."[41] It was a dramatic touch of Lenin's old insight. The torch of revolution, abandoned by western Europe, had been taken up by peoples of Asia and Africa formerly dependent, in name or in fact, on the European Powers. The changed shape of the world today, and the changed relations between western Europe and the advanced English-speaking countries on the one hand, and the rest of the world on the other, are a tribute to the historical significance of the Russian revolution.

Much more, however, was involved in the change than a mere geographical transposition. The Marxist revolution

[41] Lenin, *Polnoe Sobranie Sochinenii*, 5th ed. xlv 404; a few weeks earlier he had written: "Our European philistines do not dream that the future revolutions in countries of the east . . . will display undoubtedly greater peculiarities than the Russian revolution." (*Ibid.* 381.)

reached the peoples of Asia and Africa in its Leninist incarnation. Industrialization had to be pursued in these countries in conditions far closer to those experienced in the Soviet Union than to those envisaged by Marx. The victory of a proletarian revolution in predominantly peasant Russia was explained by Lenin as a provisional stage, at the end of which the mass of poorer peasants would have been assimilated to a proletariat. What happened in Russia in October 1917 could still be plausibly called a proletarian revolution, though not in the full Marxist sense. But in China the predominantly peasant character and leadership of the revolution was undisguised; and in many undeveloped countries a proletariat was altogether lacking. More significant still was the weakness, or sometimes total absence, of a bourgeoisie or of any of the concepts of a bourgeois society. In these countries, the bourgeois revolution, still unfinished in the Russia of 1917, had not even begun. Here the Russian problem was reproduced in an extreme form, and could be met only by the Leninist solution of a small intellectual elite to assume the leadership of the revolution. Many of these new leaders had received their education, and made their first acquaintance with Marxism, in western countries or under western auspices. But, in practice, local conditions made Marxism applicable only in its Leninist transformation. The absence of a bourgeoisie and of an established bourgeois tradition meant the rejection, in practice if not in theory, of bourgeois liberal democracy and a return to Rousseauistic or Jacobin conceptions of democracy; and the influence of the USSR appeared in many of these countries to predominate over that of the west.

This predominance is, however, not unqualified. The revolt of nationalism against imperialism has almost everywhere succeeded in winning political independence. But this has made the persistence of an unavoidable economic dependence all the more galling and inspires constant complaints of "neo-colonialism." The example of the USSR, which, thanks to its natural resources and by gigantic efforts, made itself economically independent of the west, excites envy and admiration. But all these countries, with the exception of China, know that such a task is beyond their powers. "Economic aid" has become an indispensable factor of national life. At first it seemed less invidious and less dangerous to receive aid from the Soviet Union than from the west. But gradually consciousness dawned that exclusive economic dependence either on one side or on the other carried a threat to national independence; taunts of Soviet "colonialism" or "imperialism" did not altogether miss their mark. Hence the policies of "non-alignment" followed more or less actively by most of these countries, inspired partly by a desire to obtain aid from both sides, and partly by a desire to maintain a maximum degree of independence. In China non-alignment has been extended to the point of acute hostility to both camps.

It is perhaps too early to attempt to place these ambiguous events in historical perspective. What is clear is that the Russian revolution has triggered off a revolutionary movement of revolt in Asia and Africa against the nineteenth-century capitalist order, in which the challenge is directed not against the exploitation of the industrial workers of the advanced countries, but against the exploitation of backward colonial peoples. It never occurred to Lenin, and was never admitted later, that revolution under these auspices, while it might be directed against capitalism, and have aims that could be described as socialist, had moved far away from the Marxist premises. The post-Leninist re-orientation of the socialist revolution implied that the final overthrow of capitalism would be the work not of its proletarian victims in the advanced countries (who had somehow become its allies), but of its colonial victims in the undeveloped countries, and that it would be the work not of an economic class, but of a political movement. The era of the French revolution ended in 1917, and a new revolutionary epoch opened. Historians of the future may debate whether that epoch ended in 1949, when the Asian and African revolution effectively began, or whether these events can be interpreted as a slightly unorthodox prolongation of the Russian revolution. Such debates about what is called "periodization" are not very fruitful, and it is unnecessary to anticipate them. But, so long as man is interested in exploring his past, nobody will doubt the credentials of the revolution of 1917 as one of the great turning-points in his history.

15

Ho Chi Minh: The Russian Revolution and Wars of National Liberation*

The October Revolution brightened the history of mankind with a new dawn.

Like the rising sun driving away the shadows, the October Revolution brightened the history of mankind with a new dawn.

Forty years ago, under the leadership of the Leninist Party, the Russian proletariat, firmly united with the working peasants, overthrew the power of the capitalists and landlords. The Soviet state, the state of proletarian dictatorship, bringing a genuine democracy to the people, has given proof of its vitality and invincible strength.

The October Revolution was the victory of the revolutionary forces of the toiling masses; it was an extremely violent upheaval creating conditions which clearly showed the creativeness of the toiling masses. The victory of the October Revolution confirmed the correctness of Marxism-Leninism; it paved the way to new victories of the working class in social life, on the basis of great loyalty to Marxist-Leninist principles. Thanks to the clear-

* Ho Chin Minh, "The October Revolution and the Liberation of the Peoples of the East," in *Selected Works,* IV (Hanoi: Foreign Languages Publishing House, 1962), pp. 260–279.

This article was written on the fortieth anniversary of the October Revolution, in November 1957.

299

sightedness and heroism of the Leninist Party, the Party of the proletarian class, the October Revolution won victory and ushered in a new era in the history of mankind and a new stage on the long and glorious path covered by the revolutionary Party of the Russian proletariat.

Owing to the success of the October Revolution, the Leninist Party was able successfully to fulfill the historical tasks of great significance entrusted to it. Peoples who were once oppressed have become masters of their own destiny. The Czarist empire was suppressed; this empire was formerly the prison of many nations and at the same time was enslaved by a handful of cosmopolitan financiers. The people were no longer the toys, the slaves, the cannon fodder of rival imperialists. The toiling masses wiped out the wretchedness of bourgeois Russia where, as in other countries, they had suffered under the dreadful yoke of the capitalists and landlords. The laboring people were the creators of all wealth but were kept in misery and ignorance— the atrocious and age-old fate of the overwhelming majority of mankind. For the first time in human history, the working people started to build a society without class exploitation and national oppression—a socialist society. With their exemplary enthusiasm in labor, high consciousness, ever-growing labor efficiency, and with boundless faithfulness to their own cause, that of their children, and of their brothers who still suffer in slavery, the Soviet people have transformed their age-old dream of happiness into a dazzling reality over a sixth of the earth.

The October Revolution has nationalized factories, mines, and principal means of communication and liaison. It has brought land to the peasants. On the basis of socialist industrialization and socialist transformation of the countryside along the path drawn by Lenin, the Soviet Union has developed its economy at a prodigious speed, at a pace hitherto unknown. The socialist economy has proved its superiority over the capitalist economy.

The fundamental law of the socialist economy is to satisfy the ever-growing material and cultural needs of the working people. It is completely contrary to the monopolistic capitalist economy, which relies on the ever-increasing exploitation of the working class, on the impoverishment of the laboring masses, and on the plundering of the enslaved peoples. The Soviet workers, peasants, and intellectuals, who have wiped out the regime of exploitation of man by man and of class antagonism on the vast Soviet territory, are constantly consolidating their socialist brotherhood, which is growing more splendid and blooming with every passing day. The glorious achievements of the Soviet people are preparing the way for the future society—a Communist society.

The October Revolution has proved the possibility of overthrowing the dictatorship of the exploiting class and establishing a socialist society that ensures the country's brilliant development at an unprecedented speed and takes the toiling masses to a dignified, glorious, and ever more prosperous life. It brings to the working people a free, happy, and powerful Fatherland and leads them toward a bright horizon, formerly undreamt of. This is an inspiring example for the working people throughout the world, especially for the peoples of the East, who were and are still being enslaved by imperialism. The monopolist imperialists want to keep the Eastern countries in a backward economic state, keeping the masses in misery and always trampling on their nationalism.

The October Revolution has opened up the era of a new foreign policy, the policy of peace and friendship among nations. On October 26, 1917—the day following the establishment of worker-peasant power—the Second Congress of Soviets adopted a decree concerning peace, which was the basis of the Soviet state's foreign policy. Since then, the Soviet Union has constantly been carrying out an active struggle for peace and against the warmongers. This policy was prompted by the very nature of the socialist Soviet state. The truth is that the working people hate all aggressive wars because, first of all, they bring profit to the exploiters and cause ravages and sufferings to the broad masses. That is why the working people's power genuinely defends peace, in which the peoples of all lands display keen interest.

The October Revolution overthrew the capitalists' and landlords' state in a vast country, shattered the imperialists' chains, and thus eliminated all power of the exploiting class for whom war is a source of profit. The Soviet Union consistently stands for peaceful co-existence among nations, whatever their political and social systems.

The Communists are convinced of the superiority of the socialist system. The Soviet Union is cogent proof of this. For this reason it does not fear peaceful competition; on the contrary it advocates it. Not long before the October Revolution, Lenin quoted the principle expressed by Engels in 1882: *"The victorious proletariat cannot impose any happiness whatever on another people without in this way undermining its own victory"*[1] and regarded this principle as indubitable and absolutely conforming to the spirit of internationalism.

At the same time the Soviet Union unceasingly supports other nations in their struggle for national independence, against imperialist enslavement and aggression. The firm peace policy of the Soviet Union constitutes a decisive mainstay for all nations in their struggle against the forces of war. This policy is of particular importance for the peoples of the East, considered by the imperialists as ready prey and as sources of manpower and material wealth for the stepping up of their predatory wars.

A bulwark of peace, the Soviet Union is at the same time an invincible force ready to repel any aggression. From 1918 to 1920, Soviet power actively supported by the international proletariat crushed the internal counterrevolutionary forces and wiped out the armies of fourteen interventionist imperialist powers. During the Second World War, the Soviet Union annihilated the huge armed forces of the fascist aggressors, which had been carefully prepared with the assistance of all imperialist countries. Thus it saved the world from the barbarous Hitlerite enslavement and dealt a decisive blow at the main forces of Japanese militarism. All the peoples, especially the peoples of the East, felt gratitude for the Soviet Union. Full of enthusiasm, the peoples of the East were aware that the imperialists who enslaved other peoples were not invincible. The fascist aggres-

[1] Lenin, "Summing up of the discussion on the right of nations to self-determination," Autumn 1916.

sors were crushed, despite their modern weapons and their long preparation before the Second World War for their criminal aggression.

The October Revolution and the building of socialism in the Soviet Union have considerably increased the revolutionary forces of the working class in the capitalist countries. The laboring peoples of many European and Asian countries have followed the example set by the Russian revolutionary proletariat.

In a short space of history, socialism has become a world system, now embracing twelve countries with more than 900 million people.

The October Revolution has shattered the fetters of imperialism, destroyed its foundation and inflicted on it a deadly blow. Like a thunderbolt, it has stirred up the Asian peoples from their centuries-old slumbers. It has opened up for them the revolutionary anti-imperialist era, the era of national liberation.

The Soviet Union is the strongest and most powerful bulwark of progress, democracy and peace. Its invincible and constantly developing strength and its consistent peace policy constitute the firmest guarantee for the independence of all nations, big and small. The Soviet Union has always made worthy efforts and has tabled practical proposals for arms reduction. It has persistently struggled for the suppression of nuclear and thermonuclear weapons which are threatening all nations. It has many a time asked other states to adopt collective security systems aimed at safeguarding peace in Europe and Asia. It has always upheld the five principles of peaceful co-existence and has endeavored to make these five principles the basis of international relations between countries throughout the world.

Contrary to the peace policy of the socialist states the aggressive warmongering imperialists, first of all the U.S. imperialists, are aggravating international tension. They refuse arms reduction, prohibition of nuclear and thermonuclear weapons, which are a terrible threat to mankind. They cherish the senseless hope of keeping the whole world under the threat of their military bases. They form aggressive blocs like fetters, in an attempt to re-shackle and re-enslave the free and independent nations. They resort to every maneuver to threaten the peoples of the

East and to re-establish colonial rule in the countries which have recovered their independence. This is the true nature of the war unleashed against Egypt by the aggressors in London and Paris, with the practical assistance of the U.S. imperialists. While fostering the aggressive schemes of the others, the U.S. imperialists make an attempt to impose their yoke on the peoples in the Near East, Southeast Asia and the Pacific, to turn those countries into new bases of aggression and to oust from these countries their allies and rivals—English, French, Dutch, etc.

The imperialists seek to sow discord and division in the great family of socialist countries. This is the very nature of their aggression against the Hungarian People's Republic, against the historic achievements of the Hungarian people, who, thanks to the heroism of the Soviet people during the Second World War, were liberated from the fascist yoke. But events have confirmed the assessment made by the 20th Congress of the Communist Party of the Soviet Union: "Thanks to the powerful socialist camp which loves peace, the forces of peace have not only moral means but also material means to check aggression."[2] Owing to this fact and the existence of a "vast zone of peace," the peace movement of the broad masses and the development of the workers' movement in the capitalist countries, today "powerful social and political forces have sufficient means to prevent the imperialists from unleashing war, and will deal them deadly blows and frustrate their adventurist plans if they venture to launch war."[3]

In Egypt, the aggressors met with ignominious defeat. The plot of subversion against the Hungarian People's Republic was foiled. Everyone sees that the powerful strength, vigilance and determination of the Soviet Union have crushed the plot of the warmongers and aggressors. At the same time this is also the victory of the cause of peace and independence of all nations.

---

[2] "Resolution of the 20th Congress of the Communist Party of the U.S.S.R.," National Political Publishing House, 1956. Russian edition, page 9.

[3] "Resolution of the 20th Congress of the Communist Party of the U.S.S.R.," page 9.

The Soviet Union does not step back when facing the imperialist maniacs who want to sow trouble among the peoples so as to easily carry out their wicked schemes. The Soviet Union is determined to defend freedom and the peaceful labor of all peoples and the security of all nations big and small. The Soviet Union constantly shows loyalty to international solidarity, sympathizes with and supports the struggle for liberation of all oppressed nations. All countries of the East, whatever their state or social regime, are deeply grateful to the Soviet Union for its peace policy and its proletarian internationalism. These policies inspire the peoples of the East with an ever-growing confidence in the great socialist ideology.

The power brought into being by the October Revolution set an example of genuine freedom and friendship between nations.

Comrade Mao Tse-tung said: "The gun-shots of the October Revolution have brought us Marxism-Leninism. It has helped the whole world and the progressive elements in China to examine the destiny of the country in the world outlook of the working class and revise their own problems: The conclusion was to follow the path of the Russians."[4]

As early as 1913, Lenin said: "Everywhere in Asia a strong democratic movement is growing, spreading and being consolidated. There the bourgeoisie is still siding with the people to fight the reactionaries. Hundreds of millions of people are rising up in life, light and liberty . . . All young Asia, that is, hundreds of millions of toiling masses in Asia have a staunch ally— the proletariat of all civilized countries. No force on earth can prevent its victory, which will liberate all the peoples of Europe as well as of Asia."[5]

In 1919, at the Eastern Communists Congress, Lenin said: "A task is laid before you here, which has previously not been laid before the communists of the whole world: basing yourselves on the general theory and practice of communism, you must, in adapting yourselves to specific conditions which do not exist in the European countries, learn how to apply this theory and this

[4] Mao Tse-tung, *On the dictatorship of people's democracy.*
[5] Lenin, *Works,* Russian edition, Vol. XIX, pages 77–78.

practice to the conditions, when the peasantry forms the basic masses, when it is necessary to settle the task of struggle not against capitalism but against medieval vestiges."[6]

Dealing a telling blow at the common enemy—imperialism, the October Revolution has brought to the Eastern peoples assistance of a decisive character; it has given them the example of the liberation struggles of the countries once oppressed by Czarism.

The October Revolution has brought to the people of all nations the right to decide their own fate and the practical means to implement this right. It is well known that Lenin attached particular importance to the recognition of the right of all nations to secession and to build up independent states. Opposing Bukharin's theories, Lenin resolutely demanded that this right should be inserted into the Party's Political program expounded at the VIIIth Congress in March 1919. The Soviet Union of the October Revolution recognized the independence of Mongolia and Finland, which seceded to build up independent states. Of course, for the formerly oppressed nations, the right to secession does not signify the obligation to secede from a state where the people have overthrown the oppressors. On the contrary, it creates conditions for a voluntary alliance between free nations on the basis of complete equality of interests. It was on this basis that in December 1922, the Union of the Soviet Socialist Republics was founded—a great example of a multi-national socialist state built on friendship, mutual confidence and good co-operation between nationalities.

Today, in the Soviet Union, thanks to the friendly assistance of the Russian people, the nationalities formerly oppressed by the Czarist regime have reached an unprecedented level of development. They are able to establish their own institutions, restore and develop their own culture in their own language. All Soviet citizens, regardless of nationality and race, enjoy complete equality and the same freedoms, not only written on paper but actually ensured. This is a situation unknown to the workers of even the most democratic bourgeois countries where acknowledged freedoms guaranteed by law are canceled out by

[6] Lenin, *Works,* Russian edition, Vol. XXX, page 140.

actual social conditions. That is why the freedoms enjoyed by the Soviet peoples have fired the hearts of millions of people who are living under colonialist oppression. The ruling circles in the imperialist countries are stifling the most elementary freedoms of the colonial and dependent peoples, while inscribing the ironic legend "Liberty, Equality, Fraternity" in jails and places where tortures are carried out.

The Soviet Union establishes the equality of peoples by basing itself on special concern for the interests and requirements of the once oppressed nationalities. It helped them build up a modern economy, sweep away the centuries-old backwardness bequeathed them by their exploiters. The national republics of the Soviet Union have developed even more rapidly than the Russian Republic in industry as well as in all other fields. The recent measures taken in the light of the decision of the XXth Congress of the Communist Party of the Soviet Union to improve the organization of industrial and construction management, bring a new contribution to the bold and ingenious policy steadily carried out by the Soviet power since the October Revolution. They will further accelerate the economic and cultural development of all the republics in the Soviet Union. The peoples of these republics are setting for the peoples of the whole world an example of socialist peoples united into a monolithic bloc in political, social and moral fields, a solidarity unknown in the conditions of the capitalist regime.

All the Soviet nationalities are animated by an ardent and genuine patriotism—a patriotism inseparable from proletarian internationalism.

For the first time in history, the national question has been solved by the victorious working class in a satisfactory way, on the basis of Marxist-Leninist principles.

Marxism-Leninism has elaborated a just and complete theory of anti-imperialist national revolution. The era of monopoly capitalism is also one where a few great powers, swayed by a handful of financiers, exercise their domination over dependent and semi-dependent countries; therefore the liberation of the oppressed countries and peoples has become an integral part of the proletarian revolution.

Hence there arise in the first place the possibility of and the need for a close fighting alliance between the colonial peoples and the proletariat of the imperialist countries, to triumph over the common enemy. The revolutionary struggle of the workers of the capitalist countries directly helps the oppressed peoples free themselves, by striking direct blows at the heart of the oppressors; this was vividly demonstrated by the October Revolution which has overthrown the power of the exploiters in Russia and resolutely abolished the oppressive colonial policy of the Czarist regime and the Russian bourgeois class. In its turn, the revolutionary struggle of colonial and semi-colonial peoples directly helps the proletariat of the capitalist countries in their fight against the ruling classes to free themselves from the yoke of capitalism. The unity of the anti-imperialist struggle carries the certainty of victory for all colonial and semi-colonial peoples and for the proletariat in the capitalist countries.

Therefore, the national question can no longer be viewed from an abstract and isolated point of view. Marxism-Leninism has shown that national movements, effectively directed against imperialism, unfailingly contribute to the general revolutionary struggle; that national claims and national movements must not be estimated according to their strictly local political and social character in a narrow-minded way, but according to the part they play against the imperialist forces in the world. Marxism-Leninism has unmasked bourgeois democracy, which dissimulated behind sermons on the abstract "equality" between nations to conceal the oppression and exploitation of the great number of nations in the world by a handful of imperialist countries. Marxism-Leninism makes a clear distinction, between "oppressed, dependent and subject nations, and the oppressing, exploiting and sovereign nations. . . ."[7]

To handle in a scientific way those problems on the basis of Marxism-Leninism and of the inexhaustible theoretical and practical experiences of the Soviet Union, at the same time to pay heed to the peculiarities of all dependent countries, is of great importance for the study of political lines, to continue the

[7] Lenin, *Works,* Russian edition, Vol. XXXI, page 123.

development of the national liberation movement and the organization of social forces in the revolutions for liberation in the Eastern countries. In 1923, Lenin wrote on the dependent countries as follows: "Our European philistines never even dream that the subsequent revolutions—in Oriental countries, which possess much vaster populations and a much vaster diversity of social conditions, will undoubtedly display even greater peculiarities than the Russian revolution."[8]

During the course of the emancipation struggles of the Eastern peoples, the Marxist-Leninist principles in the question of colonial liberation have been triumphantly confirmed. The October Revolution provided strong impetus for this struggle, and the existence of the Soviet Union constituted an important historic factor which helped that struggle develop rapidly.

The revolution in the colonial and semi-colonial countries is a national-democratic revolution. To make it successful, it is possible and necessary to form a very wide national front, uniting all social strata and classes longing for liberation from colonialist yoke. In particular, one should bear in mind that the role played by the bourgeoisie in colonial and dependent countries in general is not similar to that played by the bourgeoisie in capitalist countries. The national bourgeoisie can be won to participate actively in the national-democratic revolution.

The revolution in the colonial and semi-colonial countries is first and foremost a peasant revolution. It is inseparable from the anti-feudal revolution. The alliance of the broad peasant masses with the working class is the fundamental base on which a wide and firm national front can be formed. Consequently, agrarian reform is a fundamental task of the national-democratic revolution.

To lead the national revolution to victory and to cover the successive stages of the development of the national-democratic state, the working class and its Party must take up their role of leading the revolution.

The revolution for liberation of the oppressed countries and the revolution of the proletariat of the oppressing countries

[8] Lenin, *Works,* Russian edition, Vol. XXXIII, page 439.

must support each other. In the oppressing countries, the central task in the education of internationalism is to help the toiling people clearly understand the right of oppressed nationalities to secession and to found independent states, and in the oppressed countries this task consists in allying the various nationalities on a voluntary basis. Lenin said: "The situation which presents itself provides no other path leading to internationalism and the concord between peoples, no other path leading to this goal."[9]

The October Revolution gave an impetus to the movement of national liberation, which has become a surging wave in all Eastern countries: China, India, Indonesia, Viet Nam, etc. After the Second World War, many colonial and semi-colonial countries have shattered imperialist chains. Several of them have broken away from the capitalist system.

The victory of the Chinese revolution was a historical event of great significance. It struck a new blow at the imperialist system, the severest since the October Revolution.

Today, more than one thousand two hundred million inhabitants of Asia and Africa have already freed themselves from colonial and semi-colonial enslavement.

The colonial system of imperialism is collapsing beyond remedy; the question of total liquidation of the colonial system is the foremost one. The peoples of the East are rising up against their aggressors and are determined not to let anyone oppress them.

As Lenin had foreseen, the time has now come when, heads held high, these peoples enter the international arena.

The Vietnamese people advance towards socialism under the glorious Marxist-Leninist banner.

Thanks to the French Communist Party and the Chinese Communist Party, the Vietnamese revolutionaries have received the invigorating influence of the October Revolution and of Marxism-Leninism. That is like a thirsty and hungry traveler who, after a long journey, receives water and rice.

The Indochinese Communist Party was founded on February 3, 1930, thirteen years after the October Revolution. It became

---

[9] Lenin, *Works,* Russian edition, Vol. XXII, page 332.

the undisputed leader of the whole people in the struggle against imperialism.

In September 1930, in Nghe An province, under the leadership of the young Indochinese Communist Party, the peasants seized power and established the Soviets, marking a step in their heroic struggle. The Soviets adopted a resolution on agrarian reform which was put into effect by the peasants. But going mad before the development of the movement of national liberation and the activities of the Soviets, the French imperialists savagely repressed and terrorized the Vietnamese people. They succeeded in crushing the Soviets only by mobilizing all their available forces, bombing the liberated zones, razing whole villages to the ground, and setting up a regime of bestial terror everywhere. However, the Indochinese Communist Party throughout the country kept on struggling persistently and heroically throughout the country to lead the movement of national liberation of the Vietnamese people.

Twenty-eight years after the October Revolution the victory of the Soviet army over the Japanese imperialists created favorable conditions for the August Revolution which brought independence to Viet Nam.

But the French imperialists were not content with their defeat and wanted to re-enslave Viet Nam. For nine years, the Vietnamese people had to wage a hard and heroic resistance war against the colonialists. United in a broad patriotic front and standing around the Viet Nam Workers' Party which inherited the experiences and traditions of the Indochinese Communist Party, the Vietnamese people have defeated the forces of French and world imperialism.

In 1954, the Geneva Agreement was signed thanks to the help of the Soviet Union and China, and the support of peace-loving peoples all over the world. It put an end to the aggressive war of the colonialists. The independence, unity and territorial integrity of Viet Nam were officially recognized.

Since then the Vietnamese people have perseveringly carried on the struggle for the implementation of the Geneva Agreement to reunify the country, because South Viet Nam is still ruled by the U.S. imperialists and their henchmen. In completely liberated North Viet Nam power is in the hands of the people; this is a firm basis for the peaceful reunification of Viet Nam, a task which receives ever-growing and generous help from the Soviet Union, China and other brother countries. Thanks to this assistance, the consolidation of the North has scored good results.

The victory of the August Revolution in Viet Nam has proved once again the soundness of Marxism-Leninism on the national and colonial question, the correctness of the line mapped out by the Socialist Revolution of October 1917. It confirms that to be successful, the national revolution must:

—rely upon a broad national front against imperialism;
—solve the peasant question;
—organize a people's army;
—have the brotherly support of the people and proletariat of other countries;
—be led by the Party of the working class.

The October Revolution teaches us to unite closely the efforts of the world proletariat, of the oppressed peoples and other peace forces in the whole world to struggle against imperialism and war.

"Unless the proletariat and, following it, all the toiling masses of all countries and nations all over the world voluntarily strive for alliance and unity, victory over capitalism cannot be successfully accomplished," said Lenin.[10] And he added: "In the last analysis, the outcome of the struggle will be determined by the fact that Russia, India, China, etc., account for the overwhelming majority of the population of the globe. And it is precisely this majority that, during the past few years, has been drawn into the struggle for emancipation with extraordinary rapidity, so that in this respect there cannot be the slightest shadow of doubt as to what the final outcome of the world struggle will be. In this sense, the complete victory of socialism is fully and absolutely assured."[11]

[10] Lenin, *Works,* Russian edition, Vol. XXXI, page 128.
[11] Lenin, *Works,* Russian edition, Vol. XXXIII, page 458.

The forty years which have elapsed since the October Revolution are years of uninterrupted marching forward of socialism.

In the face of the imperialists who seek to prolong their tottering regime, detested by every people, we, revolutionaries of all countries, must at all times strengthen our unity around the U.S.S.R. and the Communist Party of the U.S.S.R. The Leninist theories of the 20th Congress strengthen this union still further, tighten the bonds of friendship and mutual trust between the socialist countries. The declaration by the Government of the Soviet Union on October 30, 1956, defined anew the relationship between socialist countries, established on principles of equality, mutual respect, confidence and friendly cooperation.

The celebration of the 40th anniversary of the great October Revolution is an opportunity to mobilize the great mass of workers of the whole world, to appeal to them to unite and struggle to achieve new and yet greater victories.

16

Maurice Meisner: The Chinese Communist Revolution*

Communist China, it is often said, is a nation imprisoned by the traditions of its historic past. "The more [Mao Tse-tung] seeks to make China new," a distinguished historian has written, "the more he seems to fall back on old Chinese ways of doing it."[1] One need not accept the view that Chinese Communism is the carrier (albeit an unconscious one) of the millennial Chinese cultural tradition to recognize that the legacies of the Chinese past weigh heavily on the Chinese revolutionary present. Institutional forms, social habits, and patterns of thought and behavior that evolved over some three thousand years cannot be so easily disposed of—not even by the most iconoclastic revolutionaries operating in the most favorable of historical environments. And, while there can be little doubt that the leaders of Communist China are revolutionary iconoclasts, they find themselves in something less than the most favorable of environments, and not for cultural reasons alone. For the survivals of the cultural past have been accompanied and supported by a terrible heri-

* Maurice Meisner, "Yenan Communism and the Rise of the Chinese People's Republic," in James B. Crowley, ed., *Modern East Asia: Essays in Interpretation* (New York: Harcourt, Brace and World, 1970), pp. 265–296. By permission.

Maurice Meisner, Professor of History at the University of Wisconsin, has written *Li Ta-chao and the Origins of Chinese Marxism*.

[1] John K. Fairbank, *China: The People's Middle Kingdom and the U.S.A.* (Cambridge, Mass.: Harvard University Press, 1967), p. 3.

tage of economic and social backwardness and massive poverty. Mao Tse-tung's famous statement that China is "poor and blank"—an expression of his great faith in the future emergence of a "new China"—is only half true. China is indeed poor, but it is hardly blank, for archaic elements of the past remain and impose cruel burdens on the present. And "cultural revolutions," however fervently pursued, are not likely to achieve a viable new culture or a "new China" unless accompanied by massive economic and social transformations.

Yet, if Chinese Communists bear the burden of "traditional China," they are also the bearers of other and more recent traditions. They carry, in their own particular fashion, the "Western" Marxist tradition—the tradition that was adopted rather than the one that was reluctantly inherited. And there is a third tradition, neither inherited nor adopted by Chinese Communists but of their own making—the Chinese Communist revolutionary tradition forged in the bitter wars and civil wars of the two decades that culminated in the establishment of the Chinese People's Republic in 1949. These two new "Chinese" traditions also bind and shackle in various ways, but they convey new values and proclaim a future different from that which the Confucian tradition of the more distant past would dictate.

It is the purpose of this essay to explore certain themes in these two new traditions to which Communist China is heir. In such an exploration, the much-celebrated Yenan period of Chinese Communism (1935–47) assumes a place of very special importance. The Yenan era not only proved decisive for the rise of Communist power in China; it also came to be seen as the heroic phase of the Chinese revolution—it is the experiences of those years that Chinese Communists today celebrate as the most pristine and noble expression of their revolutionary heritage. The Yenan period was also the time when Mao Tse-tung first seriously attempted to come to grips with Marxist theory, to understand and evaluate the Marxist-Leninist doctrine he had adopted, and to rationalize Chinese Communist political practice in terms of Marxist-Leninist theory. In the process, that theory was both explicitly and implicitly revised, and "Maoism" emerged as a distinct and distinctive variant of

Marxism, and one with enormous consequences for the future.
The now famous "thoughts of Mao Tse-tung" are in large
measure (though by no means entirely) the thoughts and writings of Mao in Yenan. And, finally, it was in the highly
nationalistic milieu of the Yenan era that Chinese Communist
theorists and historians felt the need to tie themselves to the
Chinese historical and cultural tradition, to establish a meaningful relationship with the historic past by interpreting it through
the prism of Marxist historical theory and in the light of contemporary Chinese revolutionary experience.

Much of what is distinctive about Communism and Marxism
in China, therefore, was crystallized in the Yenan period. And,
although the heroic Yenan years are now long past, the concepts, phrases, and slogans that emerged from that time are still
heard—in recent years, as crescendos announcing new revolutionary dramas.

For Chinese Communists, it is "the Yenan spirit" that is
celebrated—celebrated not only in history books but as a living
model to be emulated in the present for revolutionary tasks yet
to be completed. And for contemporary "China watchers," it is
"the Yenan syndrome" that is pondered. Why is it, they wonder, that this allegedly pathological element in the Chinese body
politic has not yet been safely buried in history books?

Whether "spirit" or "syndrome," Yenan still lives in the
present, in the minds of men both inside and outside China. To
understand why this is so, it is necessary to turn to the history
of the Yenan years, to see what "Yenan Communism" was and
how it came to be.

The Political and Psychological Significance of the Long March
The conclusion of the epic Long March marked the beginning
of the epic of Yenan. It was in October 1935 that Mao Tse-tung
led what remained of the Communist First Front Army through
the last lines of enemy soldiers guarding Mount Liup'an in
Kansu province and entered the northern portion of Shensi
province. And there, in that remote and relatively primitive area
of China's vast and sparsely populated Northwest, Chinese
Communist revolutionaries from many provinces found refuge

in the months and years to come. It was a precarious haven, to be sure, but one that provided sufficient time and opportunity to establish a new base area from which the revolution was to begin once again, grow and develop in new ways, and eventually emerge victorious.

Mao marked his arrival in Shensi with a poem that expresses something of his feelings at the time the Long March neared its end:

> Lofty the sky
> 　　and pale the clouds—
> We watch the wild geese
> 　　fly south till they vanish.
> We count the thousand
> 　　leagues already travelled.
> If we do not reach
> 　　the Great Wall we are not true men.
>
> High on the crest
> 　　of Liup'an Mountain
> Our banners billow
> 　　in the west wind.
> Today we hold
> 　　the rope in our hands.
> When shall we put bonds
> 　　upon the grey dragon?[2]

Although Mao wrote his poem in a style borrowed from the past, in the classical Chinese *tzu* form, and employed traditional phrases and allusions, the content pointed prophetically to the future. However much else was uncertain in the autumn of 1935, Mao was certain that the new battles to be fought were to be with "the grey dragon," the Japanese invaders who had occupied Manchuria and parts of North China and who threatened a full-scale war to conquer all of China. The struggle to "put bonds upon the grey dragon" was soon to begin—perhaps

[2] "Mount Liup'an," translated from the Chinese by Michael Bullock and Jerome Ch'en in Jerome Ch'en, *Mao and the Chinese Revolution* (London: Oxford University Press, 1965), p. 337.

sooner than Mao then anticipated—and was to dominate the next decade of Chinese history. As we shall have occasion to observe, this struggle was to prove of crucial importance in molding the nature of Yenan Communism and was to have critical implications for the fate of the Chinese Communist revolution.

But, while Mao anticipated something of the future in his poem, he also reflected on the year past, looking back to "count the thousand leagues already travelled"—and no doubt to count the dead and missing as well. For few of those who began that incredible, six-thousand-mile journey survived to reach "the Great Wall"—or, more precisely, the new revolutionary stronghold the Communists were to establish just to the south of that ancient northern fortress. Of the approximately 100,000 men and 35 women (80,000 soldiers and 20,000 administrative party cadres) who began with Mao from Kiangsi on the night of October 15, 1934, only about 8,000 survived the torturous trek to the north to arrive in Shensi a year later. Among the many dead—left along that circuitous and now legendary route through the treacherous mountains, rivers, and marshes of western China—were many of Mao's closest friends and comrades and one of his two younger brothers, Mao Tse-t'an, killed in one of the many bloody battles fought with pursuing Kuomintang troops and warlord armies along the way. Among the missing—and never to be found—were two of Mao's children, who remained behind with sympathetic peasant families in Kiangsi, along with many other children too young to undertake the march.

The Communists call the migration from Kiangsi to the Northwest the "Twenty-five-thousand-*li* March" (a distance of approximately eight thousand miles) and celebrate it as a great victory for the Red Army and a defeat for the Kuomintang. Actually, it was only about eighteen thousand *li,* but it was long enough and sufficiently heroic. This is not the place to relate the history of the epic or to celebrate it. The Long March will stand on its own as one of the most extraordinary chapters in the annals of military history and as a truly remarkable saga of human courage and endurance. Measuring it by any standards of human accomplishment, and quite apart from one's political persuasions, few would disagree with Edgar Snow's assessment that it was "an Odyssey unequaled in modern times."[3]

But the heroic adventures and the great human drama of the Long March should not be allowed to obscure the fact that it was born out of political failure and the prospect of military catastrophe and nearly ended in complete disaster. The Communists did not choose to leave Kiangsi but were forced to do so. Having successfully withstood Chiang Kai-shek's first four "encirclement and annihilation" campaigns (1930–33), they had neither the economic nor the military resources to resist the new "blockhouse strategy" that Chiang's imported German military advisers had devised for the fifth campaign. Surrounded by almost one million Kuomintang troops and increasingly hard pressed by the effects of an ever tightening economic blockade, the Communists found their position had become untenable by early 1934, and in the summer of that year they undertook preparations to retreat from the Soviet areas in the Southeast.

The abandonment of the Chinese Soviet Republic, which the Communists had built with such painstaking efforts for over half a decade, and the abandonment of the peasants who had supported them to the terrible reprisals the Kuomintang was to inflict, marked a political defeat of very considerable magnitude. And the fact that the largest part of the Red Army was destroyed during the ordeals of the next year can hardly be seen as a Communist victory, much less a defeat for the Kuomintang. The exhausted and ill-equipped survivors of the Long March who reached Shensi in the fall of 1935 celebrated not a military and political triumph but rather the fantastic fact that they had managed to survive at all. They were indeed heroic, but they were not victorious. Their victory was still to come, and it was to come in the context of new and very different political and historical circumstances.

Yet the Long March was the prelude to what proved to be the victorious period of the Chinese Communist revolution, and

[3] *Red Star Over China* (New York: Random House, 1938), p. 177. Snow's original account (pp. 177–96) remains the best description of the Long March to appear in English.

in that sense it was an event with momentous political and psychological consequences. Politically, the Long March is important because it was the time when Mao Tse-tung achieved effective control of the Chinese Communist party, a position of influence and authority that had eluded him during the Kiangsi period. The internal political history of the Chinese Communist party in the early and mid-1930's is much too complex a subject to deal with here, and much of the story remains obscure.[4] It is clear, however, that throughout most of the Kiangsi period Mao was engaged in an almost continuous political struggle with other Communist leaders and factions, most notably with the Comintern-supported "Twenty-eight Bolsheviks," a group of young Chinese Communists trained at Sun Yat-sen University in Moscow to do Stalin's bidding in China. Although Mao officially was chairman of the Soviet government in Kiangsi, his influence over both party and army affairs was never complete and was steadily eroded by the growing power of the Twenty-eight Bolsheviks, led by Wang Ming and Po Ku. Not only were the policies he advocated often overruled, but he sometimes found himself in the most precarious of political positions, and at no time more so than in the waning months of the Kiangsi era. In July 1934 Mao was deprived of all authority in both party and government and, according to some sources, was placed under house arrest for a time prior to the beginning of the Long March in October. Indeed, the military operations of the Long March itself were originally directed largely by a Comintern military adviser, Otto Braun, a German known by the pseudonym Li T'e. As a military strategist, the Communists' German adviser had proved a good deal inferior to the Kuomintang's German generals, von Seeckt and Falkenhausen.

It was not until the troops on the main line of the Long March stopped at the town of Tsunyi in Kweichow province in early January 1935 that the power of Li T'e and the Twenty-

[4] Much that had hitherto been obscure or unknown is detailed in John E. Rue's revealing account *Mao Tse-tung in Opposition, 1927–1935* (Stanford, Calif.: Stanford University Press, 1966) and in Stuart R. Schram's excellent biography *Mao Tse-tung* (New York: Simon & Schuster, 1967).

eight Bolsheviks was effectively broken. There Mao called an enlarged meeting of the party's Politburo, and from that fateful conference he emerged as the chairman of the Politburo and the head of the reorganized Revolutionary Military Council. His leadership was not to go unchallenged, but he was now sufficiently in control of the party (and of enough of the army) to pursue his own policies and his own strategy of revolution. The incubus of the Comintern finally had been thrown off, and Mao had achieved party supremacy in defiance of Stalin. It was an event unprecedented in the history of Communist parties in the Stalinist era and one having the greatest significance for the future course of the Chinese Communist revolution.

The Tsunyi conference also defined the destination and purpose of the Long March, hitherto unsettled matters that had provoked heated controversies among Communist leaders. "Go north and fight the Japanese" was the official battlecry that now emerged. Some dissented, most notably Chang Kuo-t'ao (and perhaps Mao's long-time comrade in arms Chu Teh). While Mao moved north, Chang led the Fourth Front Army westward to Sinkiang and Tibet,[5] although Chang and Chu eventually were to rejoin Mao in Shensi in 1936.

It is impossible to know whether Mao's determination to march to the north was motivated primarily by nationalist impulses to defend the nation against the Japanese threat or was part of a grand revolutionary design to capitalize on the growing forces of popular nationalist feelings and harness them to Communist ends. No doubt both considerations were involved, but, as events were soon to demonstrate, it was in any case a situation in which Chinese nationalist and Communist revolutionary considerations coincided. One can credit Mao with either great foresight or great luck. However that may be, the Long March had brought him to a position of supreme leadership in the Chinese Communist party and had brought the

[5] Much of this whole episode remains mysterious. According to Chu Teh's later account, he was imprisoned by Chang and forced, under threat of death, to accompany him to Sinkiang (see Agnes Smedley, *The Great Road* [New York: Monthly Review Press, 1956], pp. 328–32). Chang Kuo-t'ao was expelled from the party in 1938.

revolutionaries he now led to a geographical position from which they could both stimulate Chinese nationalist feelings and mobilize them for revolutionary purposes.

The psychological effects of the Long March are perhaps as important for the history of the Chinese Communist revolution as its political implications, although here one encounters a more intangible realm of affairs that it is difficult to assess with any degree of assurance. There can be little doubt, at least, that the experience of the Long March served to reinforce Mao's already deeply ingrained voluntaristic faith that men with the proper will, spirit, and revolutionary consciousness could conquer all material obstacles and mold historical reality in accordance with their ideas and ideals. If the Long March demonstrated anything, it was the ability of men to defy the most overwhelming odds, to triumph over the most formidable and fearsome barriers that nature could present and that other men might erect. For those who survived the ordeal—and for those who were inspired by the story of their survival—the experience, however bitter it was at the time, gave rise to a renewed sense of hope and a deepened sense of mission. These are necessary (even if not necessarily sufficient) ingredients for any successful revolutionary effort. Men must be able to hope before they can act; they must possess not only ideals and a sense of mission but hope and confidence that they will be able to realize their ideals and their mission through their own actions. More than any other event in the history of Chinese Communism, it was the Long March—and the legendary tales to which it gave rise—that provided the essential hope and confidence, the faith that determined men could prevail under even the most desperate conditions. And, more than any other individual, it was Mao Tse-tung who radiated and inspired this confidence, as is well reflected in a statement that appears in the "autobiography" he related to Edgar Snow not long after the conclusion of the Long March:

> The victorious march of the Red Army, and its triumphant arrival in Kansu and Shensi with its living forces still intact, was due first to the correct leadership of the Communist Party,

and secondly to the great skill, courage, determination and almost super-human endurance and revolutionary ardor of the basic cadres of our Soviet people. The Communist Party of China was, is, and will be, faithful to Marxism-Leninism. . . . In this determination lies one explanation of its invincibility and the certainty of its final victory.[6]

What is expressed and conveyed here (even though in Marxist-Leninist idiom) is not only confidence in the future, and in those deemed capable of molding the future in accordance with Communist hopes, but also the kinds of values that were regarded as essential to the eventual realization of those hopes. The now familiar Maoist virtues of unending struggle, heroic sacrifice, self-denial, diligence, courage, and unselfishness were values not espoused by Mao alone but carried and conveyed by all (or at least most) of "the veterans of the Long March," for they had come to regard these values as essential to their own survival and to that of the revolution to which they had devoted their lives. These values lay at the core of what later came to be celebrated as "the Yenan spirit"; they were held by the makers of the Chinese Communist revolutionary tradition, and they are still conveyed by those who have inherited that tradition.

Many more died during the Long March than survived it, and this fact alone made its peculiar contribution to "the Yenan spirit." The survivors' consciousness that they had lived while so many more had died lent an almost sacred character to their revolutionary mission and gave rise to a religious sense of dedication.

This overwhelming sense of mission and dedication may be attributed partly to what Robert Jay Lifton has referred to as "the survivor's characteristically guilt-laden need to contrast his own continuing life with others' deaths."[7] One way to attempt to transcend this feeling of guilt, or of grief, is to make an extraordinary personal commitment to a collective revolutionary effort, to create a future that will vindicate and justify the

---

[6] Cited in Snow, *Red Star Over China*, p. 167.

[7] *Revolutionary Immortality: Mao Tse-tung and the Chinese Cultural Revolution* (New York: Random House, 1968), p. 14.

sacrifices that have been made. This "survivor formulation," as Lifton has termed it, is particularly useful for understanding something of Mao Tse-tung's mentality in the Yenan period and after. Although it is doubtful that Mao has been tormented with an overriding sense of guilt, he has exhibited an acute awareness of his own defiance of death while so many of those who surrounded him were killed in the course of revolutionary struggles. Among the dead were not only untold numbers of close friends and revolutionary comrades but many members of his own family.[8] In an interview with Edgar Snow in 1965, Mao recounted his personal losses and described some of the many instances when he himself faced seemingly certain death but miraculously managed to escape. Mao found it "odd" that he had survived and commented that "death just did not seem to want him."[9] This sense of having defied death undoubtedly contributed enormously to Mao's perception of himself as a man of destiny who would lead his followers to the completion of their sacred revolutionary mission. And if others did not necessarily share Mao's special sense of destiny and infallibility, they had had similar experiences, suffered equally heavy personal losses, and acquired a similar sense of being "survivors." This psychological legacy of the Long March became one of the components of Yenan Communism, and it manifested itself in a very special commitment to carry on the revolutionary struggle.

Thus, for "the veterans of the Long March," and for those who inherited their values and sense of mission, the sheer fact of survival became a matter of enormous psychological significance. It was also a matter of great political consequence, for it was testimony not only to the validity of the mission but to the

[8] During the Long March, as we have noted, Mao lost two of his children and a younger brother. Earlier, in 1930, his younger sister and his wife, Yang K'ai-hui, the "brave Yang" Mao mourned in one of his most moving poems ("Reply to Madame Li Shu-yi," in *Poems of Mao Tse-tung*, translated and edited by Wong Man [Hong Kong: Eastern Horizon Press, 1966], p. 54), were captured and executed by Kuomintang authorities in Changsha. A second brother was killed during the Yenan period, and a son later died in battle in the Korean War.

[9] Edgar Snow, "Interview with Mao," *New Republic*, Vol. 52 (February 27, 1965), pp. 17–23.

wisdom of the leader and his policies. Indeed, the cult of Mao Tse-tung was doubtless born out of the Long March, for Mao was the prophet who had led the survivors through the wilderness. And if Shensi was not the promised land, later revolutionary successes were to seem to fulfill his prophecies. Although one does not find in the Yenan period anything resembling the more extreme forms of the worship of Mao and his "thought" witnessed in recent years, a certain mystique and sense of awe had already begun to develop around his name and person. As early as 1937, Edgar Snow reported that Mao had acquired the reputation of leading "a charmed life."[10] The "faith in Mao" that emerged from the experiences (and the legends) of the Long March, and that grew and deepened in the Yenan years, is the foundation upon which the more recent cult of Mao has been erected.

In Communist China today, no event in the history of the revolution is more celebrated than the Long March. The story is told and retold in an endless flood of memoirs, novels, films, poems, and history books. To be able to claim one was "with Chairman Mao on the Long March" is the highest of revolutionary honors. An entire floor of the Revolutionary Museum in Peking is devoted to the celebration of the epic, complete with a huge, electronically controlled map that traces the journey in minute detail. But, although the story is told in museums, the Long March has not yet been "museumified." It is not yet merely an event of historical significance to be commemorated on appropriate occasions; it remains a heroic model from the revolutionary past to be emulated on all occasions. The stories and legends of the Long March (much embellished and glorified in the retelling) convey to new generations of Chinese the past revolutionary examples of "arduous struggle," dedication, and self-sacrifice, values still deemed relevant for the revolutionary present. Its continuing symbolic significance has been manifested in various forms, but never more strikingly than in 1966 and 1967, when various Red Guard groups undertook their own exhausting "long marches" to testify to their claims to be the

[10] Snow, *Red Star Over China*, p. 67.

rightful heirs to the revolutionary tradition and to demonstrate their devotion to continuing the revolution.

In celebrating the heroism of the Long March, contemporary Chinese Communist accounts present the event as a great victory that in turn guaranteed the inevitable victory of the revolution. Victory did not seem so inevitable at the time, however. When Mao reached Shensi in October 1935, only about eight thousand haggard and half-starved men remained of the First Front Army. While they celebrated their survival, they had little else to celebrate. In assessing the situation, Mao was a good deal more candid than later Communist writers. In a report prepared in December 1936, he wrote:

> Except for the Shensi-Kansu border area, all revolutionary bases were lost, the Red Army was reduced from 300,000 to a few tens of thousands, the membership of the Chinese Communist Party was reduced from 300,000 to a few tens of thousands, and the Party organizations in Kuomintang areas were almost entirely wiped out. In short, we received an extremely great historical punishment.[11]

To be sure, Mao attributed the disaster to the ideological and political errors of his recently vanquished party opponents and duly expressed confidence in ultimate victory and in the new strategy he proposed to achieve that victory. But his appraisal of Communist fortunes at the conclusion of the Long March was bleak and accurate.

The military forces under Mao's control in Shensi were augmented in late 1935 by several thousand Communist partisans who had been engaged in guerrilla warfare in the Northwest since 1931 under the leadership of Liu Chih-tan, a Whampoa graduate and former Kuomintang army officer whose heroic exploits had given him something of a Robin Hood reputation among the peasants of his native Shensi. In addition, several thousand other Communist troops, who had abandoned a small

[11] "Strategic Problems of China's Revolutionary War," in *Selected Works of Mao Tse-tung*, Vol. I (London: Lawrence & Wishart, 1954), p. 193.

and precarious base area in Hunan province, reached Shensi in September 1935, several weeks prior to Mao's arrival. In 1936 these forces were joined by the remnants of two other armies, which had taken different, but equally difficult, routes to the North: the army under the command of Ho Lung, which had been operating in Hunan, and the troops led by Chang Kuo-t'ao and Chu Teh, which arrived from Kiangsi by way of Sinkiang. Yet by late 1936 the Red Army in Shensi numbered no more than thirty thousand men, a pitifully small and poorly equipped force compared to the pursuing Kuomintang army and various hostile warlord armies allied with Chiang Kai-shek.

The Yenan Era and Peasant Revolution

If the Communist military position in 1936 was precarious at best, the social and economic environment in which they now found themselves was hardly any more promising. Northern Shensi was one of the poorest and most backward areas of modern China. Centuries of erosion of its loess topsoil had made its lands barren and infertile, capable of supporting only a relatively small and extremely impoverished population—"a very poor, backward, underdeveloped, and mountainous part of the country," as Mao Tse-tung once remarked to a foreign visitor who had toured the province.[12] And, to Chou En-lai in 1936, it seemed a most inauspicious place to revive the revolution. He complained:

> Peasants in Shensi are extremely poor, their land very unproductive . . . . The population of the Kiangsi Soviet numbered 3,000,000 whereas here it is at most 600,000 . . . . In Kiangsi and Fukien people brought bundles with them when they joined the Red Army; here they do not even bring chopsticks; they are utterly destitute.[13]

And what of Yenan itself, the most sacred city to which pilgrimages are made to view the historic revolutionary places,

[12] Cited in Jan Myrdal, *Report from a Chinese Village* (New York: Pantheon, 1965), p. xxvii.

[13] Cited in Edgar Snow, *Random Notes on Red China, 1936–1945* (Cambridge, Mass.: Harvard University Press, 1957), pp. 60–61.

especially the austere wooden houses and cave dwellings where Mao and others lived and worked during that legendary decade? Although an ancient city, founded some three thousand years ago, it cannot claim a particularly distinguished history. As Chinese civilization moved southward over the centuries, Yenan became a remote and unknown frontier town, used mostly as an advanced military outpost to defend the northern borders against nomadic invaders from central Asia. It was little more than a dreary and impoverished market town of perhaps ten thousand people when it was occupied by Communist troops at the end of 1936 and established as the administrative capital of what was to be called the Shensi-Kansu-Ningsia Border Region. The wretched poverty of the entire area in which the Communists now operated was reflected in the bleakness of Yenan. The town's famous museums and shrines exhibit no ancient, historic glories but are products of modern revolutionary history—and, in a sense, are the result of an accident of history. ("We didn't pick it" was Mao's terse reply to a sympathetic American writer who once politely praised Yenan's harsh climate.)[14]

But it is Yenan the time, not Yenan the place, that Chinese Communists celebrate. Yet how did the time become one to celebrate when the place was so unfavorable? How did a force of thirty thousand revolutionaries, isolated in an area so remote and so lacking in economic and material resources, grow within a decade into a powerful army of more than a million men and acquire the massive peasant support upon which its momentous and overwhelming victory was to be based?

Little light is shed on these questions by pondering that most quoted of Maoist maxims: "Political power grows out of the barrel of a gun." To be sure, an important modern Chinese political reality is reflected in this slogan: The disintegration of traditional Chinese forms of political authority and sources of legitimacy had produced a twentieth-century historical situation in which the effective exercise of political power was in fact largely dependent on the control of effective military force. But

[14] Anna Louise Strong, *Tomorrow's China* (New York: Committee for a Democratic Far Eastern Policy, 1948), p. 18.

Mao Tse-tung was not the first to discover this particular secret of modern Chinese political life. Chiang Kai-shek, for one, had learned the lesson earlier, and it was, in fact, Chiang's control of an effective army in 1927 that was mainly responsible for the Communist disasters of that year. Moreover, "political power grows out of the barrel of a gun" is hardly a formula for political victory, even if it is a more or less accurate description of the character of modern Chinese politics. Still less is it an explanation for the victory prepared during the Yenan decade. For the fact remains that in 1936 the Communists in Shensi had few guns (even fewer guns than men to hold them), and they possessed what guns they had in an environment where the economic and human resources necessary for the development of military power were severely limited. It is, in short, necessary to explain how they acquired guns—and the men willing to use them—in order to understand how Communist political power did in fact grow in China.

We shall turn shortly to the many internal prerequisites for the Communist military and political success. But first it is necessary to take note of a crucial external factor—the Japanese invasion and its effects—that transformed the Chinese political scene and redefined the internal prerequisites for revolutionary victory.

For those inclined to ponder the role of "accidents" in history, the Japanese invasion of China is undoubtedly a most intriguing case. Were it not for the Japanese attempt to conquer China in 1937, it can plausibly be argued, the conditions essential to the Communist victory would not have been present. Yenan would have remained an obscure and unheralded market town in a remote Chinese province, unknown to Chinese and foreigners alike. No one in Peking today would be celebrating "the Yenan spirit," and no "China watchers" would be deliberating the implications of "the Yenan syndrome." The whole course of recent Chinese history—and indeed of world history —would probably have been profoundly different.

Those who are inclined to seek universal patterns of historical development can find in the Japanese invasion of China a classic case of one of the oldest and most persistent of historical patterns: the intimate relationship between war and revolution.

For students of communism, it is of special interest to note that all *indigenous* communist revolutions (with one dubious exception)[15] grew out of conditions created by major wars; more precisely, they grew as war and foreign invasion undermined the power and authority of existing socio-political orders. The Russian October Revolution of 1917 was in large measure the product of conditions created in Russian society by World War I. And it was the foreign invasions of World War II that produced the conditions for successful communist revolutions in Yugoslavia and Vietnam as well as in China.

However intriguing it might be to pursue the question of the relationship between war and revolution (and this is a matter that deserves the most serious consideration), there is little to be gained from viewing the Communist revolution in China solely in terms of some inevitable and universally valid model of this relationship. For the Communist success, as we shall have occasion to observe, was by no means the inevitable historical result of the Japanese invasion.

Nor can we interpret the Japanese invasion itself—and its results—as simply an "accident" of history. There were compelling political, economic, and ideological forces—as well as a variety of factors operating in the realm of international diplomacy—that led to the Japanese decision to attempt to conquer China. And that decision was not uninfluenced by the Chinese historical situation—or, more precisely, by Japanese perceptions of the weakness of China. Yet, if the invasion was not a historical accident, it was to China an external event, in the sense that it was determined by forces over which Chinese had little or no control. Neither the Nationalists (who lost a good deal of their credentials as Chinese nationalists by their feeble responses to the Japanese threat) nor the Communists (who gained considerable political capital by their consistent advocacy of national resistance to the foreign invaders) could decisively influence the course of Japanese policy in China.

It is not likely to prove fruitful to speculate about what might

[15] The exception, of course, is the revolution led by Castro in Cuba. The case is dubious because a good argument can be made that the Cuban revolution did not become communist until well after Castro had achieved state power.

or might not have happened had circumstances been different; but it is important to understand just what did happen in the existing circumstances. As we have just suggested, these circumstances—the Japanese occupation and its effects on Chinese society—proved highly favorable to the realization of Communist ends. For one thing, the Japanese undermined the foundations of the Kuomintang regime, for the Nationalists were driven from the major cities, which were their primary sources of financial and political support. For the Kuomintang, the ravages of war resulted in incredible economic chaos and bureaucratic corruption—and, eventually, in almost total demoralization. More importantly, such administrative authority as the Kuomintang had managed to exercise in the countryside was largely destroyed, and members of the gentry-landlord class, upon which that fragile authority had rested, either fled the rural areas or were left militarily and politically defenseless. At the same time, the Communists, already experienced in working in the villages among the peasantry and adept at guerrilla warfare, were given access to vast areas of the countryside. For, while the Japanese invaders were able to occupy the cities, where the Kuomintang had been based, they did not have the manpower to effectively control the countryside, where Communist guerrilla bases multiplied rapidly during the war years. The retreat of Kuomintang military forces to the west in the face of invading Japanese armies, and the concurrent collapse of Nationalist governmental authority in much of China, allowed the Communists to break out of their remote sanctuary in Shensi and expand their military and political influence through vast areas of the countryside in northern and central China. Although the increasingly powerful Yenan base area remained the political and ideological center of the Communist revolution, Communists cadres operated in many parts of rural China, gaining the political support of tens of millions of peasants and organizing many for guerrilla warfare behind Japanese lines. Some Communist organizers filtered southward from Shensi, others were survivors from earlier guerrilla bases in central China, and many more were new adherents to the Communist cause. The gradual growth of peasant-supported Communist political and military nuclei in many parts of China during the war years was to prove decisive when the revolutionary struggle with the Kuomintang was resumed with full fury in 1946 in a massive civil war.

Much of the enormous popular support the Communists gained during the war years was based on patriotic appeals for national resistance to the foreign invaders. The new banner of modern Chinese nationalism had replaced the old "Mandate of Heaven" as the symbol of political legitimacy in twentieth-century China. As that banner began to slip from old Kuomintang hands in the 1930's—at first because of their seeming unwillingness to defend the nation against the Japanese threat and then because of their obvious inability to do so—it was quickly picked up and eagerly hoisted by new Communist hands. During the war years, Yenan was not only the revolutionary center but also (for increasing numbers of Chinese) the symbol of Chinese nationalist resistance to the Japanese. From the cities many thousands of students and intellectuals migrated to Yenan to join the Communist (and now also the nationalist) cause—and there, at the Northwest Anti-Japanese Red Army University, many were trained (and also "ideologically remolded") to become important political, administrative, and military cadres for the rapidly expanding Communist base and guerrilla areas. Of far greater political importance was the Communists' ability to organize the peasantry on the basis of patriotic as well as socio-economic appeals. The Japanese occupation not only intensified the economic crisis in the countryside but gave rise to the most bitter antiforeign sentiments among the peasants. These the Communists were able to transform into a modern mass nationalist movement and utilize for revolutionary political ends. This new Communist political opportunity was greatly facilitated by the ruthless policies pursued by the Japanese invaders—the brutal and indiscriminate military forays into the villages of northern and central China, which Japanese soldiers could plunder and punish but could not hold and occupy. Indeed, in the areas to which the Communists were able to gain access, the mobilization of the peasant masses on the basis of an anti-Japanese nationalist program contributed enormously to the military and political successes of the Yenan period.

In view of the strong tendency to interpret Chinese Communism as a species of Chinese nationalism or to view the Communist revolution as a case of a new elite riding to power on a fortuitous wave of mass nationalism, it is important to keep the whole phenomenon of "peasant nationalism" in proper historical perspective. For one thing, the Chinese peasants' sense of identification with China as a political entity and resistance to foreign intruders and invaders are not phenomena that suddenly appeared on the Chinese scene in 1937; both are age-old features of Chinese history. Even armed peasant resistance to modern imperialist incursions has a rich, almost century-old history prior to the Japanese invasion, beginning with the Opium War of 1839–42. Second, it would be highly misleading either to overestimate the spontaneous origins of the peasantry's precisely modern sense of "national consciousness" or to underestimate the role of Communist cadres in instilling that modern sense of nationalism in the strategy of "people's war." The Communists did not suddenly become nationalists during the war because they had become immersed in a nationalistic rural environment; they were ardent nationalists long before 1937, and they played a crucial role (through both propaganda and organization) in transforming the elemental antiforeign response of the peasantry into a truly modern nationalist response. By forging bonds of solidarity among peasants from various localities and regions, the Communists created a nationwide movement of resistance and imbued it with a sense of national mission that otherwise would have been absent. The Chinese Communists, in large measure, brought Chinese nationalism to the countryside; they did not simply reflect it.

Furthermore, however important Communist nationalist appeals were in gaining mass peasant support, socio-economic issues were at least equally important. The war intensified the already horrendous economic burdens of the peasantry and thus increased the attractiveness of the Communist program for land reform. To be sure, the official land policy of the Yenan period was a relatively moderate one by Kiangsi standards. Instead of the outright expropriation and division of landlord holdings, the Communists adopted a program for reductions in rents and interest rates, partly to conform to the terms of the tenuous wartime alliance with the Kuomintang but more importantly as an attempt to enlist the support of landlords and "rich peasants," as well as the masses of poor peasants, in the struggle against the Japanese occupation. But the reduction of rent to no more than one-third of the crop and the elimination of the many extralegal means through which landlords and bureaucrats traditionally exploited peasants in China were hardly unappealing measures to those who had been subjected to the most merciless forms of economic, as well as social and political, oppression.

Moreover, the officially "moderate" agrarian policies were by no means universally followed. In many cases large landholdings were in fact expropriated and distributed among land-hungry peasants, especially in areas where landlords fled with retreating Kuomintang armies. Where the gentry-landlord elite remained, collaboration between Chinese landlords and Japanese occupiers was not uncommon; in exchange for political services performed—which is to say, the traditional gentry function of "social control"—the Japanese allowed the gentry their traditional economic privilege of exploiting the peasantry. In such cases, the traditional hatred of the landlord for socioeconomic reasons was intensified by new, nationalist resentments, and the Communists appealed to both feelings simultaneously, promoting class as well as national struggle. The fact of the matter, then, is that expropriation and division of gentry landholdings was a highly popular policy in much of the countryside; and where it occurred, the Communist party—if it had sufficient military predominance to guarantee the security of the peasants and their newly acquired land—won over masses of loyal peasant followers.

The view that the Communists acquired their massive peasant support in the Yenan period by a combination of nationalist appeals and moderate land policies that did not radically change existing social relationships is simply not tenable. Conditions and policies of course varied greatly from area to area. In some areas, social revolutionary actions were sacrificed to obtain the support of all rural classes in the interests of national unity; in others, radical land policies proved more effective in gaining peasant support than purely nationalist appeals; and, in still other areas, neither nationalist nor socio-economic appeals were effective. But, even where the officially moderate land policies were pursued, traditional agrarian relationships were profoundly transformed: The local political power of the gentry elite was broken, its social authority and prestige were gravely undermined, and such reduced economic power as it still held was dependent on the grace of the new holders of political and military power in the local areas—the cadres of the Chinese Communist party. In the areas under Communist control in the Yenan era, the undermining and sometimes the destruction of the power of the gentry-landlord class—the ruling elite of Chinese society for two thousand years—marked the beginning of a social revolution that was to culminate in the late 1940's and early 1950's in the elimination of the gentry as a social class throughout China. It was to be the first genuine social revolution in Chinese history since the establishment of the imperial order in 221 B.C.

Thus the Japanese invasion, by removing the Kuomintang armies and bureaucracies from vast areas of China and by undermining the power and prestige of traditional power-holders and elite groups (warlords and gentry), created conditions highly favorable to the Communists—and perhaps ones that were crucial to the eventual Communist victory. The invasion did not in itself create a revolutionary situation (for that already existed), but it did much to intensify and aggravate conditions conducive to revolution and to provide new opportunities for revolutionary action. But "revolutionary situations," however mature, do not in themselves create revolutions. Only men make revolutions—and only on the basis of their consciousness, their perception of the situation in which they find themselves, and their will and ability to transform that situation in accordance with their revolutionary goals. The war, in short, by no means guaranteed the inevitability of a Communist victory. And the successes and specific characteristics of Yenan

Communism did not spring spontaneously from any "objective" imperatives of the wartime situation. Rather, they owed much to the way in which the Chinese Communists perceived the Chinese historical situation and to the way in which they were disposed to go about changing it. Thus, to understand the Yenan era and its distinctive revolutionary and ideological legacy, it is necessary to take into account subjective as well as objective factors, particularly the intellectual and ideological predispositions of Mao Tse-tung.

The Origins of Maoism

Although "Maoism" did not crystallize into an official ideological orthodoxy until the Yenan period, its historical existence as a distinct (and distinctively Chinese) interpretation of Marxism began with the introduction of Marxism in China in 1918–19. To view Maoism as simply the ideological product or reflection of the "objective" conditions of Yenan Communism is to ignore the historical truism that men are the producers as well as the products of history, and that the way in which they make history depends, at least in part, on the way they perceive objective reality. Neither Yenan Communism nor Mao Tse-tung are exceptions to this proposition; much of what went into the making of the former was molded by the now famous "thoughts" of the latter. And Mao did not arrive in Shensi in 1935 with an empty head.

In fact, when Mao became a convert to Marxism and communism in 1919, the basic intellectual predispositions that were to mold his understanding and interpretation of Marxism and his concept of revolution were already present, and they were to be reinforced by his revolutionary experiences in the 1920's and early 1930's. While it is well beyond the scope of this essay to trace the intellectual development of Mao Tse-tung, it is possible to identify certain abiding traits of the Maoist mentality that provided the essential intellectual and ideological prerequisites for the successful Yenan strategy of revolution.

By no means the least important of Mao's early (and persisting) intellectual orientations was a profoundly voluntarist belief that the decisive factor in history is human consciousness—the ideas, the wills, and the actions of men. This faith in the ability of self-conscious men to mold objective social reality in accordance with their ideas and ideals survived the influence of the more deterministic tenets of Marxist theory, as Mao began to assimilate that theory in the 1920's and 1930's.

The survival of this fundamental voluntarist impulse, it might be noted, was greatly facilitated by the manner in which Marxism had come to China in the wake of World War I. Unlike Russia and the Western countries, China lacked a Marxist social-democratic tradition. The early Chinese converts to communism were drawn to Marxism and Leninism by the chiliastic message of the Russian Bolshevik revolution (which promised both national liberation and worldwide revolution) and were committed to a Leninist-style revolution long before they became familiar with Marxist-Leninist theory. These early communists (such as Li Ta-chao, China's first Marxist, and his disciple, Mao Tse-tung) tended to interpret Marxist theory in the light of their revolutionary expectations rather than to redefine those expectations on the basis of their new Marxist creed.

To be sure, Mao derived from the objective laws of historical development proclaimed by Marx some degree of assurance in the historical inevitability of a socialist future (and he soon learned to repeat the relevant Marxist formulas). But, in the final analysis, his faith in the achievement of that future was not based upon any real Marxist confidence in the determining, objective forces of socio-historical development; it stemmed rather from a profound confidence in the revolutionary consciousness and activism of men determined to bring about that future. For Mao, in other words, the essential factor in determining the course of history was conscious human activity, and the most important ingredients for revolution were the attitudes of men and their willingness to engage in revolutionary action.

This implied, among other things, that revolution in China need not be dependent on any predetermined levels of social and economic development and that immediate opportunities for revolutionary action need not be restricted by orthodox Marxist-Leninist formulas. It also implied a special concern for developing and maintaining "correct" ideological consciousness, the ultimately decisive factor in determining revolutionary success or failure. Correct thought, in the Maoist view, is the first and essential prerequisite for correct revolutionary action, and it is this assumption that lies behind the emphasis on the peculiarly Chinese Communist techniques of "thought reform" and "ideological remolding" developed and refined in the Yenan period. The Cheng Feng campaign of 1942–44 for the rectification of "undesirable" ideas and ideological tendencies was the most intensive application of a general Chinese Communist policy.

This whole emphasis on ideological solidarity was of central importance to the successful conduct of guerrilla warfare in the Yenan period. In a "guerrilla" situation, where centralized forms of organizational control are by definition precluded, the forging of the strongest possible commitments to a common ideology and a common manner of thinking (and thus of acting) becomes a matter of supreme importance. The fact that Maoism was already disposed to stress the importance of "subjective factors" goes a long way toward explaining why the Communists adopted the strategy of guerrilla warfare and why they were able to employ this strategy so successfully.

If Mao's voluntarism mitigated the more deterministic implications of Marxist theory, his particularly powerful nationalistic proclivities were equally important in making Marxism a more flexible ideological instrument for revolution in China. As was generally true for Chinese intellectuals who were attracted to communism and Marxism in the May Fourth period, nationalist resentments against Western imperialism and nationalist aspirations for a future "new China" were very much involved in Mao's original conversion to Marxism. Quite apart from the nationalist appeals of the Leninist theory of imperialism and specific Soviet appeals to Chinese nationalist sentiments (both of which promised China an important place in the world revolutionary process), Marxist theory itself satisfied profoundly important nationalist needs. For Mao, as for others, Marxism appeared to be the most advanced product of modern Western thought; but, unlike other Western ideologies and models, it rejected the West in its present capitalist and imperialist form (and thus also rejected the present Western imperialist impingement on China). At the same time, Marxism served to reaffirm the rejection of the already discarded "prenationalist" values of traditional China, which now could be conveniently dismissed as "feudal." In other words, Marxism had the great nationalist appeal of assigning both "precapitalist" China and the capitalist West to the same "dustbin of history" while simultaneously looking toward a "postcapitalist" future in which China would take its rightful place in a new international socialist order.

It goes without saying that Mao has always had a certain feeling of national pride in the Chinese past and that he has been at least as much concerned with the future power and glory of the Chinese nation as with the fate of the international proletarian revolution. But it might also be said that from the beginning Mao's especially deep-rooted nationalist impulses gave rise to the belief that the Chinese revolution was more or less synonymous with the world revolution—or at least that China had a very special, indeed almost messianic, role to play in the world revolutionary process. As early as 1930 Mao felt sufficiently confident to proclaim publicly that China was more revolutionary than other countries and to predict that "the revolution will certainly move towards an upsurge more quickly in China than in Western Europe."[16] In the Maoist conception of China's special place in the world revolution, genuinely internationalist aspirations and goals were no doubt inextricably intertwined with Chinese nationalist impulses. But it was in this treacherous area of "messianic revolutionary nationalism" (as Trotsky once called it) that Mao departed from other Chinese Marxists whose nationalist passions were restrained by more orthodox Western Marxist considerations.

The nationalist element in Mao's Marxist world view was reflected not only in his long-standing hostility to the Russian-dominated Comintern (and, in the late 1950's, in his open hostility toward the Soviet Union) but also, and more importantly, in his conception of revolution within China. Central to this conception was the conviction that the real enemies were

[16] "A Single Spark Can Start a Prairie Fire," in *Selected Works of Mao Tse-tung,* Vol. I, p. 118.

not so much within Chinese society as without. The real enemy was foreign imperialism, and in the face of that continuing threat China stood as a potentially proletarian nation in a hostile capitalist-imperialist world order. Although internal class divisions were important and class struggle necessary, in confronting the external foe, it was assumed that Chinese of all social classes could gather under the revolutionary nationalist umbrella held up by the Chinese Communist party—and those who could not, or would not, were excluded from membership in the nation, or at least from "the people," excommunicated as representatives of foreign imperialism. Political circumstances permitting, class struggle thus could be subordinated to national struggle—and, indeed, the two could be regarded as more or less synonymous. In fact, if the main enemy was external, then a "united front" of all Chinese opposed to foreign imperialism was not only necessary for national survival but also conducive to the eventual realization of international communist goals. In Mao's eyes, nationalist struggle was not necessarily incompatible with the pursuit of Marxist internationalist goals.

A third intellectual orientation that decisively influenced the Maoist adaptation of Marxism-Leninism to the Chinese environment may be described as essentially populist. The populist-inspired notion of a "great union of the popular masses"[17] that Mao advocated at the beginning of his revolutionary career in 1919 survived the influence of Marxism and modified the influence of Leninism. Populist impulses reinforced Mao's nationalist-inspired faith in the basic unity of the Chinese people in the face of intrusion by alien forces and led him to attribute to "the people" an almost inherent revolutionary socialist consciousness. "In the masses is embodied great socialist activism" is a recent Maoist slogan that derives from an early Maoist-populist faith, expressed in 1919 in the affirmation that "our Chinese people possesses great intrinsic energy."[18]

[17] This was the title of an article by Mao published in the summer of 1919. For a translation of extracts from the article, see *The Political Thought of Mao Tse-tung*, edited by Stuart R. Schram, rev. ed. (New York: Praeger, 1963), pp. 105–06.

[18] *Ibid.*, p. 106.

Moreover, Mao's populist impulse, with its essentially rural orientation and its romantic celebration of the rural ideal of "the unity of living and working," served to define "the people" as the peasant masses (for the peasantry, after all, constituted the overwhelming majority of the Chinese population) and led him to prize the spontaneously revolutionary energies he believed they possessed. Thus, Mao's populism drew him to the countryside at a time when the Communist revolution was still centered in the cities. In his famous (and heretical) "Hunan Report" of March 1927, he found in the Chinese peasantry an elemental revolutionary force so great that it would sweep away everything before it—including, he predicted, those revolutionary intellectuals who proved unwilling or unable to unite with the peasant masses. Then, as later, he expressed profound distrust of the "knowledge" brought by urban intellectuals and profound admiration for the innate "wisdom" of the peasantry.

Many other characteristic features of the Maoist mentality are typically populist. One might mention, for example, Mao's hostility toward occupational specialization, his acute distrust of intellectuals and specialists, his profoundly antibureaucratic orientations (and indeed his general enmity toward all forms of large-scale, centralized organization), his anti-urban bias, and his romantic mood of heroic revolutionary self-sacrifice. These, as well as many other aspects of the thought of Mao, bear striking similarities to what is generally understood by the term "populism." To be sure, Mao is not simply a populist in Marxist guise (any more than he is simply a Chinese nationalist in communist dress), but it is important to note that populist ideas and impulses have significantly influenced the manner in which Mao has understood and employed Marxism.

To understand the reasons for the Communist success in the Yenan period, it is of special importance to take into account Mao's genuinely populist faith in the peasant masses as potential bearers of socialist revolutionary consciousness. For it is this faith that permitted—and indeed dictated—the much celebrated Maoist notion of "the mass line," the various principles and rules by which Communist cadres became intimately involved and identified with the peasant masses. The Maoist maxim that intellectuals and party cadres must become the pupils of the masses before they can become their teachers was in fact widely practiced in the Yenan days. Had it been otherwise, the Communists could never have acquired the mass support and cooperation among the peasantry that was so essential to the successful employment of the strategy of "people's war."

In attributing a latent socialist consciousness to the peasantry, Mao, it should be noted, departed not only from Marx but from Lenin. For Marx, the bearers of socialist consciousness were the urban proletariat, and he rarely missed an opportunity to express his contempt for "the idiocy of rural life." And for Lenin, socialist consciousness was to be imposed on the "spontaneous" proletarian mass movement by an elite of revolutionary intellectuals organized into a highly centralized and disciplined communist party, with the peasantry playing an ambiguous auxiliary role in the revolutionary process. Mao departed from Leninism not only in his virtually total lack of interest in the urban working class but also in his conception of the nature and role of the party. The party was sacrosanct to Lenin because it was the incarnation of "proletarian consciousness." In his mind, there was no question about who should be the teachers and who the pupils. For Mao, on the other hand, this was precisely the question, and it has remained unanswered; he has never really defined the relationship between the organized "proletarian consciousness" of the party and the spontaneous "proletarian consciousness" of the masses in a purely Leninist fashion. His faith in the party as the bearer of revolutionary consciousness was never complete, for it was accompanied by the populist belief that true revolutionary knowledge and creativity ultimately emanate from the people themselves.

There were, to be sure, objective factors that influenced Mao's rather ambiguous view of the role of the party. Military power, after all, was the crucial factor in determining the outcome of the Chinese revolution, and the influence of the party as such tended to be subsumed by the Red Army. Moreover, unlike the Russian Revolution, the Chinese Communist revolution did not involve the sudden seizure of state power. It was based, rather, on the relatively gradual growth of popular support and, eventually, on the revolutionary activities of millions, often largely spontaneous, that were to take place in many local areas where communication was slow and difficult. This created a revolutionary situation that was hardly conducive to control and direction by a highly centralized party apparatus.

The voluntarist, nationalist, and populist impulses that governed Mao's understanding and interpretation of Marxism in the years after 1919 formed the essential intellectual and ideological prerequisites for the development of the Maoist strategy of peasant revolution and the successful employment of this strategy in the Yenan period. Although the Japanese invasion intensified China's socio-economic crisis and created political conditions favorable to the growth of a revolutionary movement, it was not inevitable that a revolutionary movement would in fact grow and emerge victorious. It is most unlikely that orthodox Marxist-Leninists could have appreciated fully the revolutionary opportunities offered, much less have taken advantage of them to build a communist movement on a purely peasant base. It was precisely Mao's ideological unorthodoxies that allowed the Communists to seize upon these opportunities. It was his voluntarist faith in the power of the human will and consciousness to shape historical reality that permitted him to ignore (or redefine) those Marxist socio-economic prerequisites and Marxist social-class considerations that might otherwise have restricted the possibilities for revolutionary action. It was his nationalist-populist impulses that made him look to the broadest possible sources of national revolutionary support and directed him from the cities to the countryside. And it was his populist trust in the spontaneous revolutionary energies of the peasant masses that allowed him to develop and pursue the unorthodox strategy of "people's war." Such were some of the essential ingredients in the emergence of a distinctively Chinese Marxist revolutionary mentality that proved instrumental in transforming a "revolutionary situation" into a genuine social revolution with the most momentous historical consequences.

Yenan Marxism

The Yenan era was Mao's most productive period, both as a Marxist theoretician and as a revolutionary strategist. The bulk of the writings that were later to be canonized as "the thoughts of Mao Tse-tung"—and eventually presented as universally valid revolutionary theory on as lofty a doctrinal level as the works of Marx, Engels, and Lenin—were composed during the Yenan period, especially in the years 1937–40.

A textual analysis of these writings, however, throws very little light on the much debated question "What is Maoism?" or on the problem of the relationship of "the thoughts of Mao Tse-tung" to the Marxist and Leninist traditions. The majority of Mao's Yenan writings deal with matters of military strategy— and, it is argued by some, Mao's real innovations as a "Marxist-Leninist" lie in this rather nontheoretical realm of affairs, in his long treatises on the tactics and techniques of guerrilla warfare and in his detailed discussions of the practical and specifically Chinese political and economic factors involved in the conduct of revolutionary war. Moreover, in his more theoretical writings, which are concerned with problems of Marxist theory and politics, most of the distinctive features of the Maoist version of Marxism are only implicit, and what is distinctive is often concealed and obscured by the restatement of standard Marxist-Leninist formulas. In fact, a good case can be made for the proposition that Mao's real contributions and innovations as a Marxist did not appear until the postrevolutionary period (particularly after 1955), when he directed his attention to the problems of building a socialist society in an economically backward country—especially to the problem of how to prevent the bureaucratic degeneration of a socialist revolution in the postrevolutionary era.

However that may be, Mao's Yenan writings are important for a number of reasons. First, they established Mao's reputation as an independent Marxist theoretician. Having achieved *de facto* political independence from Moscow, the Chinese Communists could now claim to have established ideological independence as well—in the form of a body of doctrine that was hailed as having applied the "universal truths" of Marxism-Leninism to the specific conditions of the Chinese historical situation. Second, Mao's treatises on "dialectics" and "contradictions" provided a rudimentary philosophical basis for the distinctive features of Maoism. Finally, the Marxist theoretical writings of the Yenan era (by Mao and others) were designed to reaffirm the Marxist-Leninist orthodoxy of the Chinese Communist party, to convey some rudimentary knowledge of that doctrine to many newly recruited members of the party, and, most importantly, to rationalize Chinese Communist political practice in terms of Marxist-Leninist theory.

Although this last task was accomplished to the satisfaction of Mao and other Chinese Communist leaders, it was done without dealing with the most crucial ideological problem raised by the Chinese Communist revolution in general and the strategy of the Yenan period in particular. The Maoist theoretical writings say virtually nothing about how a communist party almost totally separated from the cities and the urban proletariat and based entirely on peasant support could carry out a socialist revolution. This posed not only a grave Marxist theoretical dilemma but also a very practical revolutionary problem. While the peasants were very much interested in socio-economic reform and the redistribution of land, not even Mao, with all his faith in the inherent "socialist activism" of the peasant masses, really believed that the peasants as a class were inclined (spontaneously or otherwise) to socialism in the abstract, much less to the collectivization of land, which the building of a socialist order presupposed. At their radical best, the peasants were interested in the equal distribution of land on the basis of individual peasant proprietorship—an agrarian revolution, to be sure, but one that precluded a true socialist reorganization of society, by either Marxist or non-Marxist definitions. The class composition of the Chinese Communist movement and the social aspirations of the Chinese peasantry both implied that the revolution could not pass logically or practically beyond what in Marxist terms is called the "bourgeois-democratic stage." There is nothing in either Maoist ideology or Chinese social reality to suggest that the peasantry as such is the bearer of the socialist future.

Who, then, were to be the agents of socialist revolution? There are Maoist answers to this question, but they are not easily found in Maoist theoretical literature. Here we find only repetitions of the stale Marxist orthodoxy that the socialist revolution is to be led by the proletariat and the equally withered Leninist orthodoxy that the Communist party is the representative of the proletariat and the incarnation of "proletarian consciousness." This is supplemented only by the concept of "the people's democratic dictatorship," a notion that was born in the united-front strategy of the Yenan era (in Mao's essays on "new democracy" and "coalition government") and formally proclaimed in 1949, on the eve of the official establishment of the Chinese People's Republic. The formula provides for a government representing a coalition of four classes (proletariat, peasantry, petty bourgeoisie, and national bourgeoisie) but also for a coalition under "proletarian hegemony"—which is to say that political power ultimately resides in the "proletarian" Communist party.

For the purposes of the present essay, there is little to be gained by embarking upon a discussion of the political and ideological implications of these particular formulas. The fact of the matter is that during the crucial Yenan years of the revolution the Chinese Communist party lacked the active support of the Chinese urban proletariat and made very little effort to acquire it. Indeed, such an effort was largely precluded by Maoist revolutionary strategy, which, in both theory and practice, assumed that the crucial forces of revolution resided in the countryside and in the peasantry, and that the mobilization of these forces would lead to a situation in which the revolutionary rural areas would encircle and eventually occupy the nonrevolutionary cities.

What turned out to be crucial in determining that the revolution would move beyond the bourgeois-democratic stage to socialism were the "subjective factors" in history (upon which Maoism itself places such great emphasis), most particularly the conscious determination of Mao and the Chinese Communist leadership to pursue socialist goals. However unorthodox they have been in their strategy of revolution, Maoists have remained firmly committed to orthodox Marxist goals. If they have not identified themselves with the actual proletarian class, they have identified themselves with the political and social goals and the messianic, historic mission that Marx attributed to that class. And this "subjective factor" proved of enormous historical significance in determining the character and direction of the Chinese revolution.

What is thus implicit in Maoist theory, and demonstrated in Maoist practice, is the notion that the bearers of socialism are those who possess true "proletarian consciousness" and that the latter can exist quite independently of any specific social class. This consciousness is not dependent on the actual presence of the proletariat, nor, on the other hand, is it attributed to the peasantry upon whose revolutionary energies and actions the Communist success was based. Thus "proletarian consciousness" can be attributed to a revolutionary elite (the party and its leaders), which holds the socialist goal firmly in mind and directs the mass movement toward the realization of that goal. In a broader sense, "proletarian consciousness" is seen as a potential, inherent in "the people" as a whole, for all men are potentially capable of achieving (through revolutionary action) the spiritual and ideological transformation necessary to acquire a true proletarian spirit and a socialist world view.

This emphasis on the role of consciousness in the making of history and revolution reflects, of course, long-standing Maoist voluntarist and populist predispositions and also the uniquely Maoist treatment of the Marxist theory of class struggle. Mao, to be sure, has always been intensely concerned with objective class conditions in Chinese society and has been an ardent promoter of class struggle, both in theory and in practice. But he also had tended to define "class position" less on the basis of objective social class than by moral and ideological criteria. While for Marx the existence of a potentially revolutionary proletarian class was the prerequisite for the rise of revolutionary proletarian ideas, for Mao the existence of men with appropriate revolutionary ideas is sufficient to prove the existence of a revolutionary proletarian class. Perhaps the most radical ideological expression of this entire voluntarist trend is to be found in the Maoist treatises that conclude with the proposition that under certain conditions "the subjective can create the objective."

Another radical Maoist precept that dictated that the revolution would not and could not stop at the bourgeois-democratic stage, China's economic backwardness and the social composition of the Chinese Communist party notwithstanding, is the doctrine of "uninterrupted" (or "permanent") revolution. This doctrine proclaimed the necessity for a continuous process of ideological transformation and revolutionary social and political struggle, proceeding through increasingly radical phases of social development directly into the communist utopia of the future. Although the theory of permanent revolution was not formally put forward until later, it was implicit in the Maoist ideology of the Yenan era and had its philosophical roots in Mao's writings on dialectics, particularly his essays "On Practice" and "On Contradiction," which were originally speeches delivered in the summer of 1937. Here the world was seen as being in a state of eternal flux, and social and historical reality as a process of constant and inevitable change and development because of the internal contradictions inherent in all phenomena. Quite apart from the controversial question of their philosophical merits or deficiencies, the essays reflected a highly activist mentality and prophetically proclaimed the message that change, in increasingly radical directions, was permanent and necessary.

It might also be noted (and this was another prophetic pointer to the future) that Mao's emergence as an independent Marxist theoretician in the Yenan years posed a grave challenge to Moscow's authority in the world communist movement in general, and to Stalin's claim to universal Marxist-Leninist ideological and political infallibility in particular. For Mao had embarked upon "the Sinification of Marxism" (to use his own words of 1938), and the celebration of his "creative adaptation" of Marxism-Leninism to Chinese conditions and of his claims to theoretical innovation was to become increasingly explicit—and for Stalin, increasingly defiant—over the years. The celebration was to grow into claims of universal validity for "the thoughts of Mao Tse-tung"—valid, at least, for the vast non-Western areas of the world, where communist revolutions are possible and, according to the Maoist view of the world, inevitable.

The Yenan Revolutionary Tradition and Its Legacy

The Yenan period not only proved decisive for the Chinese Communist victory of 1949 but bequeathed to the victors a heroic tradition of revolutionary struggle that has since been canonized as "the Yenan spirit" and "the Yenan style." Since those who fashioned the Communist victory in the Yenan era were the ones who became the leaders of the People's Republic, it is hardly surprising that the policies they pursued and their responses to the problems of the post-1949 period have been significantly influenced by their experiences in those earlier and more heroic days. "The Yenan spirit" is not simply praised in Communist China to commemorate the heroism of days past; it has also become a model to be applied to achieve new revolutionary goals in the "postrevolutionary era." As recent political events have demonstrated dramatically, not all Chinese Communists have perceived the Yenan model in the same manner; at least, not all are convinced that it is completely relevant to contemporary Chinese needs. But many Chinese Communists, and most notably Mao Tse-tung, remain fundamentally committed to the Yenan spirit of revolutionary struggle.

In the broader sense, the Yenan revolutionary tradition includes the whole historical experience of Chinese Communism in this decisive phase of the revolution. Everything from the distinctively Chinese Communist methods of organization and tactics associated with the strategy of guerrilla warfare to Maoist philosophy and the Maoist version of Marxism-Leninism is part of this tradition.

The Yenan revolutionary tradition can be more narrowly defined as the distillation of this entire experience (as it was perceived then and reinterpreted later) into a system of social and ethical values and the concept of an ideal (and idealized) Yenan revolutionary cadre that exemplified these values. While the unique methods of organization developed in the Yenan period were enormously important in determining the manner in which political power was organized and social control exercised in China after 1949, the system of values that emerged from the Yenan era has perhaps proved to be of equally great historical significance. What Chinese Communists today celebrate as "the Yenan spirit" is in fact largely concerned with spiritual and ideological matters and, more specifically, with the kinds of social and ethical values deemed appropriately revolutionary for the present, even though they are attributed to a heroic revolutionary past.

Many of the values conveyed by "the Yenan spirit" have been mentioned earlier. Here it need only be noted that they are essentially ascetic values, which demand a highly disciplined and completely selfless life orientation. The highest and most prized virtue is struggle (and self-sacrifice) in behalf of the people. Such struggle is not necessarily seen as an end in itself; it receives its ultimate ethical sanction in the promise that it will eventually lead to the realization of the communist utopia of the future. But unselfish revolutionary struggle is in itself ethically valued and typically described in Chinese Communist writings as "saintly and divine" and the source of true happiness. In the Maoist theory of dialectics, struggle is seen as inevitable and infinite; and in Maoist moral theory, the spirit of revolutionary struggle is presented as the most sacred of revolutionary virtues.

Other Maoist moral maxims are more commonplace—hard work, diligence, self-denial, frugality, altruism, and self-discipline. Such values are attributed to "the Yenan spirit" and have been imparted to the Chinese people in various ways in recent decades. In the Yenan decade these values were in fact practiced by Chinese Communists, for they were imposed by the harsh imperatives of revolutionary struggle and the spartan and egalitarian style of life that such struggle demanded. In the Maoist view, however, men imbued with such values not only were responsible for revolutionary success in the past but remain essential for the building of a communist society in the future. The ideal, self-reliant Yenan guerrilla leader who "became one" with the people, who "combined ability with virtue" and was always ready to sacrifice his life for the revolution, became the prototype for the later model of the "new communist man" who exemplifies these ascetic values and revolutionary commitments.

The generalization and idealization of the Yenan model reflects Mao's voluntarist faith that the truly decisive factor in history is man—or, more precisely, ideologically self-conscious men motivated by the proper revolutionary will and the proper moral values. It also reflects his populist faith that all men are inherently capable of the spiritual and ideological transformation needed to make them "new communist men" and that such a transformation is the prerequisite for both the economic and political actions that will lead to the achievement of genuine Marxist goals. Such men are more important than machines and technology, in the Maoist view, and ideological-moral solidarity is more important than any artificial unity that formal bureaucratic organization can provide or impose.

This whole galaxy of Maoist beliefs owes much to the Yenan experience (although the success of the Yenan period owes much to these beliefs as well), for the Yenan experience seemed to confirm the view that determined men inspired by the correct ideology and spirit can triumph over the most formidable material obstacles. The Yenan era began with thirty thousand poorly armed revolutionary soldiers, isolated in an area that offered only the most meager material resources. A decade later, that small force had grown into a regular army of a million men, supported by several million more peasants organized in local partisan groups. More importantly, it had grown on the basis of a massive popular social revolution that involved the active and meaningful cooperation and participation of tens of millions of peasants.

At the end of World War II, when the uneasy Kuomintang-Communist truce inevitably collapsed and led to open civil war, Kuomintang armies enjoyed a four-to-one superiority in manpower over regular Communist military forces and an even greater superiority in modern military technology, largely supplied by the United States. Yet the Communist victory in the massive battles that marked the civil war of 1946–49, however bloody and difficult, was surprisingly swift. It was, as Stuart Schram has so well put it, "one of the most striking examples in history of the victory of a smaller but dedicated and well-organized force enjoying popular support over a larger but unpopular force with poor morale and incompetent leadership."[19] On October 1, 1949, Mao stood high on the Gate of Heavenly Peace in Peking to officially establish the Chinese People's Republic, while Chiang Kai-shek and those who remained in his army and bureaucracy had already fled to the island of Taiwan, there to impose their rule on a hostile population and to find a haven granted by the grace of the American Seventh Fleet.

When the peasant soldiers of the Red Army occupied Peking and the other major cities of China in 1949, it was an almost anticlimactic climax of the Chinese revolution. Though the people of the cities generally welcomed the Communists as liberators (or at least as the lesser of two evils), the urban classes had made only the most minimal contribution to the victory of that revolution. The decisive battles had been fought (and the real dramas had taken place) earlier—and in the countryside.

The dramatic Communist success in the civil war, and the whole Yenan experience on which that success was based, undoubtedly served to reinforce the Maoist belief in the primacy of moral over material forces, of men over machines, and to bolster the faith that the truly creative revolutionary forces of society resided more in the countryside than in the cities. What is more, the Chinese revolutionary experience gave rise to powerful antibureaucratic orientations and to what some writers call "an antitechnocratic bias"—the Maoist preference for the ideologically pure generalist (modeled on the ideal Yenan guerrilla leader) over the technologically proficient (but ideologically deficient) expert. This is not a bias against technology as such, it should be noted, but rather a profound concern for the social uses of modern technology and its bureaucratic and elitist implications.

These intellectual and ideological orientations, accompanied by the ascetic values associated with "the Yenan spirit" of heroic revolutionary struggle, are some of the major compo-

---

[19] *Mao Tse-tung*, p. 225.

nents of the Chinese Communist revolutionary tradition. The implications of this legacy were largely muted during the early years of the People's Republic, years that saw the final steps in the destruction of the more than two-thousand-year-old gentry ruling class and a period when the consolidation of Communist political power and economic development were the main revolutionary orders of the day. But new bureaucratic and technological elites were to emerge from the new Communist forms of political organization and economic development. And it was in response to this that the Yenan legacy was to reemerge in the years after 1955 as a harbinger of new policies and strategies of social and economic development that seemed to defy the "laws" of "the modernization process." These historically unprecedented Maoist strategies were designed to pursue economic development in a manner consistent with the realization of Marxist goals, and they have kept China in a state of virtually continuous revolutionary ferment for more than a decade. It is much too early to pass historical judgments on either the validity or the viability of this Maoist search for a uniquely Chinese route to communism.

17

Mao Tse-tung: Revolutionary War in China*

We are now engaged in a war; our war is a revolutionay war; and our revolutionary war is being waged in this semi-colonial and semi-feudal country of China. Therefore, we must study not only the laws of war in general, but the specific laws of revolutionary war, and the even more specific laws of revolutionary war in China.

It is well known that when you do anything, unless you understand its actual circumstances, its nature and its relations to other things, you will not know the laws governing it, nor know how to do it, nor be able to do it well.

War is the highest form of struggle for resolving contradictions, when they have developed to a certain stage, between classes, nations, states, or political groups and it has existed ever since the emergence of private property and of classes. Unless you understand the actual circumstances of war, its nature and its relations to other things, you will not know the laws of war, nor know how to direct war, nor be able to win victory.

Revolutionary war, whether a revolutionary class war or a revolutionary national war, has its own specific circumstances

* Mao Tse-tung, Excerpts from "Problems of Strategy in China's Revolutionary War," in *Selected Military Writings of Mao Tse-tung* (Peking: Foreign Languages Press, 1963), pp. 75–78, 87–95.

This article was written in 1936.

and nature, in addition to the circumstances and nature of war in general. Therefore, besides the general laws of war, it has specific laws of its own. Unless you understand its specific circumstances and nature, unless you understand its specific laws, you will not be able to direct a revolutionary war and wage it successfully.

China's revolutionary war, whether civil war or national war, is waged in the specific environment of China and so has its own specific circumstances and nature distinguishing it both from war in general and from revolutionary war in general. Therefore, besides the laws of war in general and of revolutionary war in general, it has specific laws of its own. Unless you understand them, you will not be able to win in China's revolutionary war.

Therefore, we must study the laws of war in general, we must also study the laws of revolutionary war, and, finally, we must study the laws of China's revolutionary war.

Some people hold a wrong view, which we refuted long ago. They say that it is enough merely to study the laws of war in general, or, to put it more concretely, that it is enough merely to follow the military manuals published by the reactionary Chinese government or the reactionary military academies in China. They do not see that these manuals give merely the laws of war in general and moreover are entirely copied from abroad, and if we copy and apply them exactly without the slightest change in form or content, we shall be "cutting the feet to fit the shoes" and be defeated. Their argument is: why should knowledge which has been acquired at the cost of blood be of no use? They fail to see that although we must cherish the earlier experience thus acquired, we must also cherish experience acquired at the cost of our own blood.

Others hold a second wrong view, which we also refuted long ago. They say that it is enough merely to study the experience of revolutionary war in Russia, or, to put it more concretely, that it is enough merely to follow the laws by which the civil war in the Soviet Union was directed and the military manuals published by Soviet military organizations. They do not see that these laws and manuals embody the specific characteristics of the civil war and the Red Army in the Soviet Union and that if we copy and apply them without allowing any change, we shall also be "cutting the feet to fit the shoes" and be defeated. Their argument is: since our war, like the war in the Soviet Union, is a revolutionary war, and since the Soviet Union won victory, how then can there be any alternative but to follow the Soviet example? They fail to see that while we should set special store by the war experience of the Soviet Union, because it is the most recent experience of revolutionary war and was acquired under the guidance of Lenin and Stalin, we should likewise cherish the experience of China's revolutionary war, because there are many factors that are specific to the Chinese revolution and the Chinese Red Army.

Still others hold a third wrong view, which we likewise refuted long ago. They say that the most valuable experience is that of the Northern Expedition of 1926–27 and that we must learn from it, or, to put it more concretely, that we must imitate the Northern Expedition in driving straight ahead to seize the big cities. They fail to see that while the experience of the Northern Expedition should be studied, it should not be copied and applied mechanically, because the circumstances of our present war are different. We should take from the Northern Expedition only what still applies today, and work out something of our own in the light of present conditions.

Thus the different laws for directing different wars are determined by the different circumstances of those wars—differences in their time, place and nature. As regards the time factor, both war and its laws develop; each historical stage has its special characteristics, and hence the laws of war in each historical stage have their special characteristics and cannot be mechanically applied in another stage. As for the nature of war, since revolutionary war and counterrevolutionary war both have their special characteristics, the laws governing them also have their own characteristics, and those applying to one cannot be mechanically transferred to the other. As for the factor of place, since each country or nation, especially a large country or nation, has its own characteristics, the laws of war for each country or nation also have their own characteristics, and here, too, those applying to one cannot be mechanically transferred to the other. In studying the laws for directing wars that occur at different historical stages, that differ in nature and that are waged in different places and by different nations, we must fix our attention on the characteristics and development of each, and must oppose a mechanical approach to the problem of war.

Nor is this all. It signifies progress and development in a commander who is initially capable of commanding only a small formation, if he becomes capable of commanding a big one. There is also a difference between operating in one locality and in many. It likewise signifies progress and development in a commander who is initially capable of operating only in a locality he knows well, if he becomes capable of operating in many other localities. Owing to technical, tactical and strategic developments on the enemy side and on our own, the circumstances also differ from stage to stage within a given war. It signifies still more progress and development in a commander who is capable of exercising command in a war at its lower stages, if he becomes capable of exercising command in its higher stages. A commander who remains capable of commanding only a formation of a certain size, only in a certain locality and at a certain stage in the development of a war shows that he has made no progress and has not developed. There are some people who, contented with a single skill or a peep-hole view, never make any progress; they may play some role in the revolution at a given place and time, but not a significant one. We need directors of war who can play a significant role. All the laws for directing war develop as history develops and as war develops; nothing is changeless. . . .

China's revolutionary war, which began in 1924, has passed through two stages, the first from 1924 to 1927, and the second from 1927 to 1936; the stage of national revolutionary war against Japan will now commence. In all three of its stages this revolutionary war has been, is and will be fought under the leadership of the Chinese proletariat and its party, the Chinese Communist Party. The chief enemies in China's revolutionary war are imperialism and the feudal forces. Although the Chinese bourgeoisie may take part in the revolutionary war at certain historical junctures, yet its selfishness and lack of political and economic independence render it both unwilling and unable to lead China's revolutionary war on to the road of complete victory. The masses of China's peasantry and urban petty bourgeoisie wish to take an active part in the revolutionary war and to carry it to complete victory. They are the main forces in the revolutionary war, but being small-scale producers they are limited in their political outlook (and some of the unemployed masses have anarchist views), so that they are unable to give correct leadership in the war. Therefore, in an era when the proletariat has already appeared on the political stage, the responsibility for leading China's revolutionary war inevitably falls on the shoulders of the Chinese Communist Party. In such an era, any revolutionary war will definitely end in defeat if it lacks, or runs counter to, the leadership of the proletariat and the Communist Party. Of all the social strata and political groupings in semi-colonial China, the proletariat and the Communist Party are the ones most free from narrow-mindedness and selfishness, are politically the most far-sighted, the best organized and the readiest to learn with an open mind from the experience of the vanguard class, the proletariat, and its political party throughout the world and to make use of this experience in their own cause. Hence only the proletariat and the Communist Party can lead the peasantry, the urban petty bourgeoisie and bourgeoisie, can overcome the narrow-mindedness of the peasantry and the petty bourgeoisie, the destructiveness of the unemployed masses, and also (provided the Communist Party does not err in its policy) the vacillation and lack of thoroughness of the bourgeoisie—and can lead the revolution and the war on to the road of victory.

The revolutionary war of 1924–27 was waged, basically speaking, in conditions in which the international proletariat and the Chinese proletariat and its party exerted political influence on the Chinese national bourgeoisie and its parties, and entered into political cooperation with them. But this revolutionary war failed at the critical juncture, primarily because the big bourgeoisie turned traitor and also because the opportunists within the revolutionary ranks voluntarily surrendered the leadership of the revolution.

The Agrarian Revolutionary War, lasting from 1927 to the

present, has been waged under new conditions. The enemy in this war is not imperialism alone but also the alliance of the big bourgeoisie and the big landlords. And the national bourgeoisie has become a tail to the big bourgeoisie. This revolutionary war is led by the Communist Party alone, which has established absolute leadership over it. The absolute leadership of the Communist Party is the most important condition enabling the revolutionary war to be carried through firmly to the end. Without this leadership, it is inconceivable that the revolutionary war could have been carried on with such perseverance.

The Chinese Communist Party has led China's revolutionary war courageously and resolutely, and for fifteen long years[1] has demonstrated to the whole nation that it is the people's friend, fighting at all times in the forefront of the revolutionary war in defense of the people's interests and for their freedom and liberation.

By its arduous struggles and by the martyrdom of hundreds of thousands of its heroic members and tens of thousands of its heroic cadres, the Communist Party of China has played a great educative role among hundreds of millions of people throughout the country. The Party's great historic achievements in its revolutionary struggles have provided the prerequisite for the survival and salvation of China at this critical juncture when she is being invaded by a national enemy; and this prerequisite is the existence of a political leadership enjoying the confidence of the vast majority of the people and chosen by them after long years of testing. Today, the people accept what the Communist Party says more readily than what any other political party says. Were it not for the arduous struggles of the Chinese Communist Party in the last fifteen years, it would be impossible to save China in the face of the new menace of subjugation.

Besides the errors of the Right opportunism of Chen Tu-hsiu[2] and the "Left" opportunism of Li Li-san,[3] the Chinese

---

[1] When Mao Tse-tung wrote this article in 1936, it was exactly fifteen years since the founding of the Chinese Communist Party in July 1921—ed.

[2] One of the founders of the Chinese Communist Party, Chen Tu-hsiu was expelled from the party in 1929—ed.

[3] The line of Li Li-san, propounded around 1930, opposed Mao's

Communist Party has committed two other errors in the course of the revolutionary war. The first error was the "Left" opportunism of 1931–34,[4] which resulted in serious losses in the Agrarian Revolutionary War so that, instead of our defeating the enemy's fifth campaign of "encirclement and suppression," we lost our base areas and the Red Army was weakened. This error was corrected at the enlarged meeting of the Political Bureau of the Central Committee at Tsunyi in January 1935. The second was the Right opportunism of Chang Kuo-tao in 1935–36[5] which developed to such an extent that it undermined the discipline of the Party and the Red Army and caused serious losses to part of the Red Army's main forces. But this error was also finally rectified, thanks to the correct leadership of the Central Committee and the political consciousness of Party members, commanders and fighters in the Red Army. Of course all these errors were harmful to our Party, to our revolution and the war, but in the end we overcame them, and in doing so our Party and our Red Army have steeled themselves and become still stronger.

The Chinese Communist Party has led and continues to lead the stirring, magnificent and victorious revolutionary war. This war is not only the banner of China's liberation, but also has international revolutionary significance. The eyes of the revolutionary people the world over are upon us. In the new stage, the stage of the anti-Japanese national revolutionary war, we shall lead the Chinese revolution to its completion and exert a profound influence on the revolution in the East and in the whole world. Our revolutionary war has proved that we need a correct Marxist military line as well as a correct Marxist political line. Fifteen years of revolution and war have hammered out such a political line and such a military line. We believe that from now

---

advocacy of the creation of rural bases for guerrilla warfare. Instead, it called for insurrections in the cities combined with attacks on these cities by the Red Army—ed.

[4] During these years the Chinese Communist Party was dominated by the so-called "Twenty-eight Bolsheviks," among whom Wang Ming and Chin Pang-hsien were the leading figures—ed.

[5] Chang Kuo-tao advocated reconciliation with the Kuomintang under Chiang Kai-shek—ed.

on, in the new stage of the war, these lines will be further developed, filled out and enriched in new circumstances, so that we can attain our aim of defeating the national enemy. History tells us that correct political and military lines do not emerge and develop spontaneously and tranquilly, but only in the course of struggle. These lines must combat "Left" opportunism on the one hand and Right opportunism on the other. Without combating and thoroughly overcoming these harmful tendencies which damage the revolution and the revolutionary war, it would be impossible to establish a correct line and win victory in the revolutionary war. It is for this reason that I often refer to erroneous views in this pamphlet.

People who do not admit, do not know, or do not want to know that China's revolutionary war has its own characteristics have equated the war waged by the Red Army against the Kuomintang forces with war in general or with the civil war in the Soviet Union. The experience of the civil war in the Soviet Union directed by Lenin and Stalin has a world-wide significance. All Communist Parties, including the Chinese Communist Party, regard this experience and its theoretical summing-up by Lenin and Stalin as their guide. But this does not mean that we should apply this experience mechanically to our own conditions. In many of its aspects China's revolutionary war has characteristics distinguishing it from the civil war in the Soviet Union. Of course it is wrong to take no account of these characteristics or deny their existence. This point has been fully borne out in our ten years of war.

Our enemy has made similar mistakes. He has not recognized that fighting against the Red Army requires a different strategy and different tactics from those used in fighting other forces. Relying on his superiority in various respects, he took us lightly and stuck to his old methods of warfare. This was the case both before and during his fourth "encirclement and suppression" campaign in 1933, with the result that he suffered a series of defeats. In the Kuomintang army a new approach to the problem was suggested first by the reactionary Kuomintang general Liu Wei-yuan and then by Tai Yueh. Their idea was eventually accepted by Chiang Kai-shek. That was how Chiang Kai-shek's

Officers Training Corps at Lushan came into being and how the new reactionary military principles applied in the fifth campaign of "encirclement and suppression" were evolved.

But when the enemy changed his military principles to suit operations against the Red Army, there appeared in our ranks a group of people who reverted to the "old ways." They urged a return to ways suited to the general run of things, refused to go into the specific circumstances of each case, rejected the experience gained in the Red Army's history of sanguinary battles, belittled the strength of imperialism and the Kuomintang as well as that of the Kuomintang army, and turned a blind eye to the new reactionary principles adopted by the enemy. As a result, all the revolutionary bases except the Shensi-Kansu Border Region were lost, the Red Army was reduced from 300,000 to a few tens of thousands, the membership of the Chinese Communist Party fell from 300,000 to a few tens of thousands, and the Party organizations in the Kuomintang areas were almost all destroyed. In short, we paid a severe penalty, which was historic in its significance. This group of people called themselves Marxist-Leninists, but actually they had not learned an iota of Marxism-Leninism. Lenin said that the most essential thing in Marxism, the living soul of Marxism, is the concrete analysis of concrete conditions. That was precisely the point these comrades of ours forgot.

Hence one can see that, without an understanding of the characteristics of China's revolutionary war, it is impossible to direct it and lead it to victory.

What then are the characteristics of China's revolutionary war?

I think there are four principal ones.

The first is that China is a vast, semi-colonial country which is unevenly developed politically and economically and which has gone through the revolution of 1924–27.

This characteristic indicates that it is possible for China's revolutionary war to develop and attain victory. We already pointed this out (at the First Party Congress of the Hunan-Kiangsi Border Area) when in late 1927 and early 1928, soon after guerrilla warfare was started in China, some comrades in the Chingkang Mountains in the Hunan-Kiangsi border area raised the question, "How long can we keep the Red Flag flying?" For this was a most fundamental question. Without answering this question of whether China's revolutionary base areas and the Chinese Red Army could survive and develop, we could not have advanced a single step. The Sixth National Congress of the Chinese Communist Party in 1928 again gave the answer to the question. Since then the Chinese revolutionary movement has had a correct theoretical basis.

Let us now analyze this characteristic.

China's political and economic development is uneven—a weak capitalist economy coexists with a preponderant semi-feudal economy; a few modern industrial and commercial cities coexist with a vast stagnant countryside; several million industrial workers coexist with several hundred millions of peasants and handicraftsmen laboring under the old system; big warlords controlling the central government coexist with small warlords controlling the provinces; two kinds of reactionary armies, the so-called Central Army under Chiang Kai-shek and "miscellaneous troops" under the warlords in the provinces, exist side by side; a few railways, steamship lines and motor roads exist side by side with a vast number of wheelbarrow paths and foot-paths many of which are difficult to negotiate even on foot.

China is a semi-colonial country—disunity among the imperialist powers makes for disunity among the ruling groups in China. There is a difference between a semi-colonial country controlled by several countries and a colony controlled by a single country.

China is a vast country—"When it is dark in the east, it is light in the west; when things are dark in the south, there is still light in the north." Hence one need not worry about lack of room for maneuver.

China has gone through a great revolution—this has provided the seeds from which the Red Army has grown, provided the leader of the Red Army, namely, the Chinese Communist Party, and provided the masses with experience of participation in a revolution.

We say, therefore, that the first characteristic of China's revolutionary war is that it is waged in a vast semi-colonial country which is unevenly developed politically and economically and which has gone through a revolution. This characteristic basically determines our military strategy and tactics as well as our political strategy and tactics.

The second characteristic is that our enemy is big and powerful.

How do matters stand with the Kuomintang, the enemy of the Red Army? It is a party that has seized political power and has more or less stabilized its power. It has gained the support of the world's principal counter-revolutionary states. It has remodeled its army which has thus become different from any other army in Chinese history and on the whole similar to the armies of the modern states; this army is much better supplied with weapons and *matériel* than the Red Army, and is larger than any army in Chinese history, or for that matter than the standing army of any other country. There is a world of difference between the Kuomintang army and the Red Army. The Kuomintang controls the key positions or lifelines in the politics, economy, communications and culture of China; its political power is nation-wide.

The Chinese Red Army is thus confronted with a big and powerful enemy. This is the second characteristic of China's revolutionary war. It necessarily makes the military operations of the Red Army different in many ways from those of wars in general and from those of the civil war in the Soviet Union or of the Northern Expedition.

The third characteristic is that the Red Army is small and weak.

The Chinese Red Army, starting as guerrilla units, came into being after the defeat of the first great revolution. This occurred in a period of relative political and economic stability in the reactionary capitalist countries of the world as well as in a period of reaction in China.

Our political power exists in scattered and isolated mountainous or remote regions and receives no outside help whatsoever. Economic and cultural conditions in the revolutionary base areas are backward compared with those in the Kuomintang areas. The revolutionary base areas embrace only rural districts and small towns. These areas were extremely small in the beginning and have not grown much larger since. Moreover, they are fluid and not stationary, and the Red Army has no really consolidated bases.

The Red Army is numerically small, its arms are poor, and it has great difficulty in obtaining supplies such as food, bedding and clothing.

This characteristic presents a sharp contrast to the preceding one. From this sharp contrast have arisen the strategy and tactics of the Red Army.

The fourth characteristic is Communist Party leadership and the agrarian revolution.

This characteristic is the inevitable consequence of the first one. It has given rise to two features. On the one hand, despite the fact that China's revolutionary war is taking place in a period of reaction in China and throughout the capitalist world, it can be victorious because it is under the leadership of the Communist Party and has the support of the peasantry. Thanks to the support of the peasantry, our base areas, small as they are, are politically very powerful and stand firmly opposed to the enormous Kuomintang regime, while militarily they place great difficulties in the way of Kuomintang attacks. Small as it is, the Red Army has great fighting capacity, because its members, led by the Communist Party, are born of the agrarian revolution and are fighting for their own interests, and because its commanders and fighters are politically united.

The Kuomintang, on the other hand, presents a sharp contrast. It opposes the agrarian revolution and therefore has no support from the peasantry. Though it has a large army, the Kuomintang cannot make its soldiers and the many lower-ranking officers, who were originally small producers, risk their lives willingly for it. Its officers and men are politically divided, which reduces its fighting capacity.

Thus the four principal characteristics of China's revolutionary war are: a vast semi-colonial country which is unevenly developed politically and economically and which has gone through a great revolution; a big and powerful enemy; a small and weak Red Army; and the agrarian revolution. These characteristics determine the line for guiding China's revolutionary war as well as many of its strategic and tactical principles. It follows from the first and fourth characteristics that it is possible for the Chinese Red Army to grow and defeat its enemy. It follows from the second and third characteristics that it is impossible for the Chinese Red Army to grow very rapidly or defeat its enemy quickly; in other words, the war will be protracted and may even be lost if it is mishandled.

These are the two aspects of China's revolutionary war. They exist simultaneously, that is, there are favorable factors and there are difficulties. This is the fundamental law of China's revolutionary war, from which many other laws ensue. The history of our ten years of war has proved the validity of this law. He who has eyes but fails to see this fundamental law cannot direct China's revolutionary war, cannot lead the Red Army to victories.

18

Mark Selden: People's War in China and Vietnam*

The contributions of the National Liberation Front of South Vietnam to the theory and practice of people's war rank among the most significant revolutionary developments of our era, yet, poring through the massive scholarly, journalistic, and official writings heralding or decrying American attempts to crush the Vietnamese resistance, one is struck by the void of information concerning the NLF and developments in the liberated areas. The enemy remains almost as elusive in the literature as is his shadowy presence in the jungles and swamps of South Vietnam. After more than a decade of fighting, the NLF is as "faceless," unknown, unfathomable as ever to the American people. Indeed, a careful search reveals not a single significant scholarly approach to the subject, not an article, no less a book.[1] In the

* Mark Selden, "People's War and the Transformation of Peasant Society: China and Vietnam," in Friedman and Selden, eds., *America's Asia: Dissenting Essays on Asian-American Relations* (New York: Vintage Books, 1971). By permission.

Mark Selden is assistant professor of history at Washington University, St. Louis, and author of *People's War and the Transformation of Chinese Society*. He is coeditor of the *Bulletin* of the Committee of Concerned Asian Scholars.

[1] Available studies have been written by government officials or under military contract for consumption by an uneasy public. Douglas Pike, *Vietcong. The Organization and Techniques of the National Liberation Front of South Vietnam* (Cambridge, Mass., M.I.T. Press, 1966). Cf.

absence of independent scholarship, the officially sanctioned work of Douglas Pike, an officer of the United States Information Service with long tenure in Vietnam, has gone virtually unchallenged. Consider Pike's conclusion about the NLF:

> The social changes brought to the liberated area [of the National Liberation Front of South Vietnam] were perhaps more apparent than real. The NLF administrative liberation association was more manipulated than participational, and such an arrangement usually carries with it the seeds of its own doom. The great emphasis on communication of ideas failed to achieve its principal goal: The rural Vietnamese, lacking informational background, often failed to understand in context the meaning of the message. The rural Vietnamese knew little about the social forces loose in his country and even less about the outside world, and he greeted NLF efforts to remedy this deficiency with indifference—the condition of parochialism in which the next village is in the other world dies hard in Asia. Finally, the effort mounted by the NLF required a type of cadre—talented, skilled, dedicated, an almost superhuman person—that did not exist in sufficient numbers to ensure success.

Michael Charles Conley, *The Communist Insurgent Infrastructure in South Vietnam; A Study of Organization and Strategy* (Washington, D.C., American University, Center for Research in Social Systems, 1967); CIA agent George Carver has written (anonymously of course) of "The Faceless Viet Cong," in *Foreign Affairs*, Vol. 44, No. 3 (April, 1966), pp. 347–72. Of the handful of American studies of the NLF, all of them government inspired and financed, Pike's is by far the most useful. Interestingly enough, critics of the war who have diligently and often brilliantly exposed official rationalizations and blatant lies have virtually ignored the NLF. The single most important exception is the Australian journalist Wilfred Burchett. However, his *Vietnam: Inside Story of the Guerrilla War* (New York, International Publishers, 1965), the most important account written by a visitor to the "liberated areas," provides only a sketchy account of the internal features of the movement. Cf. Katsuichi Honda, "The National Liberation Front," Committee for the English Publication of "Vietnam—A Voice from the Villages," available from Mrs. Reiko Ishida, 2-13-7, Nishikata, Bunkyo-ku, Tokyo. Mr. Honda, a reporter for the *Asahi Shimbun*, bases his report on a visit to an NLF area in the Mekong Delta in late 1967.

Yet the principles involved remain intact. The deeper one plunged into the study of the NLF the stronger became the feeling of being on the edge of a future social morass, only dimly seen. Here one felt was tomorrow's society, the beginning of 1984, when peace is war, slavery is freedom, the non-organization is the organization.[2]

If Pike's volume obscures more than it reveals of the dynamic of a movement which has successfully resisted the juggernaut of American military power, it is extremely illuminating of pervasive American attitudes toward revolutionary change. To be sure, Pike is more outspoken and explicit than many social scientists. Yet his premises are widely shared not only by scholars and officials, but by the media and the public as well. These premises may be summarized as follows: The power of mass nationalist movements rests primarily on their manipulative qualities including a large component of terror, and on the ruthless application of Leninist organizational skills. Placing a low value on human life, power considerations alone control the calculus of revolutionary leadership. This unbridled hostility toward radical and nationalist movements provides one ideological source of American military involvement in Vietnam and throughout the world.

Terror and organization are not the only weapons attributed

---

[2] Pike, *Vietcong*, p. 382. Since this writing Richard Minear has published the first serious critique of Pike's work, "Douglas Pike and the NLF," *Bulletin of Concerned Asian Scholars*, Vol. II, No. I (October, 1969), pp. 44–47. Pike's activities inside and outside government suggest the development of a new style of official, the counterpart of the now familiar peripatetic scientists and social scientists shuttling between their university base and Washington. In the case of Pike, whose primary career is government service, official leave of absence is taken to publish —assuring the "objectivity" of the product. Pike's "private" analysis is, of course, indistinguishable from the war-time propaganda of the American government. The convergence in recent decades of official and scholarly premises and analyses—and with it the death of critical and independent scholarship which have been noted in several essays in this volume—is thus strengthened by the professional patterns of the new scholar-official. Cf. Noam Chomsky's critique of the liberal intelligentsia in "Objectivity and Liberal Scholarship," in *American Power and the New Mandarins* (New York, Pantheon, 1969), pp. 23–158.

by American officials and social scientists to revolutionary nationalists. As Chalmers Johnson has argued in his influential study of the Chinese Communist resistance, insurgent movements may be created and legitimized by an unexpected ally— the foreign invader. In this view, the Japanese invasion of 1937 destroyed indigenous Chinese leadership (the Kuomintang and the warlords) and created a leadership vacuum. Moreover, the brutality and dislocation produced by the onslaught of the invasion inadvertently mobilized the peasant population for resistance. The conclusion is inescapable: Neither the creativity nor the dedication of the resistance, but above all the windfall of peasant nationalism springing from war-induced crisis lies behind the success of revolutionary nationalist movements.[3]

An important corollary to these perspectives is the belief that the mobilization approaches characteristic of liberation wars impede the post-independence progress of transforming peasant societies into developing nation states. John Lewis, discussing the revolutionary legacy in Chinese society, gives forceful expression to the dominant view:

> The militant preservation of the revolutionary mass line progressively alienated party leaders from the postrevolutionary realities of the Chinese state. Moreover, the process of alienation continues as Communist leaders equate current struggles for economic construction with the pre–1949 revolutionary military struggle. Reasoning by analogy, they stipulate that what worked as a leadership system in Yenan must be equally effective for the same leaders a decade or so later in Peking. Believing that the mass line method must "represent the interests of the masses," Communist cadres have underestimated and misunderstood the deterioration of popular morale and

[3] Chalmers Johnson, *Peasant Nationalism and Communist Power: The Emergence of Revolutionary China, 1937–1945.* (Stanford, Cal., Stanford Univ. Press, 1962). The book may be read as a sophisticated brief for the techniques of Special War which the United States was then initiating in South Vietnam: Its primary lesson, shortly to be ignored in Washington, is the necessity to rely on aid, advisers, and special training of native armies, and avoidance of massive commitment of American forces to crush wars of liberation.

support. Dissatisfied with exhortation without positive economic effects, harried peasants and workers have become listless and sullen according to many reliable but unconfirmed reports.[4]

This latter perspective, endorsed by scholars across the entire political and disciplinary spectrum, represents a fundamental article of faith of contemporary Western man: faith that the developmental process is a product of rational evolution directed and controlled by a technological-managerial elite. In the emphasis on the critical role of technology, Weberians and Bolsheviks, the high priests of private enterprise and their counterparts among socialist planners, concur perfectly. And indeed, examination of the major historical models of industrializing societies—from England and Germany to the United States, Russia, and Japan—does suggest the importance of new business-managerial elites in channeling resources and skills from agriculture into the most advanced industrial channels. In this respect revolutionary and gradualist approaches need not diverge; technocratic liberalism and Bolshevism lead down converging paths.

We need not concern ourselves here with the abuses of "modernization" theory as a cynical cover for the perpetuation of neo-colonial domination and what Andre Gunder Frank calls

[4] John Wilson Lewis, *Leadership in Communist China* (Ithaca, N.Y., Cornell Univ. Press, 1963), pp. 99–100. This view, already dominant, has been greatly reinforced as a result of the Great Proletarian Cultural Revolution. See, for example, A. Doak Barnett, *Cadres, Bureaucracy and Political Power in Communist China* (New York, Columbia Univ. Press, 1967), pp. 38–39, 142, 437–38; Benjamin Schwartz, "Upheaval in China," in *Communism and China: Ideology in Flux* (Cambridge, Mass., Harvard Univ. Press, 1968), pp. 205–27; Tang Tsou, "Revolution, Reintegration and Crisis in Communist China: A Framework for Analysis," in Ping-ti Ho and Tang Tsou (eds.), *China in Crisis: China's Heritage and the Communist Political System* (Chicago, Univ. of Chicago Press, 1968), Vol. I, Book I, pp. 277–347, especially pp. 343–47; Lucian Pye, *The Spirit of Chinese Politics* (Cambridge, Mass., M.I.T. Press, 1968), *passim;* Jerome Cohen, "The Chinese Communist Party and 'Judicial Independence' 1949–1959," in *Harvard Law Review*, Vol. 82, No. 5 (March, 1969), pp. 967–1006.

"the development of underdevelopment." But let us be blunt about the human costs implicit in these elitist approaches to industrialization even at their most successful. In the process the populace is deliberately subordinated to the imperatives of the machine, generations are sacrificed for the future fruits of industrialization, and a new elite, the professional manipulators of advanced technology, is created. Moreover, a common side effect of the process, particularly under capitalist auspices, has been the perpetuation of endemic pockets of poverty amidst plenty, their residents overwhelmed by the challenges of a new order. Are there alternative routes to development which are less costly in human terms?

The thesis of this essay is as follows: Out of the ashes of military strife which enveloped China and Vietnam in protracted wars of liberation emerged a radically new vision of man and society and a concrete approach to development. Built on foundations of participation and community action which challenge elite domination, this approach offers hope of more *humane* forms of development and of effectively overcoming the formidable barriers to the transformation of peasant societies. In the base areas and consolidated war zones in which the movement enjoyed its fullest growth, the redefinition of community began in the resistance to a foreign invader and continued in the struggle to overcome domestic problems of poverty and oppression. People's war implies more than a popular guerrilla struggle for national independence; it impinges directly and with profoundly revolutionary consequences on the full scope of rural life. In the course of people's war, local communities defined in response to the imperatives of defense and social change may be effectively integrated in national movements. The very intensity of the war-time experience contributes to rapid development of consciousness and organization. In people's war peasants cease to be the passive pawns of landlords and officials or to fatalistically accept the verdict of a harsh natural environment. Where the primary resource of insurgent movements is man, and where active commitment is the *sine qua non* of success, the sharing of common hardships and hopes creates powerful bonds among peasant resisters and between leaders and led. In the new institutions which emerge locally in the course of the resistance, to an unprecedented degree peasants begin to secure active control of their economic and political destinies.

Partisan leadership does not merely fill a vacuum created by the flight or demise of the landlord-official class. Nor does it achieve victory by reaping the grim rewards of terror, for it can never match the ruthlessness of the "official terror" instituted by foreign forces and their puppets. Rather, at its best, it forges new bonds of unity in which the very definitions of leader and led are recast and the beginnings of a new social basis are created. In China I call this the Yenan Way after the war-time capital of the movement. The same spirit infuses the Vietnamese resistance. In the embryonic social forms created under war-time duress are important features relevant to the future of the Third World, and indeed, to possibilities for participatory social patterns everywhere.

Let us begin with China, whose war of liberation may well provide the primary revolutionary model for the second half of the twentieth century. The starting point of this analysis—one which applies equally to Vietnam and much of the Third World —is the firm rejection of idealized images of the family and village which have permeated both the literature and popular perceptions. Samuel Popkin has referred to this as the

> "myth of the village." Peasants who have no material rewards are assumed to have spiritual rewards. When a son sticks to his father for the sake of survival, it is called filial piety. . . . Somehow the necessities and/or oppressions of one era seem to have become the traditional values of the next.[5]

The poverty and exploitation in which most peasants lived even in the best of times were the central features of Chinese rural

[5] Samuel Popkin, "Village Authority Patterns in Vietnam," unpublished paper presented to the Peace Research Society, June 3, 1968. A useful discussion dispatching many of these myths in the case of precolonial Vietnam is found in Robert Sansom, "The Economics of Insurgency in South Vietnam," unpublished Ph.D. dissertation (Oxford, 1968), pp. 519–20.

life. Built into well-articulated patterns of authority and submission were the unquestioned domination of the rich over the poor, the aged over youth, and men over women.

Yet the system, when it was functioning effectively, was not without its compensations, principally the security provided within the context of family and village, and the community of interests shared by the most humble villager and leading members of the local elite, the gentry. For if gentry were exploiters in their roles as landlords and money-lenders, and if, in the final analysis, they relied on state military power to protect their interests from the challenge of rebellious peasants, they were nevertheless united with the people in the desire to minimize government incursions on the village. The legitimation of gentry prerogatives rested primarily on their intermediary role as representative of local interests in dealing with a remote government whose primary concern was the efficient collection of taxes and the stability which that necessitated.

This balance was shattered in the chaos of the late nineteenth and early twentieth century. The demise of imperial authority undermined the aura of gentry legitimacy provided by Confucian sanction. Effective performance of brokerage roles was transformed and increasingly defined by local military force. Simultaneously the exploitative functions of the local elite were intensified and brought into public purview. First, in the absence of effective imperial rule, social control, that is the repression of rebellious peasants, fell directly to landlords and their private armies. In the absence of central authority, landlords sponsored local military forces to protect their interests. Second, particularly in South China, the development of absentee landlordism throughout the Ch'ing period (1644–1911) eliminated the social basis for a landlord-peasant community of interests. Increasingly to be found living in luxury in the towns and cities, the most prosperous of the gentry had become landlords pure and simple. Physically cut off from the village, increasingly their interest in local affairs was limited to ensuring the efficient flow of rents into the family coffers. Tensions between landlords and tenants were thus sharpened at a time when rural misery and dislocation were rising sharply.

If mounting absentee landlordism and the decline of central authority in a century of ruinous war stripped the gentry of its cloak of legitimacy, the result was no "vacuum" of leadership but rather a new power mix. Insurgents did not ineluctably replace imperial-gentry control; where they succeeded in seizing power it was only in the course of bitter struggle against entrenched interests. If the landlord-warlord local leadership of the twentieth century lacked the sanctions of time and Confucian tradition, it nevertheless offered a formidable challenge to would-be revolutionaries. At the same time, the military and political patterns which emerged out of dynastic decline, warlord ravages and foreign incursion did create and redefine opportunities for insurgents in rural China.

The proliferation of private military power included both the "legitimate" armies of landlords and warlords, and bandits roaming the hills. Both of them sapped the overstrained resources of the peasantry and both contributed to the militarization of Chinese society. The extraordinary human toll of a century of warlordism has been well analyzed in numerous studies of the era. Two tendencies seem particularly relevant to the future development of the resistance. One was the expansion of peasant horizons beyond the village or local marketing community as a result of participation in military forces, whether bandit, secret society, or official. The result was to define a defense community, to create a network of extended relationships which were vital to peasant welfare. Second, a century of military upheaval placed a premium on youthful, vigorous leadership which contrasts sharply with the mandarin style of high traditional society. In particular the military expanded opportunities for attaining power among the sons of the poor. These developments, the creation of defense communities and increasing reliance on the energies of youth and the poor, would be furthered by the war-time insurgent movement which attempted to redirect their thrust for new social and national purposes.

The critical problem confronting Communist leadership in 1937 on the eve of all-out war with Japan was this: How can a small and weak army of committed revolutionaries build a movement to resist the aggressive designs of an advanced industrial power? If the experience of guerrilla warfare during the preceding decade of civil war and land revolution provided a legacy of experience, the sobering fact was that the movement had recently been crushed and the party nearly annihilated by Kuomintang and warlord armies united if only in their opposition to social revolution. Forced by 1934 to abandon its major base areas in South and Central China, surviving Communist forces had regrouped at the conclusion of the Long March in China's remote and desolate northwest.

The Japanese invasion of 1937 posed new problems and possibilities. In place of the class war which had centered on the struggle for land, the party attempted to spearhead a *national* movement, uniting the broadest possible spectrum of Chinese in defense against foreign conquest. If that were all, there would be little to distinguish the Chinese Communist movement from its counterparts struggling for liberation from colonial domination throughout the Third World, and indeed, such an explanation is inadequate to grasp the dynamics of the wartime movement.[6] For if the Communists were not *simply* agrarian reformers, and if radical land revolution was temporarily shelved, their ability to respond boldly and effectively to war-aggravated problems of rural society lies at the heart of their extraordinary popular success during the resistance. The response to their appeal to the peasant must be understood in the context of a comprehensive and imaginative program of rural leadership and reform. Nationalism generated peasant support for the resistance only in the context of a reform program in which the peasants as a group actively participated in the effort to resolve overwhelming social, economic, and security problems endemic in late Ch'ing and warlord China and aggravated by the Japanese onslaught. The new nationalism in the countryside and the commitment to engage in guerrilla resistance are inseparable from the movement's penetration and revitalization

[6] Johnson, *Peasant Nationalism* is the classic statement of the nationalist interpretation of the Communist rise. The position was articulated initially by George Taylor, *The Struggle for North China* (New York, Institute of Pacific Relations, 1940).

of basic elements of the shattered social and economic life of the village. Both in areas where local power-holders had fled either the Japanese or the Communists, and in those in which they chose to cooperate with Communist-sponsored governments, the political monopoly of the landlord elite was challenged. For the first time the peasantry as a group was integrated into the political process and involved in new social and economic relationships leading to the restructuring of village life.

This point is critical in understanding the failure of the Kuomintang to reap the nationalist benefits which accrued from foreign invasion. The Kuomintang, as the wielder of central government power, did mobilize substantial elite nationalist support behind it in the early war years. Indeed, it was primarily in terms of nationalist appeals to resist the Japanese invader that the Kuomintang and Communists vied for support of the rural and urban elite, including student youth, the hotbed of twentieth-century Chinese nationalism. Such appeals, however, fell on deaf ears when directed to the peasantry. From the perspective of the Kuomintang ruling power, in the face of overwhelmingly superior invading armies and a major insurgent challenge from the Communist-led resistance, active popular support became essential for preserving the power. Neither astuteness in the manipulations of warlord and landlord coalitions, nor modernized, German-trained regular armies—basic ingredients of a decade of Kuomintang hegemony—sufficed under these circumstances. By 1938, driven from urban and coastal areas which had provided the bulwark of its strength, the Kuomintang proved helpless to secure control of the countryside.

The Kuomintang failure to confront the awesome problems of peasant misery, and its related inability to mobilize peasant support for the resistance should be viewed in the perspective of a familiar Third World problem. The Kuomintang approach exemplifies many of the major obstacles to transformation of peasant societies by "military modernizers" or other elite groups cut off despite nationalistic proclivities by training, experience, and world view from the vast majority of their people. It was not merely Kuomintang stubbornness, stupidity, or blind-ness (any more than it is in analogous instances in Vietnam, Thailand, Laos, and much of Latin America) which posed an obstacle in this regard. We are confronting rather a fundamental *structural* barrier implicit in the constitution of these elites. Firmly committed by power considerations as well as ideologi-cal predisposition to support of landlord hegemony, the Kuo-mintang was incapable of leading a popular movement which could withstand the onslaught of repeated Japanese attack and provide a base for resistance. In the final analysis the Kuomin-tang had little to offer the peasantry except the theft of grain, brutal seizure of young sons to man the armies of the status quo, and nationalist rhetoric which proved meaningless in the absence of a social program—in short, hunger, death, and empty words.

In attempting to lead the war-time resistance, Communist leadership faced a dilemma. On the one hand the party sought to construct a broad united front including former class enemies —landlords, rich peasants, and the bourgeoisie, linked by a common spirit of anti-Japanese nationalism. On the other its strength rested primarily on peasant support. In the interest of national unity the frontal attack on the landlord class was re-placed in 1937 with a program to "reduce rent and interest" whose principal features were a rent ceiling of 37.5 per cent and reduction of all rents by 25 per cent. The critical question was whether a rent reduction movement which preserved certain landlord rights and eschewed violence could stimulate the deep peasant commitment frequently produced by the radical land upheaval of the preceding decade.

In the early 1940's, facing crippling Japanese offensives and growing tensions within the united front, rent reduction was widely and effectively implemented in the Communist-led base areas. Developed as a mass movement at the village level rather than as a routine administrative undertaking, rent reduction campaigns assumed many features of the radical movement which swept away the landlord order after 1946; the basic psychological problem in both cases was to overcome deep-seated peasant fears of landlord reprisal. In rent reduction campaigns, the goal was a direct personal challenge of landlord excesses by every peasant. At this time it was the *excesses* of the landlord system, not the system itself, which was being challenged. Rent reduction directives thus called for mass participation in curbing landlord prerogatives, while insisting on the united front principle that reduced rents continue to flow into landlord coffers. Peasants could not anticipate the total destruction of the system, the exhilarating liberation from landlord rule (*fanshen*) which was the hallmark of the later land reform.[7]

Under these circumstances, building an effective mass movement on the basis of rent reduction presented formidable difficulties. The key lay in the creation of powerful peasant associations to confront recalcitrant landlords and to provide a focus for the subsequent protection, indeed the fundamental redefinition, of peasant interests. Group consciousness and support developed through the peasant associations were crucial for allaying fears and stirring a spirit of militancy. A critical step came as peasant associations became powerful enough to guarantee tenant rights to cultivate the land and enjoin landlords from arbitrarily repossessing their land. Thus a potential threat to peasant activists was eliminated. Yet the problems were peculiarly tenacious. There are numerous accounts of peasants vigorously denouncing landlord exploitation by day only to make supplemental rental payments secretly at night. Old attitudes, fears, and insecurity did not die quickly under these circumstances. Nevertheless, the cumulative effect is clear: these campaigns provided a focus for peasant activism and release from subordination to a landlord elite. Peasant associations which spearheaded the movement became the locus of peasant power and participation, providing an effective counterweight to landlord domination. Moreover, nationalist appeals were frequently integrally related with the effort to curb landlord power. Where landlords were linked in active complicity with the Japanese, by no means an uncommon occurrence, they became the object of anti-traitor struggle movements, and their lands were subject to outright confiscation. Thus the rent reduc-

---

[7] William Hinton, *Fanshen. A Documentary of Revolution in a Chinese Village* (New York, Monthly Review, 1966).

tion movement was carried to its logical conclusion in the case of landlord traitors.[8]

Rent reduction was an integral part of the drive to simultaneously liberate the peasantry and stimulate the economy, to strengthen the resistance movement, and to improve conditions of rural life. By 1941, facing critical supply problems in the face of blockade and intense repression, primitive efforts at economic development became an integral part of war-time mobilization. The creation of fraternity rather than hostility between cadres and peasants lay at the root of the problem of strengthening the resistance. It also opened avenues to stimulating the economy through the introduction of new ideas and techniques from outside the village and by experimentation within. Indeed it was in the heat of the resistance struggle that distinctive Chinese approaches to development emerged: emphasis on the paramount role of human labor and popular creativity in the absence of financial and technological resources, self-sufficiency, decentralization, and community planning. It was believed that the prospect of increased rewards realized through the rent reduction movement would stimulate the peasant's "productive enthusiasm" with positive effects on over-all output. But the task of overcoming poverty and agrarian stagnation was not left to individual enthusiasm alone. The key lay in the coordination and stimulation of fragmented and

[8] Ch'i Wu, *I-ko ko-ming ken-chü-ti ti ch'eng-ch'ang* (The Development of a Revolutionary Base), Peking, Jen-min, 1958, pp. 118, 124, provides data on landlord complicity with the Japanese in the Shansi-Hopeh-Shantung-Honan Border area. While the effort to rectify abuses in land tenure relationships was carried out under the general banner of rent reduction, the campaign touched a broad range of other problems. Investigation of land titles during the campaign frequently unearthed large landlord holdings which had gone unregistered in the effort to evade taxes. In some cases these became subject to redistribution. In the Shensi-Kansu-Ningsia area, the single surviving base to experience land revolution prior to the outbreak of the Resistance War, the subsequent rent reduction movement rectified instances in which landlords had illegally recovered property from peasant recipients in the earlier redistribution. These were expropriated and returned to the original recipients. Cf. *Chieh-fang Jih-pao* (Liberation Daily) (March 18, April 15, May 12, 15, June 6, July 25, 1942).

idle resources. Cooperative farming was initiated as the focus of a new village economy and a new society.

The cooperatives which spread throughout the base areas in the final years of the resistance war signified a major innovation in the approach to rural problems. Building on peasant leadership manifested in the course of guerrilla resistance and rent reduction, the cooperatives marked the first effort to create indigenous organization embedded in the economic life of the village. Cooperatives redirected peasant economic concerns from their narrow focus on the family to the larger unit of the mutual-aid group and the village itself. They also served to unify and strengthen the village as an economic and social unit, integrating it in the effort to link the resistance with new approaches to economic development throughout the base areas.

In other respects the cooperative movement marked the Party's most ambitious approach to the peasant. In contrast to movements for land redistribution or rent reduction, which had appealed by the most direct means to the needs and desires of the poor, cooperatives were unfamiliar to many peasants. Moreover they offered few immediate financial benefits, and required sustained leadership and broad commitment. In the long run, success was predicated on the creation of effective local leadership committed to cooperative principles of community and economic development. Yet unless mutual aid rapidly increased production, no amount of adept leadership could overcome peasant skepticism and resistance. Basic cooperative principles such as flexibility in adapting to local variations, decentralization, and sharply limiting the size of productive units were astutely tailored to the possibilities for organization and participation in war-time base areas. If the cooperatives were to succeed, if self-perpetuating communities committed to human and economic development were to emerge out of the chaos of war and disintegration, these principles were essential. In the numerous areas in which mutual aid successfully took root, it defined effective community channels to challenge peasant particularism, led to a basic restructuring of village economic patterns and enhanced possibilities for sustained development.

The cooperative unit was in fact a microcosm of the society

envisioned by war-time leadership, embodying not only a pro-
methean vision of man actively striving to control nature, but
confronting the full scope of rural problems. In addition to their
basic economic functions, cooperatives also served as guerrilla
units engaging in raids and combat-support operations; they
provided a focus for part-time education, education linked
closely with concrete problems of war, the economy, and rural
society; and they represented as well an autonomous and participatory political unit which continuously addressed itself to
local grievances. Above all, cooperatives embodied the resistance spirit of sharing and self-sacrifice. Mao Tse-tung's war-
time slogan captures well the simple but powerful cooperatives
spirit:

> Those who have labor give labor; those who have much give
> much; those who have little give little; human and animal
> power are put together. Thus one can avoid violating the
> seasons, and is able to plow in time, sow in time, hoe in time,
> and harvest in time.[9]

The war-time cooperatives thus embodied basic principles
subsequently developed after 1958 in the commune movement.
These principles, above all the emphasis on local community
organization, popular creativity, and self-reliance rather than
state and bureaucratic management, would constitute the heart
of the Chinese challenge to Soviet practice.

The inauguration of the cooperative movement sharply posed
the problem of relationships between leadership committed to
radical social transformation and the peasantry. As the anthro-
pologist, Eric Wolf, has suggested:

> In peaceful times revolutionary leaders may scour the coun-
> tryside in attempts to "go to the people." . . . Yet all too fre-
> quently they still do so as outsiders, as people city-bred and
> city-trained, drawing their behavior patterns and cultural
> idioms from the dominant sector. . . . These behavior pat-

[9] Quoted in Franz Schurmann, *Ideology and Organization in Communist China* (Berkeley, Univ. of California Press, 1966), p. 420.

terns and cultural idioms they must first unlearn, if they are to enter into successful contact with the peasant rebels.

What is critical, Wolf notes, is the development of

> a complex dialogue with the villagers in which the outsider learns as much, if not more about local organization and criteria of relevance, than the local inhabitants. Guerrilla warfare both speeds and deepens this learning as cadre and peasant activists synchronize their behavior and translate from one cultural idiom to the other.[10]

Preoccupation with problems of a leadership effectively integrated with the peasantry resulted in the party's first major rectification movement (*cheng-feng*) in the years 1942–44 and, simultaneously, its initial experiments in sending cadres and students to serve in the villages (*hsia-fang*) as a step toward overcoming the problems of elitist bureaucratic leadership and rural isolation. The mobilization style of leadership in the base areas required forging new relationships of solidarity between leaders and led, critical for waging a successful guerrilla struggle. As Jack Belden observed following an extensive tour of the base areas:

> . . . guerrilla warfare, which often brought the Communist cadre into the peasant's hut seeking refuge, has developed in the farmer a new sense of nearness and familiarity with government. Government has become something close to earth that the peasant can touch, shake by the hand or even slap in the face. Gone are its external trappings, the awe-inspiring uniforms, the fur-lined silk gowns of the officials, the men bearing arms before austere yamen gates. In the villages the officials dress in cotton jackets and pants like peasants, they talk like peasants, live like peasants. They are mainly peasants. There is nothing about them to distinguish them from anyone else. Nor are they any longer addressed as Officer, Old Master,

---

[10] Eric R. Wolf, "Peasant Problems and Revolutionary Welfare," unpublished paper presented to the Third Annual Socialist Scholars Conference, New York City, September 10, 1967, p. 9.

or even Elder Born. Why should they be? They were elevated to office by the votes of the peasants themselves.[11]

The solidarity forged in the guerrilla movement, in the attack on rural oppression and economic stagnation, and in new popular forms of culture and education, was the hallmark of the resistance. Its success was predicated on transforming hierarchical patterns of leadership into firm egalitarian bonds constantly renewed in the struggle against the foreign enemy and the struggle against injustices of rural life.[12] These same principles have been affirmed and developed in the course of the resistance to American forces in South Vietnam.

NLF success is rooted in nationalism linked to a creative response to Vietnamese rural problems. Mounting peasant misery during recent decades is the product of the French colonial legacy, the ravages of war, and mounting scarcity of land. The closure of the delta as a frontier in the early 1930's marked the beginning of a steady downward spiral in peasant income and welfare which brought millions to the verge of subsistence. By the 1950's more than 80 per cent of the delta's population and 60 per cent of all peasants in South Vietnam were tenants. Over 7,000,000 delta tenants and hired laborers owned no land whatsoever and millions more possessed but a fraction of that required to feed their families. With increasing

[11] Jack Belden, *China Shakes the World* (New York, Harper & Brothers, 1949), pp. 83–84. Belden's contrast to Kuomintang officialdom living high in the midst of the catastrophic famine of 1941 highlights the significance of his comments on Communist leadership. "I was ashamed to go from one Kuomintang general to another, eating special delicacies from their well-laid tables, while peasants were scraping the fields outside the yamens for roots and wild grass to stuff into their griping stomachs. But I was more than ashamed—I was overcome with a feeling of loathing—when I learned that these same generals and the Kuomintang officials were buying up land from starving farmers for arrears in taxes and were holding it to wait tenants and rainy days." (p 97.)

[12] Elsewhere I have discussed in detail the institutional developments and the transformation of leadership patterns in Communist-led resistance bases. "The Yenan Legacy: The Mass Line" in A. Doak Barnett (ed.), *Chinese Communist Politics in Action* (Seattle, Univ. of Washington Press, 1969).

competition for the land, tenants faced rising rents, generally in the realm of 40–60 per cent of the crop, while rural wages declined. Throughout the decades after 1930 French and Vietnamese absentee landlordism rose steadily and agricultural productivity remained stagnant.[13] Writing in 1959 of South Vietnam's land problems, an American land reform adviser observed that

> substantial concentration of ownership has taken place in the last two decades. The area held by individuals owning more than 100 hectares has climbed from 733,800 to 1,076,000 hectares, while the absolute number of such large owners has remained approximately the same. Where one percent of the owners held 36 percent of the total rice land in 1934, they now own 44 percent of the total.[14]

The Vietnamese rural economy thus presented a stark picture of spiraling tenancy, land concentration, absentee ownership, rising rents, and declining rural wages.[15]

The NLF was quick to address itself to South Vietnam's rural crisis, always, however, in the context of the struggle against foreign domination. Indeed, NLF land policy reflects the tension between its primary commitment to liberation from American domination as a *national* movement, and the *class* effort to strengthen peasant-based resistance through land reform. Readjustments of land inequities were evaluated in light of their potential effect on the resistance.

[13] Sansom, "The Economics of Insurgency," pp. 462–67, 475–80, 494–500, 511, 518, 529, 537. Measured exclusively in terms of tenancy rates the Vietnamese land problem was far more acute than that in North China base areas where Communist war-time resistance centered. Cf. Eric R. Wolf, *Peasant Wars of the Twentieth Century* (New York, Harper & Row, 1969), pp. 160–78.

[14] Price Gittinger, "Agrarian Reform," pp. 200–208 in Richard W. Lindholm (ed.), *Vietnam: The First Five Years* (Lansing, Michigan State Univ. Press, 1959), p. 205.

[15] Sansom, "The Economics of Insurgency," pp. 462–67, 494–500. Nguyen Khac Vien, "The Peasants' Struggle (1954–1960)," pp. 50–77, *Vietnamese Studies,* No. 8, pp. 52–53. Cf. James Hendry, *The Small World of Khanh Hau* (Chicago, Aldine Publishers, 1964), pp. 133–40.

If we have to settle cases of restoring ownership to original owners, we should rely upon their enemy-opposing achievements in reaching a decision: only those who have scored exploits in the struggle against the enemies will be given back land.[16]

In all cases the NLF emphasized increasing village solidarity based on broad acceptance of the justice of the land redistribution. The same document lays out the complex ground rules for land reform:

The immediate duty for the time being is to carry out national union, to struggle determinedly against the war-waging and aggressive imperialists, and to overthrow the Ngo Dinh Diem ruling clique. Hence, in the land problem at present, one should on the one hand wrest back land that the peasants had gotten during resistance, limit exploitation by landlords, improve the peasant's life, and intensify solidarity among the laboring peasants' ranks, and on the other hand, continue to recognize ownership rights of landlords (with the exception of the tyrannical clique of U.S.-Diemist henchmen), recognize the right of landlords to collect land rent at a determined rate. In the countryside, our tactics at present are: solidarity between landless, poor and middle peasants, alliance with rich peasants, classification of the landlord class, winning over elements more-or-less opposing the U.S.-Diemists, neutralizing half-way elements and toppling the tyrannical clique presently serving as U.S.-Diemist lackeys.

Two basic approaches have been characteristic of NLF land policy. First, as in the analogous Chinese case, was the reduction of rent. Peasants rose to reduce landlord exactions which frequently exceeded half the crop. Characteristically, the NLF offered no uniform national guidelines as to the appropriate rent levels—these were to be decided in each area on the basis of

---

[16] *Viet Cong Documents* (hereafter: *VCD*) #296. The translation is that given by Christine White in an unpublished paper, "Land Reform and Revolution: Vietnam." These and all other translated Vietnamese documents cited are available at the Chicago Central Library.

local conditions. However, a maximum rate of 15 per cent, a mere fraction of prevailing exactions, was enforced in many areas.[17] Although the landlord system was to be preserved through the continued payment of rents, heavy emphasis was placed on restricting landlord prerogatives. A significant step lay in providing safeguards for tenants against the loss of land they were cultivating.

But in many areas NLF land policy followed a second and more radical course. Particularly where the earlier Viet Minh land reform was reversed after 1954 by the Diemist restoration of landlord power, "land to the tiller" was again proclaimed. Property which had been seized by landlords was redistributed to the peasants. In addition, communal lands and the property of traitors were expropriated and redistributed. In some cases peasants received temporary rights to cultivate the land rent-free.[18]

The importance of land policy, and its integral relationship with the anti-American struggle, are vividly articulated in a widely quoted document tracing the development of the resistance in a village in Kien Phong province. After repeated failures, the report relates how the first major inroads were made in this village:

We awoke the people to the fact that if the American-Diem clique succeeded in permanently maintaining the organization of village notables and security, soon Mister H, the cruel land-

---

[17] The fifteen per cent guideline may be found in "Resolution of the Central Office for South Vietnam" of March 1966 (Press Release of United States Mission, Saigon, August 18, 1967), pp. 43–44. *VCD* #296 suggests the following guidelines: "For a *cong* of good land whose output is 15-20 *gia,* or even 30 *gia* and above, the maximum rent shall not exceed 1-1/2 *gia* per *cong.*" In this case rentals would amount to only 5–10 per cent on the best land. These criteria were designed to ensure that the rewards of increased productivity went to the tiller.

[18] *Vietnamese Studies,* No. 8, pp. 157–59. The essay "In the Liberated Zones of South Vietnam," pp. 156–79, contains a full statement of NLF land policy as of 1965. Other key NLF land documents include: *VCD* #2, pp. 296, 298, 455; "Political Program of the South Vietnam National Liberation Front," United States Mission in Vietnam, for the full texts of the 1960 and 1967 NLF programs.

lord, and others would return to the village to seize land and collect back rent. For that reason, we said, the farmers must eliminate the influence of the village notables and sweep away the security agents. . . .

As I have noted, the main interest of the farmer of XB village is in land. . . . In its political and armed struggle, in its administration of the rural area, and in other revolutionary tasks, the Party knew well how to make use of the farmers' interest in land. On it we built a mass movement. And for that reason the revolutionary movement made great progress and resulted in a great success.[19]

The NLF was not alone in viewing resolution of the land problem as a key to military victory. From the time of its intervention in Vietnam the United States has also insisted that land reform held the key to the creation of a viable government capable of resisting the inroads of insurgent movements. Wolf Ladejinsky, mastermind behind the American-sponsored agrarian reform effort in Japan and other Asian countries, as adviser to President Diem, was instrumental in introducing similar measures in South Vietnam. Since the inauguration of Diem's land reform program in 1956, American officials have continued to prod reluctant Saigon regimes to carry through land reform as the centerpiece of a program to reassert control in the countryside.[20]

[19] *VCD* #2, pp. 41–42. For lengthy excerpts see Denis Warner, *The Last Confucian* (New York, Macmillan, 1963). The report notes how subsequent resistance work was continually pegged to the issue of land as in the use of the following slogan: "To keep your land and prevent landowners from collecting rent, you must lay naily boards (used for village defense)." (p. 50.) It also offers one of the fullest accounts of the over-all program including education, social services, and defense at the local level.

[20] Wolf Ladejinsky, "Agrarian Reform in the Republic of Vietnam," in Wesley R. Fishel (ed.), *Problems of Freedom, South Vietnam Since Independence* (New York, Free Press of Glencoe, 1961), pp. 154–57. Recently, a number of "realists" centered in the RAND Corporation, among whom Charles Wolf, Jr., and Edward Mitchell are the most articulate spokesmen, have queried the American emphasis on land reform. Their "discovery" (as if the military had not been telling us this

Ironically, both the Diem land reform and the accompanying pacification program centering on strategic hamlets, created new opportunities for the NLF to strengthen the resistance on the twin pillars of nationalism and agrarian reform. Diem's land reform, leaving untouched the entire central region (his per-

---

for years) is that the key to pacification lies not with the resolution of the land problem and other rural grievances but with the provision of effective military security. The implications of Mitchell's conclusion are clear: "From the point of view of government control the ideal province in South Vietnam would be one in which few peasants operate their own land, the distribution of land holdings is unequal, no land redistribution has taken place, large French landholdings existed in the past, population density is high, and the terrain is such that mobility or accessibility is low." Edward J. Mitchell, *Land Tenure and Rebellion: A Statistical Analysis of Factors Affecting Government Control in South Vietnam.* RAND Memorandum RM-5181-ARPA.

Mitchell's work is an extraordinary blend of the super-sophistication of social scientific computerized survey methods and the crudest abuses of elementary research techniques. His entire data base is a 1965 survey of NLF and Saigon control of individual provinces, with no indication of the definition of "control" employed. Not only does he ignore totally historical and strategic factors in the development of the Viet Minh and NLF, but his single crude index of peasant discontent is that of tenancy rates. Moreover, Mitchell distorts entirely crucial questions of terrain. His data exclude entirely dense forests, paddy land and mountains.

The Vietnamese case, no more than that of China, supports a simple correlation between rural misery and revolutionary success; many other factors including the strength of counterrevolutionary forces and the terrain critically affect the course of insurgent movements. What is abundantly clear in both cases is that conditions of misery prevailing throughout the country provided fuel for insurgent movements. Whether or not the *most* wretched of the wretched have achieved the greatest success in overthrowing their domestic and foreign oppressors is irrelevant to proving or disproving the link between oppression and rebellion.

Unburdened by moral scruples which might impede the "pacification" effort, and armed with studies like Mitchell's, an alliance of military men and social science "realists" find the solution to counterinsurgency problems in endless military escalation regardless of the costs in human lives. The "final solution," unflinchingly carrying forward the implications of Mitchell's approach, is outlined by Samuel Huntington. The chairman of Harvard's government department blandly suggests that we continue to encourage the felicitous war-time trend toward "urbanization" by appropriate military means. In the end, Vietnamese faced with

sonal power base), was limited to the delta where large estates and absentee landlords dominated the rice economy. The land reform laws designated all estates exceeding 100 hectares for government purchase and sale to occupying tenants. Yet in practice, the amount of land which actually found its way into the possession of these former tenants represented but a small fraction of the total land legally subject to redistribution. As Bernard Fall observed, "after nearly two years of the reform program only 35,700 hectares had been transferred to 18,000 farmers."[21] Diem's land reform did nothing to alter landlord domination as the central fact of South Vietnamese rural life. The overwhelming number of landless farmers and tenants were completely bypassed by it. As one American expert put it with classic understatement:

> Any real crash program would be hotly resented in Saigon, and it would be resisted locally by the province and district chiefs whose principal sources of support remain the land-lords and other wealthy classes.[22]

However, to focus discussion of the land reform on such shortcomings is to miss its real significance. In many areas it served primarily to provide the cover for wresting land from the poor and restoring it to former landlords. The American-sponsored land reform was carried out primarily in areas where the Viet Minh had earlier spearheaded a successful movement to give land to the poor and landless. The return of the Diem

---

the option of migration to the city or a fiery death in the countryside cannot but choose "freedom." Since the NLF is unable to secure the cities the war will end successfully for the United States with the "de-population" of rural areas. "The Bases of Accommodation," *Foreign Affairs*, Vol. 46, No. 3 (July, 1968), pp. 642–56. Excellent critiques of Mitchell's work may be found in Sansom, "The Economics of Insurgency," pp. 580–89; and Christine White, "Land Reform and Revolution: Vietnam" (unpublished), pp. 1–3.

[21] Bernard Fall, *Vietnam Witness 1953–1966* (New York, Praeger, 1966), p. 179.

[22] John Montgomery, "Land Reform as a Means to Political Development in Viet Nam," *Orbis* (Summer, 1968), p. 24.

government meant that many who had been cultivating the land for a decade as *de facto* owners suddenly were forced to pay rent—frequently collected for a fee at gunpoint by government soldiers or officials—or they were "permitted" to purchase the land they had regarded as their own.[23] In striking contrast to Viet Minh and NLF programs, the reform was limited exclusively to tenants on large estates. Since they alone were eligible to purchase expropriated land, the great majority of the landless and the land poor were excluded from all benefits. Moreover, even where the letter of the law was scrupulously obeyed, the Diem land reform left unchallenged the economic and political supremacy of the large landlords. Retaining the legal maximum of 100 hectares after the reform, they continued to enjoy the overpowering wealth and position to ensure the subordination of local peasants including the new purchasers of small plots of land. In short, Diem's reform bolstered the power of the landlord class, did little to assist the landless and the poor, and added new antagonisms to the festering problems of village life, antagonisms to which, as we have observed, the NLF program vigorously addressed itself.[24]

The strategic hamlet conception, implemented simultaneously with Diem's land reform, while theoretically potent from a military perspective, in practice created new avenues for the resistance to transcend class and unite all villagers. The strategic hamlets, similar to Japanese programs in Manchuria and China, were explicitly modeled on British experience in Malaya. The goal was to destroy existing scattered hamlets and herd the entire local population into camps surrounded by barbed wire in an effort to control the population, to separate the fish from the

[23] Sansom, "The Economics of Insurgency," pp. 564–66; Wolf, *Peasant Wars*, pp. 197–98.

[24] A devastating liberal critique of Saigon's land reform program is found in Twentieth Report of the Committee on Government Operations, "Land Reform in Vietnam," Report No. 1142, Ninetieth Congress, 2nd Session, House of Representatives. Cf. the perceptive analyses from the other side in "The Peasants' Struggle," *Vietnamese Studies*, No. 8, pp. 55–67 and Vo Nguyen and Le Tan Danh, "In the Liberated Zones of South Vietnam," *ibid.*, pp. 156–67.

water, the people from the resistance.[25] The strategic hamlet program did take a heavy toll in Vietnamese lives. At the same time, by all accounts, the destruction of their homes and farms and forced regroupment in concentration camps under horrendous conditions provoked outrage among virtually everyone involved. An NLF report captures well the negative and unintended mobilization effect of this approach on the local population:

> The creation of "prosperity centres" ushered in a new stage of the rural masses' struggle. Now, it was no longer the poor peasants alone who saw their interests threatened, nor only former resistance members who risked at any moment, being arrested, tortured, and summarily executed. The rural population as a whole, poor or rich, opponent or neutralist, and even supporters of the regime, also suffered.[26]

As in the Japanese onslaught in rural China, such policies linked with brutal repression dramatized the message of the resistance to the entire population. Frequently middle and rich peasants, least susceptible to appeals of the Front on class issues, suffered the greatest losses in the strategic hamlet program and became NLF partisans.[27]

[25] Chong-sik Lee, *Counterinsurgency in Manchuria: The Japanese Experience, 1931–1940*. RAND Corporation Memorandum RM-5012-ARPA, 1967. Sir Robert Thompson, the architect of British counterinsurgency strategy in Malaya, and the primary inspiration of American counterinsurgency theoreticians, headed an advisory mission to Vietnam. Thompson, today Nixon's top counterinsurgency adviser, attributed the dismal results of Diem's program to administrative "adventurism" and the squandering of resources. The Diem plan called for constructing sixteen times the number of hamlets in a fraction of the time required by the British in building strategic hamlets in Malaya. Robert Thompson, *Defeating Communist Insurgency* (London, Chatto & Windus, 1966), pp. 121–40.

[26] "The Peasants' Struggle," pp. 74–75.

[27] An effective critique of the theory and practice of American counterinsurgency including an analysis of its striking analogy with Japanese counterinsurgency in China, is found in Noam Chomsky, "Objectivity and Liberal Scholarship," pp. 23–158 in *American Power and the New Mandarins,* particularly pp. 37–60. Cf. the August 1967, issue of *Asian*

Where a resistance movement successfully links the war effort to an attack on the problems of the disintegration and oppression of village life, the combination is a potent one. The slogan, "plow in one hand, rifle in the other," implies something beyond a contemporary Asian version of the American Revolution's minute man.[28] It symbolizes the commitment to a vision of national liberation which goes beyond repelling foreign invasion to elimination of economic stagnation and social repression. The implications of the combat villages, the NLF's response to Diem's strategic hamlets, transcended military concerns:

> To set up a strong struggling village is to defend the people's life and livelihood, to preserve the human, material and financial strength for the Revolution and realistically push forward the armed struggle.[29]

Survey for a multifaceted discussion of counterinsurgency in Vietnam by the social scientists and officials who design it. The single American strategic development beyond Japanese practice in China (exclusive of the application of sophisticated technology to terrorize and annihilate larger segments of the population) is the unsuccessful effort to outbid the insurgents by offering land to the tiller.

[28] "In the Liberated Zones of South Vietnam," p. 162.

[29] *VCD, #45.* In focusing on the relationship between people's war and social transformation I do not intend to imply that the egalitarian and participatory style characteristic of these movements can *only* emerge out of people's war, but that the revolutionary situation implicit in such struggle is highly conducive to this approach. The case of Cuba suggests that similar approaches may develop in the absence of a foreign invader and a people's war, though here, too, its spirit harks back to the heroic guerrilla tradition of the Sierra Maestra. Joseph Kahl, following a recent visit to Cuba, has sensitively captured the underlying spirit of the revolution:

One of the key slogans on the big billboards surrounding the Plaza of the revolution José Martí . . . (literally means) "The Road of Communism is to Create Wealth through *Conciencia.*" That last and key word conveys an amalgam of consciousness, conscience, conscientiousness, and commitment, and is perhaps the most repeated word in the Cuban language of revolution. The implication is that in the old society the mentality of money, and the motivation for work was the fear of poverty, but in the new

To be successful, the institutions of the resistance had also to fulfill the economic and political needs of the community.

Land reform marked the initial and key phase in the effort to redefine the economic life of the village. However, closely integrated with it were other approaches suggestive of the dimensions of a new society emerging in NLF areas. The major principles of cooperative farming—self-sufficiency, self-determination and community organization—were applied not only to production but to guerrilla activity and local politics, indeed to all facets of the rural program. An NLF document of late 1968 describing activities in Binh Dinh province, for instance, states that

> The acceleration of production work should go hand in hand with the development of labor mutual assistance cells in order to ensure a rational utilization of manpower to serve both production work and the front line. . . .
>
> In the lowland, work exchange cells and production cells should be organized by the Farmers' Association. In the moun-

---

society people will comprehend the need to work for the common good, and abundance will flow as a result of that understanding. Along with it will come a style of life that is cooperative and humane, and without "alienation," since work will be part of a voluntary social experience. . . .

Society is to be reshaped in the pattern of comradeship of the guerrilla fighters of the Sierra Maestra. Some of the abstractions stem from Marx, but the Cuban color comes from the mountains.

"The Moral Economy of a Revolutionary Society," pp. 30–37, *Trans-Action* (July 1969), pp. 31–32. As the writings of Debray and Guevara make plain, the guerrilla struggle against Batista followed substantially different lines from people's war in China and Vietnam. The Cuban campaign involved a much less intimate relationship between the guerrilla and the peasant population (peasant support was sought but no significant rural revolution was initiated prior to Batista's collapse). It followed a pattern more closely akin to that of roving armies than the creation of functioning administrative areas, and of course lacked the presence of a foreign invader. Cf. Noam Chomsky's superb account of the social vision and practice of the Spanish anarchist movement in the Spanish Civil War in "Objectivity and Liberal Scholarship," pp. 76–126, and Eric Wolf, *Peasant Wars, passim.*

tainous areas, cells should be established to provide labor mutual support and to guide and help one another in production work.[30]

Building on a spirit of cooperation and on expanded consciousness growing out of the resistance and anti-landlord struggles, agricultural cooperation carried these principles to the economic heart of village life.

Simultaneously self-sufficiency and self-determination were emphasized as root principles of the political and economic life of the village in the face of mounting problems posed by American destruction of crops:

> . . . the present production mission is to motivate the entire party, army and people to develop a self-sufficient spirit and to strictly implement the two-step, three-prong tactics, increase and protect production, and practice economy to quickly augment the food stock.[31]

This meant not only development of new organizational forms such as cooperatives, but involvement of the entire population, including soldiers, administrative officials and students, in production. The immediate goal was the achievement of self-sufficiency for their units or organizations and reducing the tax burden on the rural population. But here again, broader aims were involved: the breakdown of distinctions between mental and manual labor, between leadership and the mass; the awareness that within resistance communities the resolution of pressing rural problems through cooperative efforts was not only possible but a daily occurrence.

[30] "On Economic and Financial Missions from the Present Time to Early 1969," *Vietnam Documents and Research Notes,* Document No. 49 (January 1969), pp. 6, 9. For additional discussion of NLF development of cooperative agriculture see "In the Liberated Zones of South Vietnam," pp. 165–67 and "Missions, Policy and Methods to Increase the Agricultural Output in 1967–1968," translated in *Viet Cong Loss of Population Control* (United States Mission in Vietnam, Crimp Collection, December 16, 1968). Cf. Pike, *Vietcong,* pp. 293–94 (Pike describes these efforts as " 'red-ant' collectivation.")

[31] "On Economic and Financial Missions from the Present Time to Early 1969," p. 5.

Despite desperately limited resources, hand in hand with these approaches to rural economic development, has occurred impressive expansion of education and social services. One example suggests the characteristic style of educational development and its importance in the context of the larger struggle. An NLF document relates how villagers in an area abandoned by administrators of the Saigon government petitioned their district office for a school. When their request was ignored, a movement was initiated locally to build and manage the school. The result was that

> The GVN failure then appeared to the villagers as a striking contrast to their own ability to meet the need, inspiring confidence in their own capabilities. Furthermore, activities of managing the school, such as hiring teachers, deciding on curricula, and observing and evaluating its progress were an ongoing community concern. By carrying the political struggle efforts against GVN to their logical conclusion, villagers find encouraging examples of the strengths and potential of human effort in the liberation movement and simultaneously provide services to the community, which increase the involvement of the community members in new, self-sustaining integrative interactions.[32]

It is not presently possible to document the extent to which this social vision has already been institutionalized and peasant consciousness transformed in the liberated areas of South Vietnam. What is clear is that peasant consciousness and the institutional order of rural Vietnam are being reshaped in the process of waging a people's war.[33] Even so hostile an observer as

[32] Ellen Zweig, "The Role of Struggle in the People's War of Liberation South Vietnam," unpublished paper. *VCD, #*2. Cf. *VCD, #*321.

[33] In contrast to the abundant evidence available in the case of China, it is not presently possible to document satisfactorily the extent of NLF follow-up to its successful land policies along the institutional lines indicated above. In part this undoubtedly reflects the intensity of the American attack which prevents the consolidation of secure base areas on a scale comparable to those developed during the Chinese resistance. Since I am unable to read Vietnamese, it is a product also of the present neces-

Douglas Pike suggests the egalitarian possibilities of community emerging in NLF areas:

> The liberated area may be regarded as a rudimentary society, for it was an organized collection of persons working together and communicating with one another within the framework of a common culture. . . . Probably it is safe to conclude that the group norm in the liberated area was characterized by a greater sense of equalitarianism, greater social mobility with individual merit counting for more and family for less, and a greater awareness of strata, class consciousness or social solidarity.[34]

In its reliance on popular participation and initiative, in the emphasis on the contributions of man in a context of face-to-face human struggle, in the high value placed on performance of multiple roles as soldiers, farmers, cadres and teachers, in its egalitarian and selfless spirit embodied in every facet of the movement—in all these ways we find the Yenan spirit resurrected and developed in Vietnam today.

In the Chinese and Vietnamese resistance, emphasis on popular participation, the fundamental postulate of people's war, meant that strength and legitimacy rested primarily on active peasant support. This support in turn was contingent on the movement's ability to respond effectively to war-time political, economic, and security needs. As Franz Schurmann recently observed after a visit to bomb-shattered North Vietnam, the mobilization process cannot be grasped exclusively or even primarily in organizational terms. Rather

> the spirit of individuals and classes is the energy that makes organization work. Without that spirit, organization can function only through nonhuman technology, which means turning men into machines as well as making use of machines.[35]

---

sity to rely heavily on documents translated and selected by American government sources to support official interpretations of the enemy.

[34] Pike, *Vietcong*, pp. 272–73.

[35] "Our People Are a Wonder," *Liberation* (April 1968), p. 18.

Consciousness of this problem, of the danger of turning men into machines, was central to the distinctive shape of popular mobilization in China's war-time base areas as it is in the China of the cultural revolution and in Vietnam today. Under continuous crisis conditions, rigid and dogmatic tendencies toward elite domination and tight central control of war and administration were effectively challenged by populist and pragmatic impulses and the conviction that ultimate support and commitment required popular participation and initiative. This was the significance of the "mass line" style of resistance leadership with its premium on decentralization, its antagonism to bureaucratic elitism and rigidity, and its heavy reliance on popular creativity. In this spirit of involvement and participation in areas which typically had been the exclusive preserve of a remote and burdensome officialdom or a narrow local elite, in seizing the initiative to grapple with the entire range of village problems, commitment to a nationalist struggle took on an immediacy and a structure in the context of redressing fundamental grievances of peasant life. As the peasantry en masse broke the bonds of passivity and subservience, new forms of local community began to replace those eroded steadily during a century of rural disintegration, colonial and semi-colonial bondage, and war.

The resistance movements in China and Vietnam suggest significant parallels with other egalitarian rebel movements, particularly those in societies undergoing rapid change in the face of war and industrialization. The Sicilian and Andalusian peasant movements eloquently described by E. J. Hobsbawm, China's Taiping rebels, the millenarian movement in the Brazilian backlands and Zapata's Mexican peasant rebels are among the best documented of these cases.[36]

[36] E. J. Hobsbawn, *Primitive Rebels, Studies in Archaic Forms of Social Movement in the Nineteenth and Twentieth Centuries* (New York, Norton, 1959); Euclides da Cunha, *Rebellion in the Backlands* (Chicago, Univ. of Chicago Press, 1944); John Womack, Jr., *Zapata and the Mexican Revolution* (New York, Knopf, 1969). An arresting American movement with strong parallels to the above is that of the struggle of Spanish-Americans under the leadership of Reies Lopes Tijerina to secure land rights in the southwest. Cf. Stan Steiner, *La Raza: The Mexican-Americans* (New York, Harper & Row, 1970).

Reading of Zapata's "liberated area," for instance, one discovers a spirit strikingly akin to what we have found in the resistance:

> Community, together with personal freedom: . . . this belief that people can rule themselves without sacrificing either social welfare or personal freedom—this dream became reality in the small, enclosed *campesino* community of Morelos in 1914–15.
>
> Zapata and his chiefs, of course, were themselves villagers, field hands and sharecroppers; their authority sprang from local councils and rested on fidelity to the texts they were about to make forcefully real. On this basis a politics of confidence arose. . . .
>
> For the first time in Mexico, it was not a remote bureaucracy nor an all-too-present military authority that made decisions in the name of the people. The people themselves, through the cooperation of village leaders, fashioned the new levers of power and the new means of livelihood from the bottom up, unhindered by rigid programs, fusing the traditional agencies of local society and the momentum of the Revolution.[37]

Zapata's movement, and those cited above, stopped short of permanently transforming their societies. They were eventually destroyed by opponents of social revolution better able to master the military, organizational, and technological forces of the contemporary world.

In contrast to Zapata, there is a quality of modernity in the dedication of Chinese and Vietnamese revolutionaries to a vision of social transformation and development carried beyond local resistance communities and embodied on a national scale.

[37] Carlos Fuentes, "Viva Zapata," pp. 5–11, in *The New York Review of Books* (March 13, 1969), p. 8. I do not share Fuentes' optimistic view of the possibility for creation of a viable resistance community which preserves "personal freedom." Not at least in the sense of *individual* autonomy which is so valued in liberal democracies, and not in the prerogatives traditionally enjoyed by monied and powerful elites. The exhilarating sense of freedom and power experienced by peasant revolutionaries is rooted in the collectivity of participation in guerrilla units, in mutual-aid teams, in peasant associations, etc.

That conception reaffirms the creative contributions of men, above all of peasants, working in their own villages rather than the efforts of a remote technological elite or the bureaucratic organs of the state. It is linked with a pragmatic and practical effort implemented even while the fighting rages to advance concretely toward a day when the nation as a whole can reap the benefits of independence and development. Problems of peasant particularism, economic stagnation, and elitism cannot of course be eliminated in a single sweep. What is impressive is that the base areas of the resistance contain in embryo the possibilities for new forms of community life and growth consonant with these movement ideals. Theirs is not an anarchism reveling ultimately in the struggle of atomized individuals for private ends. Rather it is the freedom of all continually redefined by an accepted and cherished community. The cooperative effort to resist a ruthless oppressor is simultaneously directed toward overcoming natural and man-made barriers to change. The spirit of the resistance thus suggests new possibilities of human fulfillment while grappling with the formidable problems of poverty and economic stagnation which stalk the Third World.

VI.

TWENTIETH-CENTURY REVOLUTIONS: MEXICAN, CUBAN, ALGERIAN AND THE FRENCH STUDENT REBELLION

19

Daniel Cosío Villegas: The Mexican Revolution*

I sincerely believe that the Mexican people have long known that the Mexican Revolution is dead, although they do not know, or only half understand, why this fact is concealed instead of being proclaimed. Therefore, the question arose some time ago: If it is dead, why have the death notices not been circulated. Why, more exactly, has the Mexican Revolution not been buried in the Rotunda of the Great, or perhaps in the Monument to the Mexican Revolution, where two of its heros, Francisco Madero[1] and Venustiano Carranza,[2] already lie?

This lack of good manners in a people who boast of being paragons of courtesy—"as polite as a Mexican Indian," said Vicente Espinel in 1618—may be easily explained and even justified. Making public the death of someone arouses everyone's curiosity as to the inheritance left by the dead person, and

---

* Daniel Cosío Villegas, "The Mexican Revolution, Then and Now," in *Change in Latin America: The Mexican and Cuban Revolutions* (Lincoln: University of Nebraska Press, 1961), pp. 23–37. By permission.

Daniel Cosío Villegas is the president of El Colegio de Mexico and the author of many works in history and economics.

[1] One of the earliest leaders of the revolution, he became president in 1911 and was overthrown and assassinated in 1913—ed.

[2] One of the most important revolutionary leaders, and later president of Mexico (1914–1920)—ed.

405

excites his relatives—legitimate or spurious—to mistrust and resentment, if not to a battle to the death, a manner of speaking appropriate to a discussion of a dead person and of a death. The Mexican Revolution actually gave to the country, and especially to its leaders, an ideology and a language, and, so long as no new ideas and expressions appear, it is easier—and perhaps it has been indispensable—to continue governing with the old ideology and language. A popular saying is that it is better to endure a known evil than to risk an unknown good; so here it may perhaps be said that it is better to endure a known dead person than to risk an unknown live one.

Two attitudes very common among today's old-time Mexicans could have led to the suspicion that there was some truth in the rumors that the Revolution was dead. One of these is a tendency to proclaim to high heaven the virtues of the Mexican Revolution and to bury as deep as possible its faults. The other is to assert that it burst out of nothing, thus magnifying the breadth of its accomplishments and the brilliance of its eminence. Apart from the fact that it is very normal, very healthy and very human to find consolation in recalling lost felicity, it may be truly maintained that the Mexican Revolution was a social, economic and political movement of extraordinary magnitude and depth, in addition to having a good deal more originality than the Mexicans themselves grant it. And it is also largely true that its origins were very modest, so much so that hardly any ideologists were responsible for its conception.

In order to estimate the magnitude and originality of the Mexican Revolution it will suffice to recall, on the one hand, the scope of its destructive force, and, on the other hand, comparable movements in other places.

In effect, it totally swept away not only the political regime of Porfirio Díaz[3] but all of Porfirian society, that is, the social classes or groups together with their ideas, tastes and manners. Not only the commanders-in-chief of the army but their officers and all the soldiers disappeared without exception. Landholders, urban and especially agricultural, were almost entirely re-

[3] President of Mexico, 1876–1880 and 1884–1911, he ruled despotically and without challenge for almost the entire period—ed.

placed by new ones. Not one of the great newspapers survived. Only two out of about fifty banks continued into the new regime. Official bureaucracy—federal, state and municipal— was wholly reformed. Moreover, let us remember that in no other Latin American country has an event of such magnitude occurred in the last hundred years, except now in Cuba. Strictly speaking, I believe that the only three changes to surpass it in extent and depth are the communist revolutions of Russia and China, and perhaps in Cuba. But even as regards these three, it may be stated that the Mexican Revolution was the first political regime to achieve power and deny the validity of liberal political philosophy in order to give to the State the role of principal promoter of the nation's material and moral well-being. Speaking broadly and somewhat ironically, liberalism supposes that if you allow rich people to become richer, and richer people the richest, the poorest people may in time become simply poor— just as when it rains heavily at the top of a mountain, the valley far below will eventually receive some additional humidity. The Mexican Revolutionists believed in the early stages that rich people should not be allowed to become richer, and that all the power and resources of the State should be applied to the benefit of the poor.

Its humble origins may be expressed in a word. The Mexican Revolution, in reality, lacked great ideologists to shape it intellectually. The contribution of the so-called forerunners—especially, Flores Magón and his associates—and even of later figures such as Luis Cabrera, was of far greater moral than ideological value. It was not so much their ideas which were noteworthy as the time at which they were expressed, when almost no one protested against or disagreed with the regime then in power. There were few ideas, and most of them were critical of the failures of the Díaz regime rather than marking out the new course that the country should follow in order to improve its lot permanently. In addition, there was the unfortunate circumstance that the Flores Magón group, which had entered the revolutionary struggle earlier, could not get along with Francisco I. Madero's group, which really initiated the revolution and was to carry it to victory. And so the former had little or no influence in the military campaign and still less in the course afterwards followed by the Revolution. Although it was not always clearly stated, it seems to me that the ideological contribution of Madero was a great deal more important than is generally recognized. But even so, it was limited from the moment it was conceived, and in reality it was almost completely lost. Madero, in any case, upheld an important idea: No reform of any kind was feasible without a prior political change. He expressed this idea with the slogan of "effective suffrage and no re-election," which now seems narrow and even childish. It may be truly considered as a reaffirmation of the political principles on which all democracy is based: popular election and a time limit to the power of the elected governor.

As a matter of fact, the Mexican Revolutionists first tried to define their goals formally when the 1917 Constitution was drawn up. The history of this episode is all the more interesting in that the Carranza government offered the Constitutional Congress of Querétaro, as an aid in preparing its work, Francisco Zarco's *History of the Constitutional Congress of 1857* in a new edition which omitted Ponciano Arriaga's views on the bad distribution and worse use of land in Mexico. These two facts suggest that at least the Carranza group, then the most powerful, hoped that the new Constitution would simply be a revision of the old one, a revision that would be justified by the experience of the country during the sixty years the 1857 Constitution had been in force.

Nonetheless, two events took place in the Querétaro Congress which Carranza and his group apparently did not foresee. The Revolution's lack of ideologists is confirmed by the fact that the greatest technical-juridical influence on the writing of the new constitutional text turned out to be the book *The Constitution and the Dictatorship.* Its author, Emilio Rabasa, was beyond doubt a great jurist, a good writer and a persuasive and intelligent person. But he was also a bitter critic of the 1857 Constitution, a liberal who was committed to the reactionary regime of Porfirio Díaz, and he certainly lacked any revolutionary ideas or inclinations.

The predominant influence of Rabasa resulted in the enlarging of the powers of the executive branch at the expense of the many powers which the previous Constitution had given to the legislative branch. In this way, Mexico passed into a presidentialist regime, but not precisely because the revolutionaries believed that their idea of the State as principal promoter of public well-being required a strong and alert executive endowed with the legal authority to take prompt and direct action. The form of the new regime was actually suggested by a reactionary who wished to give posthumous justification to the dictatorial government of Porfirio Díaz. The other result of Rabasa's influence was perhaps beneficial. The critical tone of his book made the 1917 constituents see less merit in the work of their colleagues of 1857, so they felt fewer scruples at drawing away from it.

The other important event of the Querétaro Constitutional Congress could be foreseen by Carranza. It was literally impossible that a revolutionary movement which had succeeded in overthrowing the Porfirian dictatorship—decrepit, it is true, but upheld by enormous and deep-rooted interests, within and outside the country—and which had emerged stronger and more combative from the Huerta[4] counterrevolution, would be content with revising here and there a law which, whatever may have been its initial merits, had been incapable of preventing or even restraining the longest and most thorough dictatorship that the country had ever suffered. On the other hand, the constitutional text drawn up by those men of Querétaro was to serve as a pattern for the immediate future life of the country, and the pattern could channel, but also limit or shackle, any new, revitalizing—in short, revolutionary—force. A small group of constituents was determined to insert something new into the Constitution. Against an apparently general wave of feeling, it finally achieved the approval of Articles 3, 27, 123 and 130.

The essential meaning of Article 27 is that the economic interests of the State or of the Nation are above the interests of individuals or of groups, and therefore must prevail in case of

[4] President of Mexico, 1913–1914, who seized power from Madero and was pressured into resigning by the American occupation of Vera Cruz—ed.

opposition or conflict. This principle is obviously antiliberal, very modern and nevertheless also very old. It was, after all, the order in New Spain during its three hundred years as a colony. But this article gave a formal legal base to agrarian reform and, in general, to the relations of the State with the exploiters of the Nation's natural resources, particularly minerals and oil. The fact that the majority of these exploiters were foreign reveals the nationalistic and antiforeign tone of the Mexican Revolution. But this is confirmed and broadened by other provisions of the same article such as that which states that only Mexicans and Mexican corporations may acquire possession of lands, water or mining and oil resources, and that if foreigners want to obtain them, they must agree to consider themselves as Mexicans and not invoke the protection of their governments under penalty of losing their acquired wealth to the Nation. This same Article 27—but also Article 3 and even more Article 130—is anticlerical and very much in keeping with an old Mexican tradition; and it is so to a degree of insistence and detail which is truly surprising.

Article 123, is, in reality, a complete law. Rather than being new in itself, it raised labor legislation to the rank of a constitutional law, while even today it is an ordinary law in most countries. By 1917, of course, several countries of Western Europe already had provisions or special laws on labor; but the great principles that inspired them did not appear in their constitutions. Actually, as has already been said, Article 123 is a complete regulating law, since it contains such minute provisions as those specifying the number and length of special rest periods that the female worker is entitled to when she is nursing her children. The constitutional character of this Mexican labor legislation unquestionably makes Article 123 an innovation; but at the same time it raises doubts as to whether the Mexican constituents so distrusted the protection which an ordinary law might afford their revolutionary convictions that they preferred to shield them with the constitution, which is more difficult to amend and politically impossible to abolish.

It does not seem to me that the Mexican Revolution found its best expression in the spoken or written word, but in the psychology and morale of the whole country. By 1920 the Mexican Revolution had no longer a single enemy within the country, and although the United States did not recognize the government of Obregón,[5] the government and the country at large were self-confident. For the first time in ten long years it was felt that there was order and the presence of an accepted authority. The world was going through a period of prosperity which reached Mexico. But above all else, naturally, there was enormous expectation of the great reconstruction work to be initiated by the Revolution. Not "everybody" but certainly large numbers everywhere felt that exalted sensation of man turned into a god, of man with creative genius and will, with the faith that from his hands may come a new, great, brilliant, harmonious and kind world; faith, also, that nothing is impossible and that anything may be achieved by simply willing it.

The explanation of how the Mexican Revolution passed from that initial stage—exalted, secure, generous—to the one in which we now find ourselves is complicated and difficult. Although I believe that this explanation is necessary in order to know where the Revolution stands now and even in order to imagine where it may go, I shall barely attempt to sketch it.

It is a generally accepted observation that a revolution always produces a corresponding reaction; but in our case there is a particular circumstance to be considered. The drive and the energy of the Revolution were consumed much more in destroying the past than in constructing the future. As a result, the past certainly disappeared, but the new present came into being and began to develop haphazardly, so that, for lack of another image to imitate, it finally ended by becoming equal to the destroyed past. From this standpoint the reaction won a complete victory over the Revolution, since it has succeeded in taking the country back to the exact point where it was when the Revolution broke out. I mean "the exact point" where Mexico was before the Revolution in the sense of the general mental outlook prevailing now in the country, but not in the sense that the country itself is like the Mexico of 1910, and

[5] A revolutionary leader and president, 1920–1924—ed.

much less in the sense of what Mexico will be like in ten or twenty years.

Why has this happened, or why has it happened to this extent? Many factors would have to be taken into account in order to give a complete picture, but one seems to be outstanding: the lack of ideologists to formulate the Mexican Revolution, to indicate its course and, once it was under way, the unavoidable but deplorable fact that the people who were youngest, most prepared, intelligent and honest joined the government in only minor posts. Therefore, they neither truly inspired the policy or the plans of the Revolution, nor served it by criticizing them, as they would have done had they been outside the government, in congress or the press, for example. The press, for its part, from the beginning took a stand opposed to the government until the government ceased to be revolutionary and became conservative. Since then, they live as harmoniously as partners in a business enterprise.

The fact is that, in one way or another, the present situation has been reached. What is this situation?

The economy is sound, judged from a classical liberal point of view, so much so that it is often commented that Mexico has made phenomenal progress in recent years. More strictly examined, it is possible to find rather weak points in this economy, such as the fact that some official and semiofficial enterprises depend ultimately on the fiscal resources of the federal government. Mexico likewise faces the serious problem of an unpromising future for its visible exports. A declining market for its metals and principal agricultural exports, together with ever-increasing imports, places it in a difficult situation. However, it may be stated that the present economic conditions of Mexico do not create insoluble problems and that they are no more serious than those of, for example, the Latin American countries and, in general, any country in the world with similar resources and history.

Nor is the apparent social situation bad. The constant improvement of communications since 1925 has given the Mexican population a mobility which it formerly lacked, making it easier to move to places where there are prospects of better work and salaries. The general level of public health has risen, as is shown by the fall in the general mortality rate and the increase in life expectancy. A worthy effort has been made in the field of education, although not proportionate to the headlong increase in our population and the greater needs of today's children and young people. The social security services although not as broad and general as would be desired, have been extended to a notable and promising extent.

Strictly speaking, the only problem of great magnitude is the rate at which the population and the national product grow. Since demographic trends change only very slowly, it seems better to look at it from that angle, and not, as it is quite possible to do, from the point of view of readjustment of investments and production. The rate of population growth is all the more serious because, alongside a high and sustained birth rate, the infant mortality rate tends to decline slowly but surely. It is possible that this population increase may very well strain the country's physical, human and economic resources, and that if energetic measures are not taken, it may present a very serious problem. Until now, the rate of economic growth has surpassed, generally speaking, that of population. But there is more than one reason to suspect that this situation cannot be indefinitely maintained, and that even the more or less normal ups and downs of the economic development of any country may produce disproportionate disequilibria, precisely because of the lack of a margin which permits time to act during years of pause or recession.

The political situation is decidedly less satisfactory than the economic and social. The only tangible progress is the periodic and regular renewal of the Mexican rulers: the president of the Republic, the governors of the States and the municipal authorities and federal and local legislative bodies. But their election is far from popular, being decided by personalist forces that rarely or never represent the genuine interests of large human groups. The economic and political power of the president of the Republic is almost all-embracing and is exercised in the designation of public servants of almost all categories and areas of the country. And since it is impossible for one man to know the special needs of each city or town, and which person or persons are most suitable to resolve them, most of the choices of the great elector are deplorably inadequate, and in any event they do not please anyone, because they are not the result of the free play of the political interests and aspirations of the groups concerned.

Even so, it may perhaps be said that Mexico's situation today, judged in its entirety, is not inferior to the best to be found in any Latin American country. Chile, Uruguay and Costa Rica, for example, have a political life which corresponds much more closely to a real and stable democracy. But the limitations of the physical and human resources of Chile and Uruguay and the small territory of Costa Rica make their political future, in reality, less bright than might appear at first glance. Argentina will take many years to recover from the physical and moral damage inflicted on it by the Perón dictatorship. And Brazil, with physical and human elements that are far superior to Mexico's, has not progressed, for one reason or another, as was expected of her.

On Mexico's horizon, nonetheless, there is a black cloud that few Mexicans and foreigners have noticed until now. Mexico's present situation—generally good, as has been said—is the product of the Mexican Revolution, and this year, while we celebrate the fiftieth anniversary of its initiation, we have heard a great deal about it. So what, essentially, did the Mexican Revolution offer, what has it accomplished, what is there left for it to accomplish, and can it do so?

It seems to me that the essential characteristics of the Mexican Revolution were these: to entrust to the State, and not to the individual nor to private enterprise, the promotion of the general welfare of the country; to make this general welfare the principal or only goal of the action of the State so that its economic and technical resources as well as its moral influence would be used to better the lot of the farmers and laborers, the teachers and the bureaucracy, and so forth. The Mexican Revolution had, moreover, a strong popular flavor, not only in the sense already described, in attempting to satisfy first the needs of the poor, but in believing that the people, the Indians, themselves, have virtues which must be recognized, respected and enhanced. The dominant idea during the good years of the Revolution, let us say 1920–1925, was that the Mexican Indian had so many natural qualities that the problem of education lay in teaching him modern work techniques, but without contaminating him or modifying his general way of life: his traditional courtesy and reserve, his artistic sensitivity and capacity, etc. And it was also a revolution that exalted the national at the expense, naturally, of the foreign.

What is left of all this? In truth, little or nothing.

In the first place, let us look at the situation of the government in Mexican society. Its political power is almost unlimited: that of the president in all the Republic; that of the governors in their respective States as regards local matters; and that of the municipal authorities in their respective jurisdictions as regards the minor matters that they manage. What is the basis of this situation? In part, the laws themselves, since the federal Constitution gives the Executive very broad powers, and the local constitutions also give very broad powers to the governors of the States; and, in part, the fact that when legal power does not suffice, it is quite easy to find an impeccable juridical solution, even though its purpose may be clearly wrong; and when this turns out to be too complicated, the law is simply ignored. In a real democracy, there are two effective correctives to these two kinds of abuse: the administration of justice is precisely charged with enforcing the law where it should apply; and public opinion denounces the abuse and compels the authority to correct it. In Mexico these two checks function sporadically and ineffectively.

On the other hand, in the sphere of economic action, the authority and force of the State have become less and less vigorous and decisive, to the extent that it is now possible to say that the State is the prisoner of private enterprise. If it wanted to fight, the government would win, even using only legal means, such as, for example, fiscal measures. But the government does not want to fight nor even to disagree with private enterprise. It is already remarkable—and this in itself describes the situation—that a considerable increase in the number and size of public needs—which would have to be reflected in an increase in budget expenditure—has not been matched by a change in tax rates or by the creation of new taxes.

The situation has developed broadly in this way. The State rightly considered at a certain moment that Mexico could not progress very much if it relied on agriculture and mining, its two traditional occupations; therefore, the country should industrialize, at least until it would be one-third agricultural, one-third mining and one-third industrial. To achieve this goal, the State took the initiative in the establishment or expansion of certain industries. But in most cases, it waited for private enterprise to carry out the undertakings. For this purpose, and in accordance with classical liberal reasoning, the State proposed to create "a favorable climate" for private enterprise, and this was to be done, naturally, by the classical means: political and social stability; inflexible wage rates; low taxes; easy credit and other secondary aids.

The State was not mistaken either in its initial reasoning or in the methods it used to achieve industrialization, for it is estimated that in effect 60% of industrial investment to date comes from private sources. But the State made several important errors which have finally led to the situation in which we now find ourselves. One was that it never drew up a general framework of the industrial activities which were most suitable for the country, so that private enterprise would only undertake those that fitted into that general framework. In the second place, the State has been unsuccessful in restricting inflation so that the real wages of the labor force have clearly diminished, and it is the workers who ultimately are paying for the industrial progress of Mexico. In the third place, as an inevitable consequence, economic influence has begun to be converted into political influence, so that the State today would have difficulty in taking a fundamental economic policy measure without consulting the country's great banking and industrial firms or, in fact, without counting on their approval beforehand. For these reasons and some others quite as important, the final outcome is that while 16% of the Mexican families get 50% of the national income,

46% of those families got only one-seventh of such income.

I must add one word, not about the political or economic strength of the government, but about its moral authority. It has been at a low point for several years, and for many reasons. One of them is the most important, however. All men participating in the country's public life, all politicians, as they are commonly named, talk as if we were living in 1920, 1928 or 1938 at the latest. They talk as if the Mexican Revolution were very much alive, as if its original goals were still prevailing, as if large and small government policies were inspired and adopted to reach those goals in the shortest possible time and to the fullest possible measure. It seems, however, that moral authority usually rests on the man whose deeds match his word and whose words do not go beyond his deeds.

This situation explains why there has been a considerable weakening of the popular meaning and nationalist note found in the Mexican Revolution during its best period.

It is difficult to give an opinion, even a very tentative one, on whether Mexico can go back to a course more in keeping with the original objective of the Revolution, and what means it should employ to achieve this, short of a new revolution. This is perhaps the principal concern of Mexico's leading men, although I do not know whether there is an agreement, at least as to the principal points towards which the country should direct itself. It may be that the real dilemma for Mexico—as for so many countries in the world—lies in whether to grow faster at the top only, or at a slower pace, but benefiting the lower levels of the social pyramid. Whatever may be the proper way, I am quite confident that Mexico will find it soon, for my country has a real genius for getting out of a mess . . . and for getting into a mess.

20

Maurice Zeitlin: The Cuban Revolution*

The world-historical significance of the Cuban revolution is that for the first time in the western hemisphere a revolution has been put through in the name of socialism. It is the first socialist revolution led by independent radicals throughout its most decisive phases. Even when they were to identify with the international Communist movement, and to fuse with the old Communists, they retained the clear initiative within the revolutionary leadership, and gained for Cuba a singular place among Communist states. The Cuban revolution has gone further, and has more profoundly and rapidly transformed the prerevolutionary social structure than has any other "socialist" revolution anywhere. Most of the fundamental transformation of the political economy—of property relations and of the class structure—occurred within a couple of years of the revolutionaries' consolidation of power; and with the recent (March 1968) nationalization of some 55,000 small businesses, primarily in food retailing and services, virtually the entire economy is now in the public sector: In agriculture, 70 percent of the arable land is in the public sector, leaving only farms of less than 67 hectares (160 acres) to be worked by their owners.

* Maurice Zeitlin, "Cuba—Revolution Without a Blueprint," *Trans-Action,* April 1969, pp. 38–42, 61. By permission.

Associate professor of sociology at the University of Wisconsin, Maurice Zeitlin is the author of *Revolutionary Politics and the Cuban Working Class.*

What explains the rapidity and thoroughness of the Cuban revolution, compared not only to other national and social revolutions in our time, but to other "socialist" revolutions as well?—and, perhaps inseparable from this, why did it become a "socialist revolution," unlike, for instance, the social revolutions in Mexico and Bolivia?

The Cuban, Mexican, and Bolivian revolutions have certain similarities which are neither superficial nor unimportant. In each, there was a fundamental agrarian transformation that abolished the existing land tenure system and destroyed the economic base of the ruling strata in the countryside. In each, the old military apparatus was smashed and replaced with armed detachments (or militias) of peasants and workers. In each, strategic sectors of the national economy which were foreign-owned were nationalized. In Bolivia, the tin mines were occupied and run by the armed miners themselves. In Mexico, though late in the revolutionary process, the Cárdenas regime nationalized the oil industry.

These three revolutions, therefore, are unquestionably set apart from other so-called revolutions in Latin America. Nevertheless, the similarity between the Cuban revolution and the revolutions in Mexico and Bolivia is far less important than the major difference: Scarcely an aspect of the prerevolutionary social structure in Cuba has remained intact, primarily because of the expropriation of the former owning classes, the virtual elimination of private property in the system of production and distribution, and the establishment of a centrally-planned, publicly-owned economy.

What were the features of the prerevolutionary social structure in Cuba that determined the type of social structure created by the revolution? Somewhat differently: What were the constraints and the options that were given to the leaders of the Cuban revolution by the prerevolutionary social structure? What did they have to put up with, what was the social material they had to work with in order to make this revolution—in contrast, for instance, to those who led the revolutions and came to power in Russia, China, and Yugoslavia, or in Bolivia or Mexico? In the book which I wrote with Robert Scheer several years ago[1] we took the prerevolutionary social structure as given and focused on the interaction between the United States and Cuba and in what way the interchange between them radicalized the revolution. Of course, the two are really inseparable, and it is likely that the interchange was itself determined by the prerevolutionary social structure. I want now to take that interchange as given, in order to search out the relevance of the prerevolutionary social structure itself.

My leading hypothesis is: Cuba's is the first socialist revolution to take place in a capitalist country—a country in which the owning class was capitalist and the direct producers were wage-workers. The argument may be stated in the following schematic working hypotheses:

Cuba's dominant economic class was capitalist—a peculiar type of capitalist class but a capitalist class nonetheless. There were no significant feudal or seignorial elements remaining in the upper economic strata. The major elements of the dominant strata were in exporting (mainly of sugar and other primary products) and its financing, importing (mainly luxury goods), and tourism, small-scale manufacture of consumer goods for the home market; and were agents, and representatives, investors in United States-owned manufacturing firms using equipment and materials imported from the United States. These elements tended to overlap and intertwine, and to be integrated by concrete economic interests and social and familial bonds. In short they formed the capitalist class. The agrarian component of this class was export-market oriented and employed wage-labor on a large scale in the sugar mills and cane fields. As a result, the revolution did not have to be antifeudal.

Of the classes, the working class was the largest, the most cohesive, and the most politically conscious. It was an organized national class that spread throughout the country, and that had a durable revolutionary and socialist political culture set in motion by the anarcho-syndicalists and continued under the Communist leadership of the workers. This cannot be said

[1] Maurice Zeitlin and Robert Scheer, *Cuba: Tragedy in Our Hemisphere* (New York: Grove Press), 1963.

of any other country in which revolutions in our time—whether anticolonial, nationalist, or Communist—have been put through. It cannot be said of prerevolutionary Russia certainly, where the Petrograd workers were an insignificant minority (in numbers) of the total population though decisive in the revolution. Nor certainly can it be said of prerevolutionary China, nor of Mexico, Bolivia, Algeria, nor of Vietnam. This may come as something of a conceptual shock, since the image of prerevolutionary Cuba held by many, whether friends or foes of the revolution, is that of a peasant society. Nor was it, in an important sense, an "underdeveloped" country. From the standpoint of an analysis of the economic system and class structure of prerevolutionary Cuba, I believe it is much more fruitful to view it as a relatively unevenly developed or misdeveloped capitalist country of a special colonial type.

In the agrarian sector, there was no subsistence peasantry, nor the nonwage tenant-labor characteristic of the *hacienda* or manorial economy. The vast majority of the economically active population employed in agriculture were wage workers. Improved working conditions and higher wages—working-class interests—rather than "land hunger" were their essential demands and aspirations, unlike the situation in other countries where revolutions calling themselves "socialist" have occurred. Moreover, what there was of a nonwage working population in Cuba's countryside was a small proprietor stratum—the *colonos*—who were integrated into the market economy and dependent on the large, economically strategic sugar "centrals" (production centers including mills, workers' housing and transportation) for credit, milling, and marketing; in the case of tobacco and coffee cultivation, there were also small proprietors and/or tenants whose overall economic significance was marginal. The agrarian sector was based on large-scale capitalist enterprises which employed both industrial and agricultural wage workers.

What strengthened the hand of the ruling class in other social revolutions in this century was a mass social base, largely in the countryside, which they could mobilize as allies to defend their own interests. A counterrevolutionary movement in these countries was possible because the rulers still had legitimacy in and social control of the rural population. It was no historical accident that a bloody civil war was required in revolutionary Russia to put down the counterrevolution, that three decades of armed warfare preceded the triumph of the Chinese Communists, or that the Mexican revolutionaries had to violently confront and overcome the combined might of the Catholic Church and *hacendados*—the large landowners. The Cuban revolutionaries (and this is not to detract from their own extraordinary abilities) did not have to confront a similar situation. The landed upper stratum had been virtually expropriated by the development of capitalism much before the revolution.

Of course, Cuban capialism was absentee-owned, foreign-controlled, and quasi-colonial. This meant that not only did the ruling strata not have roots in the countryside but that, indeed, they had no significant independent base of economic power in the country as a whole. The so-called Cuban capitalist class was dependent on American capitalism—politically, militarily, economically. Because of this dependency, they also lacked social legitimacy. The justification of their rule stood nakedly revealed as their control of the means of violence. They stayed in power because they had a military regime (and behind it the power of the United States government) to protect them, not because anyone believed that they *deserved* power or that they had the *right* to rule. They were illegitimate in the eyes of virtually the entire population because they had shown their incapacity to rule effectively.

Contrast this for a moment with the situation of the ruling strata in Chile, since it is the only other country in the western hemisphere in which a mass-based Marxian socialist movement has had relative durability—and is rooted predominantly in the working class. Despite this, Chile's ruling strata have considerable legitimacy. A coalition of owning strata which is both landed and industrial has been able to demonstrate its capacity to rule over a period of a century without either foreign control or the intervention of the military as an autonomous social force. In the countryside, the *hacendados* ruled a peasantry involved in tenant-labor, living on the great *fundos* and exploited through seignorial and paternalistic relations. Only recently has agrarian agitation and organization begun to shake this stability. This is in contrast to the instability and massive struggles that characterized the Cuban past, and in which the struggles were directed against a class that was scarcely considered (and perhaps scarcely considered itself) Cuban.

This contrast in the capacity of these classes to rule is also shown by the fact that Chilean political stability and parliamentary democracy have been inseparable. In Cuba, the forms of political democracy associated with capitalism had, so to speak, exhausted themselves. The brief interregnum of political democracy was considered to be a sham and not substantially more relevant to the needs of Cuba as a nation and to the interests of its people than military rule. Parties and politicians associated with Cuba's "Congress" were all but universally held in contempt. Parliamentary democracy as the legitimate mode of representative government and the bounds within which major conflicts ought to be resolved and government policy determined had lost legitimacy, if indeed it ever existed; a major ideological obstacle to revolutionary change had, therefore, been eroded well before the revolutionaries took power.

Eroded also had been whatever ideological dominion over the great majority of workers and "peasants" the Catholic Church may once have possessed. The Cuban upper strata, therefore, lacked the advantage of a significant ally that ruling classes confronted by revolutionary movements have usually had—an ally whose means of social control and moral suasion supported the existing social order and clothed revolutionary movements in the guise of mammon. That is not to say that the Church hierarchy did not oppose the social revolution. But because the communicants of the Church were drawn largely from the upper and upper-middle urban strata, and little from the countryside or peasantry, its weight in the struggle was not decisive. (It was neither a large land owner nor did it have church centers, schools, monasteries or nunneries scattered throughout the country—these scarcely existed.) Moreover, it was one of the peculiar benefits (or consequences) of direct United States occupation in the founding years of the Republic that Church and State were separated, and the American presence was a secularizing and rationalizing influence.

Large-scale enterprise in the countryside and the intermingling of industrial and agricultural workers in the sugar centrals permeated the country largely with capitalist, rationalistic, secular, antitraditional values and norms of conduct. In this sense, the country was *prepared* for development—the only thing lacking being the revolution itself which took control over the economy and the means of violence from capitalists, both foreign and domestic, and put it in the hands of a sovereign Cuban state.

Whereas the ruling strata lacked legitimacy and had no independent ideology that was expressive of their own peculiar interests and that they could impose on society at large, there was in the working class of Cuba a socialist political culture (of anarcho-syndicalist and Communist elements) born in an insurrectionary past, which had already existed for no less than three decades (and far longer in segments such as the tobacco workers). The outlook of the typical worker toward the system was impregnated by socialist ideas; what is most important, the vision of a future without capitalism was most firmly and widely held by the most decisive sectors of the working class. This is what Max Weber would have called a "simple historical fact" of such significance that without taking it into account one cannot understand the socialist revolution. If it was not the vision of the majority of workers in town and country, the dominant vision among them was, nonetheless, anticapitalist, anti-imperialist, and socialist. Even the essentially reformist and middle-class leadership of the Auténtico (and later *Ortodoxo*) party which had considerable influence among workers since the aborted revolution of the 1930s, and which was the only opposition of consequence to the Communists in the working class, also clothed its actions and program in a quasi-socialist rhetoric. Its influence among workers, however, was not of the same order as Communist influence and was debilitated by the widespread corruption of the Auténtico leadership. Most working-class struggles, whatever the leadership and however narrow the economic demands, tended to take on the political slogans of anti-imperialism and anticapitalism; it was their one consistent theme. The immediate ends of the struggle and the broader political aims—however tenuously—were linked. Thus, the historically significant impact on the workers' consciousness.

The *Report on Cuba* of the International Bank for Reconstruction and Development concluded that in the years of the most clandestine activity of the Communists about one-fourth of all workers (in 1950) "were secretly sympathetic to them"; I found, when I interviewed a national sample of workers in 1962, that some 29 percent claimed to have been partisans of the Communists before the revolution. Most important, the ideas held by workers who were non-Communist, even anti-Communist, also tended to be suffused by socialist content. As the *Report* also pointed out, "nearly all the popular education of working people on how an economic system works and what might be done to improve it came first from the anarchosyndicalists, and most recently—and most effectively—from the Communists." It was, I believe, as naturally a part of the Cuban workers' conceptions of the system, their interests, and of the creation of a world which abolished their exploitation, as bread-and-butter unionism is "natural" to workers in the United States. Both resulted from given historical conditions in which the role of leadership (durable and institutional) was crucial. From the standpoint of the development of the socialist revolution, the importance of this simple historic fact cannot be exaggerated. Despite the vacillations, zigzags, and opportunism of the Communists, one thing occurred: the infusion in the workers of a vision that transcended the Communist leadership itself. The workers could, in fact, abandon the Communists for Fidel to seek the fulfillment of the vision the Communists once represented. When the Revolutionary Government was established, it had a mass working-class base that likely was beyond its leaders in its vision of the society to be created by the revolution. This is in striking contrast to the situation in other countries in which the revolutionary leaders were far beyond their own mass base. The fact of a socialist political culture in the working class—a nationally-based, cohesive working class—combined with the force of nationalism and anti-imperialism, created a potent revolutionary force waiting to be tapped by the revolutionary leaders once they took power.

Cuba, moreover, was in certain important respects a developed country. I say in important respects and emphasize at the same time the very uneven development of the country. Advanced industrial technology and primitive agricultural implements coexisted in interdependence within the same system. On the one hand, as James O'Connor has shown,[2] economic institutions generally appearing in wealthy capitalist countries were fundamental in Cuba's prerevolutionary market structure. Production and distribution tended to be controlled by a few firms and producer's associations, and output, wages, prices, and earnings were determined within the framework of such market controls. Thus, Cuba had a vast reservoir of untapped, underutilized and misutilized resources which the revolutionary government could utilize by reordering and planning the objectives of production and distribution. A relatively developed infrastructure, obviously colonial in nature and possessing its attendant problems but nonetheless of great significance, already was established in Cuba before the revolution. Both in terms of its ability to communicate with the nation as a whole and to provide it with immediate, visible, and concrete benefits from the revolution, the revolutionaries enjoyed great advantages compared to the leaders of other social revolutions in our time. The revolutionary government could do what other revolutions' leaders could not do: They could put through an immediate and significant redistribution of the national income and improve the conditions of the masses within, so to speak, the first days of taking power. The share of the national income received by wage workers was increased by roughly one-third, according to conservative estimates (such as those by Felipe Pozos, former President of the National Bank of Cuba, in exile). This provided a cement between the regime and the masses in the early phases of the revolution which other revolutionary governments could not create in this way.

The sugar-central, wage-labor, agrarian complex also made it possible to create relatively rapidly and easily a socialist agrarian sector—virtually by shifting the locus of control within it

[2] James O'Connor, *The Origins of Socialism in Cuba* (Ithaca: Cornell University Press, 1969).

and reorganizing and reordering the objectives of production. This, again, is very much in contrast to the prerevolutionary agrarian structure inherited by other revolutionaries. Most important, the labor movement in the countryside already included wage laborers within the central labor organization; industrial and agriculutural workers associated naturally in the countryside and created bonds of social solidarity. Thus, the classical revolutionary slogan of the alliance and unity of workers and peasants was already, in a very important sense, a durable social fact before the revolutionaries came to power. The factories in the field, the sugar centrals containing the sugar mills and associated lands, provided a situation in which agricultural workers living and working on the central's lands came into more or less regular contact with industrial workers. Also, the agricultural worker himself, or his brother, or friends, may have worked at one time as a cane-cutter and another in the sugar mills, providing the industrial and agricultural worker with a fund of common experiences and perceptions. Poor proprietors also often worked in similar situations.

These centrals were, in addition, not only centers of industrial production and a basis for the creation of natural social bonds between "peasants" and workers, but also centers of political agitation and education. The most important prerevolutionary political base of the Communists was here. Forty-one percent of the sugar-central workers, compared to 30 percent of urban workers who had those occupations before the revolution, said in our interviews with them in 1962 that they were prerevolutionary supporters of the Communists. Therefore, for all these reasons, the very same acts which the Revolutionary Government would have to take from the standpoint of economic rationality, that is, to spur development, were also acts that helped secure its mass social and political base.

Think for a moment of what confronted the Soviet Communists—what, from their standpoint, they found necessary to do to destroy the old agrarian structure and replace it with a modern one. The New Economic Plan, distribution of the land and then its forcible expropriation from the very same peasants upon whom the regime rested—none of this was necessary in Cuba (nor the vast chaos and destruction of civil war). On the contrary, almost the very act of taking over and nationalizing the sugar centrals cemented the already extant bonds between workers and peasants; their working conditions and living conditions were immediately and positively transformed. The immediate and long-range interests of both were identical; each needed the other in past struggles and each was affected similarly by the fluctuations in the economy. With the revolution, these common interests became even more intimately associated. Contrast this with the Mexican revolution, where the "red battalions" of Carranza's workers helped to put down peasant rebellion, or with peasants and tin miners played off against each other in Bolivia in order to maintain the *status quo*. Contrast this with the massive repression of the peasantry under Stalin, and it indicates the profound importance of the prerevolutionary social structure in determining the pace and direction of the revolution in Cuba.

The Cuban revolutionaries—whatever their extraordinary abilities, especially Fidel's—came to power in a society whose prerevolutionary social structure endowed them with vast advantages compared to the leaders of other major social revolutions in this century. Neither the capacity of the revolutionary leaders nor their actions and reaction to the United States (nor the presence of the Soviet Union as a potential ally) can be separated from the *reality* (the "real world") of the revolutionary process. However, I think that it can be shown also that the rapidity and thoroughness (as well as the humane and libertarian aspects which I have not discussed here) of the Cuban revolution, and its movement into socialism, to a great extent were the result of the prerevolutionary social structure. Once a leadership came to power in Cuba that was really committed to a national solution to her problems—once revolutionaries committed to economic development and an independent national existence took power, and would brook no interference (indeed, a highly problematic "if" provided by Fidel, Che, and their comrades), the revolution's course was profoundly influenced by the prerevolutionary social structure. Therefore, Fidel led a socialist revolution almost without knowing it and the Communists were virtually dragged into socialism by the *fidelistas* because history made this possible.

21

Frantz Fanon: The Revolutionary Transformation of the Algerian Woman*

The way people clothe themselves, together with the traditions of dress and finery that custom implies, constitutes the most distinctive form of a society's uniqueness, that is to say the one that is the most immediately perceptible. Within the general pattern of a given costume, there are of course always modifications of detail, innovations which in highly developed societies are the mark of fashion. But the effect as a whole remains homogeneous, and great areas of civilization, immense cultural regions, can be grouped together on the basis of original, specific techniques of men's and women's dress.

It is by their apparel that types of society first become known, whether through written accounts and photographic records or motion pictures. Thus, there are civilizations without neckties, civilizations with loin-cloths, and others without hats. The fact of belonging to a given cultural group is usually revealed by clothing traditions. In the Arab world, for example, the veil worn by women is at once noticed by the tourists. One may remain for a long time unaware of the fact that a Moslem does not eat pork or that he denies himself daily sexual relations during the month of Ramadan, but the veil worn by

* Frantz Fanon, "Algeria Unveiled," in *A Dying Colonialism,* New York, Grove Press, 1967. By permission.

431

the women appears with such constancy that it generally suffices to characterize Arab society.

In the Arab Maghreb, the veil belongs to the clothing traditions of the Tunisian, Algerian, Moroccan and Libyan national societies. For the tourist and the foreigner, the veil demarcates both Algerian society and its feminine component.[1] In the case of the Algerian man, on the other hand, regional modifications can be noted: the *fez* in urban centers, turbans and *djellabas*[2] in the countryside. The masculine garb allows a certain margin of choice, a modicum of heterogeneity. The woman seen in her white veil unifies the perception that one has of Algerian feminine society. Obviously what we have here is a uniform which tolerates no modification, no variant.[3]

The *haïk*[4] very clearly demarcates the Algerian colonized

---

[1] We do not here consider rural areas where the woman is often unveiled. Nor do we take into account the Kabyle woman who, except in the large cities, never uses a veil. For the tourist who rarely ventures into the mountains, the Arab woman is first of all one who wears a veil. This originality of the Kabyle woman constitutes, among others, one of the themes of colonialist propaganda bringing out the opposition between Arabs and Berbers. Such studies, devoted to the analysis of psychological modifications, neglect considerations that are properly historical. We shall presently take up this other aspect of Algerian reality in action. Here we shall content ourselves with pointing out that the Kabyle women, in the course of 130 years of domination, have developed other defense mechanisms with respect to the occupier. During the war of liberation their forms of action have likewise assumed absolutely original aspects.

[2] *djellaba*—a long, hooded cloak. (Translator's note)

[3] One phenomenon deserves to be recalled. In the course of the Moroccan people's struggle for liberation, and chiefly in the cities, the white veil was replaced by the black veil. This important modification is explained by the Moroccan women's desire to express their attachment to His Majesty Mohammed V. It will be remembered that it was immediately after the exiling of the King of Morocco that the black veil, a sign of mourning, made its appearance. It is worth noting that black, in Moroccan or Arab society, has never expressed mourning or affliction. As a combat measure, the adoption of black is a response to the desire to exert a symbolic pressure on the occupier, and hence to make a logical choice of one's own symbols.

[4] The *haïk*—the Arab name for the big square veil worn by Arab women, covering the face and the whole body. (Translator's note)

society. It is of course possible to remain hesitant before a little girl, but all uncertainty vanishes at the time of puberty. With the veil, things become well-defined and ordered. The Algerian woman, in the eyes of the observer, is unmistakably "she who hides behind a veil."

We shall see that this veil, one of the elements of the traditional Algerian garb, was to become the bone of contention in a grandiose battle, on account of which the occupation forces were to mobilize their most powerful and most varied resources, and in the course of which the colonized were to display a surprising force of inertia. Taken as a whole, colonial society, with its values, its areas of strength, and its philosophy, reacts to the veil in a rather homogeneous way. The decisive battle was launched before 1954, more precisely during the early 1930's. The officials of the French administration in Algeria, committed to destroying the people's originality, and under instructions to bring about the disintegration, at whatever cost, of forms of existence likely to evoke a national reality directly or indirectly, were to concentrate their efforts on the wearing of the veil, which was looked upon at this juncture as a symbol of the status of the Algerian woman. Such a position is not the consequence of a chance intuition. It is on the basis of the analyses of sociologists and ethnologists that the specialists in so-called native affairs and the heads of the Arab Bureaus coordinated their work. At an initial stage, there was a pure and simple adoption of the well-known formula, "Let's win over the women and the rest will follow." This definition of policy merely gave a scientific coloration to the "discoveries" of the sociologists.

Beneath the patrilineal pattern of Algerian society, the specialists described a structure of matrilineal essence. Arab society has often been presented by Westerners as a formal society in which outside appearances are paramount. The Algerian woman, an intermediary between obscure forces and the group, appeared in this perspective to assume a primordial importance. Behind the visible, manifest patriarchy, the more significant existence of a basic matriarchy was affirmed. The role of the Algerian mother, that of the grandmother, the aunt and the "old woman," were inventoried and defined.

This enabled the colonial administration to define a precise political doctrine: "If we want to destroy the structure of Algerian society, its capacity for resistance, we must first of all conquer the women; we must go and find them behind the veil where they hide themselves and in the houses where the men keep them out of sight." It is the situation of woman that was accordingly taken as the theme of action. The dominant administration solemnly undertook to defend this woman, pictured as humiliated, sequestered, cloistered . . . It described the immense possibilities of woman, unfortunately transformed by the Algerian man into an inert, demonetized, indeed dehumanized object. The behavior of the Algerian was very firmly denounced and described as medieval and barbaric. With infinite science, a blanket indictment against the "sadistic and vampirish" Algerian attitude toward women was prepared and drawn up. Around the family life of the Algerian, the occupier piled up a whole mass of judgments, appraisals, reasons, accumulated anecdotes and edifying examples, thus attempting to confine the Algerian within a circle of guilt.

Mutual aid societies and societies to promote solidarity with Algerian women sprang up in great number. Lamentations were organized. "We want to make the Algerian ashamed of the fate that he metes out to women." This was a period of effervescence, of putting into application a whole technique of infiltration, in the course of which droves of social workers and women directing charitable works descended on the Arab quarters.

The indigent and famished women were the first to be besieged. Every kilo of semolina distributed was accompanied by a dose of indignation against the veil and the cloister. The indignation was followed up by practical advice. Algerian women were invited to play "a functional, capital role" in the transformation of their lot. They were pressed to say no to a centuries-old subjection. The immense role they were called upon to play was described to them. The colonial administration invested great sums in this combat. After it had been posited that the woman constituted the pivot of Algerian society, all efforts were made to obtain control over her. The

Algerian, it was assured, would not stir, would resist the task of cultural destruction undertaken by the occupier, would oppose assimilation, so long as his woman had not reversed the stream. In the colonialist program, it was the woman who was given the historic mission of shaking up the Algerian man. Converting the woman, winning her over to the foreign values, wrenching her free from her status, was at the same time achieving a real power over the man and attaining a practical, effective means of destructuring Algerian culture.

Still today, in 1959, the dream of a total domestication of Algerian society by means of "unveiled women aiding and sheltering the occupier" continues to haunt the colonial authorities.[5]

The Algerian men, for their part, are a target of criticism for their European comrades, or more officially for their bosses. There is not a European worker who does not sooner or later, in the give and take of relations on the job site, the shop or the office, ask the Algerian the ritual questions: "Does your wife wear the veil? Why don't you take your wife to the movies, to the fights, to the café?"

---

[5] The ground is prepared in the school establishments as well. The teachers to whom the parents have entrusted their children soon acquire the habit of passing severe judgment on the fate of woman in Algerian society. "We firmly hope that you at least will be strong enough to impose your point of view. . . ." Schools for "young Moslem girls" are multiplying. At their pupils' approach to puberty, the teachers or the nuns exercise a truly exceptional activity. The mothers are first felt out, besieged, and given the mission of shaking up and convincing the father. Much is made of the young student's prodigious intelligence, her maturity; a picture is painted of the brilliant future that awaits those eager young creatures, and it is none too subtly hinted that it would be criminal if the child's schooling were interrupted. The shortcomings of colonized society are conceded, and it is proposed that the young student be sent to boarding school in order to spare the parents the criticism of "narrow-minded neighbors." For the specialist in colonial affairs, veterans and the "developed" natives are the commandos who are entrusted with destroying the cultural resistance of a colonized country. The regions are accordingly classified in terms of the number of developed "active units," in other words, agents of erosion of the national culture that they contain.

European bosses do not limit themselves to the disingenuous query or the glancing invitation. They use "Indian cunning" to corner the Algerian and push him to painful decisions. In connection with a holiday—Christmas or New Year, or simply a social occasion with the firm—the boss will invite *the Algerian employee and his wife.* The invitation is not a collective one. Every Algerian is called in to the director's office and invited by name to come with "your little family." "The firm being one big family, it would be unseemly for some to come without their wives, you understand? . . ." Before this formal summons, the Algerian sometimes experiences moments of difficulty. If he comes with his wife, it means admitting defeat, it means "prostituting his wife," exhibiting her, abandoning a mode of resistance. On the other hand, going alone means refusing to give satisfaction to the boss; it means running the risk of being out of a job. The study of a case chosen at random—a description of the traps set by the European in order to bring the Algerian to expose himself, to declare: "My wife wears a veil, she shall not go out," or else to betray: "Since you want to see her, here she is,"—would bring out the sadistic and perverse character of these contacts and relationships and would show in microcosm the tragedy of the colonial situation on the psychological level, the way the two systems directly confront each other, the epic of the colonized society, with its specific ways of existing, in the face of the colonialist hydra.

With the Algerian intellectual, the aggressiveness appears in its full intensity. The *fellah,* "the passive slave of a rigidly structured group," is looked upon with a certain indulgence by the conqueror.[6] The lawyer and the doctor, on the other hand, are severely frowned upon. These intellectuals, who keep their wives in a state of semi-slavery, are literally pointed to with an accusing finger. Colonial society blazes up vehemently against this inferior status of the Algerian woman. Its members worry and show concern for those unfortunate women, doomed "to produce brats," kept behind walls, banned.

Before the Algerian intellectual, racialist arguments spring

---

[6] *fellah*—a peasant. (Translator's note)

forth with special readiness. For all that he is a doctor, people will say, he still remains an Arab. "You can't get away from nature." Illustrations of this kind of race prejudice can be multiplied indefinitely. Clearly, the intellectual is reproached for limiting the extension of learned Western habits, for not playing his role as an active agent of upheaval of the colonized society, for not giving his wife the benefit of the privileges of a more worthy and meaningful life. . . . In the large population centers it is altogether commonplace to hear a European confess acidly that he has never seen the wife of an Algerian he has known for twenty years. At a more diffuse, but highly revealing, level of apprehension, we find the bitter observation that "we work in vain" . . . that "Islam holds its prey."

The method of presenting the Algerian as a prey fought over with equal ferocity by Islam and France with its Western culture reveals the whole approach of the occupier, his philosophy and his policy. This expression indicates that the occupier, smarting from his failures, presents in a simplified and pejorative way the system of values by means of which the colonized person resists his innumerable offensives. What is in fact the assertion of a distinct identity, concern with keeping intact a few shreds of national existence, is attributed to religious, magical, fanatical behavior.

This rejection of the conqueror assumes original forms, according to circumstances or to the type of colonial situation. On the whole, these forms of behavior have been fairly well studied in the course of the past twenty years; it cannot be said, however, that the conclusions that have been reached are wholly valid. Specialists in basic education for underdeveloped countries or technicians for the advancement of retarded societies would do well to understand the sterile and harmful character of any endeavor which illuminates preferentially a given element of the colonized society. Even within the framework of a newly independent nation, one cannot attack this or that segment of the cultural whole without endangering the work undertaken (leaving aside the question of the native's psychological balance). More precisely, the phenomena of counter-acculturation must be understood as the organic impossibility of a culture to modify any one of its customs without at the same time re-evaluating its deepest values, its most stable models. To speak of counter-acculturation in a colonial situation is an absurdity. The phenomena of resistance observed in the colonized must be related to an attitude of counter-assimilation, of maintenance of a cultural, hence national, originality.

The occupying forces, in applying their maximum psychological attention to the veil worn by Algerian women, were obviously bound to achieve some results. Here and there it thus happened that a woman was "saved," and symbolically unveiled.

These test-women, with bare faces and free bodies, henceforth circulated like sound currency in the European society of Algeria. These women were surrounded by an atmosphere of newness. The Europeans, over-excited and wholly given over to their victory, carried away in a kind of trance, would speak of the psychological phenomena of conversion. And in fact, in the European society, the agents of this conversion were held in esteem. They were envied. The benevolent attention of the administration was drawn to them.

After each success, the authorities were strengthened in their conviction that the Algerian woman would support Western penetration into the native society. Every rejected veil disclosed to the eyes of the colonialists horizons until then forbidden, and revealed to them, piece by piece, the flesh of Algeria laid bare. The occupier's aggressiveness, and hence his hopes, multiplied ten-fold each time a new face was uncovered. Every new Algerian woman unveiled announced to the occupier an Algerian society whose systems of defense were in the process of dislocation, open and breached. Every veil that fell, every body that became liberated from the traditional embrace of the *haïk*, every face that offered itself to the bold and impatient glance of the occupier, was a negative expression of the fact that Algeria was beginning to deny herself and was accepting the rape of the colonizer. Algerian society with every abandoned veil seemed to express its willingness to attend the master's school and to decide to change its habits under the occupier's direction and patronage.

We have seen how colonial society, the colonial administration, perceives the veil, and we have sketched the dynamics of the efforts undertaken to fight it as an institution and the resistances developed by the colonized society. At the level of the individual, of the private European, it may be interesting to follow the multiple reactions provoked by the existence of the veil, which reveal the original way in which the Algerian woman manages to be present or absent.

For a European not directly involved in this work of conversion, what reactions are there to be recorded?

The dominant attitude appears to us to be a romantic exoticism, strongly tinged with sensuality.

And, to begin with, the veil hides a beauty.

A revealing reflection—among others—of this state of mind was communicated to us by a European visiting Algeria who, in the exercise of his profession (he was a lawyer), had had the opportunity of seeing a few Algerian women without the veil. These men, he said, speaking of the Algerians, are guilty of concealing so many strange beauties. It was his conclusion that a people with a cache of such prizes, of such perfections of nature, owes it to itself to show them, to exhibit them. If worst came to worst, he added, it ought to be possible to force them to do so.

A strand of hair, a bit of forehead, a segment of an "overwhelmingly beautiful" face glimpsed in a streetcar or on a train, may suffice to keep alive and strengthen the European's persistence in his irrational conviction that the Algerian woman is the queen of all women.

But there is also in the European the crystallization of an aggressiveness, the strain of a kind of violence before the Algerian woman. Unveiling this woman is revealing her beauty; it is baring her secret, breaking her resistance, making her available for adventure. Hiding the face is also disguising a secret; it is also creating a world of mystery, of the hidden. In a confused way, the European experiences his relation with the Algerian woman at a highly complex level. There is in it the will to bring this woman within his reach, to make her a possible object of possession.

This woman who sees without being seen frustrates the colonizer. There is no reciprocity. She does not yield herself, does not give herself, does not offer herself. The Algerian has an attitude toward the Algerian woman which is on the whole clear. He does not see her. There is even a permanent intention not to perceive the feminine profile, not to pay attention to women. In the case of the Algerian, therefore, there is not, in the street or on a road, that behavior characterizing a sexual encounter that is described in terms of the glance, of the physical bearing, the muscular tension, the signs of disturbance to which the phenomenology of encounters has accustomed us.

The European faced with an Algerian woman wants to see. He reacts in an aggressive way before this limitation of his perception. Frustration and aggressiveness, here too, evolve apace. Aggressiveness comes to light, in the first place, in structurally ambivalent attitudes and in the dream material that can be revealed in the European, whether he is normal or suffers from neuropathological disturbances.[7]

In a medical consultation, for example, at the end of the morning, it is common to hear European doctors express their disappointment. The women who remove their veils before them are commonplace, vulgar; there is really nothing to make such a mystery of. One wonders what they are hiding.

---

[7] Attention must be called to a frequent attitude, on the part of European women in particular, with regard to a special category of evolved natives. Certain unveiled Algerian women turn themselves into perfect Westerners with amazing rapidity and unsuspected ease. European women feel a certain uneasiness in the presence of these women. Frustrated in the presence of the veil, they experience a similar impression before the bared face, before that unabashed body which has lost all awkwardness, all timidity, and become downright offensive. Not only is the satisfaction of supervising the evolution and correcting the mistakes of the unveiled woman withdrawn from the European woman, but she feels herself challenged on the level of feminine charm, of elegance, and even sees a competitor in this novice metamorphosed into a professional, a neophyte transformed into a propagandist. The European woman has no choice but to make common cause with the Algerian man who had fiercely flung the unveiled woman into the camp of evil and of depravation. "Really!" the European women will exclaim, "these unveiled women are quite amoral and shameless." Integration, in order to be successful, seems indeed to have to be simply a continued, accepted paternalism.

European women settle the conflict in a much less round-about way. They bluntly affirm that no one hides what is beautiful and discern in this strange custom an "altogether feminine" intention of disguising imperfections. And they proceed to compare the strategy of the European woman, which is intended to correct, to embellish, to bring out (beauty treatments, hairdos, fashion), with that of the Algerian woman, who prefers to veil, to conceal, to cultivate the man's doubt and desire. On another level, it is claimed that the intention is to mislead the customer, and that the wrapping in which the "merchandise" is presented does not really alter its nature, nor its value.

The content of the dreams of Europeans brings out other special themes. Jean-Paul Sartre, in his *Réflexions sur la Question Juive,* has shown that on the level of the unconscious, the Jewish woman almost always has an aura of rape about her.

The history of the French conquest in Algeria, including the overrunning of villages by the troops, the confiscation of property and the raping of women, the pillaging of a country, has contributed to the birth and the crystallization of the same dynamic image. At the level of the psychological strata of the occupier, the evocation of this freedom given to the sadism of the conqueror, to his eroticism, creates faults, fertile gaps through which both dreamlike forms of behavior and, on certain occasions, criminal acts can emerge.

Thus the rape of the Algerian woman in the dream of a European is always preceded by a rending of the veil. We here witness a double deflowering. Likewise, the woman's conduct is never one of consent or acceptance, but of abject humility.

Whenever, in dreams having an erotic content, a European meets an Algerian woman, the specific features of his relations with the colonized society manifest themselves. These dreams evolve neither on the same erotic plane, nor at the same tempo, as those that involve a European woman.

With an Algerian woman, there is no progressive conquest, no mutual revelation. Straight off, with the maximum of violence, there is possession, rape, near-murder. The act assumes a para-neurotic brutality and sadism, even in a normal European. This brutality and this sadism are in fact emphasized by the frightened attitude of the Algerian woman. In the dream, the woman-victim screams, struggles like a doe, and as she weakens and faints, is penetrated, martyrized, ripped apart.

Attention must likewise be drawn to a characteristic of this dream content that appears important to us. The European never dreams of an Algerian woman taken in isolation. On the rate occasions when the encounter has become a binding relationship that can be regarded as a couple, it has quickly been transformed by the desperate flight of the woman who, inevitably, leads the male "among women." The European always dreams of a group of women, of a field of women, suggestive of the gynaeceum, the harem—exotic themes deeply rooted in the unconscious.

The European's aggressiveness will express itself likewise in contemplation of the Algerian woman's morality. Her timidity and her reserve are transformed in accordance with the commonplace laws of conflictual psychology into their opposite, and the Algerian woman becomes hypocritical, perverse, and even a veritable nymphomaniac.

We have seen that on the level of individuals the colonial strategy of destructuring Algerian society very quickly came to assign a prominent place to the Algerian woman. The colonialist's relentlessness, his methods of struggle were bound to give rise to reactionary forms of behavior on the part of the colonized. In the face of the violence of the occupier, the colonized found himself defining a principled position with respect to a formerly inert element of the native cultural configuration. It was the colonialist's frenzy to unveil the Algerian woman, it was his gamble on winning the battle of the veil at whatever cost, that were to provoke the native's bristling resistance. The deliberately aggressive intentions of the colonialist with respect to the *haïk* gave a new life to this dead element of the Algerian cultural stock—dead because stabilized, without any progressive change in form or color. We here recognize one of the laws of the psychology of colonization. In an initial phase, it is the action, the plans of the occupier that determine the centers of resistance around which a people's will to survive becomes organized.

It is the white man who creates the Negro. But it is the Negro who creates negritude. To the colonialist offensive against the veil, the colonized opposes the cult of the veil. What was an undifferentiated element in a homogeneous whole acquires a taboo character, and the attitude of a given Algerian woman with respect to the veil will be constantly related to her overall attitude with respect to the foreign occupation. The colonized, in the face of the emphasis given by the colonialists to this or that aspect of his traditions, reacts very violently. The attention devoted to modifying this aspect, the emotion the conqueror puts into his pedagogical work, his prayers, his threats, weave a whole universe of resistances around this particular element of the culture. Holding out against the occupier on this precise element means inflicting upon him a spectacular setback; it means more particularly maintaining "co-existence" as a form of conflict and latent warfare. It means keeping up the atmosphere of an armed truce.

Upon the outbreak of the struggle for liberation, the attitude of the Algerian woman, or of native society in general, with regard to the veil was to undergo important modifications. These innovations are of particular interest in view of the fact that they were at no time included in the program of the struggle. The doctrine of the Revolution, the strategy of combat, never postulated the necessity for a revision of forms of behavior with respect to the veil. We are able to affirm even now that when Algeria has gained her independence such questions will not be raised, for in the practice of the Revolution the people have understood that problems are resolved in the very movement that raises them.

Until 1955, the combat was waged exclusively by the men. The revolutionary characteristics of this combat, the necessity for absolute secrecy, obliged the militant to keep his woman in absolute ignorance. As the enemy gradually adapted himself to the forms of combat, new difficulties appeared which required original solutions. The decision to involve women as active elements of the Algerian Revolution was not reached lightly. In a sense, it was the very conception of the combat that had to be modified. The violence of the occupier, his ferocity, his delirious attachment to the national territory, induced the leaders no longer to exclude certain forms of combat. Progressively, the urgency of a total war made itself felt. But involving the women was not solely a response to the desire to mobilize the entire nation. The women's entry into the war had to be harmonized with respect for the revolutionary nature of the war. In other words, the women had to show as much spirit of sacrifice as the men. It was therefore necessary to have the same confidence in them as was required from seasoned militants who had served several prison sentences. A moral elevation and a strength of character that were altogether exceptional would therefore be required of the women. There was no lack of hesitations. The revolutionary wheels had assumed such proportions; the mechanism was running at a given rate. The machine would have to be complicated; in other words its network would have to be extended without affecting its efficiency. The women could not be conceived of as a replacement product, but as an element capable of adequately meeting the new tasks.

In the mountains, women helped the *guerrilla* during halts or when convalescing after a wound or a case of typhoid contracted in the *djebel*.[8] But deciding to incorporate women as essential elements, to have the Revolution depend on their presence and their action in this or that sector, was obviously a wholly revolutionary step. To have the Revolution rest at any point on their activity was an important choice.

Such a decision was made difficult for several reasons. During the whole period of unchallenged domination, we have seen that Algerian society, and particularly the women, had a tendency to flee from the occupier. The tenacity of the occupier in his endeavor to unveil the women, to make of them an ally in the work of cultural destruction, had the effect of strengthening the traditional patterns of behavior. These patterns, which were essentially positive in the strategy of resistance to the corrosive action of the colonizer, naturally had negative effects. The woman, especially the city woman, suffered a loss of ease and of assurance. Having been accustomed to confinement, her body did not have the normal mobility before a limitless horizon of

---

[8] *djebel*—mountain. (Translator's note)

avenues, of unfolded sidewalks, of houses, of people dodged or bumped into. This relatively cloistered life, with its known, categorized, regulated comings and goings, made any immediate revolution seem a dubious proposition. The political leaders were perfectly familiar with these problems, and their hesitations expressed their consciousness of their responsibilities. They were entitled to doubt the success of this measure. Would not such a decision have catastrophic consequences for the progress of the Revolution?

To this doubt there was added an equally important element. The leaders hesitated to involve the women, being perfectly aware of the ferocity of the colonizer. The leaders of the Revolution had no illusions as to the enemy's criminal capacities. Nearly all of them had passed through their jails or had had sessions with survivors from the camps or the cells of the French judicial police. No one of them failed to realize that any Algerian woman arrested would be tortured to death. It is relatively easy to commit oneself to this path and to accept among different eventualities that of dying under torture. The matter is a little more difficult when it involves designating someone who manifestly runs the risk of certain death. But the decision as to whether or not the women were to participate in the Revolution had to be made; the inner oppositions became massive, and each decision gave rise to the same hesitations, produced the same despair.

In the face of the extraordinary success of this new form of popular combat, observers have compared the action of the Algerian women to that of certain women resistance fighters or even secret agents of the specialized services. It must be constantly borne in mind that the committed Algerian woman learns both her role as "a woman alone in the street" and her revolutionary mission instinctively. The Algerian woman is not a secret agent. It is without apprenticeship, without briefing, without fuss, that she goes out into the street with three grenades in her handbag or the activity report of an area in her bodice. She does not have the sensation of playing a role she has read about ever so many times in novels, or seen in motion pictures. There is not that coefficient of play, of imitation, almost always present in this form of action when we are dealing with a Western woman.

What we have here is not the bringing to light of a character known and frequented a thousand times in imagination or in stories. It is an authentic birth in a pure state, without preliminary instruction. There is no character to imitate. On the contrary, there is an intense dramatization, a continuity between the woman and the revolutionary. The Algerian woman rises directly to the level of tragedy.[9]

The growth in number of the F.L.N. cells, the range of new tasks—finance, intelligence, counter-intelligence, political training—the necessity to provide for one active cell three or four replacement cells to be held in reserve, ready to become active at the slightest alert concerning the front cell, obliged the leaders to seek other avenues for the carrying out of strictly individual assignments. After a final series of meetings among leaders, and especially in view of the urgency of the daily problems that the Revolution faced, the decision to concretely involve women in the national struggle was reached.

The revolutionary character of this decision must once again be emphasized. At the beginning, it was the married women who were contacted. But rather soon these restrictions were abandoned. The married women whose husbands were militants were the first to be chosen. Later, widows or divorced women were designated. In any case, there were never any unmarried girls—first of all, because a girl of even twenty or twenty-three hardly ever has occasion to leave the family domicile unaccompanied. But the woman's duties as mother or spouse, the desire to limit to the minimum the possible consequences of her arrest and her death, and also the more and more numerous volunteering of unmarried girls, led the political leaders to make another leap, to remove all restrictions, to accept indiscriminately the support of all Algerian women.

---

[9] We are mentioning here only realities known to the enemy. We therefore say nothing about the new forms of action adopted by women in the Revolution. Since 1958, in fact, the tortures inflicted on women militants have enabled the occupier to have an idea of the strategy used by women. Today new adaptations have developed. It will therefore be understood if we are silent as to these.

Meanwhile the woman who might be acting as a liaison agent, as a bearer of tracts, as she walked some hundred or two hundred meters ahead of the man under whose orders she was working, still wore a veil; but after a certain period the pattern of activity that the struggle involved shifted in the direction of the European city. The protective mantle of the Kasbah, the almost organic curtain of safety that the Arab town weaves round the native, withdrew, and the Algerian woman, exposed, was sent forth into the conqueror's city. Very quickly she adopted an absolutely unbelievable offensive tactic. When colonized people undertake an action against the oppressor, and when this oppression is exercised in the form of exacerbated and continuous violence as in Algeria, they must overcome a considerable number of taboos. The European city is not the prolongation of the native city. The colonizers have not settled in the midst of the natives. They have surrounded the native city; they have laid siege to it. Every exit from the Kasbah of Algiers opens on enemy territory. And so it is in Constantine, in Oran, in Blida, in Bône.

The native cities are deliberately caught in the conqueror's vise. To get an idea of the rigor with which the immobilizing of the native city, of the autochthonous population, is organized, one must have in one's hands the plans according to which a colonial city has been laid out, and compare them with the comments of the general staff of the occupation forces.

Apart from the charwomen employed in the conquerors' homes, those whom the colonizer indiscriminately calls the "Fatmas," the Algerian women, especially the young Algerian women, rarely venture into the European city. Their movements are almost entirely limited to the Arab city. And even in the Arab city their movements are reduced to the minimum. The rare occasions on which the Algerian woman abandons the city are almost always in connection with some event, either of an exceptional nature (the death of a relative residing in a nearby locality), or, more often, traditional family visits for religious feasts, or a pilgrimage. In such cases, the European city is crossed in a car, usually early in the morning. The Algerian woman, the young Algerian woman—except for a very few students (who, besides, never have the same ease as their

European counterparts)—must overcome a multiplicity of inner resistances, of subjectively organized fears, of emotions. She must at the same time confront the essentially hostile world of the occupier and the mobilized, vigilant, and efficient police forces. Each time she ventures into the European city, the Algerian woman must achieve a victory over herself, over her childish fears. She must consider the image of the occupier lodged somewhere in her mind and in her body, remodel it, initiate the essential work of eroding it, make it inessential, remove something of the shame that is attached to it, devalidate it.

Initially subjective, the breaches made in colonialism are the result of a victory of the colonized over their old fear and over the atmosphere of despair distilled day after day by a colonialism that has incrusted itself with the *prospect of enduring forever.*

The young Algerian woman, whenever she is called upon, establishes a link. Algiers is no longer the Arab city, but the autonomous area of Algiers, the nervous system of the enemy apparatus. Oran, Constantine develop their dimensions. In launching the struggle, the Algerian is loosening the vise that was tightening around the native cities. From one area of Algiers to another, from the Ruisseau to Hussein-Dey, from El-Biar to the rue Michelet, the Revolution creates new links. More and more, it is the Algerian woman, the Algerian girl, who will be assuming these tasks.

Among the tasks entrusted to the Algerian woman is the bearing of messages, of complicated verbal orders learned by heart, sometimes despite complete absence of schooling. But she is also called upon to stand watch, for an hour and often more, before a house where district leaders are conferring.

During those interminable minutes when she must avoid standing still, so as not to attract attention, and avoid venturing too far since she is responsible for the safety of the brothers within, incidents that are at once funny and pathetic are not infrequent. An unveiled Algerian girl who "walks the street" is very often noticed by young men who behave like young men all over the world, but who use a special approach as the result of the idea people habitually have of one who has discarded the veil. She is treated to unpleasant, obscene, humiliating remarks. When such things happen, she must grit her teeth, walk away a few steps, elude the passers-by who draw attention to her, who give other passers-by the desire either to follow their example, or to come to her defense. Or it may be that the Algerian woman is carrying in her bag or in a small suitcase twenty, thirty, forty million francs, money belonging to the Revolution, money which is to be used to take care of the needs of the families of prisoners, or to buy medicine and supplies for the guerrillas.

This revolutionary activity has been carried on by the Algerian woman with exemplary constancy, self-mastery, and success. Despite the inherent, subjective difficulties and notwithstanding the sometimes violent incomprehension of a part of the family, the Algerian woman assumes all the tasks entrusted to her.

But things were gradually to become more complicated. Thus the unit leaders who go into the town and who avail themselves of the women-scouts, of the girls whose function it is to lead the way, are no longer new to political activity, are no longer unknown to the police. Authentic military chiefs have now begun to pass through the cities. These are known, and are being looked for. There is not a police superintendent who does not have their pictures on his desk.

These soldiers on the move, these fighters, always carry their weapons—automatic pistols, revolvers, grenades, sometimes all three. The political leader must overcome much resistance in order to induce these men, who under no circumstance would allow themselves to be taken prisoner, to entrust their weapons to the girl who is to walk ahead of them, it being up to them, if things go badly, to recover the arms immediately. The group accordingly makes its way into the European city. A hundred meters ahead, a girl may be carrying a suitcase and behind her are two or three ordinary-looking men. This girl who is the group's lighthouse and barometer gives warning in case of danger. The file makes its way by fits and starts; police cars and patrols cruise back and forth.

There are times, as these soldiers have admitted after completing such a mission, when the urge to recover their weapons is almost irresistible because of the fear of being caught short and not having time to defend themselves. With this phase, the Algerian woman penetrates a little further into the flesh of the Revolution.

But it was from 1956 on that her activity assumed really gigantic dimensions. Having to react in rapid succession to the massacre of Algerian civilians in the mountains and in the cities, the revolutionary leadership found that if it wanted to prevent the people from being gripped by terror it had no choice but to adopt forms of terror which until then it had rejected. This phenomenon has not been sufficiently analyzed; not enough attention has been given to the reasons that lead a revolutionary movement to choose the weapon that is called terrorism.

During the French Resistance, terrorism was aimed at soldiers, at Germans of the Occupation, or at strategic enemy installations. The technique of terrorism is the same. It consists of individual or collective attempts by means of bombs or by the derailing of trains. In Algeria, where European settlers are numerous and where the territorial militias lost no time in enrolling the postman, the nurse and the grocer in the repressive system, the men who directed the struggle faced an absolutely new situation.

The decision to kill a civilian in the street is not an easy one, and no one comes to it lightly. No one takes the step of placing a bomb in a public place without a battle of conscience.

The Algerian leaders who, in view of the intensity of the repression and the frenzied character of the oppression, thought they could answer the blows received without any serious problems of conscience, discovered that the most horrible crimes do not constitute a sufficient excuse for certain decisions.

The leaders in a number of cases canceled plans or even in the last moment called off the *fidaï*[10] assigned to place a given bomb. To explain these hesitations there was, to be sure, the memory of civilians killed or frightfully wounded. There was

---

[10] *fidaï*—a death volunteer, in the Islamic tradition. (Translator's note)

the political consideration not to do certain things that could compromise the cause of freedom. There was also the fear that the Europeans working with the Front might be hit in these attempts. There was thus a threefold concern: not to pile up possibly innocent victims, not to give a false picture of the Revolution, and finally the anxiety to have the French democrats on their side, as well as the democrats of all the countries of the world and the Europeans of Algeria who were attracted by the Algerian national ideal.

Now the massacres of Algerians, the raids in the countryside, strengthened the assurance of the European civilians, seemed to consolidate the colonial status, and injected hope into the colonialists. The Europeans who, as a result of certain military actions on the part of the Algerian National Army in favor of the struggle of the Algerian people, had soft-pedaled their race prejudice and their insolence, recovered their old arrogance, their traditional contempt.

I remember a woman clerk in Birtouta who, on the day of the interception of the plane transporting the five members of the National Liberation Front, waved their photographs in front of her shop, shrieking: "They've been caught! They're going to get their what-you-call'ems cut off!"

Every blow dealt the Revolution, every massacre perpetrated by the adversary, intensified the ferocity of the colonialists and hemmed in the Algerian civilian on all sides.

Trains loaded with French soldiers, the French Navy on maneuvers and bombarding Algiers and Philippeville, the jet planes, the militiamen who descended on the *douars*[11] and decimated uncounted Algerians, all this contributed to giving the people the impression that they were not defended, that they were not protected, that nothing had changed, and that the Europeans could do what they wanted. This was the period when one heard Europeans announcing in the streets: "Let's each one of us take ten of them and bump them off and you'll see the problem solved in no time." And the Algerian people, especially in the cities, witnessed this boastfulness which added insult to injury and noted the impunity of these criminals who

[11] *douar*—a village. (Translator's note)

did not even take the trouble to hide. Any Algerian man or woman in a given city could in fact name the torturers and murderers of the region.

A time came when some of the people allowed doubt to enter their minds, and they began to wonder whether it was really possible, quantitatively and qualitatively, to resist the occupant's offensives. Was freedom worth the consequences of penetrating into that enormous circuit of terrorism and counter-terrorism? Did this disproportion not express the impossibility of escaping oppression?

Another part of the people, however, grew impatient and conceived the idea of putting an end to the advantage the enemy derived by pursuing the path of terror. The decision to strike the adversary individually and by name could no longer be eluded. All the prisoners "shot and killed while trying to escape," and the cries of the tortured, demanded that new forms of combat be adopted.

Members of the police and the meeting places of the colonialists (cafés in Algiers, Oran, Constantine) were the first to be singled out. From this point on the Algerian woman became wholly and deliberately immersed in the revolutionary action. It was she who would carry in her bag the grenades and the revolvers that a *fidaï* would take from her at the last moment, before the bar, or as a designated criminal passed. During this period Algerians caught in the European city were pitilessly challenged, arrested, searched.

This is why we must watch the parallel progress of this man and this woman, of this couple that brings death to the enemy, life to the Revolution. The one supporting the other, but apparently strangers to each other. The one radically transformed into a European woman, poised and unconstrained, whom no one would suspect, completely at home in the environment, and the other, a stranger, tense, moving toward his destiny.

The Algerian *fidaï,* unlike the unbalanced anarchists made famous in literature, does not take dope. The *fidaï* does not need to be unaware of danger, to befog his consciousness, or to forget. The "terrorist," from the moment he undertakes an assignment, allows death to enter into his soul. He has a rendezvous with death. The *fidaï*, on the other hand, has a rendezvous with the life of the Revolution, and with his own life. The *fidaï* is not one of the sacrificed. To be sure, he does not shrink before the possibility of losing his life or the independence of his country, but at no moment does he choose death.

If it has been decided to kill a given police superintendent responsible for tortures or a given colonialist leader, it is because these men constitute an obstacle to the progress of the Revolution. Froger, for example, symbolized a colonialist tradition and a method inaugurated at Sétif and at Guelma in 1954.[12] Moreover, Froger's apparent power crystallized the colonization and gave new life to the hopes of those who were beginning to have doubts as to the real solidity of the system. It was around people like Froger that the robbers and murderers of the Algerian people would meet and encourage one another. This was something the *fidaï* knew, and that the woman who accompanied him, his woman-arsenal, likewise knew.

Carrying revolvers, grenades, hundreds of false identity cards or bombs, the unveiled Algerian woman moves like a fish in the Western waters. The soldiers, the French patrols, smile to her as she passes, compliments on her looks are heard here and there, but no one suspects that her suitcases contain the automatic pistol which will presently mow down four or five members of one of the patrols.

We must come back to that young girl, unveiled only yesterday, who walks with sure steps down the streets of the European city teeming with policemen, parachutists, militiamen. She no longer slinks along the walls as she tended to do before the Revolution. Constantly called upon to efface herself before a member of the dominant society, the Algerian woman avoided the middle of the sidewalk which in all countries in the world belongs rightfully to those who command.

The shoulders of the unveiled Algerian woman are thrust back with easy freedom. She walks with a graceful, measured stride, neither too fast nor too slow. Her legs are bare, not

---

[12] Froger, one of the colonialist leaders. Executed by a *fidaï* in late 1956.

confined by the veil, given back to themselves, and her hips are free.

The body of the young Algerian woman, in traditional society, is revealed to her by its coming to maturity and by the veil. The veil covers the body and disciplines it, tempers it, at the very time when it experiences its phase of greatest effervescence. The veil protects, reassures, isolates. One must have heard the confessions of Algerian women or have analyzed the dream content of certain recently unveiled women to appreciate the importance of the veil for the body of the woman. Without the veil she has an impression of her body being cut up into bits, put adrift; the limbs seem to lengthen indefinitely. When the Algerian woman has to cross a street, for a long time she commits errors of judgment as to the exact distance to be negotiated. The unveiled body seems to escape, to dissolve. She has an impression of being improperly dressed, even of being naked. She experiences a sense of incompleteness with great intensity. She has the anxious feeling that something is unfinished, and along with this a frightful sensation of disintegrating. The absence of the veil distorts the Algerian woman's corporal pattern. She quickly has to invent new dimensions for her body, new means of muscular control. She has to create for herself an attitude of unveiled-woman-outside. She must overcome all timidity, all awkwardness (for she must pass for a European), and at the same time be careful not to overdo it, not to attract notice to herself. The Algerian woman who walks stark naked into the European city relearns her body, re-establishes it in a totally revolutionary fashion. This new dialectic of the body and of the world is primary in the case of one revolutionary woman.[13]

---

[13] The woman, who before the Revolution never left the house without being accompanied by her mother or her husband, is now entrusted with special missions such as going from Oran to Constantine or Algiers. For several days, all by herself, carrying directives of capital importance for the Revolution, she takes the train, spends the night with an unknown family, among militants. Here too she must harmonize her movements, for the enemy is on the lookout for any false step. But the important thing here is that the husband makes no difficulty about letting

But the Algerian woman is not only in conflict with her body.
She is a link, sometimes an essential one, in the revolutionary
machine. She carries weapons, knows important points of
refuge. And it is in terms of the concrete dangers that she faces
that we must gauge the insurmountable victories that she has
had to win in order to be able to say to her chief, on her return:
"Mission accomplished . . . R.A.S."[14]

Another difficulty to which attention deserves to be called
appeared during the first months of feminine activity. In the
course of her comings and goings, it would happen that the
unveiled Algerian woman was seen by a relative or a friend of
the family. The father was sooner or later informed. He would
naturally hesitate to believe such allegations. Then more reports
would reach him. Different persons would claim to have seen
"Zohra or Fatima unviled, walking like a . . . My Lord, protect us! . . ." The father would then decide to demand explanations. He would hardly have begun to speak when he would
stop. From the young girl's look of firmness the father would
have understood that her commitment was of long standing.

---

his wife leave on an assignment. He will make it, in fact, a point of
pride to say to the liaison agent when the latter returns, "You see, everything has gone well in your absence." The Algerian's age-old jealousy,
his "congenital" suspiciousness, have melted on contact with the Revolution. It must be pointed out also that militants who are being sought by
the police take refuge with other militants not yet identified by the
occupier. In such cases the woman, left alone all day with the fugitive,
is the one who gets him his food, the newspapers, the mail, showing no
trace of suspicion or fear. Involved in the struggle, the husband or the
father learns to look upon the relations between the sexes in a new
light. The militant man discovers the militant woman, and jointly they
create new dimensions for Algerian society.

[14] R.A.S.—*Rien à signaler*—a military abbreviation for "Nothing to
report."

We here go on to a description of attitudes. There is, however, an
important piece of work to be done on the woman's role in the Revolution: the woman in the city, in the *djebel*, in the enemy administrations;
the prostitute and the information she obtains; the woman in prison,
under torture, facing death, before the courts. All these chapter head-
ings, after the material has been sifted, will reveal an incalculable number of facts essential for the history of the national struggle.

The old fear of dishonor was swept away by a new fear, fresh and cold—that of death in battle or of torture of the girl. Behind the girl, the whole family—even the Algerian father, the authority for all things, the founder of every value—following in her footsteps, becomes committed to the new Algeria.

Removed and reassumed again and again, the veil has been manipulated, transformed into a technique of camouflage, into a means of struggle. The virtually taboo character assumed by the veil in the colonial situation disappeared almost entirely in the course of the liberating struggle. Even Algerian women not actively integrated into the struggle formed the habit of abandoning the veil. It is true that under certain conditions, especially from 1957 on, the veil reappeared. The missions in fact became increasingly difficult. The adversary now knew, since certain militant women had spoken under torture, that a number of women very Europeanized in appearance were playing a fundamental role in the battle. Moreover, certain European women of Algeria were arrested, to the consternation of the adversary who discovered that his own system was breaking down. The discovery by the French authorities of the participation of Europeans in the liberation struggle marks a turning point in the Algerian Revolution. From that day, the French patrols challenged every person. Europeans and Algerians were equally suspect. All historic limits crumbled and disappeared. Any person carrying a package could be required to open it and show its contents. Anyone was entitled to question anyone as to the nature of a parcel carried in Algiers, Philippeville, or Batna. Under those conditions it became urgent to conceal the package from the eyes of the occupier and again to cover oneself with the protective *haïk*.

Here again, a new technique had to be learned: how to carry a rather heavy object dangerous to handle under the veil and still give the impression of having one's hands free, that there was nothing under this *haïk*, except a poor woman or an insignificant young girl. It was not enough to be veiled. One had to look so much like a "fatma" that the soldier would be convinced that this woman was quite harmless.

Very difficult. Three meters ahead of you the police challenge a veiled woman who does not look particularly suspect. From the anguished expression of the unit leader you have guessed that she is carrying a bomb, or a sack of grenades, bound to her body by a whole system of strings and straps. For the hands must be free, exhibited bare, humbly and abjectly presented to the soldiers so that they will look no further. Showing empty and apparently mobile and free hands is the sign that disarms the enemy soldier.

The Algerian woman's body, which in an initial phase was pared down, now swelled. Whereas in the previous period the body had to be made slim and disciplined to make it attractive and seductive, it now had to be squashed, made shapeless and even ridiculous. This, as we have seen, is the phase during which she undertook to carry bombs, grenades, machine-gun clips.

The enemy, however, was alerted, and in the streets one witnessed what became a commonplace spectacle of Algerian women glued to the wall, on whose bodies the famous magnetic detectors, the "frying pans," would be passed. Every veiled woman, every Algerian woman became suspect. There was no discrimination. This was the period during which men, women, children, the whole Algerian people, experienced at one and the same time their national vocation and the recasting of the new Algerian society.

Ignorant or feigning to be ignorant of these new forms of conduct, French colonialism, on the occasion of May 13th, reenacted its old campaign of Westernizing the Algerian woman. Servants under the threat of being fired, poor women dragged from their homes, prostitutes, were brought to the public square and *symbolically* unveiled to the cries of *"Vive l'Algérie française!"* Before this new offensive old reactions reappeared. Spontaneously and without being told, the Algerian women who had long since dropped the veil once again donned the *haïk,* thus affirming that it was not true that woman liberated herself at the invitation of France and of General de Gaulle.

Behind these psychological reactions, beneath this immediate and almost unanimous response, we again see the overall attitude of rejection of the values of the occupier, even if these values objectively be worth choosing. It is because they fail to grasp this intellectual reality, this characteristic feature (the famous sensitivity of the colonized), that the colonizers rage at always "doing them good in spite of themselves." Colonialism wants everything to come from it. But the dominant psychological feature of the colonized is to withdraw before any invitation of the conqueror's. In organizing the famous cavalcade of May 13th, colonialism has obliged Algerian society to go back to methods of struggle already outmoded. In a certain sense, the different ceremonies have caused a turning back, a regression.

Colonialism must accept the fact that things happen without its control, without its direction. We are reminded of the words spoken in an international assembly by an African political figure. Responding to the standard excuse of the immaturity of colonial peoples and their incapacity to administer themselves, this man demanded for the underdeveloped peoples "the right to govern themselves badly." The doctrinal assertions of colonialism in its attempt to justify the maintenance of its domination almost always push the colonized to the position of making uncompromising, rigid, static counter-proposals.

After the 13th of May, the veil was resumed, but stripped once and for all of its exclusively traditional dimension.

There is thus a historic dynamism of the veil that is very concretely perceptible in the development of colonization in Algeria. In the beginning, the veil was a mechanism of resistance, but its value for the social group remained very strong. The veil was worn because tradition demanded a rigid separation of the sexes, but also because the occupier *was bent on unveiling Algeria.* In a second phase, the mutation occurred in connection with the Revolution and under special circumstances. The veil was abandoned in the course of revolutionary action. What had been used to block the psychological or political offensives of the occupier became a means, an instrument. The veil helped the Algerian woman to meet the new problems created by the struggle.

The colonialists are incapable of grasping the motivations of the colonized. It is the necessities of combat that give rise in Algerian society to new attitudes, to new modes of action, to new ways.

22

Gabriel and Daniel Cohn-Bendit: The French Student Rebellion, 1968*

There is no such thing as an isolated revolutionary act. Acts that can transform society take place in association with others, and form part of a general movement that follows its own laws of growth. All revolutionary activity is collective, and hence involves a degree of organization. What we challenge is not the need for this but the need for a revolutionary leadership, the need for a party.

Central to my thesis is an analysis of the bureaucratic phenomenon, which I have examined from various viewpoints. For example, I have looked at the French workers' unions and parties and shown that what is wrong with them is not so much their rigidity and treachery as the fact that they have become integrated into the overall bureaucratic system of the capitalist state.

The emergence of bureaucratic tendencies on a world scale, the continuous concentration of capital, and the increasing intervention of the State in economic and social matters, have produced a new managerial class whose fate is no longer bound up with that of the private ownership of the means of production.

* Gabriel Cohn-Bendit and Daniel Cohn-Bendit, "C'est pour toi que tu fais la révolution," in *Obsolete Communism: The Left-Wing Alternative* (New York: McGraw-Hill, 1968), pp. 249–256. By permission.

It is in the light of this bureaucratization that the Bolshevik Party has been studied. Although its bureaucratic nature is not, of course, its only characteristic, it is true to say that Communists, and also Trotskyists, Maoists and the rest, no less than the capitalist State, all look upon the proletariat as a mass that needs to be directed from above. As a result, democracy degenerates into the ratification at the bottom of decisions taken at the top, and the class struggle is forgotten while the leaders jockey for power within the political hierarchy.

The objections to Bolshevism are not so much moral as sociological; what we attack is not the evil conduct of some of its leaders but an organizational set-up that has become its one and only justification.

The most forceful champion of a revolutionary party was Lenin, who in his *What Is to Be Done?* argued that the proletariat is unable by itself to reach a "scientific" understanding of society, that it tends to adopt the prevailing, i.e. the bourgeois, ideology.

Hence it was the essential task of the party to rid the workers of this ideology by a process of political education which could only come to them *from without*. Moreover, Lenin tried to show that the party can only overcome the class enemy by turning itself into a professional revolutionary body in which everyone is allocated a fixed task. Certain of its infallibility, a Party appoints itself the natural spokesman and sole defender of the interests of the working class, and as such wields power on their behalf—i.e., acts as a bureaucracy.

We take quite a different view: far from having to teach the masses, the revolutionary's job is to try to understand and express their common aspirations; far from being Lenin's "tribune of the people who uses every manifestation of tyranny and oppression . . . to explain his Socialist convictions and his Social Democratic demands," the real militant must encourage the workers to struggle on their own behalf, and show how their every struggle can be used to drive a wedge into capitalist society. If he does so, the militant acts as an agent of the people and no longer as their leader.

The setting up of any party inevitably reduces freedom of the people to freedom to agree with the party.

In other words, democracy is not suborned by bad leadership but by the very existence of leadership. Democracy cannot even exist within the Party, because the Party itself is not a democratic organization, i.e., it is based upon authority and not on representation. Lenin realized full well that the Party is an artificial creation, that it was imposed upon the working class "from without." Moral scruples have been swept aside: the party is "right" if it can impose its views upon the masses and wrong if it fails to do so. For Lenin, the whole matter ends there. In his *State and Revolution,* Lenin did not even raise the problem of the relationship between the people and the party. Revolutionary power was a matter of fact, based upon people who are prepared to fight for it; the paradox is that the party's program, endorsed by these people, was precisely: All power to the Soviets! But whatever its program, in retrospect we can see that the Party, because of its basic conception, is bound to bring in privilege and bureaucracy, and we must wash our hands of all organizations of this sort. To try and pretend that the Bolshevik Party is truly democratic is to deceive oneself, and this, at least, is an error that Lenin himself never committed.

What then is our conception of the role of the revolutionary? To begin with, we are convinced that the revolutionary cannot and must not be a leader. Revolutionaries are a militant minority drawn from various social strata, people who band together because they share an ideology, and who pledge themselves to struggle against oppression, to dispel the mystification of the ruling classes and the bureaucrats, to proclaim that the workers can only defend themselves and build a socialist society by taking their fate into their own hands, believing that political maturity comes only from revolutionary struggle and direct action.

By their action, militant minorities can do no more than support, encourage, and clarify the struggle. They must always guard against any tendency to become a pressure group outside the revolutionary movement of the masses. When they act, it must always be with the masses, and not as a faction.

For some time, the 22 March Movement was remarkable only for its radical political line, for its methods of attack—often spontaneous—and for its non-bureaucratic structure. Its objectives and the role it could play became clear only during the events of May and June, when it attracted the support of the working class. These militant students whose dynamic theories emerged from their practice, were imitated by others, who developed new forms of action appropriate to their own situation. The result was a mass movement unencumbered by the usual chains of command. By challenging the repressive nature of their own institution—the university—the revolutionary students forced the state to show its hand, and the brutality with which it did so caused a general revulsion and led to the occupation of the factories and the general strike. The mass intervention of the working class was the greatest achievement of our struggle; it was the first step on the path to a better society, a path that, alas, was not followed to the end. The militant minorities failed to get the masses to follow their example: to take collective charge of the running of society. We do not believe for a single moment that the workers are incapable of taking the next logical step beyond occupying the factories—which is to run them on their own. We are sure that they can do what we ourselves have done in the universities. The militant minorities must continue to wage their revolutionary struggle, to show the workers what their trade unions try to make them forget: their own gigantic strength. The distribution of petrol by the workers in the refineries and the local strike committees shows clearly what the working class is capable of doing once it puts its mind to it.

During the recent struggle, many student militants became hero-worshippers of the working class, forgetting that every group has its own part to play in defending its own interests, and that, during a period of total confrontation, these interests converge.

The student movement must follow its own road—only thus can it contribute to the growth of militant minorities in the factories and workshops. We do not pretend that we can be leaders in the struggle, but it is a fact that small revolutionary groups can, at the right time and place, rupture the system decisively and irreversibly.

During May and June, 1968, the emergence of a vast chain

of workers' committees and sub-committees by-passed the calcified structure of the trade unions, and tried to call together all workers in a struggle that was their own and not that of the various trade union bureaucracies. It was because of this that the struggle was carried to a higher stage. It is absurd and romantic to speak of revolution with a capital R and to think of it as resulting from a single, decisive action. The revolutionary process grows and is strengthened daily not only in revolt against the boredom of a system that prevents people from seeing the "beach under the paving stones" but also in our determination to make the beach open to all.

If a revolutionary movement is to succeed, no form of organization whatever must be allowed to dam its spontaneous flow. It must evolve its own forms and structures.

In May and June, many groups with these ideas came into being; here is a pamphlet put out by the ICO, not as a platform or program for action, but as a basis for discussion by the workers:

"The aim of this group is to unite those workers who have lost confidence in the traditional labor organizations—parties and trade unions.

"Our own experiences have shown us that modern trade unions contribute towards stabilizing and preserving the exploitative system.

"They serve as regulators of the labor market, they use the workers' struggle for political ends, they are the handmaidens of the ruling class in the modern state.

"It is up to the workers to defend their own interests and to struggle for their own emancipation.

"Workers, we must try to understand what is being done to us all, and denounce the trade unions with their spurious claims that they alone can help us to help ourselves.

"In the class struggle we intervene as workers together, and not on the basis of our job, which can only split our ranks. We are in favor of setting up committees in which the greatest number of workers can play an active part. We defend every non-sectarian and non-sectional claim of the working class, every claim that is in the declared interest of all. We support everything that widens the struggle and we oppose everything that tends to weaken it. We are in favor of international contacts, so that we may also get in touch with workers in other parts of the world and discuss our common problems with them.

"We have been led to question all exploitative societies, all organizations, and tackle such general problems as state capitalism, bureaucratic management, the abolition of the state and of wage-slavery, war, racism, 'Socialism,' etc. Each of us is entitled to present his own point of view and remains entirely free to act in whatever way he thinks best in his own factory. We believe in spontaneous resistance to all forms of domination, not in representation through the trade unions and political parties.

"The workers' movement forms a part of the class struggle because it promotes practical confrontations between workers and exploiters. It is for the workers alone to say how, why and where we are all to struggle. We cannot in any way fight for them; they alone can do the job. All we can do is give them information, and learn from them in return. We can contribute to discussions, so as to clarify our common experience, and we can also help to make their problems and struggle known to others.

"We believe that our struggles are milestones on the road to a society that will be run by the workers themselves." (*Information et Correspondance Ouvrières*)

From the views expressed by this and other groups, we can get some idea of the form that the movement of the future must take. Every small action committee, no less than every mass movement which seeks to improve the lives of all men must resolve:

(1) to respect and guarantee the plurality and diversity of political currents within the revolutionary mainstream. It must accordingly grant minority groups the right of independent action—only if the plurality of ideas is allowed *to express itself in social practice* does this idea have any real meaning;

(2) to ensure that all delegates are accountable to, and subject to immediate recall by, those who have elected them,

and to oppose the introduction of specialists and specialization at every step by widening the skill and knowledge of all;

(3) to ensure a continuous exchange of ideas, and to oppose any control of information and knowledge;

(4) to struggle against the formation of any kind of hierarchy;

(5) to abolish all artificial distinctions within labor, in particular between manual and intellectual work, and discrimination on grounds of sex;

(6) to ensure that all factories and businesses are run by those who work in them;

(7) to rid ourselves, in practice, of the Judaeo-Christian ethic, with its call for renunciation and sacrifice. There is only one reason for being a revolutionary—because it is the best way to live.

Reaction, which is bound to become more and more violent as the revolutionary movement increases its impact on society, forces us to look to our defenses. But our main task is to keep on challenging the traditional bureaucratic structures both in the government and also in the working-class movements.

How can anyone represent anyone else? All we can do is to involve them. We can try and get a few movements going, inject politics into all the structures of society, into the Youth Clubs, Youth Hostels, the YMCA and the Saturday Night dance, get out on to the streets, out on to all the streets of all the towns. To bring real politics into everyday life is to get rid of the politicians. We must pass from a critique of the university to the anti-university, open to all. Our challenge of the collective control of knowledge by the bourgeoisie must be radical and intransigent.

The multiplication of nuclei of confrontation decentralizes political life and neutralizes the repressive influence of the radio, television and party politics. Every time we beat back intimidation on the spot, we are striking a blow for freedom. To break out from isolation, we must carry the struggle to every market place and not create Messianic organizations to do the job for us. We reject the policy committee and the editorial board.

In the event, the students were defeated in their own struggle. The weakness of our movement is shown by the fact that we were unable to hold on to a single faculty—the recapture of the factories by the CRS[1] (with the help of the CGT)[2] might well have been halted by the working class, had there been a determined defense of a single "red base." But this is mere speculation. What is certain is that the movement must look carefully at its actions in May and June and draw the correct lessons for the future. The type of organization we must build can neither be a vanguard nor a rearguard, but must be right in the thick of the fight. What we need is not organization with a capital O, but a host of insurrectional cells, be they ideological groups, study groups—we can even use street gangs.

Effective revolutionary action does not spring from "individual" or "external" needs—it can only occur when the two coincide so that the distinction itself breaks down. Every group must find its own form, take its own action, and speak its own language. When all have learnt to express themselves, in harmony with the rest, we shall have a free society.

Reader, you have come to the end of this book, a book that wants to say only one thing: between us we can change this rotten society. Now, put on your coat and make for the nearest cinema. Look at their deadly love-making on the screen. Isn't it better in real life? Make up your mind to learn to love. Then, during the interval, when the first advertisements come on, pick up your tomatoes or, if you prefer, your eggs, and chuck them. Then get out into the street, and peel off all the latest government proclamations until underneath you discover the message of the days of May and June.

Stay awhile in the street. Look at the passers-by and remind yourself: the last word has not yet been said. Then act. Act with others, not for them. Make the revolution here and now. It is your own. *C'est pour toi que tu fais la révolution.*

[1] Compagnies Républicaines de Sécurité, special police under the jurisdiction of the Minister of the Interior—ed.

[2] Confédération Générale du Travail, the Communist-led confederation of trade unions—ed.

Select Bibliography*

I. GENERAL WORKS

Hannah Arendt, *On Revolution,* New York, 1963.

Shlomo Avineri, *The Social and Political Thought of Karl Marx,* Cambridge, England, 1970.

Crane Brinton, *The Anatomy of Revolution,* New York, 1938.

P. A. R. Calvert, "Revolution: The Politics of Violence," *Political Studies,* XV, 1967, pp. 1–11.

Katherine Chorley, *Armies and the Art of Revolution,* London, 1943.

Harry Eckstein (ed.), *Internal War,* New York, 1964.

Lyford P. Edwards, *The Natural History of Revolution,* Chicago, 1927.

Carl J. Friedrich (ed.), *Revolution* (Nomos VIII), New York, 1966.

Louis Gottschalk, "Causes of Revolution," *The American Journal of Sociology,* I, 1944, pp. 1–8.

Hugh D. Graham and Ted Gurr (eds.), *The National History of Violence in America,* New York, 1970.

Ted Gurr, *Why Men Rebel,* Princeton, 1970.

David Horowitz, *Empire and Revolution,* New York, 1969.

Chalmers Johnson, *Revolution and the Social System,* Stanford, 1964.

* These are works, in English, which have been helpful in the preparation of this book.

Chalmers Johnson, *Revolutionary Change,* Boston, 1966.
Thomas S. Kuhn, *The Structure of Scientific Revolutions,* Chicago, 1967.
Carl Leiden and Karl M. Schmitt, *The Politics of Violence: Revolution in the Modern World,* Englewood Cliffs, 1968.
Heinz Lubasz (ed.), *Revolutions in Modern Europe,* New York, 1966.
Arno Mayer, *Dynamics of Counterrevolution in Europe,* New York, 1971.
Herbert Marcuse, *Reason and Revolution,* Boston, 1960.
Karl Marx, *A Contribution to the Critique of Political Economy,* Chicago, 1904.
Karl Marx and Frederick Engels, *The Communist Manifesto,* Chicago, 1947.
Karl Marx and Frederick Engels, *The German Ideology,* New York, 1970.
James Meisel, *Counterrevolution: How Revolutions Die,* New York, 1966.
Norman Miller and Roderick Aya (eds.), *National Liberation, Revolution in the Third World,* New York, 1971.
Barrington Moore, Jr., *Social Origins of Dictatorship and Democracy,* Boston, 1967.
Max Nomad, *Apostles of Revolution,* New York, 1961.
Max Nomad, *Rebels and Renegades,* New York, 1932.
Clifford T. Paynton and Robert Blackey (eds.), *Why Revolution,* Cambridge, Mass., 1971.
Leon Trotsky, *The Permanent Revolution,* New York, 1969.

II. EARLY MODERN REVOLUTIONS

Trevor Aston (ed.), *Crisis in Europe, 1560–1660,* Garden City, New York, 1967.
J. S. Bromley and E. H. Kossmann (eds.), *Britain and the Netherlands,* London, 1960.
J. H. Elliott, *The Revolt of the Catalans,* Cambridge, England, 1963.
Robert Forster and Jack P. Greene (eds.), *Preconditions*

of *Revolution in Early Modern Europe,* Baltimore, 1970.

Pieter Geyl, *The Revolt of the Netherlands,* London, 1932.

J. H. Hexter, *Reappraisals in History,* Aberdeen, 1961.

H. G. Koenigsberger, "The Organization of Revolutionary Parties in France and the Netherlands," *Journal of Modern History,* XXVII, 1955, pp. 335–351.

A. D. Loublinskaya, *French Absolutism: The Crucial Phase,* Cambridge, England, 1968.

R. B. Merriman, *Six Contemporaneous Revolutions,* Oxford, 1938.

Roland Mousnier, *Peasant Uprisings in 17th Century France, Russia and China,* New York, 1971.

B. F. Porshnev, "The Legend of the 17th Century in French History," *Past and Present,* 8, 1955, pp. 15–27.

III. THE ENGLISH CIVIL WAR

H. N. Brailsford, *The Levellers and the English Revolution,* London, 1961.

D. Brunton and D. H. Pennington, *The Members of the Long Parliament,* Aberdeen, 1954.

S. R. Gardiner, *The History of the Great Civil War,* 4 vols., London, 1893.

S. R. Gardiner, *The History of the Commonwealth and Protectorate,* 4 vols., London, 1903.

William Haller, *Liberty and Reformation in the Puritan Revolution,* New York, 1955.

J. H. Hexter, *The Reign of King Pym,* Cambridge, Mass., 1941.

Christopher Hill, *God's Englishman, Oliver Cromwell and the English Revolution,* New York, 1970.

Christopher Hill, *Puritanism and Revolution,* New York, 1958.

E. W. Ives (ed.), *The English Revolution,* London, 1968.

Valerie Pearl, *London and the Outbreak of the Puritan Revolution,* Oxford, 1961.

Ivan Roots, *The Great Rebellion,* London, 1966.

Lawrence Stone, *The Crisis of the Aristocracy,* Oxford, 1965.

R. H. Tawney, "The Rise of the Gentry," *Economic History Review,* XI, 1941.

H. R. Trevor-Roper, "The Gentry, 1540–1640," *Economic History Review,* Supplement 1, 1953.

Michael Walzer, *The Revolution of the Saints,* Cambridge, Mass., 1965.

C. V. Wedgwood, *The King's Peace,* London, 1955.

C. V. Wedgwood, *The King's War,* London, 1958.

IV. THE AMERICAN REVOLUTION

Bernard Bailyn, *The Ideological Origins of the American Revolution,* Cambridge, Mass., 1967.

Charles A. Beard, *An Economic Interpretation of the Constitution of the United States,* New York, 1925.

E. James Ferguson, *The Power of the Purse,* Chapel Hill, 1961.

E. Franklin Jameson, *The American Revolution Considered as a Social Movement,* Princeton, 1967.

Merrill Jensen, *The Articles of Confederation,* Madison, 1970.

Staughton Lynd, *Class Conflict; Slavery and the U.S. Constitution,* Indianapolis, 1968.

Jackson T. Main, *The Antifederalists,* Chapel Hill, 1961.

Forest McDonald, *We the People: The Economic Origins of the Constitution,* Chicago, 1938.

Edmund and Helen Morgan, *The Stamp Act Crisis,* Chapel Hill, 1953.

Edmund Morgan, *The Birth of the Republic,* Chicago, 1956.

Gordon S. Wood, *The Creation of the American Republic,* Chapel Hill, 1969.

V. THE FRENCH REVOLUTION

Crane Brinton, *The Jacobins,* New York, 1930.

Emanuel Chill (ed.), *Power, Property and History,* New York, 1971.

Alfred Cobban, *The Social Interpretation of the French Revolution,* Cambridge, England, 1965.

Paul Farmer, *France Reviews Its Revolutionary Origins,* New York, 1944.

Louis Gottschalk, *Jean-Paul Marat,* Chicago, 1967.

E. J. Hobsbawm, *The Age of Revolution,* New York, 1962.

Jeffrey Kaplow (ed.), *New Perspectives on the French Revolution,* New York, 1965.

Georges Lefebvre, *The Coming of the French Revolution,* Princeton, 1954.

Georges Lefebvre, *The French Revolution,* 2 vols., New York, 1962, 1964.

Albert Mathiez, *The French Revolution,* New York, 1964.

R. R. Palmer, *Twelve Who Ruled,* Princeton, 1941.

R. R. Palmer, *The Age of the Democratic Revolution,* 2 vols., Princeton, 1959, 1964.

Georges Rudé, *The Crowd in the French Revolution,* Oxford, 1960.

Albert Soboul, *The Parisian Sans-Culottes and the French Revolution,* Oxford, 1964.

M. J. Sydenham, *The Girondins,* London, 1961.

J. L. Talmon, *The Rise of Totalitarian Democracy,* Boston, 1952.

J. B. Thompson, *Robespierre,* 2 vols., Oxford, 1935.

Alexis de Tocqueville, *The Old Regime and the French Revolution,* Garden City, New York, 1955.

VI. 1848

Georges Duveau, *1848: The Making of a Revolution,* New York, 1968.

Frederick Engels, *Germany: Revolution and Counter-Revolution,* New York, 1933.

Frank Eyck, *The Frankfurt Parliament,* New York, 1968.

François Fejto (ed.), *The Opening of an Era,* London, 1949.

Theodore S. Hamerow, *Restoration, Revolution, Reaction,* Princeton, 1958.

Karl Marx, *The Class Struggles in France,* New York, 1924.

Karl Marx, *The Eighteenth Brumaire of Louis Bonaparte,* New York, 1963.

Donald C. McKay, *The National Workshops,* Cambridge, Mass., 1933.

Lewis B. Namier, *1848, The Revolution of the Intellectuals,* New York, 1946.

Paul Noyes, *Organization and Revolution: Working Class Associations in the German Revolution of 1848,* Princeton, 1966.

Priscilla Robertson, *Revolutions of 1848,* Princeton, 1952.

Alexis de Tocqueville, *The Recollections,* New York, 1959.

VII.   THE PARIS COMMUNE OF 1871

Stuart Edwards, *The Paris Commune: 1871,* London, 1971.

Frank Jellinek, *The Paris Commune of 1871,* London, 1937.

Karl Marx, *The Civil War in France,* New York, 1940.

Alan B. Spitzer, *The Revolutionary Theories of Louis Auguste Blanqui,* New York, 1957.

R. L. Williams, *The French Revolution of 1870–71,* London, 1969.

VIII.   THE RUSSIAN REVOLUTION, 1917

Paul Avrich, *Kronstadt,* Princeton, 1970.

E. H. Carr, *The Bolshevik Revolution,* 3 vols., London, 1952–4.

W. H. Chamberlin, *The Russian Revolution, 1917–1921,* 2 vols., New York, 1965.

Isaac Deutscher, *Stalin,* New York, 1949.

Isaac Deutscher, *Trotsky,* 3 vols., New York, 1965.

Isaac Deutscher, *The Unfinished Revolution,* New York, 1967.

L. H. Haimson, *The Russian Marxists and the Origins of Bolshevism,* Cambridge, Mass., 1953.

Marcel Liebman, *The Russian Revolution,* London, 1970.

Rosa Luxemburg, *The Russian Revolution*, Ann Arbor, 1961.

Richard Pipes, *The Formation of the Soviet Union: Communism and Nationalism*, Cambridge, Mass., 1954.

Arthur Rosenberg, *A History of Bolshevism*, London, 1934.

Leonard Schapiro, *The Communist Party of the Soviet Union*, New York, 1960.

Leon Trotsky, *History of the Russian Revolution*, 3 vols., London, 1967.

Bertram Wolfe, *Three Who Made a Revolution*, New York, 1948.

IX. THE CHINESE COMMUNIST REVOLUTION

Jack Belden, *China Shakes the World*, New York, 1949.

Conrad Brandt, *Stalin's Failure in China*, Cambridge, Mass., 1958.

Lionel M. Chassin, *The Communist Conquest of China*, Cambridge, Mass., 1965.

Jerome Ch'en, *Mao and the Chinese Revolution*, New York, 1967.

C. P. Fitzgerald, *The Birth of Communist China*, Middlesex, 1954.

William Hinton, *Fanshen*, New York, 1966.

Harold Isaacs, *The Tragedy of the Chinese Revolution*, Stanford, 1962.

Chalmers Johnson, *Peasant Nationalism and Communist Power*, Stanford, 1962.

Maurice Meisner, *Li Ta-chao and the Origins of Chinese Marxism*, Cambridge, Mass., 1967.

John E. Rue, *Mao Tse-tung in Opposition*, Stanford, 1966.

Stuart Schram, *Mao Tse-tung*, Middlesex, 1967.

Franz Schurmann, *Ideology and Organization in Communist China*, Berkeley, 1966.

Vera Simone (ed.), *China in Revolution*, New York, 1968.

Edgar Snow, *Red Star Over China*, New York, 1938.

X. THE MEXICAN REVOLUTION

Frank R. Brandenburg, *The Making of Modern Mexico,* Englewood Cliffs, 1964.

Anita Brenner and George Leighton, *The Wind that Swept Mexico,* Austin, 1971.

Harold F. Cline, *The United States and Mexico,* Cambridge, Mass., 1953.

Ernest Gruening, *Mexico and Its Heritage,* New York, 1928.

Stanley Ross (ed.), *Is the Mexican Revolution Dead?* New York, 1966.

Frank Tannenbaum, *The Mexican Agrarian Revolution,* Washington, D.C., 1929.

Frank Tannenbaum, *Peace by Revolution,* New York, 1933.

Frank Tannenbaum, *Mexico: The Struggle for Peace and Bread,* New York, 1950.

Raymond Vernon, *The Dilemma of Mexico's Development,* Cambridge, Mass., 1963.

John Womack, Jr., *Zapata and the Mexican Revolution,* New York, 1968.

XI. THE CUBAN REVOLUTION

Regis Debray, *Revolution in the Revolution,* New York, 1967.

Che Guevara, *Guerrilla Warfare,* New York, 1969.

Che Guevara, *On Vietnam and World Revolution,* New York, 1968.

Che Guevara, *Reminiscences of the Cuban Revolutionary War,* New York, 1968.

Leo Huberman and Paul Sweezy, *Cuba: Anatomy of a Revolution,* New York, 1960.

K. S. Karol, *Guerrillas in Power: The Course of the Cuban Revolution,* New York, 1971.

James O'Connor, *The Origins of Cuban Socialism,* Ithaca, 1969.

Maurice Zeitlin, *Revolutionary Politics and the Cuban Working Class,* 1967.

Maurice Zeitlin and Robert Scheer, *Cuba: Tragedy in Our Hemisphere,* New York, 1963.

XII. THE REVOLUTION IN INDOCHINA

Nina Adams and Alfred McCoy (eds.), *Laos: War and Revolution,* New York, 1970.

Wilfred Burchett, *Inside Story of the Guerrilla War,* New York, 1965.

Committee of Concerned Asian Scholars, *The Indochina Story,* New York, 1970.

Philippe Devillers and Jean Lacouture, *End of a War,* New York, 1969.

Bernard Fall, *The Two Vietnams,* New York, 1964.

Marvin E. Gettleman (ed.), *Vietnam, History, Documents and Opinions,* New York, 1970.

Marvin and Susan Gettleman and Lawrence and Carol Kaplan (eds.), *Conflict in Indochina,* New York, 1970.

Vo Nguyen Giap, *People's War, People's Army,* New York, 1965.

Jonathan Grant, Jonathan Unger, Lawrence Moss (eds.), *Cambodia: The Widening War in Indochina,* New York, 1970.

Ellen J. Hammer, *The Struggle for Indochina,* Stanford, 1954.

Jean Lacouture, *Vietnam Between Two Truces,* New York, 1966.

Jean Lacouture, *Ho Chi Minh: A Political Biography,* New York, 1968.

Donald Lancaster, *The Emancipation of French Indochina,* New York, 1961.

John T. McAlister, *Vietnam: The Origins of Revolution,* New York, 1969.

George McT. Kahin and John Lewis, *The United States in Vietnam,* New York, 1969.

Hugh Toye, *Laos: Buffer State or Battleground,* London, 1968.

XIII. THE FRENCH STUDENT REBELLION OF 1968
Gabriel and Daniel Cohn-Bendit, *Obsolete Communism, The Left-Wing Alternative,* New York, 1968.

Barbara and John Ehrenreich, *Long March, Short Spring: The Student Uprisings at Home and Abroad,* New York, 1969.

Henri Lefebvre, *The Explosion: Marxism and the French Student Upheaval,* New York, 1969.

Patrick Seale and Maureen McConville, *Red Flag/Black Flag,* New York, 1968.

Daniel Singer, *Prelude to Revolution, France in May 1968,* New York, 1971.

Index

About the Editors

LAWRENCE KAPLAN is assistant professor of history at the City College of the City University of New York. The author of several articles on the English revolution, and coeditor of *Conflict in Indochina*, Professor Kaplan is now at work on a study of Puritan ideology during the English revolution.

CAROL KAPLAN, also a coeditor of *Conflict in Indochina*, is now enrolled in the School of Social Work, Hunter College of the City University of New York.